Collins *gem*

World Atlas

G000140973

ISBN-10: 0-00-720561-9
ISBN-13: 978-0-00-720561-5

ISBN-10: 0-06-089061-4 (in the United States)
ISBN-13: 978-0-06-089061-2
FIRST U.S. EDITION published 2006

HarperCollins books may be purchased for educational, business, or sales promotional use. For information in the United States, please write to: Special Markets Department, HarperCollins Publishers, 10 Eas 53rd Street, New York, NY 10022.

The name of the "Smithsonian," "Smithsonian Institution," and the sun burst logo are registered trademarks of the Smithsonian Institution.

Maps © Collins Bartholomew Ltd 2005

Printed and bound in Italy by Amadeus S.p.A.

10 09 08 07 06
9 8 7 6 5 4 3 2 1

Collins *gem*

World
Atlas

Collins

An Imprint of HarperCollinsPublishers

world

country profiles		8-23
countries		24-25
physical features		26-27
climate		28-29
population and cities		30-31

europe

countries	1:46 500 000	32-33
western russian federation	1:26 500 000	34-35
baltic states and moscow region	1:10 500 000	36-37
ukraine, moldova and romania	1:10 500 000	38-39
scandinavia and iceland	1:13 000 000	40-41
british isles	1:10 500 000	42-43
scotland	1:5 500 000	44
ireland	1:5 500 000	45
england and wales	1:5 500 000	46-47
northwest europe	1:5 500 000	48-49
central europe	1:10 500 000	50-51
france and switzerland	1:10 500 000	52-53
spain and portugal	1:10 500 000	54-55
italy and the balkans	1:10 500 000	56-57
southeast europe	1:10 500 000	58-59

asia

countries	1:103 000 000	60-61
southeast asia	1:40 000 000	62-63
malaysia and western indonesia	1:20 000 000	64-65
myanmar, thailand and indo-china	1:20 000 000	66-67
philippines	1:20 000 000	68
north korea and south korea	1:12 000 000	69
japan	1:13 000 000	70-71
china and mongolia	1:40 000 000	72-73
central china	1:20 000 000	74-75
southern asia	1:26 500 000	76-77
pakistan, northern india, nepal and bangladesh	1:20 000 000	78-79
central asia	1:26 500 000	80-81
arabian peninsula	1:20 000 000	82-83
eastern mediterranean	1:20 000 000	84-85
russian federation	1:55 500 000	86-87

africa

countries	1:79 500 000	88-89
northwest africa	1:34 500 000	90-91
northeast africa	1:34 500 000	92-93
central africa	1:26 500 000	94-95
southern africa	1:26 500 000	96-97
republic of south africa	1:13 000 000	98-99

oceania

countries	1:86 000 000	100-101
australia	1:33 000 000	102-103
southeast australia	1:13 000 000	104-105
new zealand	1:13 000 000	106
antarctica	1:79 500 000	107

north america

countries	1:86 000 000	108-109
canada	1:40 000 000	110-111
western canada	1:20 000 000	112-113
eastern canada	1:20 000 000	114-115
united states of america	1:33 000 000	116-117
western united states	1:14 500 000	118-119
north central united states	1:14 500 000	120-121
northeast united states	1:14 500 000	122-123
southeast united states	1:14 500 000	124-125
south central united states	1:14 500 000	126-127
mexico	1:20 000 000	128-129
the caribbean	1:26 500 000	130-131

south america

countries	1:66 000 000	132-133
northern south america	1:33 000 000	134-135
southern south america	1:33 000 000	136-137
southeast brazil	1:13 000 000	138-139

oceans

features		140-141
pacific ocean	1:123 500 000	142-143
atlantic ocean and indian ocean	1:123 500 000	144-145
arctic ocean	1:79 500 000	146

index		147-255

contents

INTRODUCTION

The atlas is introduced by details of the world's countries and regions and by maps and information on major geographical themes. The reference maps which follow this world section have been compiled to provide the best coverage for each part of the world through careful selection of scales and map projections. Maps are arranged on a continental basis, with each continent being introduced by maps and statistics on the continent's countries and capitals. Maps of the world's oceans complete the worldwide coverage.

Map symbolization

Maps show information by using symbols which are designed to reflect the features on the earth that they represent. Map symbols can be in the form of points – such as those used to show towns and airports; lines – used to represent roads and rivers; or areas – such as lakes. Variation in design of these types of symbol allows a great range of information to be shown. The symbols used in this atlas are explained here. Not all details can be shown at the small map scales used in this atlas, so information is generalized to allow easy interpretation. This generalization takes the form of selection – the inclusion of some features and the omission of others of less importance; and simplification – where lines are smoothed, areas combined, or symbols displaced slightly to add clarity. This is done in such a way that the overall character of the area mapped is retained. The degree of generalization varies, and is determined largely by the scale at which the map is drawn.

Scale

Scale is the relationship between the size of an area shown on the map and the actual size of the area on the ground. It determines the amount of detail shown on a map – larger scales show more, smaller scales show less – and can be used to measure the distance between two points, although the projection of the map must also be taken into account when measuring distances.

Geographical names

The spelling of place names on maps is a complex problem for the cartographer. There is no single standard way of converting them from one alphabet, or symbol set, to another. Changes in official languages also have to be taken into account when creating maps and policies need to be established for the spelling of names on individual atlases and maps. Such policies must take account of the local official position, international conventions or traditions, as well as the purpose of the atlas or map. The policy in this atlas is to use local name forms which are officially recognized by the governments of the countries concerned, but with English conventional name forms being used for the most well-known places. In these cases, the local form is often included in brackets on the map and also appears as a cross-reference in the index. All country names and those for international features appear in their English forms.

Boundaries

The status of nations and their boundaries are shown in this atlas as they are in reality at the time of going to press, as far as can be ascertained. Where international boundaries are the subject of disputes the aim is to take a strictly neutral viewpoint, based on advice from expert consultants.

MAP SYMBOLS

Settlements

Population		National Capital		Administrative Capital		City or Town
over 5 million	▣	**BEIJING**	◉	Tianjin	◉	**New York**
1 million – 5 million	▢	**MADRID**	○	Sydney	○	Madurai
500 000 – 1 million	▫	**BANGUI**	▫	Douala	○	**Barranquilla**
100 000 – 500 000	▫	WELLINGTON	○	Mansa	○	Yong'an
50 000 – 100 000	▫	PORT OF SPAIN	○	Lubango	○	Puruliya
under 50 000	▫	MALABO	○	Chinhoyi	○	El Tigre

Styles of lettering

Country name	**FRANCE**	Island	*Gran Canaria*
Overseas territory / Dependency	**Guadaloupe**	Lake	*Lake Erie*
Administrative name	**SCOTLAND**	Mountain	*Mt Blanc*
Area name	PATAGONIA	River	*Thames*

Physical features

▢	Freshwater lake
▢	Seasonal freshwater lake
▢	Salt lake
▢	Seasonal salt lake
▢	Dry salt lake
◌	Ice cap
—	River
≍ 2188	Mountain pass
△ 6960	Summit

Communications

════════	Major road
————————	Road
– – – – –	Track
– – – – –	Railway
✈	Main airport
··············	Canal

Other features

∴	Site of special interest
⌇⌇⌇	Wall

Boundaries

————————	International
– – – – –	International disputed
————————	Administrative (selected countries only)
··············	Ceasefire line

EUROPE COUNTRIES	area sq km	area sq miles	population	capital
ALBANIA	28 748	11 100	3 166 000	Tirana
ANDORRA	465	180	71 000	Andorra la Vella
AUSTRIA	83 855	32 377	8 116 000	Vienna
BELARUS	207 600	80 155	9 895 000	Minsk
BELGIUM	30 520	11 784	10 318 000	Brussels
BOSNIA-HERZEGOVINA	51 130	19 741	4 161 000	Sarajevo
BULGARIA	110 994	42 855	7 897 000	Sofia
CROATIA	56 538	21 829	4 428 000	Zagreb
CZECH REPUBLIC	78 864	30 450	10 236 000	Prague
DENMARK	43 075	16 631	5 364 000	Copenhagen
ESTONIA	45 200	17 452	1 323 000	Tallinn
FINLAND	338 145	130 559	5 207 000	Helsinki
FRANCE	543 965	210 026	60 144 000	Paris
GERMANY	357 022	137 849	82 476 000	Berlin
GREECE	131 957	50 949	10 976 000	Athens
HUNGARY	93 030	35 919	9 877 000	Budapest
ICELAND	102 820	39 699	290 000	Reykjavik
IRELAND, REPUBLIC OF	70 282	27 136	3 956 000	Dublin
ITALY	301 245	116 311	57 423 000	Rome
LATVIA	63 700	24 595	2 307 000	Riga
LIECHTENSTEIN	160	62	34 000	Vaduz
LITHUANIA	65 200	25 174	3 444 000	Vilnius
LUXEMBOURG	2 586	998	453 000	Luxembourg
MACEDONIA (F.Y.R.O.M.)	25 713	9 928	2 056 000	Skopje
MALTA	316	122	394 000	Valletta
MOLDOVA	33 700	13 012	4 267 000	Chişinău
MONACO	2	1	34 000	Monaco-Ville
NETHERLANDS	41 526	16 033	16 149 000	Amsterdam/The Ha
NORWAY	323 878	125 050	4 533 000	Oslo
POLAND	312 683	120 728	38 587 000	Warsaw
PORTUGAL	88 940	34 340	10 062 000	Lisbon
ROMANIA	237 500	91 699	22 334 000	Bucharest
RUSSIAN FEDERATION	17 075 400	6 592 849	143 246 000	Moscow

languages	religions	currency
...lbanian, Greek	Sunni Muslim, Albanian Orthodox, Roman Catholic	Lek
...panish, Catalan, French	Roman Catholic	Euro
...erman, Croatian, Turkish	Roman Catholic, Protestant	Euro
...elorussian, Russian	Belorussian Orthodox, Roman Catholic	Belarus rouble
...utch (Flemish), French (Walloon), German	Roman Catholic, Protestant	Euro
...osnian, Serbian, Croatian	Sunni Muslim, Serbian Orthodox, Rom. Catholic, Protestant	Marka
...ulgarian, Turkish, Romany, Macedonian	Bulgarian Orthodox, Sunni Muslim	Lev
...oatian, Serbian	Roman Catholic, Serbian Orthodox, Sunni Muslim	Kuna
...zech, Moravian, Slovak	Roman Catholic, Protestant	Czech koruna
...nish	Protestant	Danish krone
...stonian, Russian	Protestant, Estonian and Russian Orthodox	Kroon
...nnish, Swedish	Protestant, Greek Orthodox	Euro
...ench, Arabic	Roman Catholic, Protestant, Sunni Muslim	Euro
...erman, Turkish	Protestant, Roman Catholic	Euro
...eek	Greek Orthodox, Sunni Muslim	Euro
...ungarian	Roman Catholic, Protestant	Forint
...landic	Protestant	Icelandic króna
...glish, Irish	Roman Catholic, Protestant	Euro
...an	Roman Catholic	Euro
...vian, Russian	Protestant, Roman Catholic, Russian Orthodox	Lats
...rman	Roman Catholic, Protestant	Swiss franc
...uanian, Russian, Polish	Roman Catholic, Protestant, Russian Orthodox	Litas
...xeburgish, German, French	Roman Catholic	Euro
...cedonian, Albanian, Turkish	Macedonian Orthodox, Sunni Muslim	Macedonian denar
...ese, English	Roman Catholic	Maltese lira
...manian, Ukrainian, Gagauz, Russian	Romanian Orthodox, Russian Orthodox	Moldovan leu
...nch, Monegasque, Italian	Roman Catholic	Euro
...sh, Frisian	Roman Catholic, Protestant, Sunni Muslim	Euro
...rwegian	Protestant, Roman Catholic	Norwegian krone
...sh, German	Roman Catholic, Polish Orthodox	Zloty
...uguese	Roman Catholic, Protestant	Euro
...anian, Hungarian	Romanian Orthodox, Protestant, Roman Catholic	Romanian leu
...sian, Tatar, Ukrainian, local languages	Russian Orthodox, Sunni Muslim, Protestant	Russian rouble

EUROPE COUNTRIES (continued)

EUROPE COUNTRIES (continued)		area sq km	area sq miles	population	capital
SAN MARINO		61	24	28 000	San Marino
SERBIA AND MONTENEGRO		102 173	39 449	10 527 000	Belgrade
SLOVAKIA		49 035	18 933	5 402 000	Bratislava
SLOVENIA		20 251	7 819	1 984 000	Ljubljana
SPAIN		504 782	194 897	41 060 000	Madrid
SWEDEN		449 964	173 732	8 876 000	Stockholm
SWITZERLAND		41 293	15 943	7 169 000	Bern
UKRAINE		603 700	233 090	48 523 000	Kiev
UNITED KINGDOM		243 609	94 058	58 789 194	London
VATICAN CITY		0.5	0.2	472	Vatican City

EUROPE DEPENDENT TERRITORIES

EUROPE DEPENDENT TERRITORIES			area sq km	area sq miles	popul
Azores		Autonomous Region of Portugal	2 300	888	242
Faroe Islands		Self-governing Danish Territory	1 399	540	47
Gibraltar		United Kingdom Overseas Territory	7	3	2
Guernsey		United Kingdom Crown Dependency	78	30	62
Isle of Man		United Kingdom Crown Dependency	572	221	7
Jersey		United Kingdom Crown Dependency	116	45	8

ASIA COUNTRIES

ASIA COUNTRIES		area sq km	area sq miles	population	capital
AFGHANISTAN		652 225	251 825	23 897 000	Kābul
ARMENIA		29 800	11 506	3 061 000	Yerevan
AZERBAIJAN		86 600	33 436	8 370 000	Baku
BAHRAIN		691	267	724 000	Manama
BANGLADESH		143 998	55 598	146 736 000	Dhaka
BHUTAN		46 620	18 000	2 257 000	Thimphu
BRUNEI		5 765	2 226	358 000	Bandar Seri Begawa
CAMBODIA		181 000	69 884	14 144 000	Phnom Penh
CHINA		9 584 492	3 700 593	1 289 161 000	Beijing
CYPRUS		9 251	3 572	802 000	Nicosia
EAST TIMOR		14 874	5 743	778 000	Dili
GEORGIA		69 700	26 911	5 126 000	T'bilisi

uages	religions	currency
n	Roman Catholic	Euro
ian, Albanian, Hungarian	Serbian Orthodox, Montenegrin Orthodox, Sunni Muslim	Serbian dinar, Euro
ak, Hungarian, Czech	Roman Catholic, Protestant, Orthodox	Slovakian koruna
iene, Croatian, Serbian	Roman Catholic, Protestant	Tólar
ilian, Catalan, Galician, Basque	Roman Catholic	Euro
edish	Protestant, Roman Catholic	Swedish krona
man, French, Italian, Romansch	Roman Catholic, Protestant	Swiss franc
ainian, Russian	Ukrainian Orthodox, Ukrainian Catholic, Roman Catholic	Hryvnia
ish, Welsh, Gaelic	Protestant, Roman Catholic, Muslim	Pound sterling
n	Roman Catholic	Euro

tal	languages	religions	currency
ta Delgada	Portuguese	Roman Catholic, Protestant	Euro
shavn	Faroese, Danish	Protestant	Danish krone
altar	English, Spanish	Roman Catholic, Protestant, Sunni Muslim	Gibraltar pound
eter Port	English, French	Protestant, Roman Catholic	Pound sterling
glas	English	Protestant, Roman Catholic	Pound sterling
elier	English, French	Protestant, Roman Catholic	Pound sterling

uages	religions	currency
, Pushtu, Uzbek, Turkmen	Sunni Muslim, Shi'a Muslim	Afghani
enian, Azeri	Armenian Orthodox	Dram
i, Armenian, Russian, Lezgian	Shi'a Muslim, Sunni Muslim, Russ. and Armenian Orthodox	Azerbaijani manat
ic, English	Shi'a Muslim, Sunni Muslim Christian	Bahrain dinar
gali, English	Sunni Muslim, Hindu	Taka
ngkha, Nepali, Assamese	Buddhist, Hindu	Ngultrum, Indian rupee
ay, English, Chinese	Sunni Muslim, Buddhist, Christian	Brunei dollar
mer, Vietnamese	Buddhist, Roman Catholic, Sunni Muslim	Riel
darin, Wu, Cantonese, Hsiang, reg. lang.	Confucian, Taoist, Buddhist, Christian, Sunni Muslim	Yuan, Hong Kong dollar, Macau pataca
ek, Turkish, English	Greek Orthodox, Sunni Muslim	Cyprus pound
guese, Tetun, English	Roman Catholic	US dollar
g., Russ., Armen., Azeri, Osset., Abkhaz	Georgian Orthodox, Russian Orthodox, Sunni Muslim	Lari

ASIA COUNTRIES (continued)		area sq km	area sq miles	population	capital
INDIA		3 064 898	1 183 364	1 065 462 000	New Delhi
INDONESIA		1 919 445	741 102	219 883 000	Jakarta
IRAN		1 648 000	636 296	68 920 000	Tehrān
IRAQ		438 317	169 235	25 175 000	Baghdād
ISRAEL		20 770	8 019	6 433 000	Jerusalem *(De facto. Disputed)*
JAPAN		377 727	145 841	127 654 000	Tōkyō
JORDAN		89 206	34 443	5 473 000	'Ammān
KAZAKHSTAN		2 717 300	1 049 155	15 433 000	Astana
KUWAIT		17 818	6 880	2 521 000	Kuwait
KYRGYZSTAN		198 500	76 641	5 138 000	Bishkek
LAOS		236 800	91 429	5 657 000	Vientiane
LEBANON		10 452	4 036	3 653 000	Beirut
MALAYSIA		332 965	128 559	24 425 000	Kuala Lumpur/Putra
MALDIVES		298	115	318 000	Male
MONGOLIA		1 565 000	604 250	2 594 000	Ulan Bator
MYANMAR		676 577	261 228	49 485 000	Rangoon
NEPAL		147 181	56 827	25 164 000	Kathmandu
NORTH KOREA		120 538	46 540	22 664 000	P'yŏngyang
OMAN		309 500	119 499	2 851 000	Muscat
PAKISTAN		803 940	310 403	153 578 000	Islamabad
PALAU		497	192	20 000	Koror
PHILIPPINES		300 000	115 831	79 999 000	Manila
QATAR		11 437	4 416	610 000	Doha
RUSSIAN FEDERATION		17 075 400	6 592 849	143 246 000	Moscow
SAUDI ARABIA		2 200 000	849 425	24 217 000	Riyadh
SINGAPORE		639	247	4 253 000	Singapore
SOUTH KOREA		99 274	38 330	47 700 000	Seoul
SRI LANKA		65 610	25 332	19 065 000	Sri Jayewardenepur
SYRIA		185 180	71 498	17 800 000	Damascus
TAIWAN		36 179	13 969	22 548 000	T'aipei
TAJIKISTAN		143 100	55 251	6 245 000	Dushanbe
THAILAND		513 115	198 115	62 833 000	Bangkok
TURKEY		779 452	300 948	71 325 000	Ankara

guages	religions	currency
di, English, many regional languages	Hindu, Sunni Muslim, Shi'a Muslim, Sikh, Christian	Indian rupee
onesian, local languages	Sunni Muslim, Protestant, Rom. Catholic, Hindu, Buddhist	Rupiah
isi, Azeri, Kurdish, regional languages	Shi'a Muslim, Sunni Muslim	Iranian rial
abic, Kurdish, Turkmen	Shi'a Muslim, Sunni Muslim, Christian	Iraqi dinar
brew, Arabic	Jewish, Sunni Muslim, Christian, Druze	Shekel
panese	Shintoist, Buddhist, Christian	Yen
abic	Sunni Muslim, Christian	Jordanian dinar
zakh, Russian, Ukr., Ger., Uzbek, Tatar	Sunni Muslim, Russian Orthodox, Protestant	Tenge
abic	Sunni Muslim, Shi'a Muslim, Christian, Hindu	Kuwaiti dinar
rgyz, Russian, Uzbek	Sunni Muslim, Russian Orthodox	Kyrgyz som
o, local languages	Buddhist, traditional beliefs	Kip
abic, Armenian, French	Shi'a Muslim, Sunni Muslim, Christian	Lebanese pound
alay, English, Chinese, Tamil, local lang.	Sunni Muslim, Buddhist, Hindu, Christian, traditional beliefs	Ringgit
ehi (Maldivian)	Sunni Muslim	Rufiyaa
alka (Mongolian), Kazakh, local languages	Buddhist, Sunni Muslim	Tugrik (tögrög)
rmese, Shan, Karen, local languages	Buddhist, Christian, Sunni Muslim	Kyat
pali, Maithili, Bhojpuri, English, local lang.	Hindu, Buddhist, Sunni Muslim	Nepalese rupee
rean	Traditional beliefs, Chondoist, Buddhist	North Korean won
abic, Baluchi, Indian languages	Ibadhi Muslim, Sunni Muslim	Omani riyal
du, Punjabi, Sindhi, Pushtu, English	Sunni Muslim, Shi'a Muslim, Christian, Hindu	Pakistani rupee
lauan, English	Roman Catholic, Protestant, traditional beliefs	US dollar
glish, Pilipino, Cebuano, local languages	Roman Catholic, Protestant, Sunni Muslim, Aglipayan	Philippine peso
abic	Sunni Muslim	Qatari riyal
ssian, Tatar, Ukrainian, local languages	Russian Orthodox, Sunni Muslim, Protestant	Russian rouble
abic	Sunni Muslim, Shi'a Muslim	Saudi Arabian riyal
inese, English, Malay, Tamil	Buddhist, Taoist, Sunni Muslim, Christian, Hindu	Singapore dollar
rean	Buddhist, Protestant, Roman Catholic	South Korean won
halese, Tamil, English	Buddhist, Hindu, Sunni Muslim, Roman Catholic	Sri Lankan rupee
abic, Kurdish, Armenian	Sunni Muslim, Christian	Syrian pound
andarin, Min, Hakka, local languages	Buddhist, Taoist, Confucian, Christian	Taiwan dollar
ik, Uzbek, Russian	Sunni Muslim	Somoni
ai, Lao, Chinese, Malay, Mon-Khmer lang.	Buddhist, Sunni Muslim	Baht
rkish, Kurdish	Sunni Muslim, Shi'a Muslim	Turkish lira

world countries
asia

ASIA COUNTRIES (continued)		area sq km	area sq miles	population	capital
TURKMENISTAN		488 100	188 456	4 867 000	Ashgabat
UNITED ARAB EMIRATES		77 700	30 000	2 995 000	Abu Dhabi
UZBEKISTAN		447 400	172 742	26 093 000	Tashkent
VIETNAM		329 565	127 246	81 377 000	Ha Nôi
YEMEN		527 968	203 850	20 010 000	Şan'ā'

ASIA DEPENDENT AND DISPUTED TERRITORIES			area sq km	area sq miles	popul
Christmas Island		Australian External Territory	135	52	
Cocos Islands		Australian External Territory	14	5	
Gaza		Semi-autonomous region	363	140	1 203
Jammu and Kashmir		Disputed territory (India/Pakistan)	222 236	85 806	13 000
West Bank		Disputed territory	5 860	2 263	2 303

AFRICA COUNTRIES		area sq km	area sq miles	population	capital
ALGERIA		2 381 741	919 595	31 800 000	Algiers
ANGOLA		1 246 700	481 354	13 625 000	Luanda
BENIN		112 620	43 483	6 736 000	Porto-Novo
BOTSWANA		581 370	224 468	1 785 000	Gaborone
BURKINA		274 200	105 869	13 002 000	Ouagadougou
BURUNDI		27 835	10 747	6 825 000	Bujumbura
CAMEROON		475 442	183 569	16 018 000	Yaoundé
CAPE VERDE		4 033	1 557	463 000	Praia
CENTRAL AFRICAN REPUBLIC		622 436	240 324	3 865 000	Bangui
CHAD		1 284 000	495 755	8 598 000	Ndjamena
COMOROS		1 862	719	768 000	Moroni
CONGO		342 000	132 047	3 724 000	Brazzaville
CONGO, DEMOCRATIC REP. OF		2 345 410	905 568	52 771 000	Kinshasa
CÔTE D'IVOIRE		322 463	124 504	16 631 000	Yamoussoukro
DJIBOUTI		23 200	8 958	703 000	Djibouti
EGYPT		1 000 250	386 199	71 931 000	Cairo
EQUATORIAL GUINEA		28 051	10 831	494 000	Malabo
ERITREA		117 400	45 328	4 141 000	Asmara

guages		religions	currency
kmen, Uzbek, Russian		Sunni Muslim, Russian Orthodox	Turkmen manat
bic, English		Sunni Muslim, Shi'a Muslim	United Arab Emirates dirham
ek, Russian, Tajik, Kazakh		Sunni Muslim, Russian Orthodox	Uzbek som
tnamese, Thai, Khmer, Chinese, local lang.		Buddhist, Taoist, Roman Catholic, Cao Dai, Hoa Hao	Dong
bic		Sunni Muslim, Shi'a Muslim	Yemeni rial

bital	languages	religions	currency
e Settlement	English	Buddhist, Sunni Muslim, Protestant, Rom. Cath.	Australian dollar
st Island	English	Sunni Muslim, Christian	Australian dollar
ra	Arabic	Sunni Muslim, Shi'a Muslim	Israeli shekel
nagar			
	Arabic, Hebrew	Sunni Muslim, Jewish, Shi'a Muslim, Christian	Jordanian dinar, Israeli shekel

guages	religions	currency
bic, French, Berber	Sunni Muslim	Algerian dinar
rtuguese, Bantu, local languages	Roman Catholic, Protestant, traditional beliefs	Kwanza
nch, Fon, Yoruba, Adja, local languages	Traditional beliefs, Roman Catholic, Sunni Muslim	CFA franc*
glish, Setswana, Shona, local languages	Traditional beliefs, Protestant, Roman Catholic	Pula
nch, Moore (Mossi), Fulani, local lang.	Sunni Muslim, traditional beliefs, Roman Catholic	CFA franc*
undi (Hutu, Tutsi), French	Roman Catholic, traditional beliefs, Protestant	Burundian franc
nch, English, Fang, Bamileke, local lang.	Rom. Catholic, traditional beliefs, Sunni Muslim, Protestant	CFA franc*
rtuguese, creole	Roman Catholic, Protestant	Cape Verde escudo
nch, Sango, Banda, Baya, local languages	Protestant, Rom. Catholic, traditional beliefs, Sunni Muslim	CFA franc*
bic, French, Sara, local languages	Sunni Muslim, Rom. Catholic, Protestant, traditional beliefs	CFA franc*
morian, French, Arabic	Sunni Muslim, Roman Catholic	Comoros franc
nch, Kongo, Monokutuba, local lang.	Rom. Catholic, Protestant, traditional beliefs, Sunni Muslim	CFA franc*
nch, Lingala, Swahili, Kongo, local lang.	Christian, Sunni Muslim	Congolese franc
nch, creole, Akan, local languages	Sunni Muslim, Rom. Catholic, traditional beliefs, Protestant	CFA franc*
mali, Afar, French, Arabic	Sunni Muslim, Christian	Djibouti franc
abic	Sunni Muslim, Coptic Christian	Egyptian pound
anish, French, Fang	Roman Catholic, traditional beliefs	CFA franc*
rinya, Tigre	Sunni Muslim, Coptic Christian	Nakfa

AFRICA COUNTRIES (continued)		area sq km	area sq miles	population	capital
ETHIOPIA		1 133 880	437 794	70 678 000	Addis Ababa
GABON		267 667	103 347	1 329 000	Libreville
THE GAMBIA		11 295	4 361	1 426 000	Banjul
GHANA		238 537	92 100	20 922 000	Accra
GUINEA		245 857	94 926	8 480 000	Conakry
GUINEA-BISSAU		36 125	13 948	1 493 000	Bissau
KENYA		582 646	224 961	31 987 000	Nairobi
LESOTHO		30 355	11 720	1 802 000	Maseru
LIBERIA		111 369	43 000	3 367 000	Monrovia
LIBYA		1 759 540	679 362	5 551 000	Tripoli
MADAGASCAR		587 041	226 658	17 404 000	Antananarivo
MALAWI		118 484	45 747	12 105 000	Lilongwe
MALI		1 240 140	478 821	13 007 000	Bamako
MAURITANIA		1 030 700	397 955	2 893 000	Nouakchott
MAURITIUS		2 040	788	1 221 000	Port Louis
MOROCCO		446 550	172 414	30 566 000	Rabat
MOZAMBIQUE		799 380	308 642	18 863 000	Maputo
NAMIBIA		824 292	318 261	1 987 000	Windhoek
NIGER		1 267 000	489 191	11 972 000	Niamey
NIGERIA		923 768	356 669	124 009 000	Abuja
RWANDA		26 338	10 169	8 387 000	Kigali
SÃO TOMÉ AND PRÍNCIPE		964	372	161 000	São Tomé
SENEGAL		196 720	75 954	10 095 000	Dakar
SEYCHELLES		455	176	81 000	Victoria
SIERRA LEONE		71 740	27 699	4 971 000	Freetown
SOMALIA		637 657	246 201	9 890 000	Mogadishu
SOUTH AFRICA, REPUBLIC OF		1 219 090	470 693	45 026 000	Pretoria/Cape Town
SUDAN		2 505 813	967 500	33 610 000	Khartoum
SWAZILAND		17 364	6 704	1 077 000	Mbabane
TANZANIA		945 087	364 900	36 977 000	Dodoma
TOGO		56 785	21 925	4 909 000	Lomé
TUNISIA		164 150	63 379	9 832 000	Tunis
UGANDA		241 038	93 065	25 827 000	Kampala

languages	religions	currency
oromo, Amharic, Tigrinya, local languages	Ethiopian Orthodox, Sunni Muslim, traditional beliefs	Birr
rench, Fang, local languages	Roman Catholic, Protestant, traditional beliefs	CFA franc*
nglish, Malinke, Fulani, Wolof	Sunni Muslim, Protestant	Dalasi
nglish, Hausa, Akan, local languages	Christian, Sunni Muslim, traditional beliefs	Cedi
rench, Fulani, Malinke, local languages	Sunni Muslim, traditional beliefs, Christian	Guinea franc
ortuguese, crioulo, local languages	Traditional beliefs, Sunni Muslim, Christian	CFA franc*
wahili, English, local languages	Christian, traditional beliefs	Kenyan shilling
esotho, English, Zulu	Christian, traditional beliefs	Loti, S. African rand
nglish, creole, local languages	Traditional beliefs, Christian, Sunni Muslim	Liberian dollar
rabic, Berber	Sunni Muslim	Libyan dinar
alagasy, French	Traditional beliefs, Christian, Sunni Muslim	Ariary, Malagasy franc
nichewa, English, local languages	Christian, traditional beliefs, Sunni Muslim	Malawian kwacha
rench, Bambara, local languages	Sunni Muslim, traditional beliefs, Christian	CFA franc*
rabic, French, local languages	Sunni Muslim	Ouguiya
nglish, creole, Hindi, Bhojpuri, French	Hindu, Roman Catholic, Christian	Mauritius rupee
rabic, Berber, French	Sunni Muslim	Moroccan dirham
ortuguese, Makua, Tsonga, local languages	Traditional beliefs, Roman Catholic, Sunni Muslim	Metical
nglish, Afrikaans, Germ., Ovambo, loc. lang.	Protestant, Roman Catholic	Namibian dollar
rench, Hausa, Fulani, local languages	Sunni Muslim, traditional beliefs	CFA franc*
nglish, Hausa, Yoruba, Ibo, Fulani, local lang.	Sunni Muslim, Christian, traditional beliefs	Naira
inyarwanda, French, English	Roman Catholic, traditional beliefs, Protestant	Rwandan franc
ortuguese, creole	Roman Catholic, Protestant	Dobra
rench, Wolof, Fulani, local languages	Sunni Muslim, Roman Catholic, traditional beliefs	CFA franc*
nglish, French, creole	Roman Catholic, Protestant	Seychelles rupee
nglish, creole, Mende, Temne, local lang.	Sunni Muslim, traditional beliefs	Leone
omali, Arabic	Sunni Muslim	Somali shilling
frikaans, English, nine official local languages	Protestant, Roman Catholic, Sunni Muslim, Hindu	Rand
rabic, Dinka, Nubian, Beja, Nuer, local lang.	Sunni Muslim, traditional beliefs, Christian	Sudanese dinar
wazi, English	Christian, traditional beliefs	Emalangeni, S. African rand
wahili, English, Nyamwezi, local languages	Shi'a Muslim, Sunni Muslim, traditional beliefs, Christian	Tanzanian shilling
rench, Ewe, Kabre, local languages	Traditional beliefs, Christian, Sunni Muslim	CFA franc*
rabic, French	Sunni Muslim	Tunisian dinar
nglish, Swahili, Luganda, local languages	Rom. Catholic, Protestant, Sunni Muslim, traditional beliefs	Ugandan shilling

AFRICA COUNTRIES (continued)	area sq km	area sq miles	population	capital
ZAMBIA	752 614	290 586	10 812 000	Lusaka
ZIMBABWE	390 759	150 873	12 891 000	Harare

AFRICA DEPENDENT AND DISPUTED TERRITORIES		area sq km	area sq miles	populat
Canary Islands	Autonomous Community of Spain	7 447	2 875	1 694 4
Madeira	Autonomous Region of Portugal	779	301	242 0
Mayotte	French Territorial Collectivity	373	144	171 0
Réunion	French Overseas Department	2 551	985	756 0
St Helena and Dependencies	United Kingdom Overseas Territory	121	47	5 0
Western Sahara	Disputed territory (Morocco)	266 000	102 703	308 0

OCEANIA COUNTRIES		area sq km	area sq miles	population	capital
AUSTRALIA		7 692 024	2 969 907	19 731 000	Canberra
FIJI		18 330	7 077	839 000	Suva
KIRIBATI		717	277	88 000	Bairiki
MARSHALL ISLANDS		181	70	53 000	Delap-Uliga-Djarrit
MICRONESIA, FED. STATES OF		701	271	109 000	Palikir
NAURU		21	8	13 000	Yaren
NEW ZEALAND		270 534	104 454	3 875 000	Wellington
PAPUA NEW GUINEA		462 840	178 704	5 711 000	Port Moresby
SAMOA		2 831	1 093	178 000	Apia
SOLOMON ISLANDS		28 370	10 954	477 000	Honiara
TONGA		748	289	104 000	Nuku'alofa
TUVALU		25	10	11 000	Vaiaku
VANUATU		12 190	4 707	212 000	Port Vila

OCEANIA DEPENDENT TERRITORIES		area sq km	area sq miles	populat
American Samoa	United States Unincorporated Territory	197	76	67 0
Cook Islands	Self-governing New Zealand Territory	293	113	18 0
French Polynesia	French Overseas Territory	3 265	1 261	244 0
Guam	United States Unincorporated Territory	541	209	163 0
New Caledonia	French Overseas Territory	19 058	7 358	228 0

languages	religions	currency
glish, Bemba, Nyanja, Tonga, local lang.	Christian, traditional beliefs	Zambian kwacha
glish, Shona, Ndebele	Christian, traditional beliefs	Zimbabwean dollar

pital	languages	religions	currency
Cruz de Tenerife, Las Palmas	Spanish	Roman Catholic	Euro
nchal	Portuguese	Roman Catholic, Protestant	Euro
aoudzi	French, Mahorian	Sunni Muslim, Christian	Euro
Denis	French, creole	Roman Catholic	Euro
mestown	English	Protestant, Roman Catholic	St Helena pound
youne	Arabic	Sunni Muslim	Moroccan dirham

*Communauté Financière Africaine franc

languages	religions	currency
glish, Italian, Greek	Protestant, Roman Catholic, Orthodox	Australian dollar
glish, Fijian, Hindi	Christian, Hindu, Sunni Muslim	Fiji dollar
ibertese, English	Roman Catholic, Protestant	Australian dollar
glish, Marshallese	Protestant, Roman Catholic	US dollar
glish, Chuukese, Pohnpeian, local lang.	Roman Catholic, Protestant	US dollar
auruan, English	Protestant, Roman Catholic	Australian dollar
glish, Maori	Protestant, Roman Catholic	New Zealand dollar
glish, Tok Pisin (creole), local languages	Protestant, Roman Catholic, traditional beliefs	Kina
moan, English	Protestant, Roman Catholic	Tala
glish, creole, local languages	Protestant, Roman Catholic	Solomon Islands dollar
ngan, English	Protestant, Roman Catholic	Pa'anga
valuan, English	Protestant	Australian dollar
glish, Bislama (creole), French	Protestant, Roman Catholic, traditional beliefs	Vatu

pital	languages	religions	currency
gotogo	Samoan, English	Protestant, Roman Catholic	US dollar
arua	English, Maori	Protestant, Roman Catholic	New Zealand dollar
peete	French, Tahitian, Polynesian lang.	Protestant, Roman Catholic	CFP franc*
gåtña	Chamorro, English, Tapalog	Roman Catholic	US dollar
uméa	French, local languages	Roman Catholic, Protestant, Sunni Muslim	CFP franc*

OCEANIA DEPENDENT TERRITORIES (continued)			area sq km	area sq miles	popula
Niue		Self-governing New Zealand Territory	258	100	2
Norfolk Island		Australian External Territory	35	14	2
Northern Mariana Islands		United States Commonwealth	477	184	79
Pitcairn Islands		United Kingdom Overseas Territory	45	17	
Tokelau		New Zealand Overseas Territory	10	4	2
Wallis and Futuna Islands		French Overseas Territory	274	106	15

NORTH AMERICA COUNTRIES		area sq km	area sq miles	population	capital
ANTIGUA AND BARBUDA		442	171	73 000	St John's
THE BAHAMAS		13 939	5 382	314 000	Nassau
BARBADOS		430	166	270 000	Bridgetown
BELIZE		22 965	8 867	256 000	Belmopan
CANADA		9 984 670	3 855 103	31 510 000	Ottawa
COSTA RICA		51 100	19 730	4 173 000	San José
CUBA		110 860	42 803	11 300 000	Havana
DOMINICA		750	290	79 000	Roseau
DOMINICAN REPUBLIC		48 442	18 704	8 745 000	Santo Domingo
EL SALVADOR		21 041	8 124	6 515 000	San Salvador
GRENADA		378	146	80 000	St George's
GUATEMALA		108 890	42 043	12 347 000	Guatemala City
HAITI		27 750	10 714	8 326 000	Port-au-Prince
HONDURAS		112 088	43 277	6 941 000	Tegucigalpa
JAMAICA		10 991	4 244	2 651 000	Kingston
MEXICO		1 972 545	761 604	103 457 000	Mexico City
NICARAGUA		130 000	50 193	5 466 000	Managua
PANAMA		77 082	29 762	3 120 000	Panama City
ST KITTS AND NEVIS		261	101	42 000	Basseterre
ST LUCIA		616	238	149 000	Castries
ST VINCENT AND THE GRENADINES		389	150	120 000	Kingstown
TRINIDAD AND TOBAGO		5 130	1 981	1 303 000	Port of Spain
UNITED STATES OF AMERICA		9 826 635	3 794 085	294 043 000	Washington DC

capital	languages	religions	currency
Alofi	English, Polynesian	Christian	New Zealand dollar
Kingston	English	Protestant, Roman Catholic	Australian dollar
Capitol Hill	English, Chamorro, local lang.	Roman Catholic	US dollar
Adamstown	English	Protestant	New Zealand dollar
	English, Tokelauan	Christian	New Zealand dollar
Matā'utu	French, Wallisian, Futunian	Roman Catholic	CFP franc*

*Franc des Comptoirs Français du Pacifique

languages	religions	*	currency
English, creole	Protestant, Roman Catholic		East Caribbean dollar
English, creole	Protestant, Roman Catholic		Bahamian dollar
English, creole	Protestant, Roman Catholic		Barbados dollar
English, Spanish, Mayan, creole	Roman Catholic, Protestant		Belize dollar
English, French	Roman Catholic, Protestant, Eastern Orthodox, Jewish		Canadian dollar
Spanish	Roman Catholic, Protestant		Costa Rican colón
Spanish	Roman Catholic, Protestant		Cuban peso
English, creole	Roman Catholic, Protestant		East Caribbean dollar
Spanish, creole	Roman Catholic, Protestant		Dominican peso
Spanish	Roman Catholic, Protestant		El Sal. colón, US dollar
English, creole	Roman Catholic, Protestant		East Caribbean dollar
Spanish, Mayan languages	Roman Catholic, Protestant		Quetzal, US dollar
French, creole	Roman Catholic, Protestant, Voodoo		Gourde
Spanish, Amerindian languages	Roman Catholic, Protestant		Lempira
English, creole	Protestant, Roman Catholic		Jamaican dollar
Spanish, Amerindian languages	Roman Catholic, Protestant		Mexican peso
Spanish, Amerindian languages	Roman Catholic, Protestant		Córdoba
Spanish, English, Amerindian languages	Roman Catholic, Protestant, Sunni Muslim		Balboa
English, creole	Protestant, Roman Catholic		East Caribbean dollar
English, creole	Roman Catholic, Protestant		East Caribbean dollar
English, creole	Protestant, Roman Catholic		East Caribbean dollar
English, creole, Hindi	Roman Catholic, Hindu, Protestant, Sunni Muslim		Trinidad and Tob. dollar
English, Spanish	Protestant, Roman Catholic, Sunni Muslim, Jewish		US dollar

world countries
oceania, north america

NORTH AMERICA DEPENDENT TERRITORIES

			area sq km	area sq miles	populati
Anguilla		United Kingdom Overseas Territory	155	60	12 0
Aruba		Self-governing Netherlands Territory	193	75	100 0
Bermuda		United Kingdom Overseas Territory	54	21	82 0
Cayman Islands		United Kingdom Overseas Territory	259	100	40 0
Greenland		Self-governing Danish Territory	2 175 600	840 004	57 0
Guadeloupe		French Overseas Department	1 780	687	440 0
Martinique		French Overseas Department	1 079	417	393 0
Montserrat		United Kingdom Overseas Territory	100	39	4 0
Netherlands Antilles		Self-governing Netherlands Territory	800	309	221 0
Puerto Rico		United States Commonwealth	9 104	3 515	3 879 0
St Pierre and Miquelon		French Territorial Collectivity	242	93	6 0
Turks and Caicos Islands		United Kingdom Overseas Territory	430	166	21 0
Virgin Islands (U.K.)		United Kingdom Overseas Territory	153	59	21 0
Virgin Islands (U.S.A.)		United States Unincorporated Territory	352	136	111 0

SOUTH AMERICA COUNTRIES

		area sq km	area sq miles	population	capital
ARGENTINA		2 766 889	1 068 302	38 428 000	Buenos Aires
BOLIVIA		1 098 581	424 164	8 808 000	La Paz/Sucre
BRAZIL		8 514 879	3 287 613	178 470 000	Brasília
CHILE		756 945	292 258	15 805 000	Santiago
COLOMBIA		1 141 748	440 831	44 222 000	Bogotá
ECUADOR		272 045	105 037	13 003 000	Quito
GUYANA		214 969	83 000	765 000	Georgetown
PARAGUAY		406 752	157 048	5 878 000	Asunción
PERU		1 285 216	496 225	27 167 000	Lima
SURINAME		163 820	63 251	436 000	Paramaribo
URUGUAY		176 215	68 037	3 415 000	Montevideo
VENEZUELA		912 050	352 144	25 699 000	Caracas

SOUTH AMERICA DEPENDENT TERRITORIES

			area sq km	area sq miles	populati
Falkland Islands		United Kingdom Overseas Territory	12 170	4 699	3 0
French Guiana		French Overseas Department	90 000	34 749	178 0

pital	languages	religions	currency
e Valley	English	Protestant, Roman Catholic	East Caribbean dollar
anjestad	Papiamento, Dutch, English	Roman Catholic, Protestant	Arubian florin
amilton	English	Protestant, Roman Catholic	Bermuda dollar
eorge Town	English	Protestant, Roman Catholic	Cayman Islands dollar
uk	Greenlandic, Danish	Protestant	Danish krone
asse-Terre	French, creole	Roman Catholic	Euro
rt-de-France	French, creole	Roman Catholic, traditional beliefs	Euro
ymouth	English	Protestant, Roman Catholic	East Caribbean dollar
llemstad	Dutch, Papiamento, English	Roman Catholic, Protestant	Neth. Antilles guilder
an Juan	Spanish, English	Roman Catholic, Protestant	US dollar
-Pierre	French	Roman Catholic	Euro
and Turk	English	Protestant	US dollar
oad Town	English	Protestant, Roman Catholic	US dollar
arlotte Amalie	English, Spanish	Protestant, Roman Catholic	US dollar

nguages	religions	currency
anish, Italian, Amerindian languages	Roman Catholic, Protestant	Argentinian peso
panish, Quechua, Aymara	Roman Catholic, Protestant, Baha'i	Boliviano
ortuguese	Roman Catholic	Real
panish, Amerindian languages	Roman Catholic, Protestant	Chilean peso
panish, Amerindian languages	Roman Catholic, Protestant	Colombian peso
panish, Quechua, other Amerindian lang.	Roman Catholic	US dollar
nglish, creole, Amerindian languages	Protestant, Hindu, Roman Catholic, Sunni Muslim	Guyana dollar
panish, Guarani	Roman Catholic, Protestant	Guarani
panish, Quechua, Aymara	Roman Catholic, Protestant	Sol
utch, Surinamese, English, Hindi	Hindu, Roman Catholic, Protestant, Sunni Muslim	Suriname guilder
panish	Roman Catholic, Protestant, Jewish	Uruguayan peso
panish, Amerindian languages	Roman Catholic, Protestant	Bolivar

apital	languages	religions	currency
anley	English	Protestant, Roman Catholic	Falkland Islands pound
ayenne	French, creole	Roman Catholic	Euro

world countries
north america, south america

AL.	ALBANIA	JOR.	JORDAN
ARM.	ARMENIA	K.	KUWAIT
AUS.	AUSTRIA	KYR.	KYRGYZSTAN
AZ.	AZERBAIJAN	LEB.	LEBANON
B.	BURUNDI	LITH.	LITHUANIA
BE.	BENIN	LUX.	LUXEMBOURG
BEL.	BELGIUM	M.	MACEDONIA
B.H.	BOSNIA–HERZEGOVINA	MO.	MOLDOVA
BN.	BAHRAIN	NETH.	NETHERLANDS
BUR.	BURKINA	NI.	NIGERIA
CAM.	CAMEROON	POL.	POLAND
C.A.R.	CENTRAL AFRICAN REPUBLIC	Q.	QATAR
C.D'I.	COTE D'IVOIRE	R.	RWANDA
CR.	CROATIA	SLA.	SLOVAKIA
CYP.	CYPRUS	SL.	SLOVENIA
C.Z.R.	CZECH REPUBLIC	S.M.	SERBIA AND
DEN.	DENMARK		MONTENEGRO
EQ.G.	EQUATORIAL GUINEA	SUR.	SURINAME
FR.G.	FRENCH GUIANA	SW.	SWITZERLAND
GEOR.	GEORGIA	T.	TOGO
GER.	GERMANY	TAJIK.	TAJIKISTAN
GH.	GHANA	TURKM.	TURKMENISTAN
GUY.	GUYANA	U.A.E.	UNITED ARAB
HUN.	HUNGARY		EMIRATES
ISR.	ISRAEL	UZBEK.	UZBEKISTAN

1:238 000 000

0	1000	2000	3000 miles
0	2000	4000 km	

World extremes – countries

Largest country	Russian Federation	17 075 400 sq km	6 592 849 sq miles
Smallest country	Vatican City	0.5 sq km	0.2 sq miles
Largest population	China	1 289 161 000	
Smallest population	Vatican City	472	
Most densely populated country	Monaco	17 000 per sq km	34 000 per sq mile
Least densely populated country	Mongolia	2 per sq km	4 per sq mile

FACTS

The Pacific Ocean is larger than all the continents' land areas combined

52% of the earth's land surface is below 500 m / 1 644 ft

Lake Baikal, in the Russian Federation, is the world's deepest lake with a maximum depth of 1 637 m / 5 371 ft

Earth's dimensions

Total area	509 450 000 sq km	196 699 746 sq miles
Land area	148 721 931 sq km	57 421 861 sq miles
Water area	360 728 064 sq km	139 277 885 sq miles
Equatorial diameter	12 756 km	7 927 miles
Polar diameter	12 714 km	7 901 miles
Equatorial circumference	40 075 km	24 903 miles
Meridional circumference	40 008 km	24 861 miles

1:238 000 000

0   1000   2000   3000 miles
0   2000   4000 km

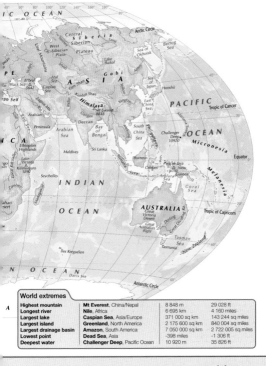

World extremes			
Highest mountain	**Mt Everest**, China/Nepal	8 848 m	29 028 ft
Longest river	**Nile**, Africa	6 695 km	4 160 miles
Largest lake	**Caspian Sea**, Asia/Europe	371 000 sq km	143 244 sq miles
Largest island	**Greenland**, North America	2 175 600 sq km	840 004 sq miles
Largest drainage basin	**Amazon**, South America	7 050 000 sq km	2 722 005 sq miles
Lowest point	**Dead Sea**, Asia	-398 miles	-1 306 ft
Deepest water	**Challenger Deep**, Pacific Ocean	10 920 m	35 826 ft

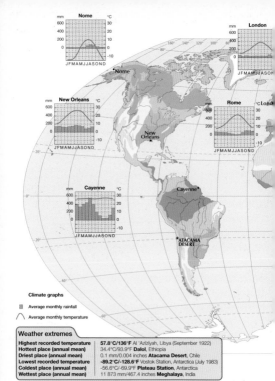

Climate graphs

▨ Average monthly rainfall

⌃ Average monthly temperature

Weather extremes

Highest recorded temperature	57.8°C/136°F Al 'Azīzīyah, Libya (September 1922)
Hottest place (annual mean)	34.4°C/93.9°F Dalol, Ethiopia
Driest place (annual mean)	0.1 mm/0.004 inches Atacama Desert, Chile
Lowest recorded temperature	-89.2°C/-128.6°F Vostok Station, Antarctica (July 1983)
Coldest place (annual mean)	-56.6°C/-69.9°F Plateau Station, Antarctica
Wettest place (annual mean)	11 873 mm/467.4 inches Meghalaya, India

1:238 000 000

0   1000   2000   3000 miles
0   2000   4000 km

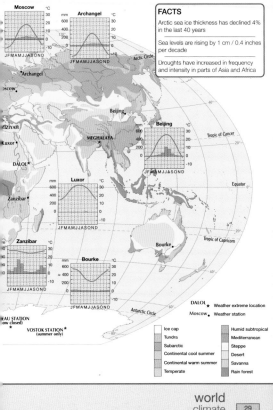

FACTS

Arctic sea ice thickness has declined 4% in the last 40 years

Sea levels are rising by 1 cm / 0.4 inches per decade

Droughts have increased in frequency and intensity in parts of Asia and Africa

Moscow °C
mm 600 400 200
JFMAMJJASOND

Archangel °C
mm 600 400 200
JFMAMJJASOND

Beijing °C
mm 600 400 200
JFMAMJJASOND

Luxor °C
mm 600 400 200
JFMAMJJASOND

Zanzibar °C
mm 600 400 200
JFMAMJJASOND

Bourke °C
mm 600 400 200
JFMAMJJASOND

Arctic Circle

Tropic of Cancer

Equator

Tropic of Capricorn

Antarctic Circle

Moscow
Archangel
Beijing
ZIYAR
Luxor
MEGHALAYA
DALOL
Zanzibar
Bourke

EAU STATION
(ow closed)

VOSTOK STATION
(summer only)

DALOL ★ Weather extreme location

Moscow ● Weather station

Ice cap
Tundra
Subarctic
Continental cool summer
Continental warm summer
Temperate

Humid subtropical
Mediterranean
Steppe
Desert
Savanna
Rain forest

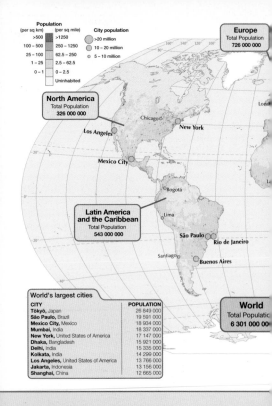

Population

(per sq km)	(per sq mile)
>500	>1250
100 – 500	250 – 1250
25 – 100	62.5 – 250
1 – 25	2.5 – 62.5
0 – 1	0 – 2.5
	Uninhabited

City population
- ⬤ >20 million
- ⬤ 10 – 20 million
- ○ 5 – 10 million

Europe
Total Population
726 000 000

North America
Total Population
326 000 000

Latin America and the Caribbean
Total Population
543 000 000

World
Total Population
6 301 000 000

London

Chicago
New York
Los Angeles
Mexico City
Bogotá
Lima
São Paulo
Rio de Janeiro
Santiago
Buenos Aires

World's largest cities	
CITY	POPULATION
Tōkyō, Japan	26 849 000
São Paulo, Brazil	19 591 000
Mexico City, Mexico	18 934 000
Mumbai, India	18 337 000
New York, United States of America	17 147 000
Dhaka, Bangladesh	15 921 000
Delhi, India	15 335 000
Kolkata, India	14 299 000
Los Angeles, United States of America	13 766 000
Jakarta, Indonesia	13 156 000
Shanghai, China	12 665 000

1:238 000 000

0   1000   2000   3000 miles
0   2000   4000 km

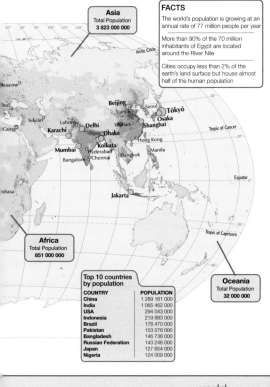

Asia
Total Population
3 823 000 000

FACTS

The world's population is growing at an annual rate of 77 million people per year

More than 90% of the 70 million inhabitants of Egypt are located around the River Nile

Cities occupy less than 2% of the earth's land surface but house almost half of the human population

Arctic Circle

Moscow

bul

Tehrān

Cairo

Tropic of Cancer

Lahore Delhi Beijing Seoul Tōkyō
Karachi Tianjin Osaka
Dhaka Wuhan Shanghai
Mumbai Kolkata Hong Kong
Hyderabad Manila
Bangalore Chennai Bangkok

shasa

Jakarta

Equator

Africa
Total Population
851 000 000

Tropic of Capricorn

Top 10 countries by population

COUNTRY	POPULATION
China	1 289 161 000
India	1 065 462 000
USA	294 043 000
Indonesia	219 883 000
Brazil	178 470 000
Pakistan	153 578 000
Bangladesh	146 736 000
Russian Federation	143 246 000
Japan	127 654 000
Nigeria	124 009 000

Oceania
Total Population
32 000 000

world
population and cities

Europe's countries		
Largest country	Russian Federation	17 075 400 sq km	6 592 812 sq miles
Smallest country	Vatican City	0.5 sq km	0.2 sq miles
Largest population	Russian Federation	143 246 000	
Smallest population	Vatican City	472	
Most densely populated country	Monaco	17 000 per sq km	34 000 per sq mile
Least densely populated country	Iceland	3 per sq km	7 per sq mile

Reykjavík **ICELAND**

Norwegian
Sea

Tórshavn Faroe
Islands
(Denmark)

Bergen Oslo

ATLANTIC

OCEAN

Glasgow Edinburgh *North*
Belfast **UNITED** *Sea*
IRELAND KINGDOM DENMARK
Dublin Manchester Copenhagen
Birmingham Hamburg
Cardiff **NETH.** Berlin
The Hague Amsterdam
English Channel London Brussels Essen
Channel Islands **BELGIUM GERMANY**
LUX. Frankfurt Pra
Nantes Paris am Main
Luxembourg Vie
Orléans Strasbourg Munich **AUST**
FRANCE Bern Zürich **LIE.** Bra
Vaduz **SLOV**
Bay of Geneva
Biscay Lyon Milan Ljubljana
Bordeaux Turin **SAN**
MARINO
IT
Andorra **MONACO**
la Vella Marseille Corsica
Oporto **ANDORRA** Rome
PORTUGAL Barcelona Vatican City
Tagus Naples
Lisbon Madrid **SPAIN** Sardinia *Tyrrhenian*
Palma *Sea*
Valencia de Mallorca
Seville *Balearic* Palermo
Islands Sicil
Cádiz Cartagena *Medite* r
Gibraltar (U.K.) **MALTA**
Valletta

Azores
(Portugal)

Madeira
(Portugal)

AFRICA

AL.	ALBANIA
B.H.	BOSNIA-HERZEGOVINA
CR.	CROATIA
CZ.R.	CZECH REPUBLIC
HUN.	HUNGARY
LIE.	LIECHTENSTEIN
LUX.	LUXEMBOURG
M.	MACEDONIA
NETH.	NETHERLANDS
S.M.	SERBIA AND MONTENEGRO
SW.	SWITZERLAND

1:46 500 000

0   150   300   450 miles
0   300   600 km

FACTS

The European Union was founded by six countries: Belgium, France, Germany, Italy, Luxembourg and the Netherlands

Europe has the 2 smallest independent countries in the world – Vatican City and Monaco

The Roman Catholic Church is based in the Vatican City, an independent country entirely within the city of Rome.

Europe's capitals

Largest capital (population)	Paris, France	9 753 000	
Smallest capital (population)	Vatican City	472	
Most northerly capital	Reykjavik, Iceland	64° 39'N	
Most southerly capital	Valletta, Malta	35° 54'N	
Highest capital	Andorra la Vella, Andorra	1 029 m	3 376 ft

europe
countries

europe
western russian federation

europe
ukraine, moldova and romania
39

RUSSIAN FEDERATION

FINLAND

Gulf of Bothnia

NORWAY

ICELAND

Arctic Circle

Norwegian Sea

North Cape (Nordkapp)

Vatnajökull

Reykjavík

Faxaflói

Arctic Circle

40   1:13 000 000

0   50   100   150 miles

0   100   200 km

europe
scandinavia and iceland

41

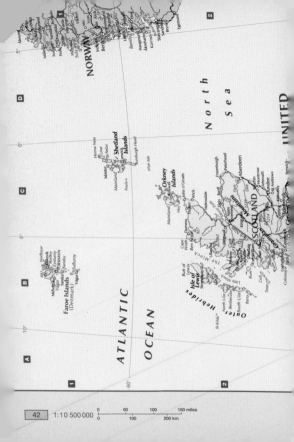

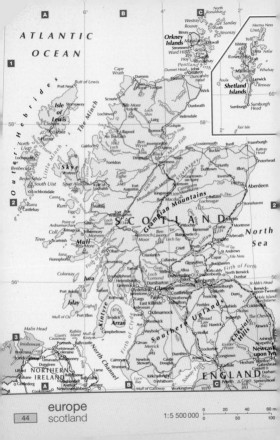

ATLANTIC OCEAN

A — **B** — **C**

SCOTLAND

Orkney Islands

Shetland Islands

Herma Ness
Unst
Yell
Mainland
Lerwick
Bressay
Sumburgh Head

Westray
North Ronaldsay
Sanday
Stronsay
Mainland
Stromness
Ward Hills
Hoy
Pentland Firth
Dunnet Head
Duncansby Head
Fair Isle

Cape Wrath
Durness
Tongue
Thurso
Wick
Loch Shin
Laing
Dunbeath
Helmsdale

Butt of Lewis
Port Nis
Stornoway
Isle of Lewis
Clisham
Tarbert
Harris
North Uist
Benbecula
South Uist
Lochboisdale
Barra
Castlebay

The Minch
Little Minch
Outer Hebrides

Gairloch
An Teallach
Loch Maree
Torridon
Ben Wyvis
Dingwall
Dornoch
Golspie
Lossiemouth
Elgin
Buckie
Fraserburgh
Rattray Head
Peterhead

Skye
Cuillin Hills
Sgurr Alasdair
Loch Lochart
Fort Augustus
Monadhliath Mountains
Grantown
Cairngorm Mountains
Aviemore
Ellon
Aberdeen

Rum
Eigg
Canna
Ben Macdui
Braemar
Lochnagar
Stonehaven

Muck
Point of Ardnamurchan
Coll
Arisaig
Fort William
Ben Nevis
Loch Linnhe
Rannoch Moor
Ben Lawers
Loch Tay
Crieff
Sidlaw Hills
Dundee
St Andrews
Firth of Tay
Arbroath
Montrose
Forfar
Brechin

Tiree
Scarinish
Iona
Fionnphort
Mull
Ben More
Oban
Loch Awe
Inveraray
Crianlarich
Callander
Glenrothes
Dunfermline
Kirkcaldy
Firth of Forth
North Berwick
Dunbar
St Abb's Head

Colonsay
Jura
Islay
Port Askaig
Port Ellen
Mull of Oa
Kintyre
Tarbert
Lochgilphead
Gigha
Arran
Campbeltown
Mull of Kintyre

Firth of Lorn
Firth of Clyde
Dunoon
Dumbarton
Glasgow
Greenock
Largs
Irvine
Kilmarnock
Ayr
Maybole
Girvan
Merrick
Dumfries
Lockerbie
Longtown
Carlisle

Bute
Paisley
East Kilbride
Hamilton
Motherwell
Coatbridge
Edinburgh
Peebles
Galashiels
Duns
Kelso
Jedburgh
The Cheviot
Alnwick

Ailsa Craig
Newton Stewart
Castle Douglas
Kirkcudbright
Workington
Solway Firth

Southern Uplands
Cheviot Hills
Hawick
Kielder Water
Newcastle upon Tyne
Hexham
Durham

NORTH SEA

SOUTHERN UPLANDS

ENGLAND

NORTHERN IRELAND

Malin Head
Inishowen
Giant's Causeway
Rathlin Island
Ballycastle
Portrush
Coleraine
Portstewart
Limavady
Ballymena
Larne
Dungiven
Ballymoney
Cookstown
Antrim
Newtownabbey
Lurgan

A — **B** — **C**

europe
italy and the balkans

57

Asia's countries			
Largest country	Russian Federation	17 075 400 sq km	6 592 812 sq miles
Smallest country	Maldives	298 sq km	115 sq miles
Largest population	China	1 289 161 000	
Smallest population	Palau	20 000	
Most densely populated country	Singapore	6 656 per sq km	17 219 per sq mile
Least densely populated country	Mongolia	2 per sq km	4 per sq mile

EUROPE

Moscow

Nizhniy
Novgorod

RUSSIA

Mediterranean Sea

Yekaterinburg

Samara

Volga

Ural Mountains

Ural'sk

Nová

Black Sea

Ankara

TURKEY   GEORGIA

Astana

Adana   Tbilisi

Nicosia   ARMENIA   Yerevan

CYPRUS

LEBANON   SYRIA   AZERBAIJAN

Beirut   Damascus   Baku

Jerusalem   Amman

ISRAEL   JORDAN

Baghdad

IRAQ

KUWAIT
Kuwait

SAUDI
ARABIA

Jeddah   Riyadh

Mecca

Aral
Sea

Caspian Sea

Tabriz

Tehrān

IRAN

Shīrāz

BAHRAIN
Manama

QATAR
Doha

U.A.E.
Abu Dhabi

Dubai

Muscat

OMAN

KAZAKHSTAN

Lake
Balkhash

Bishkek

Almaty

Tashkent   Tien Sha

TURKMENISTAN   KYRGYZSTAN

Ashgabat   Dushanbe

TAJIKISTAN

Herāt   Kabul

AFGHANISTAN

Kandahār   Islamabad

Lahore

PAKISTAN   Delhi

Hyderabad   New Delhi

Agra

Karachi

Mount Everest

NEPAL   Kathmandu

Himal

Pla
of Ti

DI
Gang

Sana'ā
YEMEN

Red Sea

AFRICA

Aden

Socotra

Arabian
Sea

Ahmadabad

Mumbai

Hyderabad

Bangalore

Laccadive
Islands

Madurai

Colombo

MALDIVES   Male

Allahabad

INDIA

Kolkata

Ba
of Be

Chennai

Sri Jayewarde
Kotte

SRI LANKA

Asia's capitals			
Largest capital (population)	Tōkyō, Japan	26 849 000	
Smallest capital (population)	Koror, Palau	14 000	
Most northerly capital	Astana, Kazakhstan	51° 10'N	
Most southerly capital	Dili, East Timor	8° 35'S	
Highest capital	Thimphu, Bhutan	2 423 m	7 949 ft

INDIAN
OCEAN

British Indian
Ocean Territory

60   1:103 000 000

0	500	1000	1500 miles
0	1000	2000 km	

CTIC OCEAN

Bering
Sea

Magadan

DERATION

Sea
of
Okhotsk

Petropavlovsk-
Kamchatskiy

Irkutsk
Lake
Baikal

MONGOLIA

Ulan Bator

Harbin

Vladivostock

Sapporo

Hakodate

Shenyang

NORTH
KOREA
(East Sea)

Sea
of
Japan

JAPAN

Beijing
Dalian

Pyŏngyang

Tōkyō

Tianjin

SOUTH
KOREA

Seoul

Osaka

Hiroshima

Lanzhou

Yellow
River

Xi'an
Nanjing
Shanghai

Yellow
Sea

Fukuoka

PACIFIC
OCEAN

CHINA

Chengdu

Yangtze
Hangzhou

Wuhan

East
China
Sea

Chongqing

Kunming

Liuzhou

Guangzhou

T'aipei

TAIWAN

Nanning

Hong Kong

Kaohsiung

NMAR
(MA)

LAOS

Ha Nôi

Hai Phong

Luzon Strait

Vientiane

THAILAND

VIETNAM

Quezon City

PHILIPPINES

on

Bangkok

CAMBODIA

Manila

Phnom
Penh

Hồ Chí Minh

South
China
Sea

PALAU

Koror

nan

Bandar Seri
Begawan

Kota
Kinabalu

Davao

bar
ds
d)

MALAYSIA

BRUNEI

Celebes
Sea

Kuala Lumpur
Putrajaya

Kuching

Borneo

Jayapura

dan

SINGAPORE
Singapore

Pontianak

New
Guinea

Sumatra

INDONESIA

Jakarta

Palembang

Banjarmasin

Makassar

OCEANIA

Bandung

Semarang

Java

Surabaya

Laut Jawa

Laut Banda

EAST TIMOR

Dili

FACTS

Over 60% of the world's
population live in Asia

Asia has 12 of the world's
20 largest cities

East Timor is Asia's newest
independent country –
founded in May 2002

asia
malaysia and western indonesia

1:20 000 000

| 0 | 100 | 200 | 300 miles |
| 0 | 150 | 300 | 450 km |

asia
myanmar, thailand and indo-china

Luzon Strait

Ibatan • Batan
Itbayat • *Batan Islands*

Babuyan
Calayan • *Babuyan Islands*
Fuga • *Camiguin*

Laoag •
Aparri
Tuguegarao •

Vigan •
Cordillera Central
Ilagan
Santiago
Mount Pulog
San Fernando •
Dagupan • Baguio •
Lingayen • San Carlos •
Tarlac • San Jose •
Angeles • Cabanatuan •
San Fernando •
Olongapo • Valenzuela • *Polillo Islands*
MANILA **Quezon City**
Batangas • Lucena • *Lamon Bay*
Calapan • San Pablo •
Mount Banahaw • Lopez •
Calapan •
Mindoro
Roxas • *Sibuyan* • *Masbate*
Roxas • *Romblon*
Busuanga • *Sibuyan Sea*
Calamian Group
Culion

Philippine Sea

PHILIPPINES

Virac •
Catanduanes

Sorsogon •
Legaspi •

Calbayog •
Samar
Catbalogan •
Tacloban •
Ormoc •
Leyte
Visayan Sea
Roxas •
Panay
Iloilo Bacolod •
San Jose de
Buenavista •
Cuyo Islands
Iloilo •
Negros
Cebu
Cebu
Tagbilaran •
Cauayan •
Tanjay •
Bayawan •
Dumaguete •
Bohol Sea
Surigao •
Siargao
Dinagat •

South China Sea

Itbayat •
Itaytay •
Dumaran
Palawan • Puerto Princesa

Mount Mantalingajan
Aborlan •

Brooke's Point •

Sulu Sea

Kudat •
Kota Belud •
Gunung Kinabalu 4095
Ranau
Beaufort •
Sandakan •
Labuan
Lamag •
MALAYSIA SABAH
BANDAR SERI BEGAWAN
Pensiangan •
INDONESIA
Tawau •
Sempora •

Banggi
Mapin
Tumindao
Sitawitawi

Balabac Strait
Balabac
Balabac

Dipolog •
Dapitan •
Ozamiz •
Oroquieta •
Zamboanga Peninsula
Pagadian •
Zamboanga
Basilan
Isabela •
Jolo
Sulu Archipelago

Cagayan de Oro •
Iligan •
Malaybalay •
Mindanao
Cotabato •
Moro Gulf
Datu Piang •
2815
Mount Apo
Digos •
Kabacan •
Davao
Mati •
Davao Gulf

General Santos •
Sarangani Islands

Buluan •
Butuan •
Tandag •

Celebes Sea

Kepulauan Nanusa
Karakelong • *Kepulauan Talaud*
Sangir
Kahunung •

INDONESIA

asia
north korea and south korea

asia
central china

75

1:26 500 000

INDIAN OCEAN

B a y
of
B e n g a l

A r a b i a n
S e a

SRI LANKA

MALDIVES

North Andaman
Middle Andaman
South Andaman
Andaman Islands (India)
Little Andaman
Ten Degree Channel
Nicobar Islands (India)
Andaman Sea
Port Blair
Cape Negrais

Bassein
Henzada
Thandwe
Kyaukpyu
Ramree Island
Yoma

Akyab
Rameswaram

Nine Degree Channel
Eight Degree Channel
Minicoy
Kalpeni
Laccadive Islands (India)
Amindivi Islands
Androt
Kavaratti
Kadmat
Kiltan

Ari Atoll
MALE
Thiladhunmathi Atoll
Miladhunmadulu Atoll
Maldhunmadulu Atoll
Male Atoll

Mumbai (Bombay)
Ulhasnagar
Nashik
Pune (Poona)
Chiplun
Ratnagiri
Kolhapur
Panaji
Margao
Madgaon
Karwar
Udupi
Mangalore
Cannanore
Calicut
Cochin
Ernakulam
Allepey
Quilon
Trivandrum
Nagercoil
Tuticorin
Tinnevelly
Colombo
Galle

Nanded
Aurangabad
Ahmadnagar
Parbhani
Latur
Nizamabad
Solapur
Gulbarga
Bidar
Karimnagar
Hyderabad
Secunderabad
Warangal
Deccan
Raichur
Bellary
Kurnool
Cuddapah
Anantapur
Bangalore
Hubli
Dharwad
Bagalkot
Bijapur
Sangli
Belgaum
Mysore
Hassan
Shimoga
Davangere
Chitradurga
Coimbatore
Erode
Salem
Tiruppur
Dharmapuri
Vellore
Dindigul
Madurai
Rajapalaiyam
Trichur
Tiruchchirappalli
Thanjavur
Pudukkottai
Cuddalore
Pondicherry
Chennai (Madras)
Chidambaram
Tindivanam
Kanchipuram

Chandrapur
Warangal
Jagdalpur
Koraput
Vizianagaram
Vishakhapatnam
Rajahmundry
Kakinada
Eluru
Vijayawada
Machilipatnam
Guntur
Ongole
Nellore

Brahmapur
Bhubaneshwar
Puri
Balasore

Gulf of Mannar
Point Pedro
Jaffna
Trincomalee
Batticaloa
Kandy
Ratnapura
Yamsukuro

90°
80°
70°
10°
20°
10°

asia
arabian peninsula

83

ROMANIA

BUCHAREST

Odesa

UKRAINE

Crimea

Black Sea

BULGARIA

SOFIA

Plovdiv

Stara Zagora

Burgas

İstanbul

Zonguldak

Samsun

GREECE

Bursa

ANKARA

TURKEY

ATHENS

İzmir

Konya

Kayseri

Malatya

Aydın Denizli

Antalya

Taurus Mountains

Adana

Gaziantep

Aleppo

Rhodes
(Ródos)

NICOSIA
(Lefkosía)

Latakia

Hamāh

SYRIA

Homs

Crete
(Kríti)

CYPRUS

Paphos

Tripoli
(Trâblous)

BEIRUT
(Beyrouth)

LEBANON

DAMASCUS
(Dimashq)

Mediterranean Sea

Alexandria
(Al Iskandarīyah)

ISRAEL

Tel Aviv-Yafo

JERUSALEM

WEST
BANK

GAZA

AMMAN

LIBYA

Libyan Plateau

CAIRO
(Al Qāhirah)

GIZA

Pyramids of Giza

EGYPT

JORDAN

Great Sand Sea

1:20 000 000

| 0 | 100 | 200 | 300 miles |

| 0 | 150 | 300 | 450 km |

86   1:55 500 000

asia
russian federation

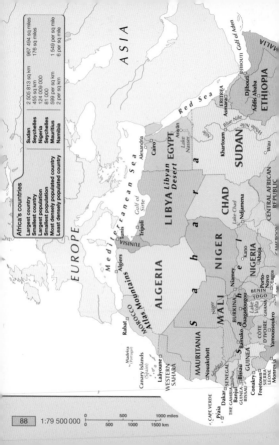

Africa's countries		
Largest country	Sudan	2 505 813 sq km	967 494 sq miles
Smallest country	Seychelles	455 sq km	176 sq miles
Largest population	Nigeria	124 009 000	
Smallest population	Seychelles	81 000	
Most densely populated country	Mauritius	599 per sq km	1 549 per sq mile
Least densely populated country	Namibia	2 per sq km	6 per sq mile

ASIA

EUROPE

Madeira (Portugal)

Canary Islands (Spain)

Mediterranean Sea

Gulf of Sirte

Red Sea

Gulf of Aden

MOROCCO
Rabat
Atlas Mountains

Algiers

TUNISIA
Tunis
Tripoli

LIBYA Libyan Desert

EGYPT
Alexandria
Cairo
Aswân
Lake Nasser

Blue Nile
White Nile

DJIBOUTI
Djibouti

ERITREA
Asmara

ETHIOPIA
Addis Ababa

SOMALIA

Laâyoune

WESTERN SAHARA

ALGERIA

S a h a r a

NIGER
Niamey

CHAD
Ndjamena

Khartoum

SUDAN

Wau

CENTRAL AFRICAN REPUBLIC

MAURITANIA
Nouakchott

MALI
Bamako

S a h e l

Timbuktu

Niger

Kano

Lake Chad

CAPE VERDE
Praia

Dakar
SENEGAL
Banjul
THE GAMBIA
GUINEA-BISSAU
Bissau

Conakry
GUINEA

Freetown
SIERRA LEONE

Monrovia

BURKINA
Ouagadougou

Lake Volta

CÔTE D'IVOIRE
Yamoussoukro

BENIN
TOGO
GHANA

NIGERIA
Abuja
Porto-Novo
Lagos

CAMEROON

88   1:79 500 000

0   500   1000 miles
0   500   1000   1500 km

ATLANTIC

OCEAN

Ascension

St Helena and
Dependencies
(U.K.)

St Helena

CONGO
GABON
Brazzaville Kinshasa
DEMOCRATIC
REPUBLIC
OF THE CONGO
Luanda

ANGOLA   Lubumbashi

Huambo

Cabinda
Okavango
Delta

NAMIBIA   BOTSWANA

Windhoek   Gaborone
Namib Desert

Cape Town
Cape of
Good Hope   Cape Agulhas

Kilimanjaro
5199
5892
RWANDA Kigali Nairobi
Kigali BURUNDI
Bujumbura
Lake Tanganyika
TANZANIA
Dodoma
Dar es Salaam
ZAMBIA
Lusaka
ZIMBABWE
Harare
Bulawayo
Pretoria
Johannesburg
REPUBLIC OF
SOUTH AFRICA
Durban
Port Elizabeth
Lilongwe
MALAWI
Lake
Nyasa
MOZAMBIQUE
Maputo
Mbabane
SWAZILAND
Maseru LESOTHO
Victoria
Lake
Victoria
KENYA
Kampala
Lake
Victoria

Victoria

SEYCHELLES

COMOROS
Moroni Dzaoudzi
Mayotte
(France)

MADAGASCAR

Antananarivo

MAURITIUS
Port Louis
St-Denis
Réunion
(France)

INDIAN

OCEAN

Zanzibar Island
Aldabra
Islands

Mozambique Channel

FACTS

Only Liberia and Ethiopia have
remained free from colonial rule
throughout their history.

Over 30% of the world's minerals,
and over 50% of the world's
diamonds, come from Africa.

9 of the 10 poorest countries in the
world are in Africa.

Africa's capitals

Largest capital (population)	Cairo, Egypt	9 462 000
Smallest capital (population)	Victoria, Seychelles	30 000
Most northerly capital	Tunis, Tunisia	36° 48' N
Most southerly capital	Cape Town, Republic of South Africa	33° 57' S
Highest capital	Addis Ababa, Ethiopia	2 408 m 7 900 ft

africa
countries

africa
northwest africa

91

1:34 500 000

africa
central africa

95

africa
republic of south africa

Wake Island
(U.S.A.)

Pagan □ Northern
Mariana Islands
(U.S.A.)

Saipan □ Capitol Hill

Guam ■ Hagåtña
(U.S.A.)

MARSHALL
ISLANDS

Gaferut

Yap˙

Chuuk   Pohnpei ■ Palikir
Caroline Islands
FEDERATED STATES
OF MICRONESIA

Kosrae

□ Delap-L
Majuro ■ Djarrit
Bairi

ASIA

Gilbert
Islands   Tarav
Kingsmill
Group

■ Yaren
NAURU

New Ireland

Rabaul   Bougainville I.

Mount   New
Wilhelm   Britain   SOLOMON ISLANDS
4509

TU

New
Guinea PAPUA
NEW
GUINEA   Solomon
Sea ■ Honiara   Malaita

Arafura
Sea

Torres Strait

Port
Moresby

Santa Cruz
Islands

Banks
Islands   Rotu

Fi

Darwin

Gulf
of
Carpentaria

Espíritu Santo

VANUATU   Malakula
Efaté
■ Port Vila

Timor Sea

Cape Lévêque

Lake
Argyle

Cairns

Coral Sea
Islands Territory
(Australia)

Coral
Sea

New
Caledonia
(France)   Îles
Loyauté

Viti I

Nouméa

INDIAN
OCEAN

Broome

North West
Cape

Townsville

AUSTRALIA

Uluru ▲   Alice Springs
867

Brisbane

Norfolk
Island
(Australia)

Lord Howe
Island
(Australia)

North Cape

Lake Eyre

Kalgoorlie

Great
Australian Bight

Lake
Torrens

Adelaide

Murray

Darling

Canberra
▲ Mount
Kosciuszko
2229

Sydney

Auckland
North
Island

Wellington

Perth

Kangaroo
Island

Melbourne

Bass Strait

Tasman
Sea

Aoraki
1754 ▲   Christ

South Island

NE
ZEAN

Cape Leeuwin

Tasmania

Hobart

Stewart Island

Auckland Islands
(N.Z.)

Campbell Island
(N.Z.)

Macquarie Island
(Australia)

Oceania's capitals		
Largest capital (population)	**Canberra**, Australia	387 000
Smallest capital (population)	**Vaiaku**, Tuvalu	5 100
Most northerly capital	**Delap-Uliga-Djarrit**, Marshall Islands	7° 7'N
Most southerly capital	**Wellington**, New Zealand	41° 18'S
Highest capital	**Canberra**, Australia	581 m 1 906 ft

100   1:86 000 000

0   500   1000   1500 miles
0   1000   2000 km

Hawaiian
Islands
(U.S.A.)

PACIFIC OCEAN

Palmyra Atoll
(U.S.A.)

Line Islands

Howland Island (U.S.A.)
Baker Island (U.S.A.)

Kiritimati

Jarvis
Island
(U.S.A.)

Phoenix
Islands

Malden
Island

K I R I B A T I

Tokelau
(N.Z.)

Penrhyn

Marquesas
Islands

American
Samoa
(U.S.A.)

Matā'utu
Sava'i
SAMOA **Apia**
Fagatogo

Nuku Hiva

Hiva Oa

Îles
Palliser

Îles du
Désappointement

TONGA
Vava'u
Group

Niue (N.Z.)
Alofi

Cook
Islands
(N.Z.)

Papeete
Tahiti

Tuamotu Islands

ua
Nuku'alofa
Tongatapu
Group

Rarotonga **Avarua**

Society Islands

**French
Polynesia**

Groupe
Actéon

Mururoa

Tubuai

Tubuai Islands

Îles Gambier

rmadec
ands
Z.)

Rapa

Pitcairn
Islands
(U.K.)

hatham
(N.Z.)

FACTS

Over 91% of Australia's population live in urban areas

The Maori name for New Zealand is Aotearoa, meaning 'land of the long white cloud'

Over 800 different languages are spoken in Papua New Guinea

Oceania's countries

Largest country	Australia	7 692 024 sq km	2 969 907 sq miles
Smallest country	Nauru	21 sq km	8 sq miles
Largest population	Australia	19 731 000	
Smallest population	Tuvalu	11 000	
Most densely populated country	Nauru	619 per sq km	1 625 per sq mile
Least densely populated country	Australia	3 per sq km	7 per sq mile

INDIAN

OCEAN

1

2

3

Timor Sea

Bathurst Island
Beagle Gulf
Melville Island
Darwin
Adelaide River
Batchelor
Pine Creek

Cape Londonderry
Joseph
Bonaparte
Gulf
Bonaparte
Archipelago
Collier
Bay
Wyndham
Timber Creek
Bar

Cape Lévêque
**Kimberley
Plateau**
Mount Ord
936
King Leopold Ranges
Derby
Halls Creek
Lajamanu
Lake
Woods

Broome
Roebuck Bay
Fitzroy
Crossing

Lagrange

Eighty Mile Beach

**T a n a m i
D e s e r t**

Lake Gregory
**NORTH
TERR**

Port Hedland
Shay Gap
Lake White

20°

Barrow Island Karratha
Roebourne
**Great Sandy
Desert**
Lake Wills

North West Cape
Onslow
Pannawonica
Chichester Range
Marble Bar
Bieralpine
Lake Mackay

Exmouth
Hamersley Range
Tom Price
Mount Meharry
1250
Newman
Lake Disappointment
Yuendumu
Mount
Liebig
Zeil
1524 1531 km
Macdonnell Ranges

Coral Bay
Paraburdoo
Gibson Desert
Lake
Macdonald
Lake
Hopkins
Alice
Amadeus
Springs
Lilbiri
(Ayers Rock)
Erldunda

Minilya
Mount Augustus
1106
Lake Maurice
Lake
Carnegie
Petermann Ranges
Mourave Range
Woodroffe 1440

Dorre
Island
Robinson Range
Wiluna
Warburton

Dirk
Hartog
Island
Meekatharra
Lake
Wells
**Great Victoria
Desert**

Kalbarri
Mount
Magnet
Leonora
Lake Carey
Lake
Maurice

Northampton
A U S T R A L I A
Leinster
Menzies

Geraldton
Mount
Barlee
Leonora

Dongara
Moora
Bonnie Rock
Southern
Cross
Coolgardie
Kalgoorlie
Rawlinna
Forrest
Hughes

Yanchep
Wongan Hills
Merredin
Norseman
Lake Cowan
Nullarbor Plain
Mundrabilla
Eucla
Fowlers Bay
Ced

Perth
Fremantle
Rockingham
Mandurah
York
Hyden
Balladonia

30°

Bunbury
Katanning
Esperance
**Great
Australian
Bight**

Busselton
Hood Point
Archipelago
of the
Recherche

Margaret River
Denmark
Albany

Cape Leeuwin
Flinders Bay
Point d'Entrecasteaux

110°
40°
120°
130°

1:33 000 000

0   150   300   450 miles

0   200   400   600 km

1:13 000 000

oceania
new zealand
1:13 000 000

1 : 79 500 000

500 · 1000 miles

500 · 1000 · 1500 km

Map labels:

SOUTH AMERICA
Falkland Islands
Cape Horn
Drake Passage
Scotia Sea
South Georgia
South Sandwich Trench
South Orkney Islands
Scotia Ridge
South Shetland Is.
Antarctic Peninsula
SOUTHERN OCEAN
American-Antarctic Ridge
Atlantic-Indian-Antarctic Basin
Larsen Ice Shelf
Palmer Land
Cape Norvegia
Weddell Sea
Southwest Pacific Basin
Alexander Island
Bellingshausen Sea
Fletcher Ice Shelf
Ronne Ice Shelf
Berkner Island
Filchner Ice Shelf
Coats Land
Lars... Ice Shelf
Queen Maud Land
Thorshavnheiane
Southeast Pacific Basin
Ellsworth Mountains
Shackleton Range
Vestfjella
Valkyrie Dome
East Antarctica
Amundsen Ridge
West Antarctica
Queen Maud Land
South Pole
Antarctic Circle
Peter I Island
Amundsen Sea
Marie Byrd Land
Transantarctic Mountains
South Geomagnetic Pole (2003)
Prince Charles Mountains
Siple Island
Ross Ice Shelf
Queen Maud Mountains
Ross Sea
Victoria Land
Antarctic Circle
Indian-Antarctic Ridge
Balleny Islands
George V Land
Adélie Land
Wilkes Land
Mill Island
Davis Sea
Vincennes Bay
South Magnetic Pole (2003)
Cape Morse
Dumont d'Urville Sea
SOUTHERN OCEAN
Indian-Antarctic Basin
Campbell Islands

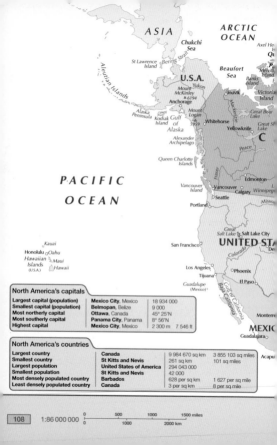

ASIA

ARCTIC OCEAN

Chukchi Sea

St Lawrence Island

Bering Strait

Axel He

Beaufort Sea

Banks Island

Melville Island

U.S.A.

Yukon

Mount McKinley △6194

Anchorage

Inuvik

Victoria Island

Aleutian Islands

Alaska Peninsula

Kodiak Island

Gulf of Alaska

Mount Logan △5959

Whitehorse

Mackenzie

Great Bear Lake

Great Sl

Yellowknife

C

Alexander Archipelago

Peace

Queen Charlotte Islands

Fraser

Edmonton

PACIFIC

OCEAN

Vancouver Island

Vancouver

Calgary

Winnipeg

Seattle

Missou

Portland

Great Salt Lake

Salt Lake City

Kauai

San Francisco

UNITED STA

Honolulu ○ Oahu

Hawaiian Islands

Maui

Colorado

Des

(U.S.A.)

Hawaii

Los Angeles

Phoenix

Tijuana

El Paso

Guadalupe (Mexico)

MEXIC

Gulf of California

Baja California

Monterre

Guadalajara○

North America's capitals		
Largest capital (population)	Mexico City, Mexico	18 934 000
Smallest capital (population)	Belmopan, Belize	9 000
Most northerly capital	Ottawa, Canada	45° 25'N
Most southerly capital	Panama City, Panama	8° 56'N
Highest capital	Mexico City, Mexico	2 300 m 7 546 ft

Acapu

North America's countries			
Largest country	Canada	9 984 670 sq km	3 855 103 sq miles
Smallest country	St Kitts and Nevis	261 sq km	101 sq miles
Largest population	United States of America	294 043 000	
Smallest population	St Kitts and Nevis	42 000	
Most densely populated country	Barbados	628 per sq km	1 627 per sq mile
Least densely populated country	Canada	3 per sq km	8 per sq mile

1:86 000 000

0	500	1000	1500 miles
0	1000	2000 km	

FACTS

Mexico City is the highest city in North America and houses approximately 18% of Mexico's population

The Panama Canal, opened in 1914, cut the journey between the Atlantic and the Pacific by over 14 000 km / 8 700 miles

The territory of Nunavut is Canada's newest administrative division, created in 1999

Greenland Sea

Greenland

Denmark Strait

Baffin Bay

Davis Strait

Baffin Island

Nuuk

Cape Farewell

Foxe Basin

Labrador Sea

Southampton Island

Hudson Strait

Hudson Bay

A D A

Belcher Islands

James Bay

Newfoundland

Île d'Anticosti

Gulf of St Lawrence

St-Pierre

St John's

St Pierre and Miquelon (France)

Lake Nipigon

Québec

Halifax

Cape Sable

Winnipeg

Thunder Bay

Great Lakes

Ottawa

Montréal

Portland

Boston

Minneapolis

Detroit

Toronto

Cleveland

New York

Chicago

Columbus

Pittsburgh

Philadelphia

OF AMERICA

Ohio

Washington D.C.

St Louis

Bermuda (U.K.)

Memphis

Atlanta

Cape Hatteras

Dallas

Jacksonville

Orlando

Houston

New Orleans

Gulf of Mexico

Miami

THE BAHAMAS

Nassau

Turks and Caicos Islands (U.K.)

Virgin Islands (U.S.A.)

Virgin Islands (U.K.)

ST KITTS AND NEVIS

ANTIGUA AND BARBUDA

Guadeloupe (France)

Havana

CUBA

Santo Domingo

Puerto Rico (U.S.A.)

DOMINICA

Cayman Islands (U.K.)

Kingston

Port-au-Prince

San Juan

ST LUCIA

Martinique (France)

BARBADOS

JAMAICA

HAITI

DOMINICAN REPUBLIC

ST VINCENT AND THE GRENADINES

Mérida

Yucatán

BELIZE

Belmopan

Caribbean Sea

GRENADA

Netherlands Antilles

TRINIDAD AND TOBAGO

ico City

Veracruz

GUATEMALA

HONDURAS

Aruba (Neth.)

Pico de Orizaba

atemala City

Tegucigalpa

San Salvador

EL SALVADOR

NICARAGUA

Managua

Lake Nicaragua

San José

COSTA RICA

Panama City

PANAMA

ATLANTIC OCEAN

SOUTH AMERICA

north america
canada

1:20 000 000

| 0 | 100 | 200 | 300 miles |
| 0 | 150 | 300 | 450 km |

north america
western canada
113

116   1:33 000 000

118 1:14 500 000

north america
western united states

122   1:14 500 000

north america
northeast united states

123

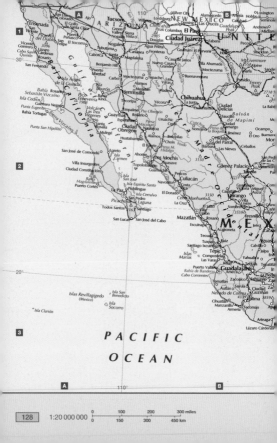

A T L A N T I C

O C E A N

THE BAHAMAS

Great
Abaco
Eleuthera
NASSAU
Cat Island
Long Island
Exuma Cays

Tropic of Cancer

Acklins
Island
Mayaguana
Great
Inagua
Turks and
Caicos Islands (U.K.)
GRAND TURK (Cockburn Town)
Caicos
Islands

W e s t   I n d i e s

Hispaniola

Leeward Islands

as Tunas
Holguín
Bayamo
Windward Passage
Guantánamo
Port-de-
Paix
Gonaïves
HAITI
Santiago
La Vega
DOMINICAN
REPUBLIC
Puerto Rico
(U.S.A.)
SAN JUAN
Virgin Is
(U.K.)
Virgin Is
(U.S.A.)
Anguilla
St-Martin
(France)
St-Maarten
(Netherlands)
ANTIGUA AND
BARBUDA

KINGSTON
Jérémie
Les
Cayes
Jacmel
PORT-
AU-PRINCE
SANTO
DOMINGO
La Romana
Ponce
BASSETERRE
ST JOHN'S

er

Montserrat
PLYMOUTH
Guadeloupe
(France)

ST KITTS AND NEVIS
BASSE-TERRE

A n t i l l e s

Lesser

DOMINICA
ROSEAU

Martinique
(France)
FORT-DE-
FRANCE

e a n   S e a

Antilles

ST LUCIA
CASTRIES

Netherlands
Antilles
Aruba
(Neth.)
Curaçao
Bonaire
ST VINCENT AND THE
GRENADINES
KINGSTOWN
BRIDGETOWN
BARBADOS

ST GEORGE'S
GRENADA

Windward Islands

Punta Gallinas
Península
de la Guajira
Golfo
de Venezuela
Isla
los Roques
La Asunción
Isla de
Margarita
Scarborough Tobago
PORT OF
SPAIN
TRINIDAD
AND
TOBAGO

Barranquilla
Santa
Marta
Riohacha
Maicaetía
Puerto
Cabello
CARACAS
Cumaná
Barcelona
Maturín
Trinidad

Cartagena
Valledupar
Maracaibo
Cabimas
Barquisimeto
Valencia
Los Teques
Zaraza
El Tigre
Ciudad
Guayana
Orinoco
Delta

Sincelejo
Magangué
Machiques
Maracaibo
Lake
Valera
Acarigua
Guanare
Tucupita

COLOMBIA
Montería
Mérida
Barinas
V E N E Z U E L A
Ciudad Bolívar
GUYANA

Cúcuta
Bucaramanga
Pamplona
Arauca
San Cristóbal
San Fernando de Apure
El Callao
Embalse
de Guri
Matakuma

C
Arauca
La Paragua
D
80°

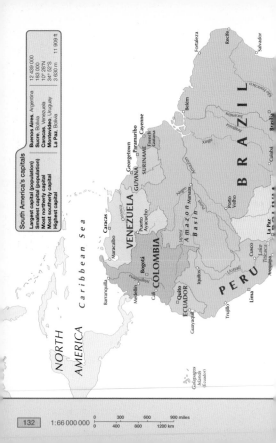

South America's capitals

Largest capital (population)	Buenos Aires, Argentina	12 439 000
Smallest capital (population)	Sucre, Bolivia	183 000
Most northerly capital	Caracas, Venezuela	10° 28'N
Most southerly capital	Montevideo, Uruguay	34° 52'S
Highest capital	La Paz, Bolivia	3 630 m	11 909 ft

NORTH
AMERICA

Caribbean Sea

VENEZUELA

Maracaibo

Caracas

Orinoco

Barranquilla

COLOMBIA

Medellín

Bogotá

Cali

Magdalena

Puerto
Ayacucho

Negro

Georgetown

GUYANA

Paramaribo

SURINAME

Cayenne

French
Guiana

Manaus

Quito

ECUADOR

Guayaquil

Galapagos
Islands
(Ecuador)

Iquitos

Japurá

Putumayo

Napo

Amazon Basin

Porto
Velho

Purus

Madeira

Belém

B R A Z I L

Cuiabá

Brasília

Xingu

Tapajós

Araguaia

Fortaleza

Recife

São Francisco

Salvador

PERU

Trujillo

Lima

Cusco

Ucayali

Arequipa

Lake
Titicaca

La Paz

1:66 000 000

| 0 | 300 | 600 | 900 miles |
| 0 | 400 | 800 | 1200 km |

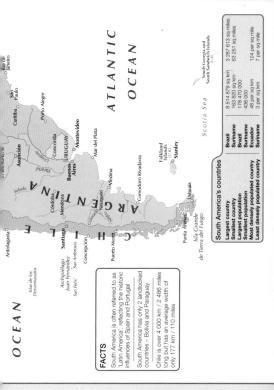

FACTS

South America is often referred to as 'Latin America', reflecting the historic influences of Spain and Portugal

South America has only 2 landlocked countries – Bolivia and Paraguay

Chile is over 4 000 km / 2 486 miles long but has an average width of only 177 km / 110 miles

South America's countries

Largest country	Brazil	8 514 879 sq miles
Smallest country	Suriname	163 820 sq miles
Largest population	Brazil	178 470 000
Smallest population	Suriname	436 000
Most densely populated country	Ecuador	46 per sq km — 124 per sq mile
Least densely populated country	Suriname	3 per sq km — 7 per sq mile

ATLANTIC

OCEAN

south america
southern south america

137

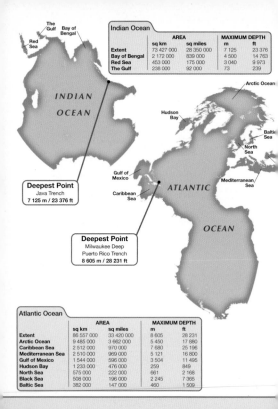

Indian Ocean

	AREA		MAXIMUM DEPTH	
	sq km	sq miles	m	ft
Extent	73 427 000	28 350 000	7 125	23 376
Bay of Bengal	2 172 000	839 000	4 500	14 763
Red Sea	453 000	175 000	3 040	9 973
The Gulf	238 000	92 000	73	239

INDIAN OCEAN

Deepest Point
Java Trench
7 125 m / 23 376 ft

ATLANTIC OCEAN

Deepest Point
Milwaukee Deep
Puerto Rico Trench
8 605 m / 28 231 ft

Atlantic Ocean

	AREA		MAXIMUM DEPTH	
	sq km	sq miles	m	ft
Extent	86 557 000	33 420 000	8 605	28 231
Arctic Ocean	9 485 000	3 662 000	5 450	17 880
Caribbean Sea	2 512 000	970 000	7 680	25 196
Mediterranean Sea	2 510 000	969 000	5 121	16 800
Gulf of Mexico	1 544 000	596 000	3 504	11 495
Hudson Bay	1 233 000	476 000	259	849
North Sea	575 000	222 000	661	2 168
Black Sea	508 000	196 000	2 245	7 365
Baltic Sea	382 000	147 000	460	1 509

FACTS

If all of Antarctica's ice melted, world sea level would rise by more than 60 m / 197 ft

The Arctic Ocean produces up to 50 000 icebergs per year

The world's greatest tidal range – 21 m / 69 ft – is in the Bay of Fundy, Nova Scotia, Canada

Deepest Point
Challenger Deep
Mariana Trench
10 920 m / 35 826 ft

Sea of Okhotsk

Bering Sea

Sea of Japan (East Sea)

East China Sea and Yellow Sea

South China Sea

PACIFIC OCEAN

Pacific Ocean

	AREA		MAXIMUM DEPTH	
	sq km	sq miles	m	ft
Extent	166 241 000	64 186 000	10 920	35 826
Bering Sea	2 261 000	873 000	4 150	13 615
Sea of Okhotsk	1 392 000	537 000	3 363	11 033
Sea of Japan (East Sea)	1 013 000	391 000	3 743	12 280
East China Sea and Yellow Sea	1 202 000	464 000	2 717	8 913
South China Sea	2 590 000	1 000 000	5 514	18 090

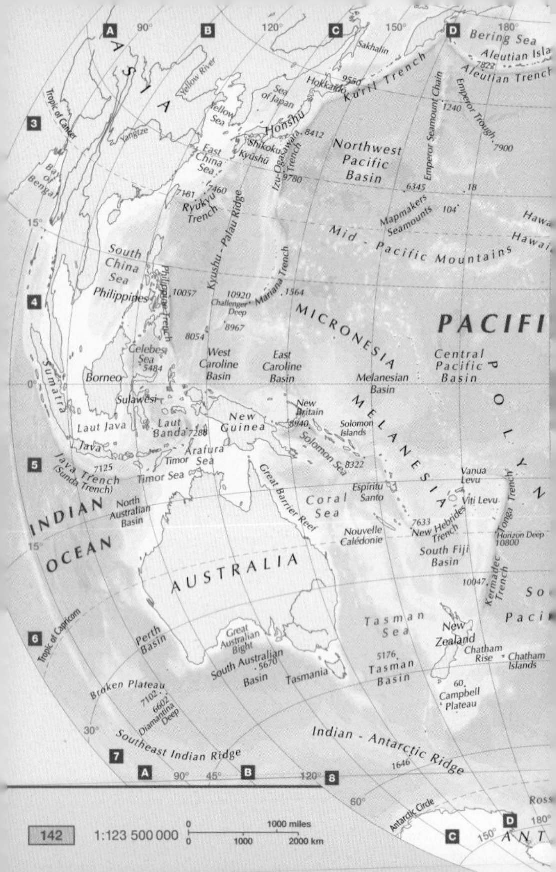
ASIA
Yellow River
Yangtze
Tropic of Cancer
Bay of Bengal
Yellow Sea
Sea of Japan
Sakhalin
Hokkaido
Honshu
Shikoku
Kyūshū
East China Sea
Kuril Trench
9550
Bering Sea
Aleutian Trench
7822
Emperor Seamount Chain
Emperor Trough
1240
7900
Izu-Ogasawara Trench
8412
9780
Northwest Pacific Basin
6345
18
104
7181
7460
Ryukyu Trench
Kyushu - Palau Ridge
Mapmakers Seamounts
Mid - Pacific Mountains
South China Sea
Philippines
Philippine Trench
10057
Mariana Trench
10920
Challenger Deep
1564
8967
8054
MICRONESIA
Celebes Sea
5484
West Caroline Basin
East Caroline Basin
Central Pacific Basin
Melanesian Basin
Borneo
Sumatra
Sulawesi
New Britain
Laut Java
Laut Banda
7288
New Guinea
8940
Solomon Islands
MELANESIA
Java
Arafura Sea
Timor
Solomon Sea
8322
7125
Java Trench (Sunda Trench)
Timor Sea
Great Barrier Reef
Vanua Levu
Espíritu Santo
Viti Levu
Tonga Trench
INDIAN OCEAN
North Australian Basin
Coral Sea
7633
New Hebrides Trench
Nouvelle Calédonie
Horizon Deep 10800
South Fiji Basin
AUSTRALIA
10047
Kermadec Trench
Tasman Sea
New Zealand
Tropic of Capricorn
Perth Basin
Great Australian Bight
South Australian Basin
5670
5176
Tasman Basin
Chatham Rise
Chatham Islands
Tasmania
60
Campbell Plateau
Broken Plateau
7102
6602
Diamantina Deep
Southeast Indian Ridge
Indian - Antarctic Ridge
1646
Antarctic Circle
90°
120°
150°
180°
15°
0°
30°
45°
60°
1:123 500 000
0
1000 miles
0
1000
2000 km

pacific ocean 143

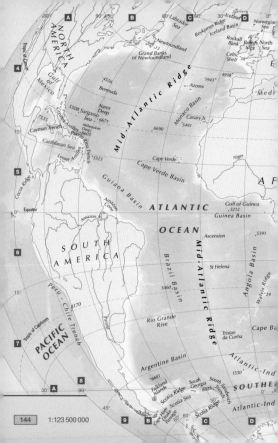

NORTH AMERICA
SOUTH AMERICA
ATLANTIC OCEAN
PACIFIC OCEAN
Mid-Atlantic Ridge
Gulf of Mexico
Caribbean Sea
Lesser Antilles
Greater Antilles
Cayman Trench
Puerto Rico Trench
Cocos Ridge
Sargasso Sea
Bermuda
Nares Deep
Milwaukee Deep
Labrador Sea
Newfoundland
Grand Banks of Newfoundland
Reykjanes Ridge
Iceland
Iceland Basin
Norwegian Sea
Rockall Bank
British Isles
North S...
Celtic Shelf
Medit...
AFR...
Azores
Monaco Basin
Canary Is
Cape Verde
Cape Verde Basin
Guiana Basin
Amazon
Amazon Cone
Equator
Tropic of Cancer
Tropic of Capricorn
Gulf of Guinea
Guinea Basin
Niger
Ascension
St Helena
Brazil Basin
Angola Basin
Walvis Ridge
Rio Grande Rise
Tristan da Cunha
Cape B...
Peru - Chile Trench
Argentine Basin
Falkland Islands
Scotia Ridge
Scotia Sea
South Georgia
South Sandwich Trench
SOUTHE...
Atlantic-Ind...
Cape Horn
Drake Passage

Depth/spot values visible: 4556, 5943, 4930, 5508, 6671, 7535, 8605, 5523, 6690, 5491, 5212, 5391, 5460, 8170, 6661, 1530, 8325, 38, 13

144   1:123 500 000

atlantic and
indian oceans

145

PACIFIC OCEAN

Bering Sea

Gulf of Alaska

Arctic Circle

Chukchi Sea

Sea of Okhotsk

ASIA

East Siberian Sea

Lena

NORTH AMERICA

Mackenzie

Beaufort Sea

Canada Basin

Mendeleyev Ridge

Laptev Sea

ARCTIC OCEAN

Lomonosov Ridge

Alpha Ridge

North Magnetic Pole (2003)

North Pole

Amundsen Basin

Arctic Mid-Ocean Ridge

Nansen Basin

Parry Islands

Victoria Island

Ellesmere Island

North Geomagnetic Pole (2003)

Franz Josef Land

Baffin Island

Baffin Bay

Kara Sea

Novaya Zemlya

Yenisey

Davis Strait

Greenland Sea

Svalbard

Barents Sea

Greenland

3884

Greenland Basin

Jan Mayen

Norwegian Basin

Denmark Strait

Norwegian Sea

Arctic Circle

Iceland

3970

ATLANTIC OCEAN

Faroe Islands

EUROPE

Baltic Sea

British Isles

North Sea

500   1000   km
500   1000   miles

INTRODUCTION TO THE INDEX

The index includes all names shown on the reference maps in the atlas. Names are referenced by page number and by a grid reference. The grid reference correlates to the alphanumeric values along the edges of each map that reflect the lines of latitude and longitude. Names are generally referenced to the largest scale map on which they appear. Each entry also includes the country or geographical area in which the feature is located. Where relevant, the index clearly indicates [inset] if a feature appears on an inset map.

Name forms are as they appear on the maps, with additional alternative names or name forms included as cross-references which refer the user to the entry for the map form of the name. Names beginning with Mc or Mac are alphabetized exactly as they appear. The terms Saint, Sainte, etc, are abbreviated to St, Ste, etc, but alphabetized as if in the full form.

Names of physical features beginning with generic geographical terms are permuted – the descriptive term is placed after the main part of the name. For example, Lake Superior is indexed as Superior, Lake; Mount Everest as Everest, Mount. This policy is applied to all languages.

Entries, other than those for towns and cities, include a descriptor indicating the type of geographical feature. Descriptors are not included where the type of feature is implicit in the name itself.

Administrative divisions are included to differentiate entries of the same name and feature type within the one country. In such cases duplicate names are alphabetized in order of administrative division. Additional qualifiers are also included for names within selected geographical areas.

INDEX ABBREVIATIONS

admin. div.	administrative division	Ger.	Germany	Port.	Portugal
Afgh.	Afghanistan	Guat.	Guatemala	prov.	province
Alg.	Algeria	h.	hill	pt.	point
Arg.	Argentina	hd	headland	r.	river
Austr.	Australia	Hond.	Honduras	reg.	region
aut. reg.	autonomous region	i.	island	Rep.	Republic
aut. rep.	autonomous republic	imp. l.	impermanent lake	resr	reservoir
Azer.	Azerbaijan	Indon.	Indonesia	rf	reef
b.	bay	is	islands	Rus. Fed.	Russian Federation
Bangl.	Bangladesh	isth.	isthmus		
B.I.O.T.	British Indian Ocean Territory	Kazakh.	Kazakhstan	S.	South
		Kyrg.	Kyrgyzstan	Serb. and Mont.	Serbia and Montenegro
Bol.	Bolivia	l.	lake	str.	strait
Bos.-Herz.	Bosnia Herzegovina	lag.	lagoon	Switz.	Switzerland
Bulg.	Bulgaria	Lith.	Lithuania	Tajik.	Tajikistan
c.	cape	Lux.	Luxembourg	Tanz.	Tanzania
Can.	Canada	Madag.	Madagascar	terr.	territory
C.A.R.	Central African Republic	Maur.	Mauritania	Thai.	Thailand
		Mex.	Mexico	Trin. and Tob.	Trinidad and Tobago
Col.	Colombia	Moz.	Mozambique	Turkm.	Turkmenistan
Czech Rep.	Czech Republic	mt.	mountain	U.A.E.	United Arab Emirates
Dem. Rep.	Democratic	mts	mountains		
Congo	Republic of the Congo	mun.	municipality	U.K.	United Kingdom
depr.	depression	N.	North	Ukr.	Ukraine
des.	desert	Neth.	Netherlands	Uru.	Uruguay
Dom. Rep.	Dominican Republic	Nic.	Nicaragua	U.S.A.	United States of America
		N.Z.	New Zealand		
esc.	escarpment	Pak.	Pakistan	Uzbek.	Uzbekistan
est.	estuary	Para.	Paraguay	val.	valley
Eth.	Ethiopia	pen.	peninsula	Venez.	Venezuela
Fin.	Finland	Phil.	Philippines	vol.	volcano
for.	forest	plat.	plateau		
g.	gulf	P.N.G.	Papua New Guinea		
		Pol.	Poland		

Aabenraa Denmark **41** B4
Aachen Ger. **48** C2
Aalborg Denmark **41** B4
Aalst Belgium **48** B2
Aarschot Belgium **48** B2
Aba China **72** C2
Aba Nigeria **91** C4
Abādān Iran **85** C2
Ābādeh Iran **85** D2
Abadla Alg. **90** B1
Abakaliki Nigeria **91** C4
Abakan Rus. Fed. **81** I3
Abakanskiy Khrebet *mts*
  Rus. Fed. **81** F1
Abancay Peru **134** B4
Abarqū Iran **85** D2
Abashiri Japan **70** D2
Ābay Wenz *r.* Eth./Sudan *see*
  Blue Nile
Abaza Rus. Fed. **81** G3
Abbasanta Italy **56** A2
Abbeville France **52** C1
Abbeville U.S.A. **124** B3
Abbot Ice Shelf Antarctica
  107 J2
Abbottabad Pak. **78** B1
Abéché Chad **91** E3
Abengourou Côte d'Ivoire **90** B4
Abeokuta Nigeria **90** C4
Aberaeron U.K. **47** B4
Aberdare U.K. **47** B4
Aberdaron U.K. **46** A3
Aberdeen S. Africa **98** B3
Aberdeen *MD* U.S.A. **123** E3
Aberdeen *SD* U.S.A. **121** D1
Aberdeen *WA* U.S.A. **118** B1
Aberdeen Lake Can. **113** F1
Aberystwyth U.K. **47** A3
Abez' Rus. Fed. **34** F2
Abhā Saudi Arabia **82** B3
Abiad, Bahr el *r.* Sudan/Uganda
  see White Nile
Abidjan Côte d'Ivoire **90** B4
Abilene *TX* U.S.A. **127** E2
Abingdon U.K. **47** C4
Abinsk Rus. Fed. **59** F1
Abitibi, Lake Can. **114** D2
Abohar India **78** B1
Abomey Benin **90** C4
Aborlan Phil. **68** A3
Absaroka Range *mts* U.S.A.
  120 A2
Abşeron Yarımadası *pen.* Azer.
  85 C1
Abū ʻArīsh Saudi Arabia **82** B3
Abu Deleiq Sudan **82** A3
Abu Dhabi U.A.E. **83** C2
Abu Hamed Sudan **92** B3
Abuja Nigeria **91** C4

Abū Kamāl Syria **85** C2
Abunā *r.* Bol. **136** B1
Abunā Brazil **134** C3
Abu Road India **78** B2
Abū Sunbul Egypt **92** B2
Abū Zabī U.A.E. *see* Abu Dhabi
Abyad' Sudan **93** A4
Acambaro Mex. **128** B2
Acaponeta Mex. **128** B2
Acapulco Mex. **128** C3
Acará Brazil **135** E3
Acaraú, Represa de *resr* Para.
  138 A3
Acarigua Venez. **134** C2
Acatlan Mex. **129** C3
Acayucán Mex. **129** C3
Accra Ghana **90** B4
Accrington U.K. **46** B3
Achalpur India **78** B2
Achicourt France **48** A2
Achill Island Ireland **45** A2
Achim Ger. **49** D1
Achuyevo Rus. Fed. **39** E2
Acıpayam Turkey **59** C3
Acireale Italy **56** C3
Acklins Island Bahamas
  131 C2
Aconcagua, Cerro *mt.* Arg.
  136 A4
A Coruña Spain **54** B1
Acqui Terme Italy **56** A1
Ács Hungary **51** D3
Actéon, Groupe *is* Fr. Polynesia
  101
Actopán Mex. **129** C2
Ada U.S.A. **127** E2
Adam Oman **83** C2
'Adan Yemen *see* Aden
Adana Turkey **84** B2
Adapazarı Turkey **59** D2
Ad Dafinah Saudi Arabia **82** B2
Ad Dahnā' *des.* Saudi Arabia
  83 B2
Ad Dakhla Western Sahara **90** A2
Ad Dammām Saudi Arabia *see*
  Dammam
Ad Dār al Ḥamrā' Saudi Arabia
  82 A2
Ad Darb Saudi Arabia **82** B3
Ad Dawādimī Saudi Arabia **82** B2
Ad Dawḥah Qatar *see* Doha
Ad Dīffah *plat.* Egypt *see*
  Libyan Plateau
Addis Ababa Eth. **93** B4
Ad Diwānīyah Iraq **85** C2
Adelaide Austr. **104** B2
Adelaide River Austr. **102** C1
Adélie Land *reg.* Antarctica
  107 G3
Aden Yemen **82** B3
Aden, Gulf of Somalia/Yemen
  83 B3
Ādigrat Eth. **92** B3
Adilabad India **79** B3

Adirondack Mountains U.S.A.
  123 F2
Adjud Romania **38** C2
Admiralty Island U.S.A. **112** B2
Admiralty Islands P.N.G. **63** D3
Adour *r.* France **52** B3
Adra Spain **54** C2
Adrar Alg. **90** B2
Adrian *TX* U.S.A. **127** D1
Adriatic Sea Europe **56** B2
Adwa Eth. **92** B3
Adygeysk Rus. Fed. **39** E3
Adzopé Côte d'Ivoire **90** B4
Aegean Sea Greece/Turkey **59**
A Estrada Spain **54** B1
Afghanistan *country* Asia **78** A1
'Afif Saudi Arabia **82** B2
Afyon Turkey **84** B2
Agadez Niger **91** C3
Agadir Morocco **90** B1
Agadyr' Kazakh. **81** E2
Agar India **78** B2
Agartala India **79** D2
Ağdam Azer. **85** C2
Agde France **53** C3
Agen France **52** C3
Aggeneys S. Africa **98** A2
Agios Dimitrios Greece **59** B3
Agios Efstratios *i.* Greece **59** C3
Agios Konstantinos Greece
  84 A2
Agios Nikolaos Greece **59** C4
Agirwat Hills Sudan **82** A3
Agnita Romania **38** B2
Agra India **79** B2
Ağrı Turkey **85** C2
Agrigento Italy **56** B3
Agrinio Greece **59** B3
Agropoli Italy **56** B2
Agua Clara Brazil **138** B2
Aguadulce Panama **130** B4
Aguanaval *r.* Mex. **128** B2
Agua Prieta Mex. **128** B1
Aguascalientes Mex. **128** B2
Aguas Formosas Brazil **139** D1
Aguilar de Campóo Spain **54** C1
Aguilas Spain **55** C2
Agulhas, Cape S. Africa **98** B3
Agulhas Negras *mt.* Brazil
  139 D2
Ağva Turkey **59** C2
Ağva Iran **85** C2
Ahaus Ger. **48** C1
Ahlat Turkey **85** C2
Ahlen Ger. **48** C2
Ahmadabad India **78** B2
Ahmadnagar India **77** B3
Ahmadpur East Pak. **78** B2
Ahome Mex. **128** B2
Ahram Iran **85** C2
Ahrensburg Ger. **49** E1
Ahvāz Iran **85** C2
Ai-Ais Namibia **98** A2
Aigio Greece **59** B3

ken U.S.A. **125** D2
morés Brazil **139** D1
morés, Serra dos hills Brazil **139** D1
in r. France **50** B3
in Azel Alg. **55** E2
in Ben Tili Maur. **90** B2
in Defla Alg. **55** D2
in Oulmene Alg. **55** E2
in Safra Alg. **90** B1
insworth U.S.A. **120** D2
intab Turkey see Gaziantep
in Taya Alg. **55** D2
in Tédélès Alg. **55** D2
in Temouchent Alg. **55** E2
irbangis Indon. **64** A1
rdrie Can. **112** D2
the-sur-l'Adour France **52** B3
asch r. Ger. **49** E3
ishihik Lake Can. **112** B1
sne r. France **48** A3
kol Romania **38** B2
ix-en-Provence France **53** D3
ix-les-Bains France **53** D2
jaccio France **53** D3
jdābīyā Libya **91** E1
mer India **78** B2
jo U.S.A. **126** B2
kçakale Turkey **84** B2
kdağmadeni Turkey **84** B2
kersberga Sweden **86** A2
keti Dem. Rep. Congo **94** C2
khalk'alak'i Georgia **35** D4
khdar, Jabal mts Oman **83** C2
khisar Turkey **59** C3
khtubinsk Rus. Fed. **35** D4
kita Japan **70** D3
kjoujt Maur. **90** A3
kkol' Kazakh. **81** E1
kmenrags pt Latvia **36** B2
kmola India **78** B2
kobo Indon. **93** B4
kola India **78** B2
kordat Eritrea **82** A3
kpatok Island Can. **111** H2
kranes Iceland **40** [inset]
krehamn Norway **42** E2
krron I.A.S.A. **122** D2
ksai Chin Terr. Asia **79** B1
ksaray Turkey **84** B2
ksay Kazakh. **80** C1
ksu China **81** F2
ksu r. Turkey **56** F2
ksehir Turkey **84** B2
ksu China **81** F2
ktsyabrski Belarus **36** C2
ktobe Kazakh. **80** C1
kure Nigeria **91** C4
kureyri Iceland **40** [inset]
kyab Myanmar see Sittwe

Alabama r. U.S.A. **125** C2
Alabama state U.S.A. **124** C2
Alacant Spain see Alicante
Alagoinhas Brazil **139** F4
Alagón Spain **55** C1
Al Aḥmadī Kuwait **83** B2
Alakol', Ozero salt l. Kazakh. **81** F2
Alakurtti Rus. Fed. **40** G2
Al 'Alayyah Saudi Arabia **82** B3
Al 'Amiriyah Egypt **84** A2
Alamo U.S.A. **119** C3
Alamogordo U.S.A. **126** C2
Alamos Sonora Mex. **128** A2
Alamos Sonora Mex. **128** B2
Alamos r. Mex. **128** B2
Alanson U.S.A. **82** B3
Åland Islands Fin. **41** D3
Alanya Turkey **86** D2
Al 'Aqabah Jordan **84** B3
Alarcón, Embalse de resr Spain **55** C2
Al 'Arīsh Egypt **84** B2
Al Arṭāwīyah Saudi Arabia **82** B2
Alas Indon. **65** C2
Alaşehir Turkey **59** C3
Alaska state U.S.A. **110** C2
Alaska, Gulf of U.S.A. **110** C3
Alaska Peninsula U.S.A. **108**
Alaska Range mts U.S.A. **110** C2
Älät Azer. **85** C2
Alatyr' Rus. Fed. **35** D3
Alausí Ecuador **134** B3
Alavus Fin. **41** E3
Alba Italy **54** A2
Albacete Spain **55** C2
Alba Iulia Romania **38** B2
Albania country Europe **58** A2
Albany Austr. **102** A3
Albany r. Can. **114** B1
Albany GA U.S.A. **125** D2
Albany NY U.S.A. **123** F2
Albany OR U.S.A. **118** B2
Albatross Bay Austr. **103** D1
Al Baydā' Libya **91** E1
Al Baydā' Yemen **82** B3
Albemarle U.S.A. **125** D1
Albemarle Sound sea chan. U.S.A. **125** E1
Albenga Italy **54** A2
Alberga watercourse Austr. **104** B1
Albert France **48** A3
Albert, Lake Dem. Rep. Congo/Uganda **95** D2
Alberta prov. Can. **112** D2
Albert Kanaal canal Belgium **48** B2
Albert Lea U.S.A. **121** E2
Albi France **52** C3
Al Bi'r Saudi Arabia **82** A2
Al Birk Saudi Arabia **82** B3

Al Biyāḍh reg. Saudi Arabia **82** B2
Alborz, Reshteh-ye mts Iran see Elburz Mountains
Albufeira Port. **54** B2
Al Buraymi U.A.E. **126** C1
Al Buraymī Oman **83** C2
Albury Austr. **105** D3
Alcalá de Henares Spain **54** C1
Alcalá la Real Spain **54** C2
Alcano Italy **56** B3
Alcañiz Spain **55** C1
Alcántara Spain **54** B2
Alcaraz, Sierra de mts Spain **54** C2
Alcázar de San Juan Spain **54** C2
Alchevs'k Ukr. **39** E2
Alcobaça Brazil **139** E1
Alcoy-Alcoi Spain **55** C2
Alcúdia Spain **55** D2
Aldabra Islands Seychelles **93** C5
Aldan Rus. Fed. **87** K3
Aldan r. Rus. Fed. **87** K2
Alderney i. Channel Is **47** B5
Aleg Maur. **90** A3
Alegrete Brazil **136** C3
Aleksandrovsk-Sakhalinskiy Rus. Fed. **87** L3
Aleksandry, Zemlya i. Rus. Fed. **86** F1
Alekseyevka Belgorodskaya Oblast' Rus. Fed. **39** E1
Alekseyevka Belgorodskaya Oblast' Rus. Fed. **39** E1
Aleksin Rus. Fed. **37** E3
Aleksinac S.M. **58** B2
Alèmbé Gabon **94** B3
Além Paraíba Brazil **139** D2
Alençon France **52** C2
Aleppo Syria **84** B2
Alerta Peru **134** B4
Alès France **53** C3
Aleşd Romania **38** B2
Alessandria Italy **56** A2
Ålesund Norway **40** B3
Aleutian Islands U.S.A. **142** E1
Aleutian Range mts U.S.A. **120**
Alevina, Mys c. Rus. Fed. **87** M3
Alexander Archipelago is U.S.A. **112** B2
Alexander Bay S. Africa **98** A2
Alexander City U.S.A. **125** C2
Alexander Island Antarctica **107** K2
Alexandra Austr. **105** D3
Alexandra N.Z. **106** A4
Alexandria Egypt **92** A1
Alexandria Romania **38** B2
Alexandria LA U.S.A. **124** B2
Alexandria MN U.S.A. **121** D1
Alexandria VA U.S.A. **123** D3
Alexandrina, Lake Austr. **104** B3

Alexandroupoli Greece 59 C2
Alexis r. Can. 115 E1
Aleysk Rus. Fed. 81 F1
Alfaro Spain 55 C1
Al Fayyūm Egypt 84 B2
Alfeld (Leine) Ger. 49 D2
Alfenas Brazil 139 C2
Al Fujairah U.A.E. see Fujairah
Algeciras Spain 54 B2
Algemesí Spain 55 C2
Algena Eritrea 82 A3
Alger Alg. see Algiers
Algeria country Africa 90 C2
Al Ghaydah Yemen 83 C3
Alghero Italy 56 A2
Al Ghurdaqah Egypt 92 B2
Al Ghwaybiyah Saudi Arabia 83 B2
Alhama de Murcia Spain 55 C2
Al Hammām Egypt 84 A2
Al Hanākīyah Saudi Arabia 82 B2
Al Hasakah Syria 85 D2
Al Hayy Iraq 85 C2
Al Hazm al Jawf Yemen 82 B3
Al Hibāk des. Saudi Arabia 83 C3
Al Hillah Saudi Arabia 82 B2
Al Hoceima Morocco 54 C2
Al Hudaydah Yemen see
  Hodeidah
Al Hufūf Saudi Arabia 83 B2
Al Hulayq al Kabir hills Libya
  91 D2
'Alīābād Iran 85 D3
Aliağa Turkey 59 C3
Alicante Spain 55 C2
Alice U.S.A. 127 D3
Alice Springs Austr. 102 C2
Aligarh India 79 B2
Alihe China 73 E1
Alima r. Congo 94 B3
Aliova r. Turkey see Çakıt
Ali Sabieh Djibouti 93 C3
Al Iskandarīyah Egypt see
  Alexandria
Al Jaghbūb Libya 91 E2
Al Jahrah Kuwait 83 B2
Al Jawf Libya 91 E2
Al Jawf Saudi Arabia 82 A2
Aljezur Port. 54 B2
Al Jubayl Saudi Arabia 83 B2
Al Junaynah Saudi Arabia 82 B2
Aljustrel Port. 54 B2

Al Karak Jordan 84 B2
Al Khābūrah Oman 83 C2
Al Khamāsin Saudi Arabia 82 B2
Al Khārijah Egypt 92 B2
Al Khasab Oman 83 C2
Al Khawr Qatar 83 C2
Al Khufrah Libya 92 A2
Al Khums Libya 91 D1
Al Khunn Saudi Arabia 83 B2
Alkmaar Neth. 48 B1
Al Kūt Iraq 85 C2
Al Kuwayt Kuwait see Kuwait
Al Lādhiqīyah Syria see Latakia
Allahabad India 79 C2
Allakh-Yun' Rus. Fed. 87 L2
'Allāqī, Wādī al watercourse
  Egypt 82 A2
Allegheny r. U.S.A. 123 E2
Allegheny Mountains U.S.A.
  123 D3
Allen, Lough i. Ireland 45 B1
Allende Coahuila Mex. 129 B2
Allende Nuevo León Mex. 129 B2
Allentown U.S.A. 123 E2
Alleppey India 77 B4
Aller r. Ger. 49 D1
Alliance NE U.S.A. 120 C2
Al Lith Saudi Arabia 82 B2
Alloa U.K. 44 C2
Almada Port. 54 B2
Almadén Spain 54 C2
Al Madīnah Saudi Arabia see
  Medina
Al Majma'ah Saudi Arabia 83 B2
Almanor, Lake U.S.A. 118 B2
Almansa Spain 55 C2
Al Mansūrah Egypt 84 B2
Al Mariyyah U.A.E. 83 C2
Al Marj Libya 91 E1
Almaty Kazakh. 81 E2
Almazán Spain 54 C1
Almeirim Brazil 135 D3
Almelo Neth. 48 C1
Almenara Brazil 139 D1
Almendra, Embalse de resr
  Spain 54 B1
Almería Spain 54 C2
Almería, Golfo de b. Spain 54 C2
Al'met'yevsk Rus. Fed. 35 E3
Al Mindak Saudi Arabia 82 B2
Al Minyā Egypt 92 B2
Al Mish'āb Saudi Arabia 83 B2
Almonte Spain 54 B2
Al Mubarrez Saudi Arabia 83 B2
Al Mudawwarah Jordan 84 B3
Al Mukallā Yemen see Mukalla
Al Mukhā Yemen see Mocha
Almuñécar Spain 54 C2
Al Muwaylih Saudi Arabia 82 A2
Almyros Greece 59 B3
Alness U.K. 44 B2
Alnwick U.K. 46 C2
Alofi Niue 101

Along India 66 A1
Alonnisos i. Greece 59 B3
Alor, Kepulauan is Indon. 63 C3
Alor Setar Malaysia 64 B1
Alozero Rus. Fed. 40 G2
Alpena U.S.A. 122 D1
Alpine U.S.A. 127 D2
Alps mts Europe 53 D2
Al Qa'āmīyāt reg. Saudi Arabia
  83 B3
Al Qaddāhiyah Libya 91 D1
Al Qāhirah Egypt see Cairo
Al Qā'īyah Saudi Arabia 82 B2
Al Qāmishlī Syria 85 C2
Al Qatn Yemen 83 B3
Al Qunfidhah Saudi Arabia 82 B3
Al Quwayrah Saudi Arabia 82 B2
Alsfeld Ger. 49 D2
Alta Norway 40 F2
Altaelva r. Norway 40 F2
Altai Mountains Asia 81 F2
Altamaha r. U.S.A. 125 D2
Altamira Brazil 135 D3
Altamura Italy 57 C2
Altay China 81 F2
Altay Mongolia 72 C1
Altdorf Switz. 53 D2
Altenburg Ger. 49 F2
Altıntaş Turkey 59 D3
Altiplano plain Bol. 136 B2
Alto Araguaia Brazil 138 B1
Alto de Moncayo mt. Spain
  55 C1
Alto Garças Brazil 138 B1
Altoona U.S.A. 123 E2
Alto Taquari Brazil 138 B1
Altötting Ger. 50 C3
Altun Shan mts China 81 F3
Alturas U.S.A. 118 B2
Altus U.S.A. 127 E2
Alūksne Latvia 36 C2
Al 'Ulā Saudi Arabia 82 A2
Al 'Uqaylah Libya 91 D1
Al Uqsur Egypt see Luxor
Alushta Ukr. 39 D3
Alva U.S.A. 127 E1
Alvarado Mex. 129 C3
Älvdalen vall. Sweden 41 C3
Älvik Norway 42 E1
Älvsbyn Sweden 40 E2
Al Wajh Saudi Arabia 82 A2
Alwar India 78 B2
Al Widyān plat. Iraq/Saudi Arabia
  85 C2
Alxa Youqi China see Ehen Hudag
Alyangula Austr. 103 C1
Alytus Lith. 36 B3
Alzada U.S.A. 120 C1
Alzey Ger. 48 D3
Amadeus, Lake salt flat Austr.
  102 C2
Amadora Port. 54 B2
Amā'ir Saudi Arabia 82 B3
Åmål Sweden 41 C4

aliada Greece **59** B3
amapare Indon. **63** D3
ambai Brazil **138** A2
ambai r. Brazil **138** D2
ambai, Serra de hills
razil/Para. **138** A2
ami-shotō is Japan **73** E3
antea Italy **57** C3
apá Brazil **135** D2
areleja Port. **54** B2
arillo U.S.A. **127** D1
asya Turkey **84** B1
azon r. S. America **134** D2
azon, Mouths of the Brazil
35 E2
azonas r. S. America see
mazon
bada India **78** B1
bato Ecuador **134** B3
bato Boeny Madag.
7 [inset] D1
bato Finandrahana Madag.
7 [inset] D2
batolampy Madag.
7 [inset] D1
batondrazaka Madag.
7 [inset] D1
berg Ger. **49** E3
bergris Cay i. Belize **130** B3
bikapur India **79** C2
bilobe Madag. **97** [inset] D1
bleside U.K. **46** B2
boasary Madag. **97** [inset] D2
bon Indon. **63** C3
boni. Indon. **63** C3
bovombe Madag. **97** [inset] D2
briz Angola **94** B3
do China **79** D1
eca Mex. **128** B2
eland i. Neth. **48** B1
erican Falls U.S.A. **118** D2
erican Falls Reservoir U.S.A.
18 D2
erican Fork U.S.A. **118** D2
erican Samoa terr.
. Pacific Ocean **101**
ericus U.S.A. **125** D2
ersfoort Neth. **48** B1
ery Ice Shelf Antarctica
07 E3
es U.S.A. **121** E2
ga Rus. Fed. **87** K2
guid Alg. **91** C2
gun' r. Rus. Fed. **87** L3
herst Can. **115** D2
iens France **52** C2
indivi Islands India **77** B3
inuis Namibia **98** A1
isk Lake Can. **113** E2
istad Reservoir Mex./U.S.A.
27 D3
mān Jordan **84** B2
massalik Greenland **111** J2
ol Iran **85** D2

Amorgos i. Greece **59** C3
Amory U.S.A. **124** C2
Amos Can. **114** C2
Amoy China see Xiamen
Amparo Brazil **139** C2
Amposta Spain **55** D1
Amqui Can. **123** G1
Amravati India **79** B2
Amritsar India **78** B1
Amstelveen Neth. **48** B1
Amsterdam Neth. **48** B1
Amstetten Austria **50** C3
Am Timan Chad **91** E3
Amudar'ya r. Asia **80** C2
Amund Ringnes Island Can.
Amundsen Gulf Can. **110** D2
Amuntai Indon. **65** C2
Amur r. China/Rus. Fed. see Heilong Jiang
'Amur, Wadi watercourse Sudan **82** A3
Anabanua Indon. **65** D2
Anabarskiy Zaliv b. Rus. Fed.
87 J2
Anaconda U.S.A. **118** D1
Anadolu Dağları mts Turkey
84 B1
Anadyr' r. Rus. Fed. **87** N2
'Ānah Iraq **85** C2
Anáhuac Mex. **129** B2
Anamur Turkey **84** B2
Anan Japan **71** B4
Anantapur India **77** B3
Anan'yiv Ukr. **38** C2
Anapa Rus. Fed. **39** E3
Anápolis Brazil **138** C1
Añatuya Arg. **136** B3
Ancenis France **52** B2
Anchorage U.S.A. **110** C2
Ancona Italy **56** B2
Ancud Chile **137** A5
Andalsnes Norway **40** B3
Andalucía aut. comm. Spain
54 C2
Andalusia U.S.A. **124** C2
Andaman Islands India **77** D3
Andaman Sea Indian Ocean
67 A2
Andapa Madag. **97** [inset] D1
Andenes Norway **40** D2
Andenne Belgium **48** B2
Anderlecht Belgium **48** B2
Anderson r. Can. **110** D2
Anderson AK U.S.A. **110** C2
Anderson IN U.S.A. **122** C2
Anderson SC U.S.A. **125** D2
Andes mts S. America **136** A1
Andfjorden sea chan. Norway
Andhra Pradesh state India
Andijon Uzbek. **81** E2
Andilamena Madag. **97** [inset] D1
Andilanatoby Madag.
97 [inset] D1
Andizhan Uzbek. see Andijon
Andoany Madag. **97** [inset] D1
Andong S. Korea **69** B2

Andorra country Europe **52** C3
Andorra la Vella Andorra **52** C3
Andover U.K. **47** C4
Andradina Brazil **138** B2
Andrews U.S.A. **127** D2
Andria Italy **57** C2
Androka Madag. **97** [inset] D2
Andros i. Bahamas **130** C2
Andros i. Greece **59** B3
Andros Town Bahamas **125** E4
Andrott i. India **77** B3
Andrushivka Ukr. **38** C1
Andselv Norway **40** D2
Andújar Spain **54** C2
Andulo Angola **96** A1
Anéfis Mali **90** C3
Aney Niger **91** D3
Angarsk Rus. Fed. **72** C1
Ange Sweden **41** D3
Ángel de la Guarda, Isla i. Mex.
128 A2
Angeles Phil. **68** B2
Ängelholm Sweden **41** C4
Angermanälven r. Sweden **40** D3
Angermünde Ger. **49** G1
Angers France **52** B2
Angikuni Lake Can. **113** F1
Anglesey i. U.K. **46** A3
Angoche Moz. **97** C1
Angola country Africa **94** B4
Angoon U.S.A. **112** B2
Angoulême France **52** C2
Angren Uzbek. **81** E2
Anguilla terr. West Indies **131** D3
Angul India **79** C2
Anholt i. Denmark **41** C4
Anhui prov. China **74** B2
Anicuns Brazil **138** C1
Aniva, Mys c. Rus. Fed. **70** D1
Aniva, Zaliv b. Rus. Fed. **70** D1
Ankang China **74** A2
Ankara Turkey **35** C5
Anlu China **74** B2
Anna Rus. Fed. **37** F3
Annaba Alg. **91** C1
Annaberg-Buchholtz Ger. **49** F2
An Nafūd des. Saudi Arabia
82 B2
An Najaf Iraq **85** C2
Annan U.K. **44** C3
Annapolis U.S.A. **123** E3
Annapurna I mt. Nepal **79** C2
Ann Arbor U.S.A. **122** D2
Anna Regina Guyana **134** D2
An Nāşiriyah Iraq **85** C2
Annecy France **53** D2
Anniston U.S.A. **125** C2
An Nu'ayriyah Saudi Arabia **83** B2
Anorontany, Tanjona hd Madag.
97 [inset] D1
Ano Viannos Greece **59** C3
Anqing China **75** B2
Ansan S. Korea **69** B2
Ansbach Ger. **49** E3

Anshan China **74** C1
Anshun China **75** A3
An Sirhān, Wādī watercourse Saudi Arabia **82** A1
Ansongo Mali **90** C3
Antakya Turkey **84** B2
Antalaha Madag. **97** [inset] E1
Antalya Turkey **84** B2
Antalya Körfezi g. Turkey **84** B2
Antananarivo Madag. **97** [inset] D1
Antarctica **107**
Antarctic Peninsula Antarctica **107** K3
An Teallach mt. U.K. **44** B2
Antequera Spain **54** C2
Anthony U.S.A. **126** B2
Anti Atlas mts Morocco **90** B2
Antibes France **53** D3
Anticostì, Île d' i. Can. **115** D2
Antigonish Can. **115** D2
Antigua and Barbuda country West Indies **131** D3
Antigua-Morelos Mex. **129** C2
Antikythira i. Greece **59** B3
Antipodes Islands N.Z. **100**
Antofagasta Chile **136** A3
Antrim U.K. **45** C1
Antrim Hills U.K. **45** C1
Antsalova Madag. **97** [inset] D1
Antsirabe Madag. **97** [inset] D1
Antsirañana Madag. **97** [inset] D1
Antsohihy Madag. **97** [inset] D1
Antwerp Belgium **48** B2
Anuradhapura Sri Lanka **77** C3
Anxi China **72** C2
Anxious Bay Austr. **104** C3
Anyang China **74** B2
Aomori Japan **70** D2
Aosta Italy **56** A1
Apalachee Bay U.S.A. **125** D3
Apaporis r. Col. **134** C3
Aparecida do Tabuado Brazil **138** B2
Aparri Phil. **68** B2
Apatity Rus. Fed. **34** C2
Apatzingán Mex. **128** B3
Apeldoorn Neth. **48** B1
Apen Ger. **48** C1
Apennines mts Italy **56** A2
Apia Samoa **101**
Apiaí Brazil **138** C2
Apo, Mount vol. Phil. **68** B3
Apolda Ger. **49** E2
Apollo Bay Austr. **104** C3
Apopka, Lake U.S.A. **125** D3
Aporé r. Brazil **138** B1
Appalachian Mountains U.S.A. **117** D3
Appleton U.S.A. **122** C2
Apsheronsk Rus. Fed. **39** E3
Apucarana Brazil **138** B2

Apucarana, Serra da hills Brazil **138** B2
Aqaba, Gulf of Asia **88** A2
Aqqikkol Hu salt l. China **79** C1
Aquidauana Brazil **138** A2
Aquidauana r. Brazil **138** A1
Ara India **79** C2
Arab, Bahr el watercourse Sudan **93** A4
Arabian Gulf Asia see The Gulf
Arabian Peninsula Asia **92** C5
Arabian Sea Indian Ocean **145** G4
Aracaju Brazil **135** F4
Aracati Brazil **135** F3
Araçatuba Brazil **138** B2
Aracruz Brazil **139** D1
Araçuaí Brazil **139** D1
Arad Romania **38** B2
Arada Chad **91** C3
Arafura Sea Austr./Indon. **63** C3
Aragarças Brazil **138** B1
Aragón r. Spain **55** C1
Araguaia r. Brazil **135** E3
Araguaína Brazil **135** E3
Araguari Brazil **138** C1
Arak Alg. **90** C2
Arāk Iran **85** C2
Arakan Yoma mts Myanmar **66** A1
Arak's r. Armenia **85** C1
Aral Sea salt l. Kazakh./Uzbek. **80** D2
Aral'sk Kazakh. **80** D2
Aranda de Duero Spain **54** C1
Arandelovac S.M. **58** B2
Aran Islands Ireland **45** B2
Aranjuez Spain **54** C1
Aranos Namibia **98** A1
Aransas Pass U.S.A. **127** E3
Arapiraca Brazil **135** F3
Arapongas Brazil **138** B2
Araquari Brazil **138** C3
'Ar'ar Saudi Arabia **82** B1
Araraquara Brazil **138** C2
Araras Brazil **135** D3
Araras, Serra das mts Brazil **138** B3
Ararat Austr. **104** C3
Ararat, Mount Turkey **85** C2
Araruama, Lago de lag. Brazil **139** D2
Araua Col. **134** B2
Araxá Brazil **138** C1
Arbil Iraq **85** C2
Arbroath U.K. **44** C2
Arbu Lut, Dasht-e des. Afgh. **78** A2
Arcachon France **52** B3
Arcata U.S.A. **118** B2
Archangel Rus. Fed. **34** D2
Archer r. Austr. **103** D1
Arco U.S.A. **118** D2
Arcos de la Frontera Spain **54** C2

Arctic Bay Can. **111** G2
Arctic Ocean **146**
Arctic Red r. Can. **112** B1
Ardabil Iran **85** C2
Ardahan Turkey **85** C1
Årdalstangen Norway **41** B3
Ardennes plat. Belgium **48** B3
Ardestān Iran **85** D2
Ardlethan Austr. **105** D2
Ardmore U.S.A. **127** E2
Ardnamurchan, Point of pt U.K.
Ardrossan Austr. **104** B2
Ardrossan U.K. **44** B3
Arena, Point U.S.A. **119** B3
Arendal Norway **41** B4
Arequipa Peru **134** B4
Arévalo Spain **54** C1
Arezzo Italy **56** B2
Argentan France **52** B2
Argentina country S. America **137** B4
Argentino, Lago l. Arg. **137** A6
Argenton-sur-Creuse France **52** C2
Arges r. Romania **38** C3
Arghandab r. Afgh. **78** A1
Argolikos Kolpos b. Greece **59**
Argos Greece **59** B3
Argostoli Greece **59** B3
Arguín r. China/Rus. Fed. **73** E
Argyle, Lake Austr. **102** B1
Ar Horqin Qi China see Tianshan
Århus Denmark **41** C4
Ariamsvlei Namibia **98** A2
Ari Atoll Maldives **77** B4
Arica Chile **134** B4
Arinagour U.K. **44** A2
Arinos Brazil **139** C1
Aripuanã Brazil **134** D4
Aripuanã r. Brazil **134** C3
Ariquemes Brazil **134** C3
Ariranhã r. Brazil **138** B1
Arizona state U.S.A. **126** B2
Arjeplog Sweden **40** D2
Arkadelphia U.S.A. **124** B2
Arkalyk Kazakh. **81** D1
Arkansas r. U.S.A. **124** B2
Arkansas state U.S.A. **124** B1
Arkansas City U.S.A. **121** D3
Arkhangel'sk Rus. Fed. see Archangel
Arklow Ireland **45** C2
Arkona, Kap c. Ger. **50** C2
Arkticheskogo Instituta, Ostrova is Rus. Fed. **86** H1
Arles France **53** C3
Arlit Niger **91** C3
Arlon Belgium **48** B3
Armagh U.K. **45** C1
Armant Egypt **92** B2
Armavir Rus. Fed. **39** F2
Armenia country Asia **85** C1

enia Col. **134** B2
eria Mex. **128** B3
idale Austr. **105** E2
strong Can. **114** B1
ayans'k Ukr. **84** B1
aud r. Can. **115** D1
em Neth. **48** B2
em, Cape Austr. **103** C1
em Bay Austr. **103** C1
o r. Italy **56** B2
o Bay Austr. **104** B2
sberg Ger. **48** D2
stadt Ger. **49** E2
ab Namibia **98** A2
na Italy **56** A1
en r. Mex. **128** B2
Ramādī Iraq **85** C2
an i. U.K. **44** B3
Raqqah Syria **84** B2
as France **52** C1
agá Mex. **129** C3
Rimāl reg. Saudi Arabia **83** C2
Riyāḍ Saudi Arabia see Riyadh
Rustāq Oman **83** C2
ḩutbah Iraq **84** C2
enajān Iran **85** D3
en'yev Rus. Fed. **70** B2
a Greece **59** B3
aaga Mex. **128** B3
em Rus. Fed. **70** B2
mivs'k Ukr. **39** E2
annay France **52** C2
esia U.S.A. **136** D2
nur Point Austr. **103** E2
nur's Pass N.Z. **106** B3
nur's Town Bahamas **125** E4
gas Uru. **136** C4
llery Lake Can. **113** E1
syz Ukr. **38** C2
ux China **81** E3
win Turkey **85** C1
i, Kepulauan is Indon. **63** C3
a Uganda **95** D2
ba terr. West Indies **131** D3
sha Tanz. **95** D3
ayheer Mongolia **72** C1
iat Can. **113** F1
idsjaur Sweden **40** D2
lika Sweden **41** C4
amas Rus. Fed. **35** D3
ew Alg. **55** C2
feld Ger. **48** D2
Czech Rep. **49** F2
nhi-dake vol. Japan **70** D2
ahikawa Japan **70** D2
ansol India **79** C2
iat Can. **113** E2
ension Bol. **136** B2
ension i. S. Atlantic Ocean **99** A5
ensión, Bahía de la b. Mex. **129** D3
chaffenburg Ger. **49** D3
chersleben Ger. **49** E2

Ascoli Piceno Italy **56** B2
Åsele Sweden **40** D3
Asenovgrad Bulg. **58** B2
Ashburton watercourse Austr. **102** A2
Ashburton N.Z. **106** B3
Ashdown U.S.A. **124** B2
Asheville U.S.A. **125** D1
Ashford U.K. **47** D4
Ashgabat Turkm. **80** C2
Ashington U.K. **46** C2
Ashkhabad Turkm. see Ashgabat
Ashland KY U.S.A. **122** D3
Ashland OH U.S.A. **122** D2
Ashland OR U.S.A. **118** B2
Ashland WI U.S.A. **122** B1
Ashmyany Belarus **36** C3
Ash Sharawrah Saudi Arabia **82** B3
Ash Shāriqah U.A.E. see Sharjah
Ash Shaṭrah Iraq **85** C2
Ash Shiḥr Yemen **83** B3
Ash Shināṣ Oman **83** C2
Ash Shu'bah Saudi Arabia **82** B2
Ashuanipi Lake Can. **115** D1
Asilah Morocco **54** B2
Asinara, Golfo dell' b. Italy **56** A2
Asino Rus. Fed. **86** H3
Asipovichy Belarus **36** C3
'Asir reg. Saudi Arabia **82** B2
Askim Norway **41** C4
Asmara Eritrea **82** B3
Åsnen l. Sweden **41** C4
Aspang-Markt Austria **51** D3
Aspen U.S.A. **120** B3
Aspiring, Mount N.Z. **106** A3
Assab Eritrea **93** C3
As Salamīyah Saudi Arabia **83** B2
As Samāwah Iraq **85** C2
Aṣ Ṣanām reg. Saudi Arabia
83 C2
Aṣ Sarīr reg. Libya **91** E2
Assen Neth. **48** C1
Assesse Belgium **48** B2
Assiniboia Can. **113** E3
Assis Brazil **138** B2
Assisi Italy **53** D3
Aṣ Ṣubayḩīyah Kuwait **83** B2
Aṣ Ṣulaymānīyah Iraq **85** C2
As Sulayyil Saudi Arabia **82** B2
As Sūq Saudi Arabia **82** B2
As Suwaydā' Syria **84** B2
As Suwayq Egypt see Suez
Astakos Greece **59** B3
Astana Kazakh. **81** E1
Āstārā Iran **85** C2
Asti Italy **56** A2
Astorga Spain **54** B1
Astoria U.S.A. **118** B1
Astrakhan' Rus. Fed. **35** D4
Astravyets Belarus **36** C3
Astypalaia i. Greece **59** C3
Asunción Para. **136** C3
Aswān Egypt **92** B2

Asyūṭ Egypt **92** B2
Atacama, Desierto de des. Chile
see Atacama Desert
Atacama, Salar de salt flat Chile
136 B3
Atacama Desert Chile **136** B3
Atakpamé Togo **90** C4
Atamyrat Turkm. **81** D3
'Ataq Yemen **82** B3
Atâr Maur. **90** A2
Atascadero U.S.A. **119** B3
Atasu Kazakh. **81** E2
Atbara Sudan **92** B3
Atbara r. Sudan **92** B3
Atbasar Kazakh. **81** D1
Atchison U.S.A. **121** D3
Ath Belgium **48** A2
Athabasca Can. **112** D2
Athabasca r. Can. **113** D2
Athabasca, Lake Can. **113** E2
Athens Greece **59** B3
Athens GA U.S.A. **125** D2
Athens OH U.S.A. **125** D1
Athens TN U.S.A. **125** D1
Athens TX U.S.A. **127** E2
Athina Greece see Athens
Athlone Ireland **45** C2
Athos mt. Greece **59** B2
Athy Ireland **45** C2
Ati Chad **91** D3
Atikokan Can. **114** A2
Atlanta U.S.A. **125** D2
Atlantic U.S.A. **121** D2
Atlantic City U.S.A. **123** F3
Atlantic Ocean **144**
Atlantis S. Africa **98** A3
Atlas Mountains Africa **90** B1
Atlas Saharien mts Alg. **90** C1
Atlin Can. **112** B2
Atlin Lake Can. **112** B2
Atmore U.S.A. **124** C2
Atoka U.S.A. **127** E2
Atrai r. India **79** C2
Aṭ Ṭā'if Saudi Arabia **82** B2
Attapu Laos **67** B2
Attavyros mt. Greece **59** C3
Attawapiskat Can. **114** B1
Attawapiskat r. Can. **114** B1
Attawapiskat Lake Can.
114 B1
Aṭ Ṭur Egypt **92** B2
Aṭ Turbah Yemen **82** B3
Atyrau Kazakh. **80** C2
Aubenas France **53** C3
Auburn AL U.S.A. **125** C2
Auburn CA U.S.A. **119** B3
Auburn NE U.S.A. **121** D2
Auburn NY U.S.A. **123** E2
Aubusson France **52** C2
Auch France **52** C3
Auckland N.Z. **106** B2
Auckland Islands N.Z. **100**
Audo Range mts Eth. **95** E2
Aue Ger. **49** F2

Augsburg Ger. **50** C3
Augusta Italy **56** C3
Augusta *GA* U.S.A. **125** D2
Augusta *ME* U.S.A. **123** G2
Augustus, Mount Austr. **102** A2
Aulnoye-Aymeries France **48** A2
Aunglan Myanmar **66** A2
Aurangabad India **78** B3
Aurich Ger. **48** C1
Aurillac France **52** C3
Aurora *CO* U.S.A. **120** C3
Aurora *IL* U.S.A. **122** C2
Aus Namibia **98** A2
Austin *MN* U.S.A. **121** E2
Austin *NV* U.S.A. **119** C3
Austin *TX* U.S.A. **127** E2
Australes, Îles *is* Fr. Polynesia *see*
  Tubuai Islands
Australia *country* Oceania **102**
Australian Capital Territory
  admin. div. Austr. **105** D3
Austria *country* Europe **50** C3
Autlán Mex. **128** B3
Autun France **53** C2
Auxerre France **53** C2
Avallon France **53** C2
Avalon Peninsula Can. **115** E2
Avaré Brazil **138** C2
Avarua Cook Is **101**
Aveiro Port. **54** B1
Avellino Italy **56** B2
Avesnes-sur-Helpe France **48** A2
Avesta Sweden **41** D3
Avezzano Italy **56** B2
Avignon France **53** C3
Ávila Spain **54** C1
Avilés Spain **54** B1
Avola Italy **56** C3
Avon *r. England* U.K. **47** C4
Avon *r. England* U.K. **47** B3
Avranches France **52** B2
Awanui N.Z. **106** B2
Āwash Eth. **93** C3
Āwash *r.* Eth. **93** C3
Awbārī Libya **91** D2
Aweil Sudan **93** A4
Awka Nigeria **94** A2
Axel Heiberg Island Can. **110** F1
Ay France **48** B3
Ayacucho Peru **134** B4
Ayagoz Kazakh. **81** F2
Ayakkum Hu *salt l.* China **72** B2
Ayamonte Spain **54** B2
Ayan Rus. Fed. **87** L3
Ayaviri Peru **134** B4
Āybak Afgh. **78** A1
Aydar *r.* Ukr. **39** D2
Aydın Turkey **59** C3
Ayeat, Gora *h.* Kazakh. **81** D2
Ayers Rock *h.* Austr. *see* Uluṟu
Aylesbury U.K. **47** C4
Ayllón Spain **54** C1

Aylmer Lake Can. **113** E1
Ayod Sudan **93** B4
Ayon, Ostrov *i.* Rus. Fed. **87** N2
'Ayoûn el 'Atroûs Maur. **90** B3
Ayr Austr. **103** D1
Ayr U.K. **44** B3
Ayre, Point of *pt* Isle of Man
  46 A2
Ayteke Bi Kazakh. **80** D2
Aytos Bulg. **58** D2
Ayutthaya Thai. **67** B2
Ayvacık Turkey **59** C3
Ayvalık Turkey **59** C3
Azaouâgh, Vallée de *watercourse*
  Mali/Niger **90** C3
Azerbaijan *country* Asia **85** C1
Azores *aut. reg.* Port. **32**
Azores *terr.* N. Atlantic Ocean **32**
Azov, Sea of Rus. Fed./Ukr. **39** E2
Azraq, Baḩr el *r.* Eth./Sudan *see*
  Blue Nile
Azuaga Spain **54** B2
Azuero, Península de *pen.*
  Panama **130** B4
Azul Arg. **137** C4
Az Zaġāzīġ Egypt **84** B2
Az Zarqā' Jordan **84** B2
Az Zaydīyah Yemen **82** B3
Azzel Matti, Sebkha *salt pan* Alg.
  90 C2
Az Zuqur *i.* Yemen **82** B3

B

Baardheere Somalia **93** C4
Bābā, Kūh-e *mts* Afgh. **78** A1
Babadag Romania **58** C2
Babaeski Turkey **59** C2
Bāb al Mandab *str.* Africa/Asia
  82 B3
Babana Indon. **65** C2
Babar *i.* Indon. **63** C3
Babati Tanz. **95** D3
Babayevo Rus. Fed. **37** E2
Babine *r.* Can. **112** C2
Babine Lake Can. **112** C2
Babo Indon. **63** C3
Bābol Iran **85** D2
Babruysk Belarus **36** C3
Babuyan *i.* Phil. **68** B2
Babuyan Islands Phil. **68** B2
Bacabal Brazil **135** E3
Bacan *i.* Indon. **63** C3
Bacău Romania **58** C2
Bacchus Marsh Austr. **104** C3
Bachu China **81** E3
Back *r.* Can. **113** F1
Bac Liêu Vietnam **67** B3
Bacolod Phil. **68** B2
Bacqueville, Lac *l.* Can. **114** C1
Badajoz Spain **54** B2

Badarpur India **66** A1
Bad Berleburg Ger. **49** D2
Bad Bevensen Ger. **49** E1
Bad Ems Ger. **48** C2
Baden Austria **51** D3
Baden-Baden Ger. **50** B3
Bad Freienwalde Ger. **49** G1
Bad Harzburg Ger. **49** E2
Bad Hersfeld Ger. **49** D2
Bad Hofgastein Austria **50** C3
Bad Homburg vor der Höhe Ger.
  49 D2
Badin Pak. **78** A2
Bad Ischl Austria **53** E2
Bādiyat ash Shām *des.* Asia *see*
  Syrian Desert
Bad Kissingen Ger. **49** E2
Bad Kreuznach Ger. **48** C3
Bad Lauterberg im Harz Ger.
  49 E2
Bad Liebenwerda Ger. **49** F2
Bad Mergentheim Ger. **49** D3
Bad Nauheim Ger. **49** D2
Bad Neuenahr-Ahrweiler Ger.
  48 C2
Bad Neustadt an der Saale Ger.
  49 E2
Bad Oldesloe Ger. **49** E1
Bad Pyrmont Ger. **49** D2
Badr Ḩunayn Saudi Arabia
  82 A2
Bad Salzuflen Ger. **49** D1
Bad Salzungen Ger. **49** E2
Bad Schwartau Ger. **50** C2
Bad Segeberg Ger. **50** C2
Badulla Sri Lanka **77** C4
Bad Zwischenahn Ger. **48** D1
Bafatá Guinea-Bissau **90** A3
Baffin Bay *sea* Can./Greenland
  111 H2
Baffin Island Can. **111** H2
Bafia Cameroon **94** B2
Bafing *r.* Guinea/Mali **90** A3
Bafoulabé Mali **90** A3
Bafoussam Cameroon **94** B2
Bāfq Iran **85** D2
Bafra Turkey **84** B1
Bāft Iran **83** C2
Bafwasende Dem. Rep. Congo
  95 C2
Bagamoyo Tanz. **95** D3
Bagani Namibia **96** B3
Bagansiapiapi Indon. **64** B1
Bagé Brazil **136** C4
Baghdād Iraq **85** C2
Baghlān Afgh. **78** A1
Bagnères-de-Luchon France
  52 C3
Bagrationovsk Rus. Fed. **36** B3
Bagrax China *see* Bohu
Baguio Phil. **68** B2
Bagzane, Monts *mts* Niger **91**
Baharampur India **79** C2
Bahawalpur Pak. **78** B2

...nía, Islas de la *is* Hond. **30** B3
...nía Blanca Arg. **137** B4
...nía Kino Mex. **128** A2
...hir Dar Eth. **93** B3
...nraich India **79** C2
...riyah, Wāḩat *al oasis* Egypt **92** A2
...nū Kālāt Iran **83** D2
...a Mare Romania **38** B2
...cheng China **73** E1
...le-Comeau Can. **115** D2
...he China **69** B3
...kal, Lake Rus. Fed. **73** D1
...le Átha Cliath Ireland *see* Dublin
...lești Romania **38** B3
...ma China **72** C2
...bridge U.S.A. **125** D2
...ker *OR* U.S.A. **118** B2
...ker *CA* U.S.A. **119** C3
...ker *MT* U.S.A. **120** C1
...riki Kiribati **100**
...rin Youqi China *see* Daban
...rnsdale Austr. **105** D3
...shan China **69** B1
...lstvo Rus. Fed. **74** A2
...yda Desert Sudan **92** B3
...jawa Indon. **65** D2
...kel Senegal **90** A3
...ker *CA* U.S.A. **119** C3
...ker Island *terr.*
   S. Pacific Ocean **101**
...ker Lake Can. **113** F1
...ker Lake *l.* Can. **113** F1
...kersfield U.S.A. **119** C3
...khchysaray Ukr. **39** D3
...khorden Turkm. **80** C3
...khmach Ukr. **39** D1
...ku Azer. *see* Baku
...kırköy Turkey **59** C2
...kkaflói *b.* Iceland **40** [inset]
...ku Azer. **85** C1
...labac Phil. **68** A3
...labac *i.* Phil. **68** A3
...labac Strait Malaysia/Phil.
   65 C1
...laikerkuak Indon. **65** C2
...lakava Austr. **104** B2
...laklava Ukr. **39** D3
...laklıya Ukr. **39** E2
...lakovo Rus. Fed. **35** D3
...la Morghāb Afgh. **78** A1
...lan Dağı *h.* Turkey **59** C3
...lashov Rus. Fed. **35** D3
...laton, Lake Hungary **51** D3
...lbina, Represa de *resr* Brazil
   134 D3
...lbriggan Ireland **45** C2

Balcanoona Austr. **104** B2
Balchik Bulg. **58** C2
Balclutha N.Z. **106** A4
Baldock Lake Can. **113** F2
Baldy Mountain h. Can. **113** E2
Baldy Peak U.S.A. **126** C2
Baleares, Islas *is* Spain *see*
   Balearic Islands
Balearic Islands *is* Spain **55** D2
Baleia, Ponta da *pt* Brazil **139** E1
Baleine, Grande Rivière de la *r.*
   Can. **114** C1
Baleine, Rivière à la *r.* Can.
   115 D1
Baleshwar India **79** C2
Bali *i.* Indon. **79** C2
Bali, Laut *sea* Indon. **65** C2
Balige Indon. **64** A1
Baliguda India **79** C2
Balıkesir Turkey **59** C3
Balıkpapan Indon. **65** C2
Balimo P.N.G. **63** D3
Bali Sea Indon. *see* Bali, Laut
Balkanabat Turkm. **80** C3
Balkan Mountains Bulg./S.M.
   58 B2
Balkhash Kazakh. **81** E2
Balkhash, Lake Kazakh. **81** E2
Balladonia Austr. **102** B3
Ballangen Norway **40** D2
Ballarat Austr. **104** C3
Ballard, Lake *salt flat* Austr.
   102 B2
Ballater U.K. **44** C2
Ballina Austr. **105** E1
Ballina Ireland **45** B1
Ballinasloe Ireland **45** B2
Ballinger U.S.A. **127** E2
Ballycastle U.K. **45** C1
Ballyclare U.K. **45** C1
Ballymena U.K. **45** C1
Ballymoney U.K. **45** C1
Ballyshannon Ireland **45** B1
Balonne *r.* Austr. **103** D2
Balotra India **78** B2
Balrampur India **79** C2
Balranald Austr. **104** C2
Balş Romania **38** B3
Balsas Mex. **129** C3
Balta Ukr. **38** C2
Bălţi Moldova **38** C2
Baltic Sea *g.* Europe **41** D4
Baltimore U.S.A. **123** E3
Baltiysk Rus. Fed. **36** A3
Balvi Latvia **36** C2
Balykchy Kyrg. **81** E2
Balykshi Kazakh. **80** C2
Bam Iran **83** C2
Bamaga Austr. **103** D1
Bamaji Lake Can. **114** A1
Bamako Mali **90** B3
Bambari C.A.R. **94** C2
Bamberg Ger. **49** E3
Bambouti C.A.R. **95** C2

Bambuí Brazil **139** C2
Bamenda Cameroon **94** B2
Bāmīān Afgh. **78** A1
Bam Posht, Kūh-e *mts* Iran
   78 A2
Bañados del Izozog *swamp* Bol.
   136 D2
Banamal, Ilha do *i.* Brazil **135** D4
Banas *r.* India **78** B2
Banaz Turkey **59** C3
Ban Ban Laos **66** B2
Banbridge U.K. **45** C1
Banbury U.K. **47** C3
Banda Dem. Rep. Congo **95** C2
Banda India **79** C2
Banda, Laut *sea* Indon. **63** C3
Banda Aceh Indon. **64** A1
Bandar-e 'Abbās Iran **83** C2
Bandar-e Anzalī Iran **85** C2
Bandar-e Emām Khomeynī Iran
   85 C2
Bandar-e Lengeh Iran **83** C2
Bandar-e Maqām Iran **83** C2
Bandar Lampung Indon. **64** B2
Bandar Seri Begawan Brunei
   65 C1
Banda Sea Indon. *see*
   Banda, Laut
Bandeiras, Pico de *mt.* Brazil
   139 D2
Bandelierkop S. Africa **99** C1
Banderas, Bahía de *b.* Mex.
   128 B2
Bandırma Turkey **59** C2
Bandundu Dem. Rep. Congo
   94 B3
Bandung Indon. **64** B2
Banff Can. **112** D2
Banff U.K. **44** C2
Banfora Burkina **90** B3
Banga Phil. **68** B3
Bangalore India **77** B3
Bangassou C.A.R. **94** C2
Banggai Indon. **65** D2
Banggai, Kepulauan *is* Indon.
   65 D2
Banggi *i.* Malaysia **65** C1
Bangka *i.* Indon. **64** B2
Bangkalan Indon. **65** C2
Bangkinang Indon. **64** B1
Bangko Indon. **64** B2
Bangkok Thai. **67** B2
Bangladesh *country* Asia **79** C2
Bangor Northern Ireland U.K.
   45 D1
Bangor Wales U.K. **46** A3
Bangor U.S.A. **123** G2
Bang Saphan Yai Thai. **67** A2
Bangui C.A.R. **94** B2
Bangweulu, Lake Zambia **97** B1
Ban Huai Khon Thai. **66** B2
Bani Mazār Egypt **80** B3
Bani Walid Libya **91** D1
Bāniyās Syria **84** B2

Banja Luka Bos.-Herz. **57** C2
Banjarmasin Indon. **65** C2
Banjul Gambia **90** A3
Banks Island *B.C.* Can. **112** B2
Banks Island *N.W.T.* Can. **110** D2
Banks Lake Can. **113** F1
Banks Peninsula N.Z. **106** B3
Bankura India **79** C2
Banmauk Myanmar **66** A1
Bann *r.* U.K. **45** C1
Ban Napè Laos **66** B2
Ban Na San Thai. **67** A3
Bannerman Town Bahamas **125** E4
Bannu Pak. **78** B1
Banswara India **78** B2
Ban Tha Kham Thai. **67** A3
Bantry Ireland **45** B3
Bantry Bay Ireland **45** B3
Banyuwangi Indon. **65** C2
Baochang China **74** B1
Baoji China **74** A2
Bao Lôc Vietnam **67** B2
Baoqing China **70** B1
Baoshan China **66** A1
Baotou China **74** B1
Baotou Shan *mt.* China/N. Korea **69** B1
Bapaume France **48** A2
Ba'qûbah Iraq **85** C2
Bar S.M. **58** A2
Baracoa Cuba **131** C2
Baradine Austr. **105** D2
Baram *r.* Malaysia **65** C1
Baranavichy Belarus **36** C3
Baranis Egypt **82** A2
Baranivka Ukr. **38** C1
Barankul Kazakh. **90** C2
Baranof Island U.S.A. **112** B2
Barat Daya, Kepulauan *is* Indon. **63** C3

Barbacena Brazil **139** D2
Barbados *country* West Indies **131** E3
Barbastro Spain **55** D1
Barcaldine Austr. **103** D2
Barcelona Spain **55** D1
Barcelona Venez. **134** C1
Barcelos Brazil **134** C2
Barcs Hungary **51** D3
Barddhaman India **79** C2
Bardejov Slovakia **51** E3
Bardsīr Iran **83** C2
Bareilly India **79** C2
Barentin France **47** D5
Barentu Eritrea **82** A3
Barents Sea Arctic Ocean **34** D1
Barfleur, Pointe de *pt* France **47** C5
Bar Harbor U.S.A. **123** G2
Bari Italy **57** C2
Barika Alg. **55** E2

Barinas Venez. **134** B2
Baripada India **79** C2
Barisal Bangl. **79** D2
Barisan, Pegunungan *mts* Indon. **64** B2
Barito *r.* Indon. **65** C2
Barkā Oman **83** C2
Barkly Tableland *reg.* Austr. **103** C1
Barkol China **72** C2
Bârlad Romania **38** C2
Bar-le-Duc France **53** D2
Barlee, Lake *salt flat* Austr. **102** A2
Barletta Italy **57** C2
Barmedman Austr. **105** D2
Barmer India **78** B2
Barmouth U.K. **47** A3
Barnaul Rus. Fed. **81** F1
Barneveld Neth. **48** B1
Barnsley U.K. **46** C3
Barnstaple U.K. **47** A4
Barquisimeto Venez. **134** C1
Barra *i.* U.K. **44** A2
Barraba Austr. **105** E2
Barra do Corda Brazil **135** D3
Barra do Garças Brazil **138** B2
Barra do São Manuel Brazil **134** D3
Barranca Lima Peru **134** B4
Barranca *Loreto* Peru **134** B3
Barranquilla Col. **134** B1
Barreiras Brazil **135** E4
Barretos Brazil **138** C2
Barrie Can. **114** C2
Barrier Range *hills* Austr. **104** C2
Barrington, Mount Austr. **105** E2
Barringun Austr. **105** D1
Barrow *r.* Ireland **45** C2
Barrow U.S.A. **110** B2
Barrow, Point U.S.A. **110** B2
Barrow Creek Austr. **102** C2
Barrow-in-Furness U.K. **46** B2
Barrow Island Austr. **102** A2
Barry U.K. **47** B4
Barrys Bay Can. **114** C2
Barsalpur India **78** B2
Barstow U.S.A. **119** C4
Bar-sur-Aube France **53** D2
Bartın Turkey **84** B1
Bartle Frere, Mount Austr. **103** D1
Bartlesville U.S.A. **127** E1
Bartoszyce Pol. **51** E2
Barung *i.* Indon. **65** C2
Baruun-Urt Mongolia **73** D1
Barvinkove Ukr. **39** E2
Barwon *r.* Austr. **105** D2
Barysaw Belarus **36** C3
Basarabi Romania **38** C3
Basel Switz. **53** D2
Bashtanka Ukr. **39** D2

Basilan *i.* Phil. **68** B3
Basildon U.K. **47** D4
Basingstoke U.K. **47** C4
Baskatong, Réservoir *resr* Can. **114** C2
Basle Switz. *see* Basel
Basoko Dem. Rep. Congo **94** C2
Basra Iraq **85** C2
Bassein Myanmar **66** A2
Basse-Terre Guadeloupe **131** D3
Basseterre St Kitts and Nevis **131** D3
Bass Strait Austr. **103** D3
Bastak Iran **83** C2
Basti India **79** C2
Bastia France **53** D3
Bastogne Belgium **48** B2
Bastrop U.S.A. **124** B2
Bata Equat. Guinea **94** A2
Batagay Rus. Fed. **87** K2
Bataguassu Brazil **138** B2
Batan *i.* Phil. **68** B1
Batangas Phil. **68** B2
Batangharī *r.* Indon. **64** B2
Batan Islands Phil. **68** B1
Batavia U.S.A. **123** E2
Bataysk Rus. Fed. **39** E2
Batchawana Mountain *h.* Can. **114** B2
Batchelor Austr. **102** C1
Bathinda India **78** B1
Bathurst Austr. **105** D2
Bathurst Can. **111** H3
Bathurst Inlet Can. **110** E2
Bathurst Inlet *inlet* Can. **110** E2
Bathurst Island Austr. **102** C1
Bathurst Island Can. **110** F1
Bātin, Wādī al *watercourse* Asia **82** E1
Batman Turkey **85** C2
Batna Alg. **91** C1
Baton Rouge U.S.A. **124** B2
Batopilas Mex. **128** B2
Batouri Cameroon **94** B2
Båtsfjord Norway **40** F1
Batticaloa Sri Lanka **77** C4
Battipaglia Italy **56** B2
Battle *r.* Can. **113** E2
Battle Creek U.S.A. **122** C2
Batu *mt.* Eth. **93** B4
Batu, Pulau-pulau *is* Indon. **64** A2
Batudaka *i.* Indon. **65** D2
Bat'umi Georgia **85** C1
Batu Pahat Malaysia **64** B1
Baubau Indon. **65** D2
Bauchi Nigeria **91** C3
Bauru Brazil **138** C2
Bauska Latvia **36** B2

156

itzen Ger. **50** C2
ispe *r.* Mex. **128** B2
ly Rus. Fed. **35** E3
vean *i.* Indon. **65** C2
amo Cuba **131** C2
anhongor Mongolia **72** C1
an Hot China **74** A2
an Obo Kuangqu China
74 A1
an Ul Hot China **74** B1
awan Phil. **68** B3
kal Rus. Fed. *see*
kal, Ozero *l.* Rus. Fed. *see*
ikal, Lake
kal'skiy Khrebet *mts*
s. Fed. **87** J3
rnak Rus. Fed. **35** E3
rnaoua France **52** B3
ramiç Turkey **59** C3
reuth Ger. **49** E3
dar Pak. **78** A2
män Iran **83** D2
mān, Kūh-e *mt.* Iran **83** D2
chy Head U.K. **47** D4
con Bay S. Africa **99** C3
gle Gulf Austr. **102** B1
lanana Madag. **97** [inset] D1
rdmore Can. **114** B2
er Paw Mountain U.S.A.
18 E1
trice U.S.A. **121** D2
ty U.S.A. **119** C3
udesert Austr. **105** E1
ufort Austr. **104** C3
ufort Malaysia **65** C1
ufort U.S.A. **125** D2
ufort Sea Can./U.S.A. **110** D2
ufort West S. Africa **98** B3
uly *r.* U.K. **44** B2
umont Belgium **48** B2
umont N.Z. **106** A4
umont U.S.A. **127** F2
ume France **53** C2
uraing Belgium **48** B2
uséjour Can. **113** F2
uvais France **52** C2
uval Can. **113** E2
ver *r.* Can. **113** E2
ver U.S.A. **119** D3
ver Creek Can. **112** A1
ver Dam U.S.A. **122** C2
ver Hill Lake Can. **113** F2
ver Island U.S.A. **122** C1
verlodge Can. **112** D2
wár India **78** B2
edouro Brazil **138** C2

Bebra Ger. **49** D2
Béchar Alg. **90** B1
Beckley U.S.A. **122** D3
Bedford U.K. **47** C3
Bedford U.S.A. **122** C3
Beecraft Peninsula Austr.
105 E2
Beenleigh Austr. **105** E1
Beersheba Israel **84** B2
Beeville U.S.A. **127** E3
Bega Austr. **105** D3
Begur, Cap de *c.* Spain **55** D1
Behshahr Iran **85** D2
Bei'an China **73** E1
Beihai China **75** A3
Beijing China **74** B2
Beilen Neth. **48** C1
Beinn Mhòr *h.* U.K. **44** A2
Beira Moz. **97** C1
Beirut Lebanon **84** B2
Beja Port. **54** B2
Bejaïa Alg. **91** C1
Béjar Spain **54** B1
Beji *r.* Pak. **78** A2
Bekdash Turkm. **80** C2
Békéscsaba Hungary **51** E3
Bekily Madag. **97** [inset] D2
Bela Pak. **78** A2
Bela-Bela S. Africa **99** C1
Bela Crkva S.M. **58** B2
Belaga Malaysia **65** C1
Belarus country Europe **36** C3
Bela Vista Brazil **138** A2
Bela Vista Moz. **99** D2
Belawan Indon. **64** A1
Belaya *r.* Rus. Fed. **87** N2
Belaya Glina Rus. Fed. **39** F2
Belaya Kalitva Rus. Fed. **39** F2
Bełchatów Pol. **51** D2
Belcher Islands Can. **111** G3
Beledweyne Somalia **93** C4
Belém Brazil **135** E3
Belen U.S.A. **126** C2
Belev Rus. Fed. **37** E3
Belfast U.K. **45** D1
Belfast U.S.A. **123** G2
Belfort France **53** D2
Belgaum India **77** B3
Belgium country Europe **48** B2
Belgorod Rus. Fed. **39** E1
Belgrade S.M. **58** B2
Beli Nigeria **91** D4
Belinyu Indon. **64** B2
Belitung *i.* Indon. **64** B2
Belize Belize **130** B3
Belize country Central America
130 B3
Bella Bella Can. **112** C2
Bellac France **52** C2
Bellata Austr. **105** D1
Belle Fourche U.S.A. **120** C2
Belle Fourche *r.* U.S.A. **120** C2
Belle Glade U.S.A. **125** D3
Belle-Île *i.* France **52** B2

Belle Isle *i.* Can. **115** E1
Belle Isle, Strait of Can. **115** E1
Belleville U.S.A. **121** D3
Bellevue U.S.A. **118** B1
Bellingham U.S.A. **118** B1
Bellinzona Switz. **53** D2
Belluno Italy **56** B1
Bellville S. Africa **98** A3
Belmonte Brazil **139** E1
Belmopan Belize **130** B3
Belmullet Ireland **45** B1
Belogorsk Rus. Fed. **73** E1
Belo Horizonte Brazil **139** D1
Beloit U.S.A. **122** C2
Belomorsk Rus. Fed. **34** C2
Belorechensk Rus. Fed. **39** E3
Beloretsk Rus. Fed. **35** E3
Beloyarskiy Rus. Fed. **34** F2
Beloye, Ozero *l.* Rus. Fed. **37** E1
Beloye More Rus. Fed. *see*
White Sea
Belozersk Rus. Fed. **37** E1
Belukha, Gora *mt.*
Kazakh./Rus. Fed. **81** F2
Belush'ye Rus. Fed. **34** D2
Belyy Rus. Fed. **37** D2
Belyy, Ostrov *i.* Rus. Fed. **34** G1
Bemidji U.S.A. **121** E1
Benalla Austr. **105** D3
Benavente Spain **54** B1
Benbecula *i.* U.K. **44** A2
Bend U.S.A. **118** B2
Bendearg *mt.* S. Africa **99** C3
Bendigo Austr. **104** C3
Bene Moz. **97** C1
Benešov Czech Rep. **50** C3
Benevento Italy **56** B2
Bengal, Bay of sea Indian Ocean
77 C3
Bengbu China **74** B2
Benghazi Libya **91** E1
Bengkayang Indon. **64** B1
Bengkulu Indon. **64** B2
Benguela Angola **96** A1
Ben Hope *h.* U.K. **44** B1
Beni *r.* Bol. **136** B2
Beni Dem. Rep. Congo **95** C2
Beni-Abbès Alg. **90** B1
Benidorm Spain **55** C2
Beni Mellal Morocco **90** B1
Benin country Africa **90** C4
Benin, Bight of *g.* Africa **90** C4
Benin City Nigeria **91** C4
Beni-Saf Alg. **55** C2
Benjamim Constant Brazil
134 C3
Benjamin Hill Mex. **128** A1
Ben Lawers *mt.* U.K. **44** B2
Ben Macdui *mt.* U.K. **44** C2
Ben More *h.* U.K. **44** A2
Benmore, Lake N.Z. **106** B3
Ben More Assynt *h.* U.K. **44** B1
Bennett Can. **112** B2
Ben Nevis *mt.* U.K. **44** B2

Bennington U.S.A. **123** F2
Benoni S. Africa **99** C2
Benson U.S.A. **126** B2
Bentong Indon. **65** D2
Benton Harbor U.S.A. **122** C2
Bentonville U.S.A. **124** B1
Benue r. Nigeria **91** C4
Benwee Head Ireland **45** B1
Ben Wyvis mt. U.K. **44** B2
Benxi China **74** C1
Beograd S.M. see Belgrade
Beohari India **79** C2
Beppu Japan **71** B4
Berane S.M. **58** A2
Berat Albania **59** A2
Berbera Somalia **93** C3
Berberati C.A.R. **94** B2
Berck France **52** C1
Berdyans'k Ukr. **39** E2
Berdychiv Ukr. **38** C2
Berehove Ukr. **38** B2
Berens River Can. **113** F2
Berezhany Ukr. **38** B2
Berezivka Ukr. **38** D2
Berezne Ukr. **38** C1
Bereznik Rus. Fed. **34** D2
Berezniki Rus. Fed. **34** E3
Berga Spain **55** D1
Bergama Turkey **59** C3
Bergamo Italy **56** A1
Bergen *Mecklenburg-Vorpommern* Ger. **50** C2
Bergen *Niedersachsen* Ger. **49** D1
Bergen Norway **41** B3
Bergen op Zoom Neth. **48** B2
Bergerac France **52** C3
Bergheim (Erft) Ger. **48** C2
Bergisch Gladbach Ger. **48** C2
Bergland Namibia **96** A1
Bergsviken Sweden **40** E2
Beringen Belgium **48** B2
Bering Sea N. Pacific Ocean **87** N3
Bering Strait Rus. Fed./U.S.A. **87** O2
Berkeley U.S.A. **119** B3
Berkner Island Antarctica **107** A2
Berkovitsa Bulg. **58** B2
Berlevåg Norway **40** F1
Berlin Ger. **49** F1
Bermagui Austr. **105** E3
Bermejo Bol. **136** B3
Bermen, Lac l. Can. **115** D1
Bermuda *terr.* N. Atlantic Ocean **144** B3
Bern Switz. **53** D2
Bernau Ger. **49** F1
Bernburg (Saale) Ger. **49** E2
Bernkastel-Kues Ger. **48** C3
Beroroha Madag. **97** [inset] D2
Berounka r. Czech Rep. **49** G3
Berri Austr. **104** C2
Berrouaghia Alg. **55** D2

Berry Islands Bahamas **131** C3
Bersenbrück Ger. **48** D1
Bershad' Ukr. **38** C2
Berté, Lac l. Can. **115** D1
Bertoua Cameroon **94** B2
Beruri Brazil **134** C3
Berwick-upon-Tweed U.K. **46** C2
Beryslav Ukr. **39** D2
Besalampy Madag. **97** [inset] D1
Besançon France **53** D2
Bessemer U.S.A. **124** C2
Besshoky, Gora h. Kazakh. **80** C2
Betanzos Spain **54** B1
Bethanie Namibia **98** A2
Bethlehem S. Africa **99** C2
Bethlehem U.S.A. **123** E2
Béthune France **48** A2
Betioky Madag. **97** [inset] D2
Betpak-Dala plain Kazakh. **81** E2
Betroka Madag. **97** [inset] D2
Betsiboka r. Madag. **97** [inset] D1
Bettendorf U.S.A. **121** E2
Bettiah India **79** C2
Betul India **79** B2
Betwa r. India **79** B2
Betws-y-coed U.K. **46** B3
Beverley U.K. **46** C3
Beverungen Ger. **49** D2
Beverwijk Neth. **48** B1
Bexhill U.K. **47** D4
Beykoz Turkey **59** C2
Beyla Guinea **90** B4
Beyneu Kazakh. **80** C2
Beypazarı Turkey **84** B1
Beyrouth Lebanon see Beirut
Beyşehir Turkey **84** B2
Beyşehir Gölü l. Turkey **84** B2
Beysug r. Rus. Fed. **39** E3
Bezhetsk Rus. Fed. **37** E2
Béziers France **53** C3
Bhadrak India **79** C2
Bhadravati India **77** B3
Bhagalpur India **79** C2
Bhairi Hol mt. Pak. **78** A2
Bhamo Myanmar **66** A1
Bhanjanagar India **79** C2
Bharatpur India **78** B2
Bharuch India **78** B2
Bhavnagar India **78** B2
Bhekuzulu S. Africa **99** D2
Bhilwara India **78** B2
Bhima r. India **77** B3
Bhiwani India **78** B2
Bhopal India **78** B2
Bhubaneshwar India **79** C2
Bhuj India **78** A2
Bhumiphol Dam Thai. **66** A2
Bhusawal India **78** B2
Bhutan country Asia **79** D2
Bia, Phou mt. Laos **66** B1
Biak i. Indon. **63** D3
Biała Podlaska Pol. **51** E2
Białogard Pol. **51** D2

Białystok Pol. **51** E2
Bianco Italy **57** C3
Biarritz France **52** B3
Biberach an der Riß Ger. **50** B3
Bida Nigeria **91** C4
Biddeford U.S.A. **123** F2
Bideford U.K. **47** A4
Bideford Bay U.K. **47** A4
Biedenkopf Ger. **49** D2
Biel Switz. **53** D2
Bielefeld Ger. **49** D1
Biella Italy **56** A1
Bielsko-Biała Pol. **51** D3
Biên Hoa Vietnam **67** B2
Bienville, Lac l. Can. **114** C1
Bifoun Gabon **94** B3
Biga Turkey **59** C2
Big Bend Swaziland **99** D2
Big Hole r. U.S.A. **118** D1
Bighorn r. U.S.A. **120** B1
Bighorn Mountains U.S.A. **120** B2
Big Lake U.S.A. **127** C2
Big Rapids U.S.A. **122** C2
Big Sand Lake Can. **113** F2
Big Sioux r. U.S.A. **121** D2
Big Spring U.S.A. **127** D2
Big Timber U.S.A. **118** E1
Big Trout Lake Can. **114** B1
Big Trout Lake l. Can. **114** A1
Bihać Bos.-Herz. **57** C2
Bihar Sharif India **79** C2
Bihor, Vârful mt. Romania **38** B2
Bijär Iran **85** C2
Bijeljina Bos.-Herz. **57** C2
Bijelo Polje S.M. **58** A2
Bijie China **75** A3
Bikaner India **78** B2
Bikin Rus. Fed. **70** B1
Bikin r. Rus. Fed. **70** B1
Bikoro Dem. Rep. Congo **94** B3
Bilaspur India **79** C2
Bila Tserkva Ukr. **38** D2
Bilauktaung Range mts Myanmar/Thai. **67** A2
Bilbao Spain **54** C1
Bilecik Turkey **59** C2
Bileċ Pol. **51** E2
Bilhorod-Dnistrovs'kyy Ukr. **38** D2
Bili Dem. Rep. Congo **95** C2
Bilibino Rus. Fed. **87** N2
Billings U.S.A. **118** E1
Bill of Portland hd U.K. **47** B4
Bilma Niger **91** D3
Biloela Austr. **103** E2
Bilohirs'k Ukr. **38** D3
Bilohir"ya Ukr. **38** C1
Bilopillya Ukr. **39** D1
Bilovods'k Ukr. **39** E2
Biloxi U.S.A. **124** C2
Bilpa Morea Claypan salt flat Austr. **103** C2
Bilshausen Ger. **49** E2

ne Chad 91 E3
ayivka Ukr. 38 D2
ni Islands Bahamas 125 E3
-Etawa India 79 B2
-Eja, Gunung mt. Indon.
 C3
Mura Zimbabwe 97 C1
ara Austr. 105 E1
en am Rhein Ger. 48 C3
hamfon U.S.A. 123 E2
ol Turkey 85 C2
ai Indon. 64 B2
uhan Indon. 64 B2
ulu Malaysia 65 C1
hou China 74 B2
o i. Equat. Guinea 94 A2
arad na Moru Croatia 56 C2
sville Austr. 107 C2
cik Turkey 84 B2
un Indon. 64 A1
anj Nepal 79 C2
an mt. Eth. 93 B3
gûl Brazil 138 B2
and Iran 80 C3
onhead U.K. 46 B3
ningham U.S.A. 47 E2
iingham U.S.A. 124 C2
Mogrein Maur. 90 A2
in-Kebbi Nigeria 90 C3
in Konni Niger 90 C1
oidzhan Rus. Fed. 73 E1
ay U.K. 44 C1
-Shalatayn Egypt 82 A2
ai Lith. 36 B2
ay, Bay of sea France/Spain
 B2
hofshofen Austria 50 C3
otasi Lake Can. 114 B2
o S. Africa 99 C3
op U.S.A. 119 C3
al China 73 E1
ra Alg. 91 C1
narck U.S.A. 120 C1
narck Archipelago is P.N.G.
arck U.S.A. 120 C1
fontein S. Africa 98 A3
rroot r. U.S.A. 118 D1
rroot Range mts U.S.A.
 C1
ug r. Rus. Fed. 37 C3
Nigeria 91 D3

Biwa-ko l. Japan 71 C3
Biysk Rus. Fed. 81 F1
Bizerte Tunisia 91 C1
Bjargtangar hd Iceland 40 [inset]
Bjästa Sweden 40 D3
Bjerkvik Norway 40 D2
Bjørnøya i. Arctic Ocean 86 D2
Black r. U.S.A. 124 B1
Blackall Austr. 103 D2
Blackburn U.K. 46 B3
Blackfoot U.S.A. 118 D2
Black Forest mts Ger. 50 B3
Black Hills U.S.A. 120 C2
Black Isle pen. U.K. 44 B2
Black Lake r. Can. 113 C2
Black Lake l. Can. 113 C2
Black Mountains U.K. 47 B4
Blackpool U.K. 46 B3
Black River r. Vietnam 66 B1
Black River Falls U.S.A. 122 B2
Blacksburg U.S.A. 123 D3
Black Sea Asia/Europe 84 B1
Blacksod Bay Ireland 45 A1
Blackstairs Mountains Ireland
 45 C2
Blackwater r. Ireland 45 C2
Blackwater Lake Can. 112 C1
Blackwood r. Austr. 102 A3
Blagoevgrad Bulg. 58 B2
Blagoveshchensk Rus. Fed.
 73 E1
Blair U.S.A. 121 D2
Blairgowrie U.K. 44 C2
Blakely U.S.A. 125 D2
Blanca, Bahía b. Arg. 137 B4
Blanche, Lake salt flat Austr.
 104 B1
Blanco r. Bol. 136 B2
Blanda r. Iceland 40 [inset]
Blanding U.S.A. 119 E3
Blanes Spain 55 D1
Blangkejeren Indon. 64 A1
Blankenheim Ger. 48 C2
Blansko Czech Rep. 51 D3
Blantyre Malawi 97 C1
Blaydon U.K. 46 C2
Blayney Austr. 105 D2
Blenheim N.Z. 106 B3
Blida Alg. 90 C1
Bloemfontein S. Africa 99 C2
Bloemhof S. Africa 99 C2
Bloemhof Dam S. Africa 99 C2
Blönduós Iceland 40 [inset]
Bloody Foreland pt Ireland 45 B1
Bloomfield U.S.A. 126 C1
Bloomington Il. U.S.A. 122 C2
Bloomington In. U.S.A. 122 C3
Blosseville Kyst coastal area
 Greenland 111 K2
Bluefield U.S.A. 122 D3
Bluefields Nic. 130 B3
Blue Mountains Austr. 105 D2
Blue Mountains U.S.A. 118 C1
Blue Nile r. Eth./Sudan 93 B3

Blue Ridge mts U.S.A. 125 D1
Blue Stack Mountains Ireland
 45 B1
Bluff N.Z. 106 A4
Bluff U.S.A. 119 E3
Blumenau Brazil 138 C3
Blyth U.K. 46 C2
Blythe U.S.A. 119 D4
Blytheville U.S.A. 124 C1
Bo Sierra Leone 90 A4
Boac Phil. 68 B2
Boa Esperança, Açude resr
 Brazil 135 E3
Boa Vista Brazil 134 C3
Bobadah Austr. 105 D2
Bobai China 75 B3
Bobaomby, Tanjona c. Madag.
 97 [inset] D1
Bobo-Dioulasso Burkina 90 B3
Bobrov Rus. Fed. 37 F3
Bobrovytsya Ukr. 39 D1
Bobrynets' Ukr. 39 D2
Boby mt. Madag. 97 [inset] D2
Boca do Acre Brazil 134 C3
Bocaiúva Brazil 139 D1
Bochnia Pol. 51 F3
Bocholt Ger. 48 C2
Bochum Ger. 48 C2
Bochum S. Africa 99 C1
Bockenem Ger. 49 E1
Boda C.A.R. 94 B2
Bodaybo Rus. Fed. 87 J3
Bodélé reg. Chad 91 D3
Boden Sweden 40 E2
Bodmin U.K. 47 A4
Bodmin Moor moorland U.K.
 47 A4
Bodø Norway 40 C2
Bodrum Turkey 59 C3
Boende Dem. Rep. Congo 94 C3
Bogalusa U.S.A. 124 C2
Bogda Shan mts China 81 F2
Boggabilla Austr. 105 E1
Boggeragh Mountains Ireland
 45 B2
Bog of Allen reg. Ireland 45 C2
Bogong, Mount Austr. 105 D3
Bogor Indon. 64 B2
Bogoroditsk Rus. Fed. 37 E3
Bogotá Col. 134 B2
Bogotol Rus. Fed. 86 H3
Boguchany Rus. Fed. 87 I3
Boguchar Rus. Fed. 39 F2
Bo Hai g. China 74 B2
Bohai Wan b. China 74 B2
Bohicong S. Africa 99 C2
Böhmer Wald mts Ger. 49 F1
Bohodukhiv Ukr. 39 E1
Bohol i. Phil. 68 B3
Bohol Sea Phil. 68 B3
Bohu China 81 F2
Bois r. Brazil 138 B1
Boise U.S.A. 118 C2
Boise City U.S.A. 127 D1

Boitumelong S. Africa 99 C2
Boizenburg Ger. 49 E1
Bojnūrd Iran 85 D2
Bokatola Dem. Rep. Congo 94 B3
Bokele Dem. Rep. Congo 94 C3
Boknafjorden sea chan. Norway 41 B4
Bokoro Chad 93 C3
Bokovskaya Rus. Fed. 39 F2
Boksitogorsk Rus. Fed. 37 D2
Bokspits S. Africa 98 B2
Bolama Guinea-Bissau 90 A3
Bolangir India 79 C2
Bolbec France 52 C2
Bole China 81 F2
Boleko Dem. Rep. Congo 94 B3
Bolgatanga Ghana 90 B3
Boli China 70 B1
Bolintin-Vale Romania 38 C3
Bolivia country S. America 136 B2
Bolkhov Rus. Fed. 37 E3
Bollène France 53 C3
Bollnäs Sweden 41 D3
Bollon Austr. 105 D1
Bolmen l. Sweden 41 C4
Bolobo Dem. Rep. Congo 94 B3
Bologna Italy 56 B2
Bologovo Rus. Fed. 37 D2
Bologoye Rus. Fed. 37 D2
Bolomba Dem. Rep. Congo 94 B3
Bolovens, Phouphieng plat. Laos 67 B2
Bol'shaya Martinovka Rus. Fed. 39 F2
Bol'shevik, Ostrov i. Rus. Fed. 87 I1
Bol'shezemel'skaya Tundra lowland Rus. Fed. 34 E2
Bol'shoy Aluy r. Rus. Fed. 87 M2
Bol'shoy Kamen' Rus. Fed. 70 D2
Bol'shoy Kavkaz mts Asia/Europe see Caucasus
Bolsward Neth. 48 B1
Bolton U.K. 46 B3
Bolu Turkey 84 B1
Bolzano Italy 56 B1
Boma Dem. Rep. Congo 94 B3
Bomaderry Austr. 105 E2
Bombala Austr. 105 D3
Bombay India see Mumbai
Bom Despacho Brazil 139 C1
Bomdila India 79 D2
Bom Jesus da Lapa Brazil 135 E4
Bømlo i. Norway 42 B2
Bonaire i. Neth. Antilles 131 D3
Bonaparte Archipelago is Austr. 102 B1
Bonavista Can. 115 E2
Bonavista Bay Can. 115 E2
Bondo Dem. Rep. Congo 94 C2

Bondoukou Côte d'Ivoire 90 B4
Bone, Teluk b. Indon. 65 D2
Bonerate, Kepulauan is Indon. 65 D2
Bongaigaon India 79 D2
Bongandanga Dem. Rep. Congo 94 C2
Bongo, Massif des mts C.A.R. 94 C2
Bongor Chad 91 D3
Bongouanou Côte d'Ivoire 90 B4
Bông Son Vietnam 67 B2
Bonham U.S.A. 127 E2
Bonifacio France 53 D3
Bonifacio, Strait of France/Italy 56 A2
Bonito Brazil 138 A2
Bonn Ger. 48 C2
Bonners Ferry U.S.A. 118 C1
Bonnie Rock Austr. 102 A3
Bonnyville Can. 113 D2
Bontoc Phil. 68 B2
Bontosunggu Indon. 65 C2
Bontrup S. Africa 99 C3
Booligal Austr. 104 C2
Boomah Austr. 105 E1
Boone U.S.A. 121 E2
Boone NC U.S.A. 122 D3
Booneville U.S.A. 124 C2
Boorowa Austr. 105 D2
Boothia, Gulf of Can. 111 G2
Boothia Peninsula Can. 110 F2
Boppard Ger. 48 C2
Boquilla, Presa de la resr Mex. 128 B2
Bor S.M. 58 B2
Bor Sudan 93 B4
Boraha, Nosy i. Madag. 97 [inset] E1
Borås Sweden 41 C4
Borāzjān Iran 85 D3
Borba Brazil 134 D3
Bordeaux France 52 B3
Bordertown Austr. 104 C3
Bordj Bou Arréridj Alg. 55 D2
Bordj Bounaama Alg. 55 D2
Bordj Messaouda Alg. 91 C1
Bordj Omer Driss Alg. 91 C2
Borðoy i. Faroe Is 42 B1
Borgarnes Iceland 40 [inset]
Borisoglebsk Rus. Fed. 39 F1
Borisovka Rus. Fed. 39 E1
Borken Ger. 48 C1
Borkum Ger. 48 C1
Borkum i. Ger. 48 C1
Borlänge Sweden 41 D3
Borna Ger. 49 F2
Borneo i. Asia 65 C1
Bornholm i. Denmark 41 C4
Bornova Turkey 59 C3
Borodyanka Ukr. 38 C1
Borohoro Rus. Fed. 37 D2
Borovichi Rus. Fed. 37 D2
Borovsk Rus. Fed. 37 E2

Borroloola Austr. 103 C1
Borşa Romania 38 B2
Borshchiv Ukr. 38 C2
Borssele Neth. 75 D1
Borshchovochnyy Khrebet mts Rus. Fed. 73 D1
Borüjerd Iran 85 C2
Boryslav Ukr. 38 B2
Boryspil' Ukr. 38 D1
Borzna Ukr. 39 D1
Borzya Rus. Fed. 73 D1
Bosanska Dubica Bos.-Herz. 57 C1
Bosanska Gradiška Bos.-Herz. 57 C1
Bosanski Novi Bos.-Herz. 57 C1
Bosa China 75 A3
Boshof S. Africa 99 C2
Bosnia-Herzegovina country Europe 57 C2
Bosobolo Dem. Rep. Congo 94 B2
Bosporus str. Turkey 59 C2
Bossangoa C.A.R. 94 B2
Bossembélé C.A.R. 94 B2
Bosten Hu l. China 81 F2
Boston U.K. 46 C3
Boston U.S.A. 123 F2
Boston Mountains U.S.A. 124
Botany Bay Austr. 105 E2
Botev mt. Bulg. 58 B2
Botevgrad Bulg. 84 A1
Bothnia, Gulf of Fin./Sweden 41 D3
Botoşani Romania 38 C2
Botshabelo S. Africa 99 C2
Botswana country Africa 96 B3
Botte Donato, Monte mt. Italy 57 C3
Bottrop Ger. 48 C2
Botucatu Brazil 138 C2
Bouaké Côte d'Ivoire 90 B4
Bouar C.A.R. 94 B2
Bouârfa Morocco 90 B1
Bougaa Alg. 55 E2
Bougainville Island P.N.G. 100
Bougaroûn, Cap c. Alg. 55 E2
Bougouni Mali 90 B3
Bouillon Belgium 48 B3
Bouira Alg. 55 D1
Boujdour Western Sahara 90 A2
Boulder U.S.A. 120 B2
Boulder City U.S.A. 119 D3
Boulogne-Billancourt France 52 C2
Boulogne-sur-Mer France 47 D
Boumango Gabon 94 B3
Boumba r. Cameroon 94 B2
Boumerdes Alg. 55 D2
Bouna Côte d'Ivoire 90 B4
Boundiali Côte d'Ivoire 90 B4
Bountiful U.S.A. 118 D2
Bourem Mali 90 B3
Bourg-en-Bresse France 53 D2
Bourges France 52 C2

urke Austr. **105** D2
urnemouth U.K. **47** C4
u Saâda Alg. **91** C1
usso Chad **91** D3
utilimit Maur. **90** A3
w r. Can. **113** D3
wen Austr. **103** D2
wy Island Can. **113** D3
wling Green KY U.S.A. **122** C3
wling Green OH U.S.A.
122 D2
wman U.S.A. **120** C1
xberg Ger. **49** D3
xtel Neth. **48** B2
yabat Turkey **84** B1
yang China **75** B3
yle Ireland **45** B2
yne r. Ireland **45** C2
ysen Reservoir U.S.A. **120** B2
yuibe Bol. **136** B3
zdağ mt. Turkey **59** C3
azı Dağları mts Turkey **59** C3
zeman C.A.R. **94** B2
zoum C.A.R. **94** B2
züyük Turkey **59** D3
aĉ i. Croatia **56** B2
achet, Lac au l. Can. **115** D2
acknell U.K. **47** C4
adenton U.S.A. **125** D3
adford U.K. **46** C3
ady U.S.A. **127** E2
aga Port. **54** B1
agança Brazil **135** E3
agança Port. **54** B1
agança Paulista Brazil **139** C2
ahin Belarus **37** D3
ahmanbaria Bangl. **66** A1
ahmapur India **77** C3
ahmaputra r. China/India **66** A1
äila Romania **38** C2
ainerd U.S.A. **121** E1
aintree U.K. **47** D4
ake (Unterweser) Ger. **49** D1
akwater Namibia **98** A1
amsche Ger. **48** D1
anco r. Brazil **134** C3
andenburg Ger. **49** F1
andon Can. **113** F3
andon Mountain h. Ireland
45 A2
andvlei S. Africa **98** B3
anilwo Pol. **51** D2
anco Brazil **139** B3
as d'Or Lake Can. **115** D2
asil, Planalto do plat. Brazil
asil Brazil **138** C1
asilândia Brazil **138** C1
asilia Brazil **138** C1
asilia de Minas Brazil **139** D1
aslaw Belarus **36** C2
asov Romania **38** C2
atislava Slovakia **51** D3
atsk Rus. Fed. **87** I3
aunau am Inn Austria **50** C3

Braunschweig Ger. **49** E1
Brautarholt Iceland **40** [inset]
Bråviken inlet Sweden **36** A2
Bravo del Norte, Rio r.
  Mex./U.S.A. see Rio Grande
Brawley U.S.A. **119** C4
Bray Ireland **45** C2
Brazil country S. America **135** D3
Brazos r. U.S.A. **127** E3
Brazzaville Congo **94** B3
Brčko Bos.-Herz. **57** C2
Brechin U.K. **44** C2
Brecht Belgium **48** B2
Breckenridge U.S.A. **127** E2
Břeclav Czech Rep. **51** D3
Brecon U.K. **47** B4
Brecon Beacons reg. U.K. **47** B4
Breda Neth. **48** B2
Bredasdorp S. Africa **98** B3
Bregenz Austria **50** B3
Breivikbotn Norway **40** E1
Brekstad Norway **40** B3
Bremen Ger. **49** D1
Bremerhaven Ger. **49** D1
Bremerton U.S.A. **118** B1
Bremervörde Ger. **49** D1
Brenham U.S.A. **127** E2
Brennero Italy **50** C3
Brenner Pass Austria/Italy **50** C3
Brentwood U.K. **47** D4
Brescia Italy **56** B1
Bressanone Italy **56** B1
Bressay i. U.K. **44** [inset]
Bressuire France **52** B2
Brest Belarus **36** C1
Brest France **52** B2
Breton Sound b. U.S.A. **124** C3
Breves Brazil **135** D3
Brewarrina Austr. **105** D1
Brewster U.S.A. **118** C1
Brewton U.S.A. **125** C2
Breytovo Rus. Fed. **37** E2
Brezovo Polje plain Croatia
  57 C1
Bria C.A.R. **94** C2
Briançon France **53** D3
Briceni Moldova **38** C2
Bridgend U.K. **47** B4
Bridgeport CT U.S.A. **123** F2
Bridgeport NE U.S.A. **120** C2
Bridgetown Barbados **131** E3
Bridgewater Can. **115** D2
Bridgwater U.K. **47** B4
Bridlington U.K. **46** C3
Bridlington Bay U.K. **46** C2
Brig Switz. **53** D2
Brigham City U.S.A. **118** D2
Brighton N.Z. **106** B4
Brighton U.K. **47** C4
Brignoles France **53** D3
Brilon Ger. **49** D2
Brindisi Italy **57** C2
Brisbane Austr. **105** E1
Bristol U.K. **47** B4
Bristol U.S.A. **125** D1

Bristol Bay U.S.A. **87** P3
Bristol Channel est. U.K. **47** A4
British Columbia prov. Can.
  112 C2
British Indian Ocean Territory
  terr. Indian Ocean **61**
Britstown S. Africa **98** B3
Brittany reg. France **52** B2
Brive-la-Gaillarde France **52** C2
Brno Czech Rep. **51** D3
Broad r. U.S.A. **125** D2
Broadback r. Can. **114** C1
Broad Law h. U.K. **44** C3
Broadus U.S.A. **120** B1
Brochet Can. **113** E2
Brochet, Lac l. Can. **113** E2
Brockville Can. **114** C2
Brodick U.K. **44** B3
Brodnica Pol. **51** D2
Brody Ukr. **38** C1
Broken Arrow U.S.A. **127** E1
Broken Hill Austr. **104** C2
Bromsgrove U.K. **47** B3
Brønderslev Denmark **41** B4
Brønnøysund Norway **40** C2
Brooke's Point Phil. **68** A3
Brookhaven U.S.A. **124** B2
Brookings OR U.S.A. **118** B2
Brookings SD U.S.A. **121** D2
Brooks Can. **113** D2
Brooks Range mts U.S.A. **110** C3
Brooksville U.S.A. **125** D3
Broom, Loch inlet U.K. **44** B2
Broome Austr. **102** B1
Brothers U.S.A. **118** B2
Brovary Ukr. **38** D1
Brownfield U.S.A. **127** D2
Browning U.S.A. **112** D3
Brownsville TN U.S.A. **124** C1
Brownsville TX U.S.A. **127** E3
Brownwood U.S.A. **127** E2
Bru Iceland **40** [inset]
Bruay-la-Bussière France **52** C1
Bruchsal Ger. **49** D3
Bruges Belgium see Brugge
Brugge Belgium **48** A2
Brühl Ger. **49** D3
Bruint India **66** A1
Brumado Brazil **138** E4
Brumunddal Norway **41** C3
Brunei country Asia **65** C1
Brunico Italy **50** C3
Brunswick GA U.S.A. **125** D2
Brunswick ME U.S.A. **123** G2
Brush U.S.A. **120** C2
Brussels Belgium **48** B2
Bruxelles Belgium see Brussels
Bryan U.S.A. **127** E2
Bryansk Rus. Fed. **37** D3
Bryne Norway **42** E2
Bryn'kovskaya Rus. Fed. **39** E2
Bryukhovetskaya Rus. Fed.
  39 E2
Brzeg Pol. **51** D2

Bucaramanga Col. **134** B2
Buchanan Liberia **90** A4
Bucharest Romania **38** C3
Bucholz in der Nordheide Ger. **49** D1
Bucin, Pasul *pass* Romania **38** C2
Bückeburg Ger. **49** D1
Buckeye U.S.A. **126** B2
Buckhaven U.K. **44** C2
Buckie U.K. **44** C3
Buckland Tableland *reg.* Austr. **103** D2
Bucureşti Romania *see* Bucharest
Buda-Kashalyova Belarus **37** D3
Budapest Hungary **51** D3
Budaun India **79** B2
Bude U.K. **47** A4
Budennovsk Rus. Fed. **35** D4
Budoni Italy **56** A2
Buea Cameroon **94** A2
Buenaventura Mex. **128** B2
Buendia, Embalse de *resr* Spain **54** C1
Buenópolis Brazil **139** D1
Buenos Aires Arg. **137** C4
Buffalo *NY* U.S.A. **123** E2
Buffalo *SD* U.S.A. **120** C1
Buffalo *WY* U.S.A. **120** B2
Buffalo Narrows Can. **110** E3
Buffels *watercourse* S. Africa **98** A2
Buftea Romania **38** C3
Bug *r.* Pol. **51** E2
Bugel, Tanjung *pt* Indon. **65** C2
Bugojno Bos.-Herz. **57** C2
Bugurusian Rus. Fed. **35** E3
Buhuşi Romania **38** C2
Builth Wells U.K. **47** B3
Buir Nur *l.* Mongolia **73** D1
Buitepos Namibia **98** A1
Bujanovac S. M. **58** B2
Bujumbura Burundi **95** C3
Bukavu Dem. Rep. Congo **95** C3
Bukhara Uzbek. *see* Buxoro
Bukittinggi Indon. **64** B2
Bukoba Tanz. **95** D3
Bulahdelal Austr. **105** E2
Bulawayo Zimbabwe **97** B2
Buldan Turkey **59** C3
Bulembu Swaziland **99** D2
Bulgan Mongolia **72** C1
Bulgaria *country* Europe **58** B2
Buller *r.* N.Z. **106** B3
Büllsport Namibia **98** A1
Bulukumba Indon. **65** D2
Bulungu Dem. Rep. Congo **94** B3
Bumba Dem. Rep. Congo **94** B3
Bumhkang Myanmar **66** A1
Buna Dem. Rep. Congo **94** B3
Bunbury Austr. **102** A3
Buncrana Ireland **45** C1
Bunda Tanz. **95** D3

Bundaberg Austr. **103** E2
Bundarra Austr. **105** E2
Bundi India **78** B2
Bungo-suidō *sea chan.* Japan **71** B4
Bunia Dem. Rep. Congo **95** D2
Bunlanga Dem. Rep. Congo **94** C3
Buôn Mê Thuôt Vietnam **67** B2
Bura Kenya **95** E3
Buraydah Saudi Arabia **82** B2
Burbach Ger. **48** D2
Burco Somalia **93** C4
Burdur Turkey **84** B2
Burē Eth. **93** B3
Bure *r.* U.K. **47** D3
Burgas Bulg. **58** C2
Burg bei Magdeburg Ger. **49** E1
Burgdorf Ger. **49** E1
Burgeo Can. **115** E2
Burgersfort S. Africa **99** D1
Burglengenfeld Ger. **49** F3
Burgos Spain **54** C1
Burhaniye Turkey **59** C3
Burhanpur India **78** B2
Burhave (Butjadingen) Ger. **49** D1
Burin Can. **115** E2
Buritis Brazil **139** C1
Burketown Austr. **103** C1
Burkina *country* Africa **90** B3
Burley U.S.A. **118** D2
Burlington *CO* U.S.A. **120** C3
Burlington *IA* U.S.A. **121** E2
Burlington *NC* U.S.A. **125** E1
Burma *country* Asia *see* Myanmar
Burney U.S.A. **118** B2
Burnie Austr. **103** D4
Burnley U.K. **46** B3
Burns U.S.A. **118** C2
Burns Lake Can. **112** C2
Burqin China **81** F2
Burra Austr. **104** B2
Burrel Albania **58** B2
Burren *reg.* Ireland **45** B2
Burrendong Reservoir Austr. **105** D2
Burren Junction Austr. **105** D2
Burriana Spain **55** C2
Burrinjuck Reservoir Austr. **105** D2
Burro, Serranías del *mts* Mex. **128** B2
Bursa Turkey **59** C2
Bûr Sa'îd Egypt **92** B1
Bûr Sa'îd Egypt *see* Port Said
Burton, Lac *l.* Can. **114** C1
Burtonport Ireland **45** B1
Burton upon Trent U.K. **46** C3
Buru *i.* Indon. **63** C3
Bururi Burundi **95** C3
Burwash Landing Can. **112** B1

Buryn' Ukr. **39** D1
Bury St Edmunds U.K. **47** D3
Busanga Dem. Rep. Congo **94** C3
Büsheher Iran **85** D3
Bushenyi Uganda **95** D3
Businga Dem. Rep. Congo **94** C2
Busselton Austr. **102** A3
Bustamante Mex. **127** D3
Busuanga Phil. **68** A2
Buta Dem. Rep. Congo **94** C2
Butare Rwanda **95** C3
Butha-Buthe Lesotho **99** C2
Butoni *i.* Indon. **65** D2
Butte U.S.A. **118** D1
Butterworth Malaysia **64** B1
Butt of Lewis *hd* U.K. **44** A1
Button Bay Can. **113** F2
Butuan Phil. **68** B3
Buturlinovka Rus. Fed. **37** E3
Butwal Nepal **79** C2
Butzbach Ger. **49** D2
Buulobarde Somalia **93** C4
Buur Gaabo Somalia **93** C5
Buurhabaka Somalia **93** C4
Buxoro Uzbek. **80** C3
Buxtehude Ger. **49** D1
Buy Rus. Fed. **37** F2
Buynaksk Rus. Fed. **35** D4
Büyükmenderes *r.* Turkey **59** C3
Buzai Gumbad Afgh. **78** B1
Buzău Romania **38** C2
Buzuluk Rus. Fed. **35** E3
Byala Bulg. **58** C2
Byalynichy Belarus **36** C3
Byarezina *r.* Belarus **36** D3
Byaroza Belarus **36** B3
Bydgoszcz Pol. **51** D2
Byerazino Belarus **36** C3
Byeshankovichy Belarus **36** C2
Bykhaw Belarus **37** D3
Bylot Island Can. **111** G2
Byrkjelo Norway **42** E1
Byrock Austr. **105** D2
Byron Bay Austr. **105** E1
Bytom Pol. **51** D2

C

Caaguazú, Cordillera de *hills* Para. **138** A3
Caarapó Brazil **138** B2
Caazapá Para. **138** A3
Cabanatuan Phil. **68** B2
Cabeceira Rio Manso Brazil **138** A1
Cabimas Venez. **134** B1
Cabinda Angola **94** B3
Cabinda *prov.* Angola **94** B3
Cabo Frio Brazil **139** D2
Cabo Frio, Ilha do *i.* Brazil **139** D2

onga, Réservoir resr Can.
...4 C2
ooiture Austr. 105 E1
o Pantoja Peru 134 B3
ora Bassa, Lake resr Moz.
...7 C1
orca Mex. 128 A1
oot Strait Can. 115 D2
ora i. Spain 55 D2
orera, Sierra de la mts Spain
...4 B1
oriel r. Spain 55 C2
cador Brazil 138 B3
oak S.M. 58 B2
eres Brazil 135 D4
eres Spain 54 B2
he Creek Can. 112 C2
cheu Guinea-Bissau 90 A3
shimbo, Serra do hills Brazil
...39 D2
hoeira Alta Brazil 138 B1
hoeiro de Itapemirim Brazil
...39 D2
cine Guinea-Bissau 90 A3
colo Angola 94 B4
go Brazil 138 B1
ica Slovakia 51 D3
denberge Ger. 49 D1
dereyta Mex. 129 B2
dillac U.S.A. 122 C2
diz Spain 54 B2
diz, Golfo de g. Spain 54 B2
ernarfon U.K. 46 A3
ernarfon Bay U.K. 46 A3
afayate Arg. 136 B3
gayan de Oro Phil. 68 B3
gliari Italy 56 A3
gliari, Golfo di b. Italy 56 A3
ha Mountains Ireland 45 B3
air Ireland 45 C2
hore Point Ireland 45 C2
hors France 93 C3
hul Moldova 38 C2
a Moz. 97 C1
abis, Serra dos hills Brazil
...35 D4
anda Angola 96 B1
apo, Serra do mts Brazil
...38 B1
apônia Brazil 138 B1
cos Islands
arks and Caicos Is 131 C2
rngorm Mountains U.K.
...4 C2
rnryan U.K. 44 B3
rns Austr. 103 D1
ro Egypt 92 B1
undo Angola 96 A1
amarca Peru 134 B3
covec Croatia 57 C1
abar Nigeria 94 A2
lafat Romania 38 B3
ahorra Spain 55 C1

Calais France 52 C1
Calais U.S.A. 123 G1
Calama Chile 136 B3
Calamian Group is Phil. 68 A2
Calamocha Spain 55 C1
Calandula Angola 94 B3
Calang Indon. 64 A1
Calanscio Sand Sea des. Libya
91 E1
Calapan Phil. 68 B2
Călăraşi Romania 38 C3
Calatayud Spain 55 C1
Calau Ger. 49 F2
Calayan i. Phil. 68 B2
Calbayog Phil. 68 B2
Calcanhar, Ponta do pt Brazil
135 F3
Calçoene Brazil 135 D2
Calcutta India see Kolkata
Caldas da Rainha Port. 54 B2
Caldas Novas Brazil 138 C1
Caldera Chile 136 A3
Caldwell U.S.A. 118 C2
Caledon r. Lesotho/S. Africa
99 C3
Caleta Olivia Arg. 137 B5
Calf of Man i. Isle of Man 46 A2
Calgary Can. 112 D2
Cali Col. 134 B2
Calicut India 77 B3
Caliente U.S.A. 119 D3
California state U.S.A. 118 B2
California, Gulf of Mex. 119 D4
California Aqueduct canal U.S.A.
119 B3
Callabonna, Lake salt flat Austr.
104 C1
Callander U.K. 44 B2
Callao Peru 134 B4
Caltagirone Italy 56 C3
Caltanissetta Italy 56 C3
Caluquembe Angola 96 A1
Caluula Somalia 90 D3
Calvi France 53 D3
Calvià Spain 55 D2
Calvillo Mex. 128 B2
Calvinia S. Africa 98 A3
Calvo, Monte mt. Italy 57 C2
Camacho Mex. 128 B2
Camacupa Angola 96 A1
Camagüey Cuba 130 C2
Camana Peru 134 B4
Camapuã Brazil 138 B1
Ca Mau Vietnam 67 B3
Ca Mau, Mui c. Vietnam 67 B3
Cambodia country Asia 67 B2
Camborne U.K. 47 A4
Cambrai France 53 C1
Cambrian Mountains U.K. 47 B3
Cambridge N.Z. 106 C2
Cambridge U.K. 47 C3
Cambridge MA U.S.A. 123 F2
Cambridge MD U.S.A. 123 E3
Cambridge MN U.S.A. 121 E1

Cambridge OH U.S.A. 122 D2
Camden Austr. 105 E2
Camden AR U.S.A. 124 B2
Camden ME U.S.A. 123 G2
Cameroon country Africa 94 B2
Cametá Brazil 135 E3
Camiguin i. Phil. 68 B2
Camiri Bol. 136 B3
Camocim Brazil 135 E3
Camooweal Austr. 103 C1
Camorta i. India 67 A3
Campana, Isla i. Chile 137 A5
Campbell, Cape N.Z. 106 B3
Campbell Island N.Z. 100
Campbell River Can. 112 C2
Campbellsville U.S.A. 122 C3
Campbellton Can. 123 G1
Campbeltown U.K. 44 B3
Campeche Mex. 129 C3
Campeche, Bahía de g. Mex.
129 C3
Camperdown Austr. 104 C3
Câmpina Romania 38 C2
Campina Grande Brazil 135 F3
Campinas Brazil 138 C2
Campina Verde Brazil 138 C1
Campobasso Italy 56 B2
Campo Belo Brazil 139 C2
Campo Grande Brazil 138 B2
Campo Maior Brazil 135 E3
Campo Mourão Brazil 138 B2
Campos Brazil 139 D2
Campos Altos Brazil 139 C1
Câmpulung Romania 38 C2
Camp Verde U.S.A. 126 B2
Cam Ranh Vietnam 67 B2
Camrose Can. 113 D2
Camsell Portage Can. 113 E2
Çan Turkey 59 C2
Canada country N. America
Canadian U.S.A. 127 D1
Canadian r. U.S.A. 127 E1
Çanakkale Turkey 59 C2
Cananea Mex. 128 A1
Canary Islands terr.
N. Atlantic Ocean 90 A2
Canastra, Serra da mts Brazil
139 C1
Canatlán Mex. 128 B2
Canaveral, Cape U.S.A. 125 D3
Canavieiras Brazil 139 E1
Canberra Austr. 105 D3
Cancún Mex. 129 D2
Candelaria Mex. 129 C3
Cangamba Angola 96 B1
Cangas del Narcea Spain 54 B1
Canguçu Brazil 136 C2
Cangzhou China 74 B2
Caniapiscau Can. 115 D1
Caniapiscau r. Can. 115 D1
Caniapiscau, Lac l. Can. 115 C1
Cañitas de Felipe Pescador
Mex. 128 B2

Çankırı Turkey **84** B1
Canna i. U.K. **44** A2
Cannanore India **77** B3
Cannes France **53** D3
Cann River Austr. **105** D3
Canoas Brazil **136** D3
Canoinhas Brazil **138** B3
Canon City U.S.A. **120** B3
Canowindra Austr. **105** D2
Cantábrica, Cordillera mts Spain **54** C1
Cantábrico, Mar sea Spain **54** B1
Canterbury U.K. **47** D4
Canterbury Bight b. N.Z. **106** B3
Canterbury Plains N.Z. **106** B3
Cần Thơ Vietnam **67** B2
Canton China see **Guangzhou**
Canton MS U.S.A. **124** C2
Canton OH U.S.A. **122** D2
Canyon U.S.A. **127** C1
Canyon Ferry Lake U.S.A. **118** D1
Cao Bằng Vietnam **66** B1
Capão Bonito Brazil **138** C2
Caparaó, Serra de mts Brazil **139** D2
Capbreton France **52** B3
Cape Barren Island Austr. **103** D4
Cape Borda Austr. **104** B3
Cape Breton Island Can. **115** D2
Cape Coast Ghana **90** B4
Cape Cod Bay U.S.A. **123** F2
Cape Dorset Can. **111** G2
Cape Fear r. U.S.A. **125** E2
Cape Girardeau U.S.A. **121** F3
Capelle aan den IJssel Neth. **48** B2
Capim r. Brazil **135** E3
Capitol Hill N. Mariana Is **63** D1
Čapljina Bos.-Herz. **57** C2
Capraia, Isola di i. Italy **56** A2
Caprara, Punta pt Italy **56** A2
Capri, Isola di i. Italy **56** B2
Caprivi Strip reg. Namibia **96** B1
Caquetá r. Col. **134** C3
Caracal Romania **38** B3
Caracas Venez. **134** C1
Caraguatatuba Brazil **139** D1
Caransebeş Romania **38** B2
Caratasca, Laguna de lag. Hond. **130** B3
Caratinga Brazil **139** D1
Carauari Brazil **134** C3
Caravaca de la Cruz Spain **55** C2
Caravelas Brazil **139** E1
Carberry Can. **113** F3

Carbó Mex. **128** A2
Carbondale CO U.S.A. **120** B3
Carbondale IL U.S.A. **122** C3
Carbonear Can. **115** E2
Carbonia Brazil **139** D1
Carcaixent Spain **55** C2
Carcassonne France **52** C3
Carcross Can. **112** B1
Cárdenas Mex. **129** C3
Cardiff U.K. **47** B4
Cardigan U.K. **47** A3
Cardigan Bay U.K. **47** A3
Cardston Can. **118** D1
Carei Romania **38** B2
Carentan France **52** B2
Carey, Lake salt flat Austr. **102** B2
Cariacica Brazil **139** D2
Caribbean Sea N. Atlantic Ocean **130** B3
Caribou U.S.A. **123** G1
Caribou Lake Can. **114** B1
Caribou Mountains Can. **112** D2
Carignan France **48** B3
Carinda Austr. **105** D2
Cariñena Spain **55** C1
Carleton Peak Can. **114** C2
Carletonville S. Africa **99** C2
Carlingford Lough inlet Ireland/U.K. **45** C1
Carlisle U.K. **46** B2
Carlisle U.S.A. **123** E2
Carlos Chagas Brazil **139** D1
Carlow Ireland **45** C2
Carlsbad CA U.S.A. **119** C4
Carlsbad NM U.S.A. **128** C2
Carlyle Can. **120** C1
Carmacks Can. **112** B1
Carman Can. **113** F3
Carmarthen U.K. **47** A4
Carmarthen Bay U.K. **47** A4
Carmaux France **52** C3
Carmen Guat. **129** C3
Carmen, Isla i. Mex. **128** A2
Carnac France **52** B2
Carnarvon S. Africa **98** B3
Carn Eige mt. U.K. **44** B2
Car Nicobar i. India **67** A3
Carnot France **52** B2
Carnot, Cape Austr. **104** B2
Carnsore Point Ireland **45** C2
Caroline Islands N. Pacific Ocean **63** D2
Carpathian Mountains Europe **38** A2
Carpentaria, Gulf of Austr. **103** C1
Carpentras France **53** D3
Carrantuohill mt. Ireland **45** B3
Carrara Italy **53** E3
Carrickmacross Ireland **45** C2

Carrick-on-Shannon Ireland **45** B2
Carrick-on-Suir Ireland **45** C2
Carrington U.S.A. **121** D1
Carrizo Springs U.S.A. **127** C3
Carrizozo U.S.A. **120** C2
Carroll U.S.A. **121** E2
Carrollton U.S.A. **125** C2
Carrot River Can. **113** F2
Carson City U.S.A. **119** C3
Cartagena Col. **134** B1
Cartagena Spain **55** C2
Cartago Costa Rica **130** B4
Carthage MO U.S.A. **121** E3
Caruarú Brazil **135** F3
Casablanca Morocco **90** B1
Casa de Janos Mex. **128** B1
Casa Grande U.S.A. **126** B2
Casale Monferrato Italy **56** A1
Casarano Italy **57** C2
Cascade U.S.A. **118** C2
Cascade Range mts Can./U.S.A. **118** B2
Cascavel Brazil **138** B2
Caserta Italy **56** B2
Cashel Ireland **45** C2
Casino Austr. **105** E1
Caspe Spain **55** C1
Casper U.S.A. **120** B2
Caspian Lowland Kazakh./Rus. Fed. **80** B2
Caspian Sea l. Asia/Europe **80** B2
Cássia Brazil **138** C2
Cassiar Can. **112** C2
Cassiar Mountains Can. **112** C2
Cassilândia Brazil **138** B1
Cassino Italy **56** B2
Castanhal Brazil **135** E3
Castaño r. Arg. **136** B4
Castaños Mex. **128** B2
Casteljaloux France **52** C3
Castelló de la Plana Spain **55** C2
Castelo Branco Port. **54** B2
Castelvetrano Italy **56** B3
Casterton Austr. **104** C3
Castlebar Ireland **45** B2
Castlebay U.K. **44** A2
Castleblayney Ireland **45** C1
Castlederg U.K. **45** C1
Castle Douglas U.K. **44** C3
Castlegar Can. **112** D3
Castleisland Ireland **45** B2
Castlemaine Austr. **104** C3
Castle Mountain Can. **112** B1
Castlereagh r. Austr. **105** D2
Castle Rock U.S.A. **120** C3
Castres France **52** C3
Castries St Lucia **131** D3
Castro Brazil **138** C2
Castro Chile **137** A5

astrovillari Italy **57** C3
tacaos Peru **134** A3
taguases Brazil **139** D2
talão Brazil **138** C1
taluña *aut. comm.* Spain **55** D1
tamarca Arg. **136** B3
tanduanes *i.* Phil. **68** B2
tanzaro Italy **57** C3
tania Italy **56** C3
tanzaro Italy **57** C3
tarman Phil. **68** B2
tbalogan Phil. **68** B2
therine, Mount Egypt *see*
Kâtrinā, Jabal
t Island Bahamas **131** C2
toche, Cabo *c.* Mex. **129** D2
tskill Mountains U.S.A.
123 F2
uayan Phil. **68** B3
ubvick, Mount Can. **115** D1
uca *r.* Col. **134** B2
ucaia Brazil **135** F3
ucasus *mts* Asia/Europe **85** C1
uedry France **48** A2
ulonia Italy **57** C3
uuspascal Can. **115** D2
van Ireland **45** C2
uvernoso, Serra de *mts* Brazil
138 B3
uxias Brazil **135** E3
uxias do Sul Brazil **136** C3
xito Angola **94** B3
yman Islands *terr.* West Indies
130 B3
zombo Angola **96** B1
ballos Mex. **128** B2
bu Phil. **68** B2
bu *i.* Phil. **68** B2
cil Plains Austr. **105** E1
cina Italy **56** B2
dar City U.S.A. **122** D2
dar Falls U.S.A. **121** E2
dar Lake Can. **113** E2
dar Rapids U.S.A. **121** E2
dros, Isla *i.* Mex. **128** A2
duna Austr. **102** C3
eldheere Somalia **93** C4
egeabaje Somalia **93** C5
falú Italy **56** B3
faya Mex. **129** B2
ebes *i.* Indon. **65** D2
ebes Sea Indon./Phil. **62** C2
ebes Sea Indon. **129** C2
lle Ger. **49** E1
ltic Sea Ireland/U.K. **43** B3
ntral, Cordillera *mts* Col.
134 B2
ntral, Cordillera *mts* Peru
134 B4
ntral, Cordillera *mts* Phil.
8 B2

Central African Republic *country*
Africa **94** C2
Central Brahui Range *mts* Pak.
78 A2
Central City U.S.A. **121** D2
Centralia *IL* U.S.A. **122** C3
Centralia *WA* U.S.A. **118** B1
Central Makran Range *mts* Pak.
78 A2
Central Range *mts* P.N.G. **63** D3
Central Russian Upland *hills*
Rus. Fed. **37** E3
Central Siberian Plateau
Rus. Fed. **87** J2
Cephalonia *i.* Greece **59** B3
Ceram Sea Indon. *see*
Seram, Laut
Ceres S. Africa **98** A3
Céret France **52** C3
Cerezo de Abajo Spain **54** C1
Cerignola Italy **56** C2
Cernavodă Romania **38** G1
Cerralvo, Isla *i.* Mex. **128** B2
Cerritos Mex. **129** B2
Cerro Azul Brazil **138** C2
Cerro Azul Mex. **129** C2
Cerro de Pasco Peru **134** B4
Cervione France **53** D3
Cervo Spain **54** B1
Cesena Italy **56** D2
Cēsis Latvia **36** C2
České Budějovice Czech Rep.
50 C3
Český Les *mts* Czech Rep./Ger.
49 F3
Çeşme Turkey **59** C3
Cessnock Austr. **105** E2
Cetinje S.M. **58** A2
Cetraro Italy **57** C3
Ceuta N. Africa **54** B2
Cévennes *mts* France **53** C3
Chābahār *Iran* **83** D2
Chabyêr Caka *salt l.* China **79** C1
Chachapoyas Peru **134** B3
Chachersk Belarus **37** D3
Chachoengsao Thai. **67** B2
Chad *country* Africa **91** D3
Chad, Lake Africa **91** D3
Chadaasan Mongolia **72** C1
Chadan Rus. Fed. **81** G1
Chadron U.S.A. **120** C2
Chaghcharān Afgh. **78** A1
Chagny France **50** A3
Chagoda Rus. Fed. **37** E2
Chaibasa India **79** C2
Chainat Thai. **67** B2
Chaiyaphum Thai. **67** B2
Chakonipau, Lac *l.* Can. **115** D1
Chala Peru **134** B4
Chalap Dalan *mts* Afgh. **78** A1
Chaleur Bay *inlet* Can. **115** D2
Chalisgaon India **78** B2
Chalki *i.* Greece **59** C3
Chalkida Greece **59** B3

Challans France **52** B2
Challenger Deep *sea feature*
N. Pacific Ocean **142** C4
Challis U.S.A. **118** C2
Châlons-en-Champagne France
53 C2
Chalon-sur-Saône France **53** C2
Cham Ger. **49** F3
Chama U.S.A. **126** C1
Chama Zambia **97** C1
Chaman Pak. **78** A1
Chambal *r.* India **78** B2
Chamberlain U.S.A. **121** D2
Chambéry France **53** D2
Chambeshi Zambia **97** C1
Champaign U.S.A. **122** C2
Champlain, Lake Can./U.S.A.
114 C2
Champotón Mex. **129** C3
Chañaral Chile **136** A3
Chandeleur Islands U.S.A.
124 C3
Chandigarh India **78** B1
Chandler U.S.A. **126** B2
Chandrapur India **79** B3
Chang, Ko *i.* Thai. **67** B2
Changane *r.* Moz. **97** C2
Changara Moz. **97** C1
Changbai China **69** B1
Changbai Shan *mts*
China/N. Korea **69** B1
Changchun China **69** B1
Changde China **75** B3
Ch'angdo N. Korea **69** B2
Changhua Taiwan **75** C3
Changhüng S. Korea **69** B3
Chang Jiang *r.* China *see* Yangtze
Changjin-gang *r.* N. Korea **69** B1
Changsha China **75** B3
Changsŏng S. Korea **69** B2
Changting China **75** B3
Ch'angwŏn S. Korea **69** B2
Changzhi China **74** B2
Changzhou China **74** B2
Chania Greece **59** B3
Channel Islands English Chan.
47 B5
Channel Islands U.S.A. **119** C4
Channel-Port-aux-Basques Can.
115 E2
Chanthaburi Thai. **67** B2
Chany, Ozero *salt l.* Rus. Fed.
81 E1
Chaouèn Morocco **54** B2
Chaoyang *Guangdong* China
75 B3
Chaoyang *Liaoning* China **74** C1
Chaozhou China **75** B3
Chapayev Kazakh. **80** C1
Chapecó Brazil **138** B3
Chapleau Can. **114** B2
Chaplygin Rus. Fed. **37** E3
Chaplynka Ukr. **39** D2
Charcas Mex. **129** B2

Chardzhev Turkm. *see*
    Turkmenabat
Charente *r.* France **52** B2
Chárikár Afgh. **78** A1
Charleroi Belgium **48** B2
Charles, Cape *c.* U.S.A. **123** E3
Charleston *IL* U.S.A. **122** C3
Charleston *SC* U.S.A. **125** E2
Charleston *WV* U.S.A. **122** D3
Charleston Peak U.S.A. **119** C3
Charleville Austr. **103** D2
Charleville-Mézières France
    53 C2
Charlotte U.S.A. **125** D1
Charlotte Harbor *b.* U.S.A.
    125 D3
Charlottesville U.S.A. **123** E3
Charlton Austr. **104** C3
Charlton Island Can. **114** C1
Chartres France **52** C2
Chashniki Belarus **36** C3
Chasŏng N. Korea **69** B1
Chassiron, Pointe de *pt* France
    52 B2
Châteaubriant France **52** B2
Château-du-Loir France **52** C2
Châteaudun France **52** C2
Châteaulin France **52** B2
Château-Thierry France **53** C2
Chateh Can. **112** D2
Châtelet Belgium **48** B2
Châtellerault France **52** C2
Chatham Can. **122** D2
Chatham Islands N.Z. **101**
Chattahoochee *r.* U.S.A. **125** D2
Chattanooga U.S.A. **125** C1
Châu Đốc Vietnam **67** D2
Chauk Myanmar **66** A1
Chaumont France **53** D2
Chauny France **53** C2
Chaves Brazil **135** D3
Chaves Port. **54** B1
Chavigny, Lac *l.* Can. **114** C2
Chavusy Belarus **37** D3
Chayevo Rus. Fed. **37** E2
Chaykovskiy Rus. Fed. **34** E3
Cheb Czech Rep. **50** C2
Cheboksary Rus. Fed. **35** D3
Chech'ŏn S. Korea **69** B2
Chegga Maur. **90** B2
Chehalis U.S.A. **118** B1
Cheju S. Korea **69** B3
Cheju-do *i.* S. Korea **69** B3
Cheju-haehyŏp *sea chan.*
    S. Korea **69** B3
Chekhov Rus. Fed. **37** E2
Chelan, Lake U.S.A. **118** B1
Cheleken Turkm. **85** D2
Chelghoum el Aïd Alg. **55** E2
Chélif, Oued *r.* Alg. **55** D2
Chełm Pol. **51** E2
Chełmno Pol. **51** D2

Chelmsford U.K. **47** D4
Cheltenham U.K. **47** B4
Chelyabinsk Rus. Fed. **35** F3
Chemnitz Ger. **49** F2
Chenachane Alg. **90** B2
Chengde China **74** B1
Chengdu China **74** A2
Chennai India **77** C3
Chenzhou China **75** B3
Cherbourg France **52** B2
Cheremkhovo Rus. Fed. **72** C1
Cherepovets Rus. Fed. **37** E2
Cherkasy Ukr. **39** D2
Cherkessk Rus. Fed. **35** D4
Chernihiv Ukr. **39** D1
Cherninivka Ukr. **39** E2
Chernivtsi Ukr. **38** C2
Chernyakhiv Ukr. **38** C1
Chernyakhovsk Rus. Fed. **36** B3
Chernyanka Rus. Fed. **37** E3
Chernyshevskiy Rus. Fed. **87** J2
Chernyshkovskiy Rus. Fed. **39** F2
Cherskogo, Khrebet *mts*
    Rus. Fed. **87** L2
Chertkovo Rus. Fed. **39** F2
Chervonohrad Ukr. **38** B1
Chervyen' Belarus **36** C3
Cherykaw Belarus **37** D3
Chesapeake Bay U.S.A. **123** E3
Cheshskaya Guba *b.* Rus. Fed.
    34 D2
Chester U.K. **46** B3
Chester *SC* U.S.A. **125** D2
Chesterfield U.K. **46** C3
Chesterfield, Îles *is*
    New Caledonia **103** E1
Chesterfield Inlet Can. **113** F1
Chesterfield *inlet* Can.
    113 F1
Chesuncook Lake U.S.A. **123** G1
Chetumal Mex. **129** D3
Chetwynd Can. **112** C2
Cheviot Hills U.K. **46** B2
Cheyenne *r.* U.S.A. **120** C2
Cheyenne U.S.A. **120** C2
Cheyenne Wells U.S.A. **120** C3
Chhapra India **79** C2
Chhatarpur India **79** B2
Chiai Taiwan **75** C3
Chiang Dao Thai. **66** A2
Chiang Mai Thai. **66** A2
Chiang Rai Thai. **66** A2
Chibi China **75** B3
Chiboma Moz. **97** C1
Chibougamau Can. **114** C2
Chicago U.S.A. **122** C2
Chichagof Island U.S.A. **112** B2
Chichester U.K. **47** C4
Chichester Range *mts* Austr.
    102 A2
Chickasha U.S.A. **127** E1
Chiclayo Peru **134** B2
Chico *r.* Arg. **137** B5
Chico U.S.A. **119** B3

Chicoutimi Can. **115** C2
Chieti Italy **56** B2
Chifeng China **74** B1
Chifre, Serra do *mts* Brazil
    139 D1
Chiganak Kazakh. **81** E2
Chigubo Moz. **97** C2
Chigu Co *l.* China **66** A1
Chihuahua Mex. **128** B2
Chikhachevo Rus. Fed. **36** C2
Chilanko *r.* Can. **112** C2
Chilas Jammu and Kashmir **78**
Chilcotin U.S.A. **127** D2
Chile *country* S. America **136** A
Chilika Lake India **79** C3
Chililabombwe Zambia **96** B1
Chilko *r.* Can. **112** C2
Chilko Lake Can. **112** C2
Chillán Chile **137** A4
Chillicothe *MO* U.S.A. **121** E3
Chillicothe *OH* U.S.A. **122** D3
Chilliwack Can. **112** C3
Chiloé, Isla de *i.* Chile **137** A5
Chilpancingo Mex. **129** C3
Chiltern Hills U.K. **47** C4
Chilung Taiwan **75** C3
Chimala Tanz. **95** D3
Chimbas Arg. **136** B4
Chimbote Peru **134** B3
Chimboy Uzbek. **80** C2
Chimoio Moz. **97** C1
Chimtargha, Qullai *mt.* Tajik.
    81 D3
China *country* Asia **72** B2
Chincha Alta Peru **134** B4
Chinchaga *r.* Can. **112** D2
Chinchorro, Banco *sea feature*
    Mex. **129** D3
Chinde Moz. **97** C1
Chindo S. Korea **69** B3
Chin-do *i.* S. Korea **69** B3
Chindu China **72** C2
Chindwin *r.* Myanmar **66** A1
Chinghwa N. Korea **69** B2
Chingola Zambia **96** B1
Chinguar Angola **96** A1
Chinhae S. Korea **69** B2
Chinhoyi Zimbabwe **97** C1
Chiniot Pak. **78** B1
Chinju S. Korea **69** B2
Chinko *r.* C.A.R. **94** C2
Chinle U.S.A. **126** C1
Chinmen Taiwan **75** B3
Chino Japan **71** C3
Chino Valley U.S.A. **126** B2
Chinsali Zambia **95** C3
Chioggia Italy **56** B1
Chios Greece **59** C3
Chios *i.* Greece **59** C3
Chipata Zambia **97** C1
Chipindo Angola **96** A1
Chipinge Zimbabwe **97** C2
Chiplun India **77** B3

ippenham U.K. **47** B4
ir r. Rus. Fed. **39** F2
irchiq Uzbek. **81** D2
iredzi Zimbabwe **97** C2
iriqui, Golfo de b. Panama
30 B1
iri-san mt. S. Korea **69** B3
irripo mt. Costa Rica **130** B4
irundu Zimbabwe **97** B1
isasibi Can. **114** C1
isholm U.S.A. **121** E1
isina Moldova **38** C2
ita Rus. Fed. **73** D1
itado Angola **96** A1
itato Angola **94** C3
itipa Malawi **95** D3
itradurga India **77** B3
itral Pak. **78** B1
itré Panama **130** B4
ittagong Bangl. **79** D2
ittaurgarh India **78** B2
itungwiza Zimbabwe **97** C1
iume Angola **96** B1
ivhu Zimbabwe **97** C1
izhou China **75** B2
kalovsk Rus. Fed. **37** F2
oix Mex. **128** B2
ojnice Pol. **51** D2
'ok'é Mountains Eth. **93** B3
okurdakh Rus. Fed. **87** L2
ókwé Moz. **97** C2
olet France **52** B2
omutov Czech Rep. **50** C2
ona r. Rus. Fed. **87** J2
'ŏnan S. Korea **69** B2
'ŏngjin N. Korea **69** B1
'ŏngju N. Korea **69** B2
ŏngp'yŏng N. Korea **69** B2
ongqing China **75** A3
ongqing mun. China **74** A2
ŏngŭp S. Korea **69** B2
ŏnju S. Korea **69** B2
onos, Archipiélago de los is
Chile **137** A5
opimzinho Brazil **138** B3
ornornors'ke Ukr. **39** D2
ortkiv Ukr. **38** C2
'ŏrwŏn S. Korea **69** B2
ōshi Japan **71** D3
osxczno Pol. **51** D2
'ŏŭm Maur. **90** A2
oybalsan Mongolia **73** D1
oyr Mongolia **73** D1
ristchurch N.Z. **106** B3
ristchurch U.K. **47** C4
ristian, Cape Can. **111** H2
ristiana S. Africa **99** C2
ristina, Mount N.Z. **106** A3
ristmas Island terr.
Indian Ocean **59** C4
rysi i. Greece **59** C4
ubut r. Arg. **137** B5

Chudniv Ukr. **38** C1
Chudovo Rus. Fed. **37** D2
Chugach Mountains U.S.A.
110 C2
Chūgoku-sanchi mts Japan
71 B4
Chuguyevka Rus. Fed. **70** B2
Chuhuyiv Ukr. **39** E2
Chukchi Sea Rus. Fed./U.S.A.
87 O2
Chukotskiy Poluostrov pen.
Rus. Fed. **87** O2
Chula Vista U.S.A. **119** C4
Chulym Rus. Fed. **86** J3
Chumbicha Arg. **136** B3
Chumikan Rus. Fed. **87** L3
Chumphon Thai. **67** A2
Ch'unch'ŏn S. Korea **69** B2
Chungking China see Chongqing
Chuquicamata Chile **136** B3
Chur Switz. **53** D2
Churchill Can. **113** F2
Churchill r. Man. Can. **113** F2
Churchill r. Nfld. and Lab. Can.
115 D1
Churchill, Cape Can. **113** F2
Churchill Falls Can. **115** D1
Churchill Lake Can. **113** E2
Chute-des-Passes Can. **115** C2
Chuuk is Micronesia **100**
Chuxiong China **66** B1
Ciadîr-Lunga Moldova **38** C2
Ciamis Indon. **64** B2
Cianjur Indon. **64** B2
Cianorte Brazil **138** B2
Ciechanów Pol. **51** E2
Ciego de Ávila Cuba **130** C2
Cienfuegos Cuba **130** B2
Cieza Spain **55** C2
Cigüela r. Spain **54** C2
Çıhanbeyli Turkey **84** B2
Cihuatlán Mex. **128** B3
Cijara, Embalse de resr Spain
54 C2
Cilacap Indon. **64** B2
Cimarron r. U.S.A. **127** E1
Cimişlia Moldova **38** C2
Cimone, Monte mt. Italy **56** B2
Cincinnati U.S.A. **122** D3
Çine Turkey **59** C3
Ciney Belgium **48** B2
Cintalapa Mex. **129** C3
Circle AK U.S.A. **110** C2
Circle MT U.S.A. **120** E1
Cirebon Indon. **64** B2
Cirencester U.K. **47** C4
Cirò Marina Italy **57** C3
Citrusdal S. Africa **98** A3
Città di Castello Italy **53** E3
Ciudad Altamirano Mex.
129 B3
Ciudad Bolívar Venez. **134** C2
Ciudad Camargo Mex. **128** B2

Ciudad Constitución Mex.
128 A2
Ciudad del Carmen Mex. **129** C3
Ciudad Delicias Mex. **128** B2
Ciudad de Valles Mex. **129** C2
Ciudad Guayana Venez. **134** C2
Ciudad Guerrero Mex. **128** C3
Ciudad Guzmán Mex. **128** B3
Ciudad Ixtepec Mex. **129** C3
Ciudad Juárez Mex. **128** B1
Ciudad Mante Mex. **129** C2
Ciudad Mier Mex. **129** C2
Ciudad Obregón Mex. **128** B2
Ciudad Real Spain **54** C2
Ciudad Rio Bravo Mex. **129** C2
Ciudad Rodrigo Spain **54** B1
Ciudad Victoria Mex. **129** C2
Ciutadella de Menorca Spain
55 D1
Çıvan Dağ mt. Turkey **59** C3
Civitanova Marche Italy **56** B2
Civitavecchia Italy **56** B2
Çıvray France **52** C2
Çivril Turkey **59** C3
Clacton-on-Sea U.K. **47** D4
Claire, Lake Can. **113** D2
Clanwilliam S. Africa **98** A3
Clare Austr. **104** B2
Clare Island Ireland **45** A2
Claremont U.S.A. **123** F2
Claremorris Ireland **45** B2
Clarence N.Z. **106** B3
Clarenville Can. **115** E2
Claresholm Can. **112** D2
Clarinda U.S.A. **121** D2
Clarión, Isla i. Mex. **128** A3
Clarkebury S. Africa **99** C3
Clark Fork r. U.S.A. **118** C1
Clark Hill Reservoir U.S.A.
125 D2
Clarksburg U.S.A. **123** D3
Clarksdale U.S.A. **124** B2
Clarksville AR U.S.A. **124** B1
Clarksville TN U.S.A. **124** C1
Claro r. Brazil **138** B1
Clayton U.S.A. **127** D1
Clear, Cape Ireland **45** B3
Cleare, Cape U.S.A. **110** C3
Clear Lake U.S.A. **121** E2
Clear Lake l. U.S.A. **119** B3
Clearwater Can. **112** D2
Clearwater r. Can. **113** D2
Clearwater U.S.A. **125** D3
Clearwater r. U.S.A. **118** C1
Cleburne U.S.A. **127** E2
Clermont France **48** B3
Clermont-en-Argonne France
48 B3
Clermont-Ferrand France **52** C2
Cleveland MS U.S.A. **124** B2
Cleveland OH U.S.A. **122** D2
Cleveland TN U.S.A. **125** D1
Cleveland, Mount U.S.A. **118** D1
Clewiston U.S.A. **125** D3
Clifden Ireland **45** A2

Clifton Austr. **105** E1
Clifton U.S.A. **126** C2
Clinton Can. **112** C2
Clinton *IA* U.S.A. **121** E2
Clinton *OK* U.S.A. **127** E1
Clisham *h.* U.K. **44** A2
Clitheroe U.K. **44** B3
Clonakilty Ireland **45** B3
Cloncurry Austr. **103** D3
Clonmel Ireland **45** C2
Cloppenburg Ger. **48** D1
Cloud Peak U.S.A. **120** B2
Clovis U.S.A. **127** D2
Cluff Lake Mine Can. **113** E2
Cluj-Napoca Romania **38** B2
Cluny Austr. **103** C2
Cluses France **53** D2
Clutha *r.* N.Z. **106** A4
Clyde *r.* U.K. **44** B3
Clyde, Firth of *est.* U.K. **44** B3
Clydebank U.K. **44** B3
Clyde River Can. **111** H2
Coaldale U.S.A. **119** C3
Coal River Can. **112** C2
Coari Brazil **134** C3
Coari *r.* Brazil **134** C3
Coastal Plain U.S.A. **124** B2
Coast Mountains Can. **112** C2
Coast Ranges *mts* U.S.A. **118** B2
Coatbridge U.K. **44** B3
Coats Island Can. **113** C1
Coats Land *reg.* Antarctica **107** A2
Coatzacoalcos Mex. **129** C2
Cobán Guat. **130** A3
Cobar Austr. **105** D2
Cóbh Ireland **45** B3
Cobija Bol. **136** B2
Cobourg Can. **123** E2
Cobourg Peninsula Austr. **102** C1
Cobram Austr. **105** D3
Coburg Ger. **49** E2
Cochabamba Bol. **136** B2
Cochem Ger. **48** C2
Cochin India **77** B4
Cochrane Can. **114** B2
Cockburn Austr. **104** C2
Cockburn Town Turks and Caicos Is *see* Grand Turk
Cockscomb *mt.* S. Africa **98** B3
Coco *r.* Hond./Nic. **130** B3
Cocos Islands *terr.* Indian Ocean **62** A3
Cod, Cape U.S.A. **123** F2
Codigoro Italy **56** B2
Cod Island Can. **115** D1
Codó Brazil **135** E3
Cody U.S.A. **120** B2
Coesfeld Ger. **48** C2
Coeur d'Alene U.S.A. **118** C1
Coffee Bay S. Africa **99** C3
Coffeyville U.S.A. **121** D3

Coffs Harbour Austr. **105** E2
Cognac France **52** B2
Cohuna Austr. **104** C3
Coiba, Isla de *i.* Panama **130** B4
Coihaique Chile **137** A5
Coimbatore India **77** B3
Coimbra Port. **54** B1
Colac Austr. **104** C3
Colatina Brazil **139** D1
Colby U.S.A. **120** C3
Colchester U.K. **47** D4
Cold Lake Can. **113** D2
Coldstream U.K. **44** C3
Coleman U.S.A. **127** E2
Coleraine U.K. **45** C1
Colesberg S. Africa **99** C3
Colima Mex. **128** B3
Colima, Nevado de *vol.* Mex. **128** B3
Coll *i.* U.K. **44** A2
Collarenebri Austr. **105** D1
Collier Bay Austr. **102** B1
Collingwood N.Z. **106** B3
Collo Alg. **55** E2
Collooney Ireland **45** B1
Colmar France **53** D2
Cologne Ger. **48** C2
Colômbia Brazil **138** C2
Colombia *country* S. America **134** B2
Colombo Sri Lanka **77** B4
Colomiers France **52** C3
Colón Panama **130** C4
Colonna, Capo *c.* Italy **57** C3
Colonsay *i.* U.K. **44** A2
Colorado *r.* Arg. **137** B4
Colorado *r.* Mex./U.S.A. **126** A2
Colorado *r.* U.S.A. **127** E3
Colorado *state* U.S.A. **120** B3
Colorado Plateau U.S.A. **120** B3
Colorado Springs U.S.A. **120** C3
Côlpin Ger. **49** F1
Columbia *MO* U.S.A. **121** E3
Columbia *SC* U.S.A. **125** D2
Columbia *TN* U.S.A. **124** C1
Columbia *r.* U.S.A. **118** B1
Columbia, Mount Can. **112** D2
Columbia Falls U.S.A. **118** D1
Columbia Mountains Can. **112** C2
Columbia Plateau U.S.A. **118** C1
Columbus *GA* U.S.A. **125** D2
Columbus *IN* U.S.A. **122** C3
Columbus *MS* U.S.A. **124** C2
Columbus *NE* U.S.A. **121** D2
Columbus *NM* U.S.A. **126** C2
Columbus *OH* U.S.A. **122** D3
Colville U.S.A. **118** C1
Colville *r.* U.S.A. **110** B2
Colville Lake Can. **110** D2
Colwyn Bay U.K. **46** B3
Comacchio Italy **56** B2
Comalcalco Mex. **129** C3
Comănești Romania **38** C2

Comencho, Lac *l.* Can. **114** C1
Comeragh Mountains Ireland **45** C2
Comilla Bangl. **79** D2
Comines Belgium **48** A2
Comino, Capo *c.* Italy **56** A2
Comitán de Domínguez Mex. **129** C3
Como Italy **56** A1
Como, Lake Italy **56** A1
Comodoro Rivadavia Arg. **137** B5
Comoros *country* Africa **97** D1
Compiègne France **52** C2
Compostela Mex. **128** B2
Comrat Moldova **38** C2
Conakry Guinea **90** A4
Conceição da Barra Brazil **139** E1
Conceição do Araguaia Brazil **135** E3
Concepción Arg. **136** B3
Concepción Chile **137** A4
Concepción Mex. **128** B2
Conception, Point U.S.A. **119** B3
Conchas Lake U.S.A. **126** D1
Conchos *r.* Nuevo León/Tamaulipas Mex. **129** C2
Conchos *r.* Mex. **128** B2
Concord *CA* U.S.A. **119** B3
Concord *NH* U.S.A. **123** F2
Concordia Arg. **136** C4
Concordia U.S.A. **121** D3
Condobolin Austr. **105** D2
Condom France **52** C3
Condon U.S.A. **118** B1
Conegliano Italy **56** B1
Conflict Group *is* P.N.G. **103** E1
Congdü China **79** C2
Congo *country* Africa **94** B3
Congo *r.* Congo/Dem. Rep. Congo **94** C3
Congo, Democratic Republic of the *country* Africa **94** C3
Conklin Can. **113** D2
Conn, Lough *l.* Ireland **45** B1
Connaught *reg.* Ireland **45** B2
Connecticut *r.* U.S.A. **123** F2
Connecticut *state* U.S.A. **123** F2
Connemara *reg.* Ireland **45** B2
Conrad U.S.A. **118** D1
Conroe U.S.A. **127** E2
Conselheiro Lafaiete Brazil **139** D2
Consett U.K. **46** C2
Côn Sơn *i.* Vietnam **67** B3
Constanţa Romania **38** C3
Constantine Alg. **91** C1
Contact U.S.A. **118** D2
Contreras, Isla *i.* Chile **137** A6
Contwoyto Lake Can. **113** C1
Conway *AR* U.S.A. **124** B1
Coober Pedy Austr. **104** A1

ok, Mount N.Z. **106** B3
okeville U.S.A. **125** C1
ok Inlet *sea chan.* U.S.A.
10 B2
ok Islands *terr.*
. Pacific Ocean **101**
ok's Harbour Can. **115** E1
okstown U.K. **45** C1
ok Strait N.Z. **106** B3
oktown Austr. **103** D1
olabah Austr. **105** D2
olangatta Austr. **105** E1
olgardie Austr. **102** B3
oma Austr. **105** D3
ombah Austr. **104** D2
onabarabran Austr. **105** D2
onalpyn Austr. **104** D3
onamble Austr. **105** D2
04 B1
ooper Creek *watercourse* Austr.
04 B3
ootamundra Austr. **105** D2
palma Mex. **129** C3
penhagen Denmark **41** C4
pertino Italy **57** C2
piapó Chile **136** A3
pper Harbor U.S.A. **122** C1
ppermine Can. *see* Kugluktuk
quimbo Chile **136** A3
rabia Romania **38** B3
ração de Jesus Brazil **139** D1
ral Bay Austr. **102** A1
ral Harbour Can. **111** G2
ral Sea S. Pacific Ocean
03 E1
ral Sea Islands Territory *terr.*
ustr. **100**
rangamite, Lake U.S.A.
rcovado, Golfo de *sea chan.*
hile **137** A5
rdoba Arg. **136** B4
rdoba U.S.A. **125** D2
rdilleras Range *mts* Phil.
8 B2
rdoba Arg. **136** B4
rdoba Mex. **129** C3
rdoba, Sierras de *mts* Arg.
36 B4
rdova U.S.A. **112** A1
rfu *i.* Greece **59** A3
rfu Turkey **59** C2
rinth Spain **54** B2
rinth Greece **59** B3
rinth U.S.A. **124** C2
rinth, Gulf of *sea chan.* Greece
9 B3
rinto Brazil **139** D1
rk Ireland **45** B3
rlu Turkey **59** C2
rnélio Procópio Brazil
38 B2
rner Brook Can. **115** E2
rner Inlet *b.* Austr. **105** D3

Corning *CA* U.S.A. **118** B3
Corning *NY* U.S.A. **123** E2
Corno, Monte *mt.* Italy **56** B2
Cornwall Can. **114** C2
Cornwallis Island Can. **110** F1
Coro Venez. **134** C1
Coromandel Brazil **138** C1
Coromandel Peninsula N.Z.
106 C2
Coronation Can. **113** D2
Coronation Gulf Can. **110** E2
Coronel Oviedo Para. **136** C3
Çorovodë Albania **59** B2
Corozal Belize **129** D3
Corpus Christi U.S.A. **127** E3
Correntina Brazil **135** E4
Corrib, Lough *l.* Ireland **45** B2
Corrientes Arg. **136** C3
Corrientes, Cabo *c.* Mex. **128** B2
Corryong Austr. **105** D3
Corse *i.* France *see* Corsica
Corse, Cap *c.* France **53** D3
Corsica *i.* France **53** D3
Corsicana U.S.A. **127** E2
Corte France **53** D3
Cortegana Spain **54** B2
Cortez U.S.A. **120** B3
Cortland U.S.A. **123** E2
Cortona Italy **56** B2
Coruche Port. **54** B2
Çoruh Turkey *see* Artvin
Çorum Turkey **84** B1
Corumbá Brazil **136** C2
Corumbá *r.* Brazil **138** C1
Corvallis U.S.A. **118** B2
Corwen U.K. **46** B3
Cosamaloapan Mex. **129** C3
Cosenza Italy **57** B3
Cosne-Cours-sur-Loire France
52 C2
Costa Blanca *coastal area* Spain
55 C2
Costa Brava *coastal area* Spain
55 D1
Costa del Sol *coastal area* Spain
54 B2
Costa de Mosquitos *coastal area*
Nic. **130** B3
Costa Rica Brazil **138** B1
Costa Rica *country*
Central America **130** B3
Costa Rica Mex. **128** B2
Costeşti Romania **38** B3
Cotabató Phil. **68** B3
Côte d'Ivoire *country* Africa
90 B4
Cotopaxi, Volcán *vol.* Ecuador
134 B3
Cotswold Hills U.K. **47** B4
Cottage Grove U.S.A. **118** B2
Cottbus Ger. **50** C2
Coubre, Pointe de la *pt* France
52 B2
Coüedic, Cape de Austr. **104** B3

Council Bluffs U.S.A. **121** D2
Courland Lagoon *b.*
Lith./Rus. Fed. **36** B2
Courtenay Can. **112** C3
Coutances France **52** B2
Coutras France **52** B2
Couvin Belgium **48** B2
Coventry U.K. **47** C3
Covington U.S.A. **122** D3
Cowan, Lake *salt flat* Austr.
102 B3
Cowdenbeath U.K. **44** C2
Cowlitz *r.* U.S.A. **118** B1
Cowra Austr. **105** D2
Coxim Brazil **138** B1
Cox's Bazar Bangl. **79** D2
Cozumel Mex. **129** D2
Cozumel, Isla de *i.* Mex. **129** D2
Cradock S. Africa **99** C3
Craig U.S.A. **120** B2
Crailsheim Ger. **49** E3
Craiova Romania **38** B3
Cranberry Portage Can. **113** E2
Cranbourne Austr. **105** D3
Cranbrook Can. **112** D3
Crateús Brazil **135** E3
Crato Brazil **135** F3
Crawford U.S.A. **120** C2
Crawfordsville U.S.A. **122** C2
Crawley U.K. **47** C4
Crazy Mountains U.S.A. **118** D1
Cree *r.* Can. **113** E2
Creel Mex. **128** B2
Cree Lake Can. **113** E2
Cremona Italy **56** B1
Crépy-en-Valois France **48** A3
Cres *i.* Croatia **56** B2
Crescent City U.S.A. **118** B2
Creston U.S.A. **121** E2
Crestview U.S.A. **124** C2
Crete *i.* Greece **59** B3
Creus, Cap de *c.* Spain **55** D1
Creutzwald France **48** C3
Crewe U.K. **46** B3
Crianlarich U.K. **44** B2
Criciúma Brazil **136** D3
Crieff U.K. **44** C2
Crimea *pen.* Ukr. **39** D2
Crimmitschau Ger. **49** F2
Cristalina Brazil **138** C1
Crna Gora *aut. rep.* S.M. **58** A2
Črnomelj Slovenia **56** C1
Croagh Patrick *h.* Ireland **45** B2
Croatia *country* Europe **57** C1
Crocker, Banjaran *mts* Malaysia
65 C1
Croker Island Austr. **63** C3
Cromer U.K. **46** D3
Cromwell N.Z. **106** A4
Crookston U.S.A. **121** D1
Crookwell Austr. **105** D2
Cross City U.S.A. **125** D3
Crossett U.S.A. **124** B2
Cross Fell *h.* U.K. **46** B2

169

Cross Lake Can. 113 F2
Crotone Italy 57 C2
Crowley U.S.A. 124 E2
Crownsest Pass Can. 112 D3
Cruz Alta Brazil 136 C3
Cruz del Eje Arg. 136 B4
Cruzeiro Brazil 139 D2
Cruzeiro do Sul Brazil 134 B3
Crystal Brook Austr. 104 B2
Crystal Falls U.S.A. 122 C1
Csongrád Hungary 51 E3
Cuando r. Angola/Zambia 96 B1
Cuangar Angola 96 A1
Cuango r. Angola/
  Dem. Rep. Congo 94 B3
Cuanza r. Angola 96 A1
Cuatro Ciénegas Mex. 127 D3
Cuauhtémoc Mex. 128 B2
Cuautla Mex. 129 C3
Cuba country West Indies 130 B2
Cubal Angola 96 A1
Cubango r. Angola/Namibia 96 B1
Cúcuta Col. 134 B2
Cuddalore India 77 B3
Cuddapah India 77 B3
Cuemba Angola 96 A1
Cuenca Ecuador 134 B3
Cuenca Spain 55 C1
Cuenca, Serranía de mts Spain
  55 C1
Cuernavaca Mex. 129 C3
Cuiabá Brazil 138 A1
Cuillin Sound sea chan. U.K.
  44 A2
Cuilo Angola 94 B3
Cuito r. Angola 96 B1
Cuito Cuanavale Angola 96 A1
Cukai Malaysia 64 B1
Culcairn Austr. 105 D3
Culgoa r. Austr. 105 D1
Culiacán Mex. 128 B2
Culion i. Phil. 68 A2
Cullera Spain 55 C2
Cullman U.S.A. 124 C2
Culuene r. Brazil 135 D4
Cumaná Venez. 134 C1
Cumberland r. U.S.A. 122 C3
Cumberland Lake Can. 113 E2
Cumberland Peninsula Can.
  111 H2
Cumberland Plateau U.S.A.
  125 C1
Cumberland Sound sea chan.
  Can. 111 H2
Cumnauld U.K. 44 C3
Cummings U.S.A. 118 B3
Cunene r. Angola 96 A1
Cuneo Italy 56 A2
Cunnamulla Austr. 105 D1
Cupar U.K. 44 C2
Curaçao i. Neth. Antilles 131 D3
Curicó Chile 137 A4
Curitiba Brazil 138 C3
Curitibanos Brazil 138 B3

Curnamona Austr. 104 B2
Currie Austr. 103 D3
Curtis Island Austr. 103 E2
Curuá r. Brazil 135 D3
Cururupu Brazil 135 E3
Curvelo Brazil 139 D1
Cusco Peru 134 B4
Cut Bank U.S.A. 118 D1
Cuttack India 79 C1
Cuxhaven Ger. 49 D1
Cuyo Islands Phil. 68 B2
Cuzco Peru see Cusco
Cyangugu Rwanda 95 C3
Cyclades is Greece 59 B3
Cypress Hills Can. 113 D3
Cyprus country Asia 92 B1
Cyprus i. Asia 84 B2
Czech Republic country Europe
  50 C3
Częstochowa Pol. 51 D2

D

Daban China 74 B1
Dacca Bangl. see Dhaka
Dachau Ger. 50 C3
Dadu Pak. 78 A2
Daet Phil. 68 B2
Dagana Senegal 92 A3
Dagupan Phil. 68 B2
Da Hinggan Ling mts China
  74 B1
Dahlak Archipelago is Eritrea
  92 C3
Dahlem Ger. 48 C2
Dahm, Ramlat des.
  Saudi Arabia/Yemen 82 B3
Dahme Ger. 49 F2
Daik Indon. 64 B2
Dakar Senegal 90 A3
Dakoro Niger 91 C3
Dakota Shet' watercourse Eth.
  95 D2
Dākhilah, Wāḥāt al oasis Egypt
  92 A2
Dakhla Oasis Egypt see
  Dākhilah, Wāḥāt al
Dakoank India 67 A3
Đakovica S.M. 58 B2
Đakovo Croatia 57 C1
Dala Angola 96 B1
Dalain Hob China 72 C2
Dalaman Turkey 59 C3
Dalaman r. Turkey 59 C3
Dalandzadgad Mongolia 72 C2
Đa Lat Vietnam 67 B2
Dalbandin Pak. 78 A2
Dalby Austr. 105 E1
Dale Hordaland Norway 42 E1
Dale Sogn og Fjordane Norway
  42 E1

Dale Hollow Lake U.S.A. 125 C
Dalgety Austr. 105 D3
Dalhart U.S.A. 127 D1
Dalhousie Can. 123 G1
Dali China 66 B1
Dalian China 73 C2
Dalkeith U.K. 44 C3
Dallas U.S.A. 127 E2
Dall Island U.S.A. 112 B2
Dalmatia reg. Bos.-Herz./Croatia
  57 C2
Dal'negorsk Rus. Fed. 70 C2
Dal'nerechensk Rus. Fed. 70 B
Daloa Côte d'Ivoire 90 B4
Dalrymple, Mount Austr. 103 D
Dalsmynni Iceland 40 [inset]
Daltenganj India 79 C2
Dalton U.S.A. 125 D2
Daly r. Austr. 102 C1
Daly Waters Austr. 102 C1
Daman India 78 B2
Damanhūr Egypt 84 B2
Damascus Syria 84 B2
Damaturu Nigeria 91 D3
Damghan Iran 85 D2
Dammam Saudi Arabia 83 C2
Damoh India 79 B2
Damongo Ghana 90 B4
Dampir, Selat sea chan. Indon.
  63 C3
Damroh India 66 A1
Damxung China 79 C1
Danané Côte d'Ivoire 90 B4
Đa Nẵng Vietnam 67 B2
Danbury U.S.A. 123 F2
Dandong China 74 B2
Danilov Rus. Fed. 37 F2
Danilovskaya Vozvyshennost'
  hills Rus. Fed. 37 E2
Dankov Rus. Fed. 37 E3
Dannenberg (Elbe) Ger. 49 E1
Dannevirke N.Z. 106 C3
Dan Sai Thai. 66 B2
Dantu China 74 B2
Danube r. Austria/Ger. 50 D3
Danube r. Bulg./Croatia/S.M.
  58 C2
Danube r. Hungary 51 D3
Danube r. Romania 58 C2
Danube Delta Romania/Ukr.
  38 C2
Danville IL U.S.A. 122 C2
Danville KY U.S.A. 122 D3
Danville VA U.S.A. 123 E3
Danzhou China 75 A4
Daoxian China 75 B3
Dapaong Togo 90 C3
Da Qaidam Zhen China 72 C2
Daqing China 73 E1
Dar'ā Syria 84 B2
Dārāb Iran 85 D3
Daraj Libya 91 D1

rān Iran 85 D2
Rāng, Sông r. Vietnam 67 B2
rbhanga India 79 C2
es Salaam Tanz. 95 D3
rfur reg. Sudan 93 A3
rgai Pak. 78 B1
rgaville N.Z. 106 B2
rgun Mongolia 72 D1
rién, Golfo del g. Col. 134 B2
rjiling India 79 C2
rlag China 72 C2
rling r. Austr. 104 C2
rling Downs hills Austr.
05 D1
rling Range hills Austr. 102 A3
rlington U.K. 46 C2
rlington Point Austr. 105 D2
rlowo Pol. 51 D2
rmstadt Ger. 49 D3
rnah Libya 91 E1
rnick Austr. 104 C2
roca Spain 55 C1
rtford U.K. 47 D4
rtmoor hills U.K. 47 A4
rtmouth Can. 115 D2
rtmouth U.K. 47 B4
ru P.N.G. 68 D3
rvaza Turkm. 80 C2
rwin Austr. 102 C1
rwha Pak. 78 B2
rtadian Indon. 65 C1
tca Turkey 59 C3
tong China 74 A1
tu Piang Phil. 68 B3
ud Khel Pak. 78 B1
ugava r. Latvia 36 B2
ugavpils Latvia 36 C2
un Ger. 48 C2
uphin Can. 113 E2
uphin Lake Can. 113 F2
vangere India 77 B3
vao Phil. 68 B3
venport U.S.A. 121 E2
veyton S. Africa 99 C2
vid Panama 130 B4
vlu China 72 C2
r France 52 B3
r Xueshan mts China 72 C2
yr az Zawr Syria 84 C2
yton U.S.A. 122 D3

Daytona Beach U.S.A. 125 D3
Daytona canal China 74 B2
Dazhou China 74 A2
De Aar S. Africa 98 B3
Dead Sea salt l. Asia 84 B2
De'an China 75 B3
Deán Funes Arg. 136 B4
Dease Lake Can. 112 C2
Death Valley depr. U.S.A. 119 C3
Deauville France 52 C2
Debar Macedonia 59 B2
Debrecen Hungary 51 E3
Debre Markos Eth. 93 B3
Debre Zeyit Eth. 93 B4
Deccan plat. India 77 B3
Děčín Czech Rep. 50 C2
Dedovichi Rus. Fed. 36 C2
Dedza Malawi 97 C1
Dee r. England/Wales U.K. 46 B3
Dee r. Scotland U.K. 44 C2
Deepwater Austr. 105 E1
Deer Lodge U.S.A. 118 D1
Defiance U.S.A. 122 D2
Dêgê China 72 C2
Deggendorf Ger. 50 C3
Degtevo Rus. Fed. 39 F2
Dehra Dun India 79 B1
Dehri India 79 C2
Dehui China 73 E2
Deinze Belgium 48 A2
Dej Romania 38 B2
De Kalb U.S.A. 122 C2
Dekese Dem. Rep. Congo 94 C3
Delano U.S.A. 119 C3
Delano Peak U.S.A. 119 D3
Delap-Uliga-Djarrit Marshall Is.
100
Delārām Afgh. 78 A1
Delaronde Lake Can. 113 E2
Delaware U.S.A. 122 D2
Delaware r. U.S.A. 123 E3
Delaware state U.S.A. 123 E3
Delaware Bay U.S.A. 123 E3
Delegate Austr. 105 D3
Delémont Switz. 53 D2
Delft Neth. 48 B1
Delfzijl Neth. 48 C1
Delgado, Cabo c. Moz. 95 E4
Delhi India 78 B2
Deli r. Indon. 64 B2
Déljne Can. 112 C1
Delitzsch Ger. 49 F2
Dellys Alg. 55 D2
Delmenhorst Ger. 49 D1
Delnice Croatia 56 B1
De-Longa, Ostrova is Rus. Fed.
87 M1
Deloraine Can. 113 E3
Delphi tourist site Greece 59 B3
Del Rio U.S.A. 127 C3
Delta CO U.S.A. 120 B3
Delta UT U.S.A. 119 D3

Delta Junction U.S.A. 110 C2
Delvinë Albania 59 B3
Demanda, Sierra de la mts Spain
54 C1
Demba Dem. Rep. Congo 94 C3
Dembi Dolo Eth. 93 B4
Demidov Rus. Fed. 37 D2
Deming U.S.A. 126 C2
Demirci Turkey 59 C3
Demmin Ger. 50 C2
Demopolis U.S.A. 124 C2
Dempo, Gunung vol. Indon.
64 B2
Demyansk Rus. Fed. 37 D2
De Naawte S. Africa 98 B3
Denakil reg. Eritrea/Eth. 93 C3
Den Burg Neth. 48 B1
Dendermonde Belgium 48 B2
Dengkou China 74 A1
Dengzhou China 74 B2
Den Haag Neth. see The Hague
Denham Austr. 102 A2
Den Helder Neth. 48 B1
Deniliquin Austr. 104 C3
Denio U.S.A. 118 C2
Denison IA U.S.A. 121 D2
Denison TX U.S.A. 127 E2
Denizli Turkey 59 C3
Denman Austr. 105 E2
Denmark Austr. 102 A3
Denmark country Europe 41 C4
Denmark Strait
Greenland/Iceland 111 K2
Denpasar Indon. 65 C2
Denton U.S.A. 127 E2
D'Entrecasteaux, Point Austr.
102 A3
Denver U.S.A. 120 B3
Deogarh Orissa India 79 C2
Deogarh Rajasthan India 78 B2
Deoghar India 79 C2
Deputatskiy Rus. Fed. 87 L2
Dêqên China 66 A1
De Queen U.S.A. 124 B2
Dera Ghazi Khan Pak. 78 B1
Dera Ismail Khan Pak. 78 B1
Derbent Rus. Fed. 35 D4
Derby Austr. 102 B1
Derby U.K. 46 C3
Dereham U.K. 47 D3
Derg, Lough l. Ireland 45 B2
Derhachi Ukr. 39 E1
De Ridder U.S.A. 124 B2
Derkul r. Rus. Fed./Ukr. 39 E2
Dérub China 79 B1
Derudeb Sudan 92 B3
De Rust S. Africa 98 B3
Derventa Bos.-Herz. 57 C2
Derwent r. U.K. 46 C3
Derzhavinsk Kazakh. 81 D1
Desaguadero r. Bol. 136 B2
Désappointement, Îles du is
Fr. Polynesia 101
Deschambault Lake Can. 113 E2

Deschutes *r.* U.S.A. **118** B1
Des Eth. **93** B3
Deseado Arg. **137** B5
Deseado *r.* Arg. **137** B5
Des Moines U.S.A. **121** E2
Des Moines *r.* U.S.A. **121** E2
Desna *r.* Rus. Fed./Ukr. **37** D1
Desnogorsk Rus. Fed. **37** D3
Dessau Ger. **49** F2
Destruction Bay Can. **112** B1
Desventurados, Islas de los *is*
S. Pacific Ocean **133**
Detmold Ger. **49** D2
Detroit U.S.A. **122** D2
Detroit Lakes U.S.A. **121** D1
Deurne Neth. **48** B2
Deva Romania **36** B2
Deventer Neth. **48** C1
Deveron *r.* U.K. **44** C2
Devét Skal *h.* Czech Rep. **51** D3
Devil's Lake U.S.A. **121** C1
Devil's Paw *mt.* U.S.A. **112** B2
Devli India **78** B2
Devnya Bulg. **58** C2
Devon Can. **112** D2
Devon Island Can. **111** F1
Devonport Austr. **103** D4
Dewas India **78** B2
Deyang China **74** A2
Deyong, Tanjung *pt* Indon. **63** D3
Dezful Iran **85** C2
Dezhou China **74** B2
Dhahran Saudi Arabia **83** C2
Dhaka Bangl. **79** D2
Dhamār Yemen **82** B3
Dhamtari India **79** C2
Dhanbad India **79** C2
Dhankuta Nepal **79** C2
Dharmanagar India **66** A1
Dharmjaygarh India **79** C2
Dharwad India **77** B3
Dhule India **78** B2
Diablo, Picacho del *mt.* Mex.
128 A1
Diamantina *watercourse* Austr.
103 C2
Diamantina, Chapada *plat.* Brazil
135 E4
Diamantino Brazil **135** D4
Diapaga Burkina **90** C3
Dibā al Ḥiṣn U.A.E. **83** C2
Dibrugarh India **76** D2
Dickinson U.S.A. **120** C1
Dickson U.S.A. **124** C1
Dicle *r.* Turkey *see* Tigris
Die France **53** D3
Diefenbaker, Lake Can. **113** C2
Diéma Mali **90** B3
Diepholz Ger. **49** D1
Dieppe France **52** C2
Diffa Niger **91** D3
Digby Can. **115** D2
Digne-les-Bains France **53** D3

Digoin France **53** C2
Digos Phil. **68** B3
Digul *r.* Indon. **63** D3
Dijon France **53** D2
Dikhil Djibouti **93** C3
Dikili Turkey **59** C3
Dila Eth. **93** B4
Dili East Timor **63** C3
Dillenburg Ger. **49** D2
Dillon U.S.A. **118** D1
Dilolo Dem. Rep. Congo **94** C4
Dimapur India **66** A1
Dimashq Syria *see* Damascus
Dimitrovgrad Bulg. **58** C2
Dimitrovgrad Rus. Fed. **35** D3
Dinagat *i.* Phil. **68** B2
Dinan France **52** B2
Dinant Belgium **48** B2
Dinar Turkey **84** B2
Dīnār, Kūh-e *mt.* Iran **85** D2
Dindigul India **77** B3
Dingelstädt Ger. **49** E2
Dingle Ireland **45** A2
Dingle Bay Ireland **45** A2
Dingwall U.K. **44** B2
Dinkelsbühl Ger. **49** E3
Dionísio Cerqueira Brazil
138 B3
Diourbel Senegal **90** A3
Dipolog Phil. **68** B3
Dīr Pak. **78** B1
Direction, Cape Austr. **103** D1
Dirē Dawa Eth. **93** C4
Dirico Angola **96** B1
Dirk Hartog Island Austr. **102** A2
Dirranbandi Austr. **105** D1
Dirs Saudi Arabia **82** B3
Disappointment, Cape
S. Georgia **137** E6
Disappointment, Lake *salt flat*
Austr. **102** B2
Discovery Bay Austr. **104** C3
Dismal Swamp U.S.A. **123** E3
Diss U.K. **47** D3
Dittaino *r.* Italy **56** C3
Diu India **78** B2
Divinópolis Brazil **139** D2
Divo Côte d'Ivoire **90** B4
Dixon U.S.A. **122** C2
Diyarbakır Turkey **84** C2
Djado Niger **91** D2
Djado, Plateau du Niger **91** D2
Djambala Congo **94** B3
Djanet Alg. **91** C2
Djelfa Alg. **91** C1
Djéma C.A.R. **95** C2
Djenné Mali **90** B3
Djibo Burkina **90** B3
Djibouti *country* Africa **93** C3
Djibouti Djibouti **93** C3
Dmitriyevka Rus. Fed. **37** F3

Dmitriyev-L'govskiy Rus. Fed.
37 E3
Dmitrov Rus. Fed. **37** E2
Dnepr *r.* Rus. Fed. *see* Dnieper
Dnieper *r.* Rus. Fed. **37** D3
Dnieper *r.* Ukr. **39** D2
Dniester *r.* Ukr. **38** C2
Dnipro *r.* Ukr. *see* Dnieper
Dniprodzerzhyns'k Ukr. **39** D2
Dnipropetrovs'k Ukr. **39** D2
Dniprorudne Ukr. **39** D2
Dnister *r.* Ukr. *see* Dniester
Dno Rus. Fed. **36** C2
Doba Chad **91** D4
Dobele Latvia **36** B2
Döbeln Ger. **49** F2
Doberai, Jazirah *pen.* Indon.
63 C3
Dobo Indon. **63** C3
Doboj Bos.-Herz. **57** C2
Dobrich Bulg. **58** C2
Dobrinka Rus. Fed. **37** F3
Dobrush Belarus **37** D3
Dodecanese *is* Greece *see*
Dodekanisos
Dodekanisos *is* Greece *see*
Dodecanese
Dodge City U.S.A. **120** C3
Dodoma Tanz. **95** D3
Doetinchem Neth. **48** C2
Dogai Coring *salt l.* China **79** C1
Dōgo *i.* Japan **71** B3
Doğubeyazıt Turkey **85** C2
Doha Qatar **83** C2
Dokkum Neth. **48** B1
Dokshytsy Belarus **36** C3
Dokuchayevs'k Ukr. **39** E2
Dolak, Pulau *i.* Indon. **63** D3
Dole France **53** D2
Dolgellau U.K. **47** B3
Dolinsk Rus. Fed. **73** F1
Dolisie Congo *see* Loubomo
Dolomites *mts* Italy **56** B1
Dolo Odo Eth. **93** C4
Dolyna Ukr. **38** B2
Domažlice Czech Rep. **50** C3
Dombås Norway **41** B3
Dombóvár Hungary **51** D3
Dome Creek Can. **112** C2
Dominica *country* West Indies
131 D3
Dominican Republic *country*
West Indies **131** C3
Domodedovo Rus. Fed. **37** E2
Domokos Greece **59** B3
Dompu Indon. **65** C2
Don *r.* Rus. Fed. **37** E2
Don *r.* U.K. **44** C2
Donald Austr. **104** C3
Donau *r.* Austria/Ger. *see* Danube
Donauwörth Ger. **50** C3
Don Benito Spain **54** B2
Doncaster U.K. **46** C3
Dondo Angola **94** B3
Dondo Moz. **97** C1

ndra Head Sri Lanka **77** C4
negal Ireland **45** B1
negal Bay Ireland **45** B1
nets'k Ukr. **39** E2
nets'kyy Kryazh *hills*
lus. Fed./Ukr. **39** E2
ngara Austr. **102** A2
ngchuan China **75** A3
ngfang China **75** A4
ngfanghong China **70** B1
nggala Indon. **65** C2
nggang China **69** A2
ngguan China **75** B3
ng Hồi Vietnam **66** B2
ngou Congo **94** B2
ngsheng China *see* Ordos
ngtai China **74** C2
ngting Hu *l.* China **75** B3
ngying China **74** B2
nnellys Crossing N.Z. **106** B2
nostia - San Sebastián Spain
55 C1
oxo Nugaaleed *val.* Somalia

orchester U.K. **47** B4
ordabis Namibia **98** A1
ordogne *r.* France **52** B2
ordrecht Neth. **48** B2
oré Lake Can. **113** E2
oring *r.* S. Africa **98** A3
ornoch U.K. **44** B2
ornoch Firth *est.* U.K. **44** B2
orogobuzh Rus. Fed. **37** D3
orohoi Romania **38** C2
öröö Nuur *salt l.* Mongolia
72 C1
protea Sweden **40** D3
orre Island Austr. **102** A2
orrigo Austr. **105** E2
orsale Camerounaise *slope*
Cameroon/Nigeria **94** B2
ortmund Ger. **48** C2
os Bahías, Cabo *c.* Arg. **137** B5
osse *r.* Ger. **49** F1
osso Niger **90** C3
othan U.S.A. **125** C2
ouai France **52** C1
ouala Cameroon **94** A2
ouarnenez France **52** B2
oubtful Sound N.Z. **106** A4
ouentza Mali **90** B3
ouglas Isle of Man **46** A2
ouglas S. Africa **98** B2
ouglas *AK* U.S.A. **112** B3
ouglas *AZ* U.S.A. **126** C2
ouglas *GA* U.S.A. **125** D2
ouglas *WY* U.S.A. **120** B2
ourada, Serra *hills* Brazil
138 B2
ourados Brazil **138** B2
ourados, Serra dos *hills* Brazil
138 B2
ouro *r.* Port. **54** B1

Dover U.K. **47** D4
Dover U.S.A. **123** E3
Dover, Strait of France/U.K. **43** D3
Downpatrick U.K. **45** D1
Dowshi Afgh. **78** A1
Dōzen *is* Japan **71** B3
Dozois, Réservoir *resr* Can. **114** C2
Dracena Brazil **138** B2
Drachten Neth. **48** C1
Drăgăneşti-Olt Romania **38** B3
Drăgăşani Romania **38** B3
Drahichyn Belarus **36** C3
Drakensberg *mts*
Lesotho/S. Africa **99** C2
Drakensberg *mts* S. Africa **99** C2
Drake Passage S. Atlantic Ocean **107** L4
Drama Greece **59** B2
Drammen Norway **41** C4
Drau *r.* Austria **56** B1
Drava *r.* Europe **56** C1
Drepano, Akra *pt* Greece **59** B3
Dresden Ger. **49** F2
Dreux France **52** C2
Drina *r.* Bos.-Herz./S.M. **57** C2
Drniš Croatia **56** C2
Drobeta - Turnu Severin Romania **38** B3
Drochtersen Ger. **49** D1
Drogheda Ireland **45** C2
Drohobych Ukr. **38** B2
Drosh Pak. **78** B1
Drouin Austr. **105** D3
Drummond Island U.S.A. **122** D1
Drummondville Can. **115** C2
Druskininkai Lith. **36** B3
Druzhkivka Ukr. **39** E2
Dryden Can. **114** A2
Drysdale *r.* Austr. **102** B1
Dubā Saudi Arabia **82** A2
Dubai U.A.E. **83** C2
Dubawnt Lake Can. **113** E1
Dubayy U.A.E. *see* Dubai
Dubbagh, Jabal al *mt.*
Saudi Arabia **82** A2
Dubbo Austr. **105** D2
Dublin Ireland **45** C2
Dublin U.S.A. **125** D2
Dubno Ukr. **38** C1
Du Bois U.S.A. **123** E2
Dubrovnik Croatia **57** C2
Dubrovytsya Ukr. **38** C1
Dubrowna Belarus **37** D3
Dubuque U.S.A. **121** E2
Duck Bay Can. **113** E2
Đức Trong Vietnam **67** B2
Duderstadt Ger. **49** E2
Dudinka Rus. Fed. **86** H2
Dudley U.K. **47** B3
Duero *r.* Spain **54** B1
Duffreboy, Lac *l.* Can. **115** C1
Dufftown U.K. **44** C2

Dugi Rat Croatia **57** C2
Duisburg Ger. **48** C2
Dukathole S. Africa **99** C3
Dukhān Qatar **83** C2
Dulan China **72** C2
Dulce *r.* Arg. **136** B4
Dülmen Ger. **48** C2
Dulovo Bulg. **58** C2
Duluth U.S.A. **121** E1
Dumaguete Phil. **68** B3
Dumai Indon. **64** B1
Dumaran *i.* Phil. **68** B2
Dumas *AR* U.S.A. **124** B2
Dumas *TX* U.S.A. **127** D1
Dumbarton U.K. **44** B3
Dumfries U.K. **44** C3
Duna *r.* Hungary *see* Danube
Dunakeszi Hungary **51** D3
Dunărea *r.* Romania *see* Danube
Dunaújváros Hungary **51** D3
Dunayivtsi Ukr. **38** C2
Dunbar U.K. **44** C2
Dunbeath U.K. **44** C1
Duncan Can. **112** C3
Duncan U.S.A. **127** E2
Duncansby Head U.K. **44** C1
Dundalk Ireland **45** C1
Dundalk Bay Ireland **45** C2
Dundas Greenland **111** H1
Dundee S. Africa **99** D2
Dundee U.K. **44** C2
Dunedin N.Z. **106** B4
Dunfermline U.K. **44** C2
Dungannon U.K. **45** C1
Dungarvan Ireland **45** C2
Dungeness *hd* U.K. **47** D4
Dungiven U.K. **45** C1
Dungog Austr. **105** E2
Dungu Dem. Rep. Congo **95** C2
Dungun Malaysia **64** B1
Dunhua China **70** B1
Dunhuang China **72** C2
Dunkerque France *see* Dunkirk
Dunkirk France **52** C1
Dunkirk U.S.A. **123** E2
Dún Laoghaire Ireland **45** C2
Dunmurry U.K. **45** C1
Dunnet Head U.K. **44** C1
Duns U.K. **44** C3
Dupnitsa Bulg. **58** B2
Dupree U.S.A. **120** C1
Durack *r.* Austr. **102** B1
Durango Mex. **128** B2
Durango Spain **54** C1
Durango U.S.A. **120** B3
Durant U.S.A. **127** E2
Durazno Uru. **137** C4
Durban S. Africa **99** D2
Durban-Corbières France **52** C3
Durbanville S. Africa **98** A3
Düren Ger. **48** C2
Durg India **79** C2
Durham U.K. **46** C2
Durham U.S.A. **125** E1

Duri Indon. **64** B1
Durmitor mt. S.M. **58** A2
Durness U.K. **44** B2
Durrës Albania **59** A2
Dursey Island Ireland **45** A3
Dursunbey Turkey **59** C3
D'Urville, Tanjung pt Indon. **63** D3
D'Urville Island N.Z. **106** B3
Dushan China **75** A3
Dushanbe Tajik. **81** D3
Düsseldorf Ger. **48** C2
Duyun China **75** A3
Dvorichna Ukr. **39** E2
Dwarka India **78** A2
Dworshak Reservoir U.S.A. **118** C1
Dyat'kovo Rus. Fed. **37** D3
Dyce U.K. **44** C2
Dyer, Cape Can. **111** H2
Dyersburg U.S.A. **124** C1
Dyfrdwy r. *England/Wales* U.K. *see* **Dee**
Dyje r. *Austria/Czech Rep.* **51** D3
Dylewska Góra h. Pol. **51** D2
Dymytrov Ukr. **39** E2
Dzamin Üüd Mongolia **73** D2
Dzaoudzi Mayotte **97** D1
Dzhanga Turkm. **85** D1
Dzhangala Kazakh. **80** C2
Dzhankoy Ukr. **39** D2
Dzhizak Uzbek. *see* **Jizzax**
Dzhuhga Rus. Fed. **39** E3
Dzhugdzhur, Khrebet mts Rus. Fed. **87** L3
Dzhungarskiy Alatau, Khrebet mts *China/Kazakh.* **81** E2
Dzhusaly Kazakh. **80** C2
Działdowo Pol. **51** E2
Dzuunmod Mongolia **72** D2
Dzyarzhynsk Belarus **36** C3

E

Eagle r. Can. **115** E1
Eagle Cap mt. U.S.A. **118** C1
Eagle Lake Can. **114** A1
Eagle Lake U.S.A. **118** B2
Eagle Pass U.S.A. **127** D3
Eagle Plain Can. **110** C2
Ear Falls Can. **114** A1
East Antarctica reg. Antarctica **107** F2
Eastbourne U.K. **47** D4
East China Sea N. Pacific Ocean **73** E2
East End Can. **118** C1
Eastern Cape prov. S. Africa **99** C3

East Falkland i. Falkland Is **137** C6
East Frisian Islands Ger. **48** C1
East Kilbride U.K. **44** B3
Eastleigh U.K. **47** C4
East Liverpool U.S.A. **123** D2
East London S. Africa **99** C3
Eastmain Can. **114** C1
Eastmain r. Can. **114** C1
Eastman U.S.A. **125** D2
East Sea N. Pacific Ocean *see* **Japan, Sea of**
East St Louis U.S.A. **122** B3
East Timor country Asia **61**
Eau Claire U.S.A. **122** B2
Eau Claire, Lac à l' l. Can. **114** C1
Eauripik atoll Micronesia **63** D2
Ebano Mex. **129** C2
Ebbw Vale U.K. **47** B4
Eberswalde-Finow Ger. **49** F1
Eboli Italy **56** C2
Ebolowa Cameroon **94** B2
Ebro r. Spain **55** C1
Ech Chélif Alg. **90** C1
Echeverría, Pico mt. Mex. **128** A2
Echoing r. Can. **113** F2
Echternach Lux. **48** C3
Echuca Austr. **104** C3
Écija Spain **54** B2
Eckernförde Ger. **50** B2
Ecuador country S. America **134** B3
Ed Eritrea **94** C1
Ed Damazin Sudan **93** B3
Ed Damer Sudan **92** B3
Ed Debba Sudan **92** B3
Ed Dueim Sudan **92** B3
Eddystone Point Austr. **103** D4
Ede Neth. **48** B1
Edea Cameroon **94** B2
Edéia Brazil **138** C1
Eden Austr. **105** D3
Eden r. U.K. **46** B2
Edenburg S. Africa **99** C2
Edenderry Ireland **45** C2
Edenhope Austr. **104** C3
Edessa Greece **59** B2
Edgeøya i. Svalbard **86** D1
Edinburg U.S.A. **127** E3
Edinburgh U.K. **44** C3
Edirne Turkey **58** C2
Edmonton Can. **112** D2
Edmundston Can. **123** G1
Edremit Turkey **59** C3
Edson Can. **112** D2
Edward's Creek Austr. **104** A1
Edwards Plateau U.S.A. **127** D2
Effingham U.S.A. **122** C3
Egan Range mts U.S.A. **119** D3

Eger Hungary **51** E3
Egersund Norway **41** B4
Egilsstaðir Iceland **40** [inset]
Eğirdir Turkey **84** B2
Eğirdir Gölü l. Turkey **84** B2
Égletons France **52** C2
Egvekinot Rus. Fed. **87** O2
Egypt country Africa **92** A2
Ehen Hudag China **74** A2
Eibergen Neth. **48** C1
Eifel hills Ger. **48** C2
Eigg i. U.K. **44** A2
Eight Degree Channel India/Maldives **77** B4
Eighty Mile Beach Austr. **102** B1
Eilat Israel **84** B3
Eilenburg Ger. **49** F2
Einbeck Ger. **49** D2
Eindhoven Neth. **48** B2
Eirunepé Brazil **134** C3
Eiseb watercourse Namibia **96** B1
Eisenach Ger. **49** E2
Eisenhüttenstadt Ger. **50** C2
Eisenstadt Austria **51** D3
Eisleben Lutherstadt Ger. **49** E2
Eivissa Spain **55** D2
Eivissa i. Spain *see* **Ibiza**
Ejea de los Caballeros Spain **55** C1
Ejeda Madag. **97** [inset] D2
Ekenäs Fin. **41** E4
Ekibastuz Kazakh. **81** E1
Ekostrovskaya Imandra, Ozero Rus. Fed. **40** G2
Eksjö Sweden **41** C4
Ekwan r. Can. **114** B1
Ela Myanmar **66** A2
Elassona Greece **59** B3
Elazığ Turkey **84** B2
Elba, Isola d' i. Italy **56** B2
El Bayadh Alg. **90** C1
Elbasan Albania **59** B2
El Bequf France **52** C2
Elbistan Turkey **84** B2
Elbląg Pol. **51** D2
El'brus mt. Rus. Fed. **35** D4
Elburz Mountains Iran **85** C2
El Callao Venez. **134** C2
El Campo U.S.A. **127** E3
El Centro U.S.A. **119** C4
El Cerro Bol. **136** B2
Elche-Elx Spain **55** C2
Elda Spain **55** C2
Eldorado Arg. **138** B3
El Dorado AR U.S.A. **124** B2
El Dorado KS U.S.A. **121** D3
El Eglab plat. Alg. **90** B2
Elgin U.K. **44** C2
Elgin U.S.A. **118** C1
El Eulma Alg. **55** E2
Eleuthera i. Bahamas **131** C2

Fasher Sudan **93** A3
Fuerte Mex. **128** B2
Geneina Sudan **93** A3
gin U.K. **44** C2
gin U.S.A. **123** F2
Goléa Alg. **90** C1
Golfo de Santa Clara Mex.
128 A1
gon, Mount Uganda **95** D2
Hammâmi *reg.* Maur. **90** A2
Higo Mex. **129** C2
Hom Alg. **90** C2
Horn U.S.A. **110** B2
hista Rus. Fed. **35** D4
lizabeth U.S.A. **123** F2
lizabeth City U.S.A. **125** E1
lizabethtown U.S.A. **122** C3
l Jadida Morocco **90** B1
k Pol. **51** E2
k City U.S.A. **127** E1
khovo Bulg. **58** C2
ko Can. **112** D3
ko U.S.A. **118** C2
k Point Can. **110** B2
llon U.K. **44** C2
llsworth U.S.A. **123** G2
llsworth Mountains Antarctica
107 K2
imalı Turkey **59** C3
l Milia Alg. **55** F2
lmira U.S.A. **123** E2
amshorn Ger. **49** D1
n Muglad Sudan **93** A3
N Obeid Sudan **93** A3
l Oro Mex. **128** D2
l Oued Alg. **91** C1
l Paso U.S.A. **126** C2
l Porvenir Mex. **126** D2
l Prat de Llobregat Spain
55 D1
l Progreso Hond. **129** D3
l Reno U.S.A. **127** E1
Isa Can. **112** B1
l Salado Mex. **129** B2
l Salto Mex. **128** B2
l Salvador *country*
Central America **130** B3
l Sauz Mex. **128** C1
l Socorro Mex. **128** A1
lsterwerda Ger. **49** F2
lva Estonia **36** C2
lvas Port. **54** B2
lverum Norway **41** C3
l Wak Kenya **95** E2
ly U.K. **47** D3
ly MN U.S.A. **121** E1

Ely NV U.S.A. **119** D3
Emämrüd Iran **85** D2
Eman *r.* Sweden **41** D4
Emba Kazakh. **80** C2
Emba *r.* Kazakh. **80** C2
Embalenhle S. Africa **99** C2
Emborcação, Represa de *resr*
Brazil **138** C1
Embu Kenya **95** D3
Emden Ger. **48** C1
Emerald Austr. **103** D2
Emet Turkey **59** C3
eMijindini S. Africa **99** D2
Emi Koussi *mt.* Chad **91** D3
Emine, Nos *pt* Bulg. **58** C2
Emirdağ Turkey **59** C3
Emmaste Estonia **36** B2
Emmeloord Neth. **48** B1
Emmen Neth. **48** C1
Emory Peak U.S.A. **127** D3
Empalme Mex. **128** A2
Empangeni S. Africa **99** D2
Empoli Italy **56** B2
Emporia *KS* U.S.A. **123** D3
Emporia *VA* U.S.A. **123** E3
Emzinoni S. Africa **99** C2
Encarnación Mex. **128** B2
Encarnación Para. **136** C3
Encruzilhada Brazil **139** D1
Ende Indon. **65** D2
Endicott Mountains U.S.A.
110 B2
Enerhodar Ukr. **39** D2
Engel's Rus. Fed. **35** D3
Enggano *i.* Indon. **64** B2
England *admin. div.* U.K. **46** C3
English Channel France/U.K.
47 C5
Enid U.S.A. **127** E1
Enkhuizen Neth. **48** B1
Enköping Sweden **41** D4
Enna Italy **56** B3
Ennadai Lake Can. **113** E1
En Nahud Sudan **93** A3
Ennedi, Massif *mts* Chad **91** E3
Enngonia Austr. **105** D1
Ennis Ireland **45** B2
Ennis U.S.A. **127** E2
Enniscorthy Ireland **45** C2
Enniskillen U.K. **45** C1
Enns *r.* Austria **50** C3
Enontekiö Fin. **40** E2
Ensay Austr. **105** D3
Enschede Neth. **48** C1
Ensenada Mex. **128** A1
Enshi China **75** A2
Enterprise Can. **112** D1
Enterprise *AL* U.S.A. **125** C2
Enterprise *OR* U.S.A. **118** C1
Entroncamento Port. **54** B2
Enugu Nigeria **91** C4
Épernay France **48** A3
Épinal France **53** D2
Epsom U.K. **47** C4

Equatorial Guinea *country* Africa
94 A2
Erbendorf Ger. **49** F3
Erbeskopf *h.* Ger. **48** C3
Erciş Turkey **59** C2
Erdao Jiang *r.* China **69** B1
Erdek Turkey **59** C2
Erdemli Turkey **84** B2
Erechim Brazil **136** C3
Ereğli *Konya* Turkey **84** B2
Ereğli *Zonguldak* Turkey **84** B1
Erenhot China **74** B1
Erevan Armenia *see* Yerevan
Erfurt Ger. **49** E2
Ergani Turkey **84** B2
'Erg Chech *des.* Alg./Mali **90** B2
Ergene *r.* Turkey **59** C2
Erie *r.* U.S.A. **122** D2
Erie, Lake Can./U.S.A. **122** D2
Erimo-misaki *c.* Japan **70** D2
Eritrea *country* Africa **92** B3
Erkner Ger. **49** F1
Erlangen Ger. **49** E3
Erldunda Austr. **102** C2
Ermelo S. Africa **99** C2
Ermoupoli Greece **59** B3
Ernakulam India **77** B4
Erode India **77** B3
Er Rachidia Morocco **90** B1
Er Rahad Sudan **93** B3
Errigal *h.* Ireland **45** B1
Erris Head Ireland **45** A1
Érsekë Albania **59** B2
Ertil' Rus. Fed. **37** F3
Erwitte Ger. **49** D2
Erzgebirge *mts* Czech Rep./Ger.
50 C2
Erzincan Turkey **84** B2
Erzurum Turkey **35** D5
Esbjerg Denmark **41** B4
Escalante U.S.A. **119** D3
Escanaba U.S.A. **122** C1
Escárcega Mex. **129** C3
Escatrón Spain **55** C1
Escaut *r.* Belgium **48** A2
Eschede Ger. **49** E1
Esch-sur-Alzette Lux. **48** B3
Eschwege Ger. **49** E2
Eschweiler Ger. **48** C2
Escondido U.S.A. **119** C4
Escuinapa Mex. **128** B2
Eşen Turkey **59** C3
Eşfahān Iran **85** D2
Esikhawini S. Africa **99** D2
Esk *r.* U.K. **46** B2
Esker Can. **115** D1
Eskifjörður Iceland **40** [inset]
Eskilstuna Sweden **41** D4
Eskişehir Turkey **84** B2
Eslāmābād-e Gharb Iran **85** C2
Esler Dağı *mt.* Turkey **59** C3
Eşme Turkey **59** C3
Esmeraldas Ecuador **134** B2
Espakeh Iran **83** D2

Espalion France **52** C3
Espanola Can. **114** B2
Espanola U.S.A. **126** C1
Esperance Austr. **102** B3
Esperanza Mex. **128** C2
Espichel, Cabo c. Port. **54** B2
Espinhaço, Serra do mts Brazil **139** D1
Espíritu Santo i. Vanuatu **142** D6
Espíritu Santo, Isla i. Mex. **128** A2
Espoo Fin. **41** E3
Esquel Arg. **137** A5
Essaouira Morocco **90** B1
Es Semara Western Sahara **90** A2
Essen Ger. **48** C2
Essequibo r. Guyana **134** D2
Esso Rus. Fed. **87** M3
Estados, Isla de los i. Arg. **137** C6
Estância Brazil **135** F4
Estcourt S. Africa **99** C2
Estella Spain **55** C1
Estepona Spain **54** B2
Esterhazy Can. **113** E2
Esteros Para. **136** B3
Estevan Can. **120** C1
Estherville U.S.A. **121** E2
Eston Can. **113** E2
Estonia country Europe **36** C2
Estrela, Serra da mts Port. **54** B1
Estremoz Port. **54** B2
Etadunna Austr. **104** B1
Étain France **48** B3
Étampes France **52** C2
Étaples France **52** C1
Etawah India **79** B2
eThandakukhanya S. Africa **99** D2
Ethiopia country Africa **93** B3
Etna, Monte vol. Italy **56** C3
Etne Norway **42** E2
Etolin Island U.S.A. **112** D2
Etosha Pan salt pan Namibia **96** A1
Ettelbruck Lux. **48** C3
Etten-Leur Neth. **48** B2
Euabalong Austr. **105** D2
Euboea i. Greece see **Evvoia**
Eucla Austr. **102** B3
Eufaula U.S.A. **125** C2
Eufaula Lake resr U.S.A. **127** E1
Eugene U.S.A. **118** B2
Eugenia, Punta pt Mex. **128** A2
Eulo Austr. **105** D1
Eunice U.S.A. **124** B2
Euphrates r. Asia **84** C2
Eureka CA U.S.A. **118** B2
Eureka MT U.S.A. **118** C1
Eureka NV U.S.A. **119** C3
Euriowie Austr. **104** C2
Euroa Austr. **105** D3

Europa Point Gibraltar **54** B2
Eutsuk Lake Can. **112** C2
Evans, Lac l. Can. **114** C1
Evans Head Austr. **105** E1
Evans Strait Can. **113** G1
Evanston U.S.A. **120** A2
Evansville U.S.A. **122** C3
Evaton S. Africa **99** C2
Everard, Lake salt flat Austr. **104** B2
Everest, Mount China/Nepal **79** C2
Everett U.S.A. **118** B1
Evergem Belgium **48** A2
Everglades swamp U.S.A. **125** D3
Evinayong Equat. Guinea **94** B2
Evje Norway **41** B4
Évora Port. **54** B2
Évreux France **52** C2
Evros r. Greece/Turkey **59** C2
Evrotas r. Greece **59** B3
Evrychou Cyprus **59** B3
Evvoia i. Greece **59** B3
Exaltación Bol. **136** B2
Exe r. U.K. **47** B4
Exeter U.K. **47** B4
Exmoor hills U.K. **47** B4
Exmouth U.K. **47** B4
Exmouth Gulf Austr. **102** A2
Exuma Cays is Bahamas **131** C2
Eya r. Rus. Fed. **39** E2
Eyl Somalia **93** C4
Eyre, Lake salt flat S.A. Austr. **104** B1
Eyre, Lake salt flat S.A. Austr. **104** B1
Eyre Peninsula Austr. **104** B2
Eysturoy i. Faroe Is **42** B1
Ezakheni S. Africa **99** D2
Ezhou China **75** B2
Ezhva Rus. Fed. **34** E2
Ezine Turkey **59** C3

F

Fabens U.S.A. **126** C2
Fåborg Denmark **50** C1
Fabriano Italy **56** B2
Fachi Niger **91** D3
Fada-N'Gourma Burkina **90** C3
Faenza Italy **56** B2
Fafanlap Indon. **63** C3
Făgăraş Romania **38** B2
Fagatogo American Samoa **101**
Fagernes Norway **41** B3
Fagersta Sweden **41** D4
Fagubline, Lac l. Mali **90** B3
Fagurhólsmýri Iceland **40** [inset]
Fairbanks U.S.A. **110** C2
Fairfield U.S.A. **119** B3
Fair Isle i. U.K. **44** [inset]

Fairmont MN U.S.A. **121** E2
Fairmont WV U.S.A. **123** D3
Fairweather, Mount Can./U.S.A. **112** B2
Fais i. Micronesia **63** D2
Faisalabad Pak. **78** B1
Faith U.S.A. **120** C1
Faizabad India **79** C2
Faku China **69** A1
Falcon Lake Mex./U.S.A. **127** E3
Falfurrias U.S.A. **127** E3
Falher Can. **112** D2
Falkenberg Ger. **49** F2
Falkenberg Sweden **41** C4
Falkensee Ger. **49** F1
Falkirk U.K. **44** C3
Falkland Islands terr. S. Atlantic Ocean **137** C6
Falköping Sweden **41** C4
Fallon U.S.A. **119** C3
Fall River U.S.A. **123** F2
Falls City U.S.A. **121** D2
Falmouth U.K. **47** A4
False Bay S. Africa **98** A3
Falster i. Denmark **41** C5
Fălticeni Romania **38** C2
Falun Sweden **41** D3
Fameck France **48** C3
Fangzheng China **73** E1
Fano Italy **56** B2
Fan Si Pan mt. Vietnam **66** B1
Faradje Dem. Rep. Congo **95** C2
Farafangana Madag. **97** [inset] D3
Farāfirah, Wāḩāt al oasis Egypt **92** A2
Farāh Afgh. **78** A1
Farah Rūd watercourse Afgh. **78** A1
Faranah Guinea **90** A3
Farasān, Jazāʼir is Saudi Arabia **82** B3
Farewell, Cape Greenland **111** J2
Farewell, Cape N.Z. **106** B3
Fargo U.S.A. **121** D1
Farg'ona Uzbek. **81** E2
Faribault U.S.A. **121** E2
Faribault, Lac l. Can. **115** C1
Farmington NM U.S.A. **126** C1
Faro Port. **54** B2
Fårö i. Sweden **42** D2
Faroe Islands terr. N. Atlantic Ocean **42** B1
Farwell U.S.A. **127** D2
Fāryāb Iran **83** C2
Fasā Iran **83** D3
Fasano Italy **57** C2
Fastiv Ukr. **38** C1
Fatehgarh India **79** B2
Fatehpur India **79** C2
Fauske Norway **40** D2
Faxaflói b. Iceland **40** [inset]
Faya Chad **91** D3
Fayetteville AR U.S.A. **124** B1

yetteville NC U.S.A. **125** E1
zilka India **78** B1
érik Maur. **90** A2
ar, Cape U.S.A. **125** E2
atherton N.Z. **106** C3
camp France **52** C2
nmarri. Ger. **50** C2
lia, Lagoa lag. Brazil **139** D2
ajó Brazil **134** B3
nding N.Z. **106** C3
ra de Santana Brazil **135** F4
anitx Spain **55** D2
dberg Ger. **49** F1
iipe C. Puerto Mex. **129** D3
lixlândia Brazil **139** D1
xstowe U.K. **47** D4
isberg Ger. **49** D2
munden r. Norway **41** C3
nie C. de Alg. **56** A3
gus Falls U.S.A. **121** D1
mo Italy **56** B2
rmont Can. **115** D1
rnoy Ireland **45** B2
mandina Beach U.S.A.
25 D2
nandópolis Brazil **138** B3
rnie Can. **112** D3
ro, Capo c. Italy **56** A2
rol Spain **54** B1
wert Neth. **48** B1
la Morocco **90** B1
shi Dem. Rep. Congo **94** B3
stus U.S.A. **121** C3
thiye Turkey **59** C3
dar i. U.K. **44** [inset]
ucht Ger. **49** E3
villes, Rivière aux r. Can.
14 C1
uyzábád Afgh. **78** B1
z Morocco see Fes
naranstowd Madag. **97** [inset]

r. Albania **59** A2
e Ness r. U.K. **44** C2
eac France **52** C3
jueira da Foz Port. **54** B1
queres Spain **55** D1
uig Morocco **90** B1
country S. Pacific Ocean **100**
Eth. **95** E2
delfia Para. **136** B3
hner Ice Shelf Antarctica
07 A2
y U.K. **46** C2
dhorn r. U.K. **44** C2
dlay U.S.A. **122** D2

Fingal Austr. **103** D4
Finger Lakes U.S.A. **123** E2
Finisterre, Cape Spain **54** B1
Finland country Europe **40** F3
Finland, Gulf of Europe **41** E4
Finlay r. Can. **112** C2
Finley Austr. **105** D3
Finne ridge Ger. **49** E2
Finnmarksvidda reg. Norway
40 E2
Finspång Sweden **41** D4
Finsterwalde Ger. **49** F2
Fionnphort U.K. **44** A2
Firenze Italy see Florence
Firminy France **53** C2
Firozabad India **79** B2
Firozpur India **78** B1
Fīrūzābād Iran **85** D3
Fish watercourse Namibia **98** A2
Fish r. S. Africa **98** B3
Fisher Strait Can. **113** G1
Fishguard U.K. **47** A4
Fisterra, Cabo c. Spain see
Finisterre, Cape
Fitchburg U.S.A. **123** F2
Fitzgerald Can. **112** D2
Fitzroy Crossing Austr. **102** B1
Fizi Dem. Rep. Congo **95** C2
Fjällsjöälven r. Sweden **40** D3
Flagstaff S. Africa **99** C3
Flagstaff U.S.A. **126** B1
Flaherty Island Can. **114** C1
Flamborough Head U.K. **46** C2
Flåming hills Ger. **49** F1
Flaming Gorge Reservoir U.S.A.
120 B2
Flathead r. U.S.A. **118** D1
Flathead Lake U.S.A. **118** D1
Flattery, Cape Austr. **103** D1
Flattery, Cape U.S.A. **118** B1
Fleetwood U.K. **46** B3
Flekkefjord Norway **41** B4
Flensburg Ger. **50** B1
Flers France **52** B2
Flinders r. Austr. **103** D1
Flinders Bay Austr. **102** A3
Flinders Island Austr. **103** D3
Flinders Ranges mts Austr.
104 B2
Flin Flon Can. **113** E2
Flint U.S.A. **122** D2
Florac France **53** C1
Florence Italy **56** B2
Florence AL U.S.A. **124** C2
Florence AZ U.S.A. **126** B2
Florence OR U.S.A. **118** B2
Florence SC U.S.A. **125** E2
Florencia Col. **134** B2
Flores Guat. **130** B3
Flores i. Indon. **65** D2
Flores, Laut sea Indon. **65** C2
Flores Sea Indon. see Flores, Laut
Floresta Brazil **135** F3
Floriano Brazil **135** E3

Florianópolis Brazil **138** C3
Florida Uru. **137** C4
Florida state U.S.A. **125** D2
Florida, Straits of
Bahamas/U.S.A. **130** B2
Florida Keys is U.S.A. **125** D4
Florina Greece **59** B2
Florø Norway **41** B3
Foča Bos.-Herz. **57** C2
Focșani Romania **38** C2
Foggia Italy **56** C2
Fogo Island Can. **115** E2
Foix France **52** C3
Fokino Rus. Fed. **37** D3
Foleyet Can. **114** B2
Foligno Italy **56** B2
Folkestone U.K. **47** D4
Folkston U.S.A. **125** D2
Follonica Italy **56** B2
Fond-du-Lac Can. **110** E3
Fond du Lac r. Can. **113** E2
Fond du Lac U.S.A. **122** C2
Fondevila Spain **54** B1
Fondi Italy **56** B2
Fonseca, Golfo de b.
Central America **130** B3
Fonte Boa Brazil **134** C3
Fontenay-le-Comte France
52 B2
Fontur pt Iceland **40** [inset]
Forbes Austr. **105** D2
Forchheim Ger. **49** E3
Forde Norway **41** B3
Fords Bridge Austr. **105** D1
Fordyce U.S.A. **124** B2
Forest U.S.A. **124** C2
Forest Hill Austr. **105** D3
Forestville Can. **115** D2
Forfar U.K. **44** C2
Forks U.S.A. **118** B1
Forlì Italy **56** B2
Formentera i. Spain **55** D2
Formentor, Cap de c. Spain
55 D2
Formiga Brazil **139** C2
Formosa Arg. **136** C3
Formosa Brazil **138** C1
Forrest Austr. **102** B3
Forrest City U.S.A. **124** B1
Forssa Fin. **41** E3
Forster Austr. **105** E2
Forsyth U.S.A. **118** E1
Fort Abbas Pak. **78** B2
Fort Albany Can. **114** B1
Fortaleza Brazil **135** F3
Fort Augustus U.K. **44** B2
Fort Benton U.S.A. **118** D1
Fort Bragg U.S.A. **119** B3
Fort Chimo Can. see Kuujjuaq
Fort Chipewyan Can. **113** D2
Fort Collins U.S.A. **120** B2
Fort-de-France Martinique
131 D3
Fort Dodge U.S.A. **121** E2

Fort Frances Can. **114** A2
Fort George Can. *see* Chisasibi
Fort Good Hope Can. **110** D2
Forth *r.* U.K. **44** C2
Forth, Firth of *est.* U.K. **44** C2
Fortín Madrejón Para. **136** C3
Fort Lauderdale U.S.A. **125** D3
Fort Liard Can. **112** C1
Fort Mackay Can. **113** D2
Fort McMurray Can. **113** D2
Fort McPherson Can. **110** D2
Fort Morgan U.S.A. **120** C2
Fort Myers U.S.A. **125** D3
Fort Nelson Can. **112** C2
Fort Nelson *r.* Can. **112** C2
Fort Payne U.S.A. **125** C2
Fort Peck U.S.A. **120** B1
Fort Peck Reservoir U.S.A. **120** B1
Fort Pierce U.S.A. **125** D3
Fort Providence Can. **112** D1
Fort Qu'Appelle Can. **113** E2
Fort Resolution Can. **112** D1
Fort Rupert Can. *see* Waskaganish
Fort Saskatchewan Can. **112** D2
Fort Scott U.S.A. **121** E3
Fort Severn Can. **114** B1
Fort-Shevchenko Kazakh. **80** C2
Fort Simpson Can. **112** C1
Fort Smith Can. **113** D1
Fort Smith U.S.A. **124** B1
Fort St James Can. **112** E2
Fort St John Can. **112** C2
Fort Stockton U.S.A. **127** D2
Fort Sumner U.S.A. **126** D2
Fort Vermilion Can. **112** D2
Fort Walton Beach U.S.A. **124** C2
Fort Wayne U.S.A. **122** D2
Fort William U.K. **44** B2
Fort Worth U.S.A. **127** E2
Fort Yukon U.S.A. **110** D2
Foshan China **75** C3
Fosna *pen.* Norway **40** C3
Foss Iceland **40** [inset]
Fossá Iceland **40** [inset]
Fossano Italy **56** A2
Foster Austr. **105** D3
Fougères France **52** B2
Foula *i.* U.K. **44** [inset]
Fourmi *i.* Greece **59** C3
Fouta Djallon *reg.* Guinea **90** A3
Foveaux Strait N.Z. **106** A4
Fowler U.S.A. **120** C3
Fowlers Bay Austr. **102** C3
Fox Creek Can. **112** D2
Foxe Basin *g.* Can. **111** G2
Foxe Channel Can. **111** G2
Fox Glacier N.Z. **106** B3
Fox Mountain Can. **112** B1
Foxton N.Z. **106** C3
Foyle, Lough *b.* Ireland/U.K. **45** C1

Foz de Areia, Represa de *resr* Brazil **138** B3
Foz do Iguaçu Brazil **138** B3
Foz do Iguaçu Brazil **138** B3
Fraga Spain **55** F1
Franca Brazil **138** C2
France *country* Europe **52** C2
Franceville Gabon **94** B3
Francis Case, Lake U.S.A. **121** D2
Francisco Sá Brazil **139** D1
Francistown Botswana **96** B2
François Lake Can. **112** C2
Frankenberg (Eder) Ger. **49** D2
Frankenhöhe *hills* Ger. **49** E3
Frankenwald *mts* Ger. **49** E2
Frankfort U.S.A. **122** D3
Frankfurt am Main Ger. **49** D2
Frankfurt an der Oder Ger. **50** C2
Fränkische Alb *hills* Ger. **50** C3
Fränkische Schweiz *reg.* Ger. **49** E3
Franklin D. Roosevelt Lake *resr* U.S.A. **118** C1
Franklin Mountains Can. **112** C1
Frantsa-Iosifa, Zemlya *is* Rus. Fed. **86** F1
Franz Josef Glacier N.Z. **106** B3
Frasca, Capo della *c.* Italy **56** A3
Frascati Italy **53** E3
Fraser *r.* B.C. Can. **112** C3
Fraser *r.* Nfld. and Lab. Can. **115** D1
Fraserburg S. Africa **98** B3
Fraserburgh U.K. **44** C2
Fraserdale Can. **114** B2
Fraser Island Austr. **103** E2
Fray Bentos Uru. **137** C4
Fredericia Denmark **41** B4
Frederick U.S.A. **127** E2
Fredericksburg *VA* U.S.A. **123** E3
Frederick Sound *sea chan.* U.S.A. **112** B2
Fredericton Can. **111** H3
Frederikshavn Denmark **41** C4
Frederikstad Norway **41** C4
Freeport *IL* U.S.A. **122** C2
Freeport *TX* U.S.A. **127** E3
Freeport City Bahamas **130** C2
Free State *prov.* S. Africa **99** C2
Freetown Sierra Leone **90** A4
Freiburg U.S.A. **49** F2
Freiburg im Breisgau Ger. **50** B3
Freising Ger. **49** E3
Freistadt Austria **50** C3
Freital Ger. **49** F2
Fréjus France **53** D3
Fremantle Austr. **102** A3
Fremont *NE* U.S.A. **121** D2

Fremont *OH* U.S.A. **122** D2
French Guiana *terr.* S. America **135** D2
Frenchman *r.* U.S.A. **118** E1
French Polynesia *terr.* S. Pacific Ocean **101**
Frenda Alg. **55** D2
Fresnillo Mex. **128** B2
Fresno U.S.A. **119** C3
Freu, Cap des *c.* Spain **55** D2
Freyming-Merlebach France **53** D2
Frías Arg. **136** B3
Friedland Ger. **49** F1
Friedrichshafen Ger. **50** B3
Friesack Ger. **49** F1
Friesoythe Ger. **48** C1
Frobisher Bay Can. *see* Iqaluit
Frolovo Rus. Fed. **35** D4
Frome, Lake *salt flat* Austr. **104** B2
Frome Downs Austr. **104** B2
Frontera Mex. **129** C3
Fronteras Mex. **128** B1
Frosinone Italy **56** B2
Freya *i.* Norway **40** B3
Frýdek-Místek Czech Rep. **51** D3
Fu'an China **75** B3
Fuding Spain **54** C1
Fuengirola Spain **54** C2
Fuerte Olimpo Para. **136** C3
Fuerteventura *i.* Canary Is **90** A1
Fuga *i.* Phil. **68** B2
Fujairah U.A.E. **83** C2
Fuji Japan **71** C3
Fujian *prov.* China **75** B3
Fuji-san *vol.* Japan **71** C3
Fukui Japan **71** C3
Fukuoka Japan **71** B4
Fukushima Japan **71** D3
Fulda Ger. **49** D2
Fulda *r.* Ger. **49** D2
Fuling China **75** A3
Fulton U.S.A. **121** E3
Fumay France **53** C2
Funchal Madeira **90** A1
Fundy, Bay of *g.* Can. **115** D2
Funhalouro Moz. **99** D1
Funing *Yunnan* China **75** A3
Funtua Nigeria **91** C3
Fürgun, Küh-e *mt.* Iran **83** C2
Furmanov Rus. Fed. **37** F2
Furnas, Represa *resr* Brazil **139** C2
Furneaux Group *is* Austr. **103** D3
Fürstenwalde Ger. **49** G1
Fürth Ger. **49** E3
Furth im Wald Ger. **49** F3
Furukawa Japan **70** D3
Fushun China **74** C1
Fusong China **69** B1
Fuwayriṭ Qatar **83** C2
Fuxin China **74** C1
Fuyang China **74** B2
Fuyu China **73** E1
Fuyun China **72** A1

zhou *Fujian* China **75** B3
zhou *Jiangxi* China **75** B3
î *i.* Denmark **41** C4

alkacyo Somalia **93** C4
bela Angola **96** A1
bès Tunisia **91** D1
bès, Golfe de *g.* Tunisia **91** D1
gaba, Wadi *watercourse*
udan **82** A2
oon *country* Africa **94** B3
orone Botswana **99** C1
rovo Bulg. **58** C2
rovo Botswana **99** C1
dag India **77** B3
debusch Ger. **49** E1
dsden U.S.A. **125** C2
 gaba, Wadi Tunisia **38** C3
eta Italy **56** B2
ferut *i.* Micronesia **106** E6
ffney U.S.A. **125** D1
fsa Tunisia **91** C1
frane, Lac Fed. **37** E2
gnoa Côte d'Ivoire **90** B4
gnon Can. **115** D1
gra Georgia **85** C1
iab *watercourse* Namibia **98** A2
illac France **52** C3
inesville *FL* U.S.A. **125** D3
inesville *GA* U.S.A. **125** D2
inesville *TX* U.S.A. **127** C2
insborough U.K. **46** C3
irdner, Lake *salt flat* Austr.
104 B2
irloch U.K. **44** B2
itana *r.* Kenya **95** E3
itapagos Islands Ecuador **132**
lashiels U.K. **44** C3
iati Romania **38** C2
idhapiggen *mt.* Norway **41** B3
ilena Bay Can. **112** D2
ilesburg U.S.A. **122** B2
ileshewe S. Africa **98** B2
ilich Rus. Fed. **37** F2
ilichskaya Vozvyshennost' *hills*
us. Fed. **37** F2
ilicia *aut. comm.* Spain **54** B1
ililee, Sea of *l.* Israel **80** B3
ille Sri Lanka **77** C4
illinas, Punta *pt* Col. **134** B1
illipoli Italy **57** D2
illipoli Turkey **59** C2
illivare Sweden **40** E2
illup U.S.A. **126** C1
iltat Zemmour Western Sahara
90 A2
iltymore *h.* Ireland **45** B3
ilveston U.S.A. **127** F3
ilveston Bay U.S.A. **127** F3
ilway Ireland **45** B2
ilway Bay Ireland **45** B2

Gamā Brazil **138** C2
Gamalakhe S. Africa **99** D3
Gambia, The *country* Africa
90 A3
Gambier, Îles *is* Fr. Polynesia
101
Gambier Islands Austr. **104** C3
Gamboma Congo **94** B3
Ganado U.S.A. **126** C1
Ganāveh Iran **85** D3
Gâncă Azer. **85** C1
Gandadiwata, Bukit *mt.* Indon.
65 C2
Gandajika Dem. Rep. Congo
94 C3
Gander Can. **115** E2
Gander *r.* Can. **115** E2
Gandesa Spain **55** D1
Gandhidham India **78** B2
Gandhinagar India **78** B2
Gandhi Sagar *resr* India **78** B2
Gandía Spain **55** C2
Ganga *r.* Bangl./India **79** D2
Ganganagar India **78** B2
Gangca China **72** C2
Gangdisê Shan *mts* China
79 C1
Ganges, Mouths of the
Bangl./India **79** C2
Gangtok India **79** C2
Gannett Peak U.S.A. **120** B2
Gansbaai S. Africa **98** A3
Gansu *prov.* China **74** A2
Ganzhou China **75** B3
Gao Mali **90** B3
Gap France **53** D3
Gap Carbon *hd* Alg. **55** C2
Gar China **79** C1
Garah Austr. **105** D1
Garanhuns Brazil **135** F3
Garbaaharrey Somalia **95** E2
Garbahaarrey U.S.A. **118** B2
Garbsen Ger. **49** D1
Garça Brazil **138** C2
Garda, Lake Italy **56** B1
Gardelegen Ger. **49** E1
Garden City U.S.A. **120** C3
Gardēz Afgh. **78** A1
Gargždai Lith. **36** B2
Gariep Dam *resr* S. Africa
99 C3
Garies S. Africa **98** A3
Garissa Kenya **95** D3
Garmisch-Partenkirchen Ger.
50 C3
Garnpung Lake *imp. l.* Austr.
104 C2
Garonne *r.* France **52** B3
Garoowe Somalia **93** C4
Garoua Cameroon **94** B2
Garry Lake Can. **113** E1
Garsen Kenya **95** E3
Garut Indon. **64** B2
Gary U.S.A. **122** C2

Garza García Mex. **129** E2
Garzê China **72** C2
Gascony, Gulf of France **52** B3
Gascoyne *r.* Austr. **102** A2
Gashua Nigeria **91** D3
Gaspé Can. **115** D2
Gaspé, Péninsule de *pen.* Can.
115 D2
Gaston, Lake U.S.A. **125** E1
Gastonia U.S.A. **125** D1
Gata, Cabo de *c.* Spain **55** C2
Gatchina Rus. Fed. **36** D2
Gateshead U.K. **46** C2
Gatesville U.S.A. **127** E2
Gatineau *r.* Can. **114** C2
Gatton Austr. **105** E1
Gauer Lake Can. **113** F2
Gausta *mt.* Norway **41** B4
Gauteng *prov.* S. Africa **99** C2
Gavdos *i.* Greece **59** B4
Gävle Sweden **41** D3
Gavrilov-Yam Rus. Fed. **37** E2
Gawai Myanmar **66** A1
Gawler Austr. **104** B2
Gawler Ranges *hills* Austr.
104 B2
Gaya India **79** C2
Gaya Niger **90** C3
Gaylord U.S.A. **122** D1
Gaza Gaza **84** B2
Gaza *terr.* Asia **84** B2
Gaz-Achak Turkm. **80** D2
Gazandzhyk Turkm. **80** C2
Gaziantep Turkey **92** D1
Gbarnga Liberia **90** B4
Gdańsk Pol. **51** D2
Gdov Rus. Fed. **36** C2
Gdynia Pol. **51** D2
Gedaref Sudan **92** B3
Gediz *r.* Turkey **59** C3
Gedser Denmark **50** C2
Geel Belgium **48** B2
Geelong Austr. **104** C3
Geesthacht Ger. **49** E1
Ge'gyai China **79** C1
Geikie *r.* Can. **110** F3
Geilo Norway **41** B3
Gejiu China **75** A3
Gela Italy **56** B3
Gelendzhik Rus. Fed. **39** E3
Gelibolu Turkey *see* Gallipoli
Gelsenkirchen Ger. **48** C2
Gemena Dem. Rep. Congo **94** B2
Gemlik Turkey **59** C2
Gemona del Friuli Italy **53** E2
Genalē Wenz *r.* Eth. **93** C4
General Acha Arg. **137** B4
General Alvear Arg. **137** B4
General Roca Arg. **137** B5
General Santos Phil. **68** B3
Genesee *r.* U.S.A. **123** E2
Geneva Switz. **53** D2

Geneva, Lake France/Switz. **53** D2
Genève Switz. *see* Geneva
Genil r. Spain **50** D4
Genk Belgium **48** B2
Genoa Italy **56** A2
Genova Italy *see* Genoa
Gent Belgium *see* Ghent
Genthin Ger. **49** F1
George r. Can. **115** D1
George S. Africa **98** B3
George, Lake *FL* U.S.A. **125** D3
George, Lake *NY* U.S.A. **123** F2
Georgetown Guyana **135** D2
George Town Malaysia **64** B1
Georgetown *SC* U.S.A. **125** E2
Georgetown *TX* U.S.A. **127** E2
George V Land reg. Antarctica **107** H3
Georgia country Asia **85** C1
Georgia state U.S.A. **125** D2
Georgian Bay Can. **123** D1
Georgina watercourse Austr. **103** C2
Georgiyevka Kazakh. **81** F2
Georgiyevsk Rus. Fed. **35** D4
Gera Ger. **49** F2
Geral, Serra mts Brazil **138** C3
Geraldine N.Z. **106** B3
Geraldton Austr. **102** A2
Gerede Turkey **84** B1
Gereshk Afgh. **78** A1
Gerlachovský štít mt. Slovakia **51** E3
Germany country Europe **50** B2
Gersfeld (Rhön) Ger. **49** D2
Gêrzê China **79** C1
Gettysburg *SD* U.S.A. **120** D1
Gevgelija Macedonia **59** B2
Ghaap Plateau S. Africa **98** B2
Ghadāmis Libya **91** C1
Ghaghara r. India **79** C2
Ghana country Africa **90** B4
Ghanzi Botswana **96** B2
Ghardaïa Alg. **90** C1
Gharyān Libya **91** D1
Ghatal India **79** C2
Ghazaouet Alg. **55** C2
Ghaziabad India **79** B2
Ghazipur India **79** C2
Ghazni Afgh. **78** A1
Ghent Belgium **48** A2
Gherla Romania **38** B2
Ghisonaccia France **53** D3
Giaginskaya Rus. Fed. **39** F3
Giant's Causeway lava field U.K. **45** C1

Gichgeniyn Nuruu mts Mongolia **72** C1
Gidolē Eth. **93** B4
Gien France **52** C2
Gießen Ger. **49** D2
Gifhorn Ger. **49** E1
Gifu Japan **71** C3
Gigha i. U.K. **44** B3
Gijón-Xixón Spain **54** B1
Gila r. U.S.A. **126** B2
Gila Bend U.S.A. **126** B2
Gilbert r. Austr. **103** D1
Gilbert Islands Kiribati **100**
Gilgandra Austr. **105** D2
Gilgit Jammu and Kashmir **78** B1
Gilgit r. Jammu and Kashmir **78** B1
Gillam Can. **113** F2
Gillette U.S.A. **120** E2
Gillingham U.K. **47** D4
Gilmour Island Can. **114** C1
Gimli Can. **113** F2
Ginir Eth. **93** C4
Ginosa Italy **57** C2
Gippsland reg. Austr. **105** D3
Girdar Dhor r. Pak. **78** A2
Girdi Iran **83** D1
Giresun Turkey **84** B1
Girona Spain **55** D1
Girvan U.K. **44** B3
Gisborne N.Z. **106** C2
Gitarama Rwanda **95** C3
Giulianova Italy **56** B2
Giurgiu Romania **38** C3
Giuvala, Pasul pass Romania **38** C2
Givors France **53** C2
Giyani S. Africa **99** D1
Giza Egypt **92** B2
Gjirokastër Albania **59** B2
Gjoa Haven Can. **110** F2
Gjøvik Norway **41** C3
Glace Bay Can. **115** E2
Glacier Peak vol. U.S.A. **118** B1
Gladstone Austr. **103** E2
Gláma mts Iceland **40** [inset]
Glan r. Ger. **48** C3
Glanaruddery Mountains Ireland **45** B2
Glasgow U.K. **44** B3
Glasgow *KY* U.S.A. **122** C3
Glasgow *MT* U.S.A. **118** E1
Glauchau Ger. **49** F2
Glazov Rus. Fed. **34** E3
Glazunovka Rus. Fed. **37** E3
Glen Coe val. U.K. **44** B2
Glendale U.S.A. **126** B2
Glendive U.S.A. **120** C1
Glenelg r. Austr. **104** C3
Glen Innes Austr. **105** E1
Glenmorgan Austr. **105** D1
Glennallen U.S.A. **110** C2
Glenrothes U.K. **44** C2

Glens Falls U.S.A. **123** F2
Glen Shee val. U.K. **44** C2
Glenwood U.S.A. **126** C2
Glenwood Springs U.S.A. **120** B3
Gliwice Pol. **51** D2
Globe U.S.A. **126** B2
Głogów Pol. **51** D2
Glomfjord Norway **40** C2
Glomma r. Norway **41** C4
Gloucester Austr. **105** E2
Gloucester U.K. **47** B4
Glubokoye Kazakh. **81** F1
Glückstadt Ger. **49** D1
Gmünd Austria **50** C3
Gmunden Austria **50** C3
Gnarrenburg Ger. **49** D1
Gniezno Pol. **51** D2
Gnjilane S.M. **58** B2
Goalpara India **79** D2
Goba Eth. **93** C4
Gobabis Namibia **98** A1
Gobi des. China/Mongolia **74** A1
Goch Ger. **48** C2
Gochas Namibia **98** A1
Godavari r. India **77** C3
Goderich Can. **114** B2
Godhra India **78** B2
Gods r. Can. **113** F2
Gods Lake Can. **113** F2
Godthåb Greenland *see* Nuuk
Godwin Austen mt. China/Jammu and Kashmir *see* K2
Goéland, Lac au l. Can. **114** C2
Goélands, Lac aux l. Can. **115** D1
Goes Neth. **48** A2
Goiânia Brazil **138** C1
Goiás Brazil **138** C1
Goio-Erê Brazil **138** B2
Gökçeada i. Turkey **59** C2
Gokwe Zimbabwe **97** B1
Gol Norway **41** C3
Golaghat India **66** A1
Gol'chikha Rus. Fed. **34** H1
Gölcük Turkey **59** C2
Goldap Pol. **51** E2
Goldberg Ger. **49** F1
Gold Coast Austr. **105** E1
Gold Coast coastal area Ghana **90** B4
Golden Can. **112** D2
Golden Bay N.Z. **106** B3
Golden Hinde mt. Can. **112** C3
Goldfield U.S.A. **119** C3
Gold River Can. **112** C3
Goldsboro U.S.A. **125** E1
Goleta U.S.A. **119** C4
Golmud China **72** C2
Golpāyegān Iran **85** D2
Golspie U.K. **44** C2
Goma Dem. Rep. Congo **95** C3
Gomati r. India **79** C2
Gombe Nigeria **91** D3

mez Palacio Mex. 128 B2
naives Haiti 131 C3
nbad-e Kavus Iran 85 D2
nder Eth. 93 B3
ndia India 79 C2
nen Turkey 59 C2
ngola r. Nigeria 91 B4
ngolgon Austr. 105 D2
ngzhuling China 69 A1
nzáles Mex. 129 C2
nzales U.S.A. 127 E3
ood Hope, Cape of S. Africa 98 A3
oding U.S.A. 118 D2
odland U.S.A. 120 C3
odooga Austr. 105 D1
ole U.K. 46 C3
olgowi Austr. 105 D2
olwa Austr. 104 B3
ondiwindi Austr. 105 E1
oose Lake U.S.A. 118 B2
oppingen Ger. 50 B3
rakhpur India 79 C2
ražde Bos.-Herz. 57 C2
ré Chad 91 D4
re N.Z. 106 A4
rey Ireland 45 C2
rgän Iran 85 D2
ri Georgia 85 C1
rlice Pol. 51 E3
rlitz Ger. 50 C2
rnji Vakuf Bos.-Herz. 57 C2
rno-Altaysk Rus. Fed. 81 F1
rnotrakiyska Nizina lowland Bulg. 58 C2
rnyak Rus. Fed. 81 F1
roka P.N.G. 63 D3
rokhovets Rus. Fed. 37 F2
rom Gorom Burkina 90 B3
rontalo Indon. 65 D1
rshechnoye Rus. Fed. 37 E3
rumna Island Ireland 45 C2
ryachiy Klyuch Rus. Fed. 89 E3
rzów Wielkopolski Pol. 50 D2
sford Austr. 105 E2
shogawara Japan 70 D2
slar Ger. 49 E2
spić Croatia 56 C2
sport U.K. 47 C4
stivar Macedonia 58 B2
teborg Sweden see Gothenburg
tha Ger. 49 E2
thenburg Sweden 41 C4
thenburg U.S.A. 120 C2
tland i. Sweden 41 D4
tse Delchev Bulg. 59 B2
tska Sandón i. Sweden 41 D4
tsu Japan 71 F4
ttingen Ger. 49 D2
tt Peak Can. 112 C4
uda Neth. 48 B1

Gouin, Réservoir resr Can. 114 C2
Goulburn Austr. 105 D2
Goulburn r. N.S.W. Austr. 105 C3
Goulburn r. Vic. Austr. 105 C3
Goundam Mali 90 B3
Gouraya Alg. 55 D2
Gourdon France 52 C3
Gouré Niger 91 D3
Gourits r. S. Africa 98 B3
Gourma-Rharous Mali 90 B3
Gourock Range mts Austr. 105 D3
Governador Valadares Brazil 139 B1
Governor's Harbour Bahamas 125 E3
Goví Altayn Nuruu mts Mongolia 72 C2
Gower pen. U.K. 47 A4
Goya Arg. 136 C3
Göyçay Azer. 85 C1
Gozha Co salt l. China 79 C1
Graaf-Reinet S. Africa 98 B3
Grabow Ger. 49 E1
Grachevka Rus. Fed. 35 E3
Gräfenhainichen Ger. 49 F2
Grafton Austr. 105 E1
Grafton U.S.A. 121 D1
Graham U.S.A. 127 E2
Graham Island Can. 112 B2
Graham Land reg. Antarctica 107 K3
Grahamstown S. Africa 99 C3
Grajaú Brazil 135 E3
Grammos mt. Greece 59 B2
Grampian Mountains U.K. 44 B2
Granada Nic. 130 B3
Granada Spain 54 C2
Granby Can. 123 F1
Gran Canaria i. Canary Is 90 A2
Gran Chaco reg. Arg./Para. 136 B3
Grand r. U.S.A. 120 F2
Grand Bahama i. Bahamas 130 C2
Grand Bank Can. 115 E2
Grand Canal China see Da Yunhe
Grand Canyon U.S.A. 126 B1
Grand Canyon gorge U.S.A. 126 B1
Grand Cayman i. Cayman Is 130 B3
Grand Coulee U.S.A. 118 C1
Grande r. Bol. 136 B2
Grande r. Brazil 139 B2
Grande, Bahía b. Arg. 137 B6
Grande, Ilha i. Brazil 139 D2
Grande Cache Can. 112 D2
Grande Comore i. Comoros see Njazidja
Grande Prairie Can. 112 D2

Grand Erg de Bilma des. Niger 91 D3
Grand Erg Occidental des. Alg. 90 B1
Grand Erg Oriental des. Alg. 91 C2
Grande-Rivière Can. 115 D2
Grand Falls N.B. Can. 123 G1
Grand Falls Nfld. and Lab. Can. 115 E2
Grand Forks Can. 112 D3
Grand Forks U.S.A. 121 D1
Grandin, Lac l. Can. 112 D1
Grand Island U.S.A. 121 D2
Grand Isle U.S.A. 124 B3
Grand Junction U.S.A. 120 B3
Grand-Lahou Côte d'Ivoire 90 B4
Grand Lake N.B. Can. 115 D2
Grand Lake Nfld. and Lab. Can. 115 E2
Grand Marais U.S.A. 121 E1
Grândola Port. 54 B2
Grand Rapids Can. 113 F2
Grand Rapids MI U.S.A. 122 C2
Grand Rapids MN U.S.A. 121 E1
Grand Teton mt. U.S.A. 120 A1
Grand Turk Turks and Caicos Is 131 C2
Grangeville U.S.A. 118 C1
Granite Peak U.S.A. 118 E3
Granitola, Capo c. Italy 56 B3
Gränna Sweden 41 C4
Gransee Ger. 49 F1
Grantham U.K. 46 C3
Grantown-on-Spey U.K. 44 C2
Grants U.S.A. 126 C1
Grants Pass U.S.A. 118 B2
Granville France 52 B2
Granville Lake Can. 113 E2
Grão Mogol Brazil 139 D1
Grarem Alg. 55 E2
Graskop S. Africa 99 D1
Grasse France 53 D3
Grave, Pointe de pt France 52 B2
Gravesend Austr. 105 E1
Gravesend U.K. 47 D4
Graz Austria 51 D3
Great Abaco i. Bahamas 131 C2
Great Australian Bight g. Austr. 102 B3
Great Barrier Island N.Z. 106 C2
Great Barrier Reef Austr. 103 D1
Great Basin U.S.A. 119 C3
Great Bear Lake Can. 112 D1
Great Belt sea chan. Denmark 41 C4
Great Bend U.S.A. 121 D3
Great Coco Island Cocos Is 67 A2
Great Dividing Range mts Austr. 105 C3
Greater Antilles is Caribbean Sea 130 B2

Great Falls U.S.A. **118** D1
Great Fish *r.* S. Africa **99** C3
Great Fish Point S. Africa **99** C3
Great Inagua *i.* Bahamas **131** C2
Great Karoo *plat.* S. Africa **98** B3
Great Kei *r.* S. Africa **99** C3
Great Malvern U.K. **47** B3
Great Namaqualand *reg.* Namibia **98** A2
Great Nicobar *i.* India **67** A3
Great Ouse *r.* U.K. **47** D3
Great Rift Valley Africa **95** D3
Great Ruaha *r.* Tanz. **95** D3
Great Salt Lake U.S.A. **118** D2
Great Salt Lake Desert U.S.A. **118** D2
Great Sand Sea *des.* Egypt/Libya **92** A2
Great Sandy Desert Austr. **102** B2
Great Slave Lake Can. **112** D1
Great Smoky Mountains U.S.A. **125** D3
Great Victoria Desert Austr. **102** B2
Great Yarmouth U.K. **47** D3
Gredos, Sierra de *mts* Spain **54** B1
Greece *country* Europe **59** B3
Greeley U.S.A. **120** C3
Greem-Bell, Ostrov *i.* Rus. Fed. **86** G1
Green *r.* Can. **122** G1
Green *r.* KY U.S.A. **125** C1
Green *r.* WY U.S.A. **120** B3
Green Bay U.S.A. **122** C2
Green Bay *b.* U.S.A. **122** C1
Greenbrier *r.* U.S.A. **125** D4
Greeneville U.S.A. **125** D1
Greenfield U.S.A. **123** D3
Green Lake Can. **113** E2
Greenland *terr.* N. America **111** J2
Greenland Sea Greenland/Svalbard **86** B2
Greenock U.K. **44** B3
Green River *r.* U.S.A. **119** D3
Green River WY U.S.A. **120** B3
Greensburg *PA* U.S.A. **123** E2
Green Swamp U.S.A. **125** E2
Green Valley U.S.A. **126** D2
Greenville Liberia **90** B4
Greenville *AL* U.S.A. **124** C2
Greenville *MS* U.S.A. **124** B2
Greenville *NC* U.S.A. **125** E1
Greenville *SC* U.S.A. **125** D2
Greenville *TX* U.S.A. **127** D2
Greenwell Point Austr. **105** E2
Greenwood U.S.A. **125** D2
Gregory, Lake Austr. **104** A1
Gregory Range *hills* Austr. **103** D1
Greifswald Ger. **50** C2
Greiz Ger. **49** F2
Grenå Denmark **41** C4
Grenada U.S.A. **124** C2
Grenada *country* West Indies **131** D3
Grenfell Austr. **105** D2
Grenfell Can. **113** E2
Grenoble France **53** D2
Grenville, Cape Austr. **103** D1
Grenville, Ger. Austr. **118** B1
Gresham U.S.A. **118** B1
Greven Ger. **48** C1
Grevena Greece **59** B2
Grevenbroich Ger. **48** C2
Greybull U.S.A. **120** B2
Grey Hunter Peak Can. **112** B1
Grey Islands Can. **115** E1
Greymouth N.Z. **106** B3
Grey Range *hills* Austr. **104** C1
Greystones Ireland **45** C2
Gribanovskiy Rus. Fed. **39** F1
Griffin U.S.A. **125** D2
Griffith Austr. **105** D2
Grimma Ger. **49** F2
Grimmen Ger. **50** C2
Grimsby U.K. **46** C3
Grímsey *i.* Iceland **40** [inset]
Grimsstaðir Iceland **40** [inset]
Griquland East *reg.* S. Africa **99** C3
Griqualand West *reg.* S. Africa **98** B2
Grise Fiord Can. **111** J1
Groblersdal S. Africa **99** C2
Groblershoop S. Africa **98** B2
Groix, Île de *i.* France **52** B2
Gronau (Westfalen) Ger. **48** C1
Grong Norway **40** C3
Groningen Neth. **48** C1
Groote Eylandt *i.* Austr. **103** C1
Grootfontein Namibia **98** A1
Groot Karas Berg *plat.* Namibia **98** A2
Groot Swartberge *mts* S. Africa **98** B3
Groot Winterberg *mt.* S. Africa **99** C3
Großer Rachel *mt.* Ger. **49** F3
Grosser Speikkogel *mt.* Austria **56** D1
Grosseto Italy **56** B2
Groß-Gerau Ger. **49** D3
Großglockner *mt.* Austria **50** C3
Groß-Hesepe Ger. **48** C1
Gross Ums Namibia **98** A1
Grosvater Bay Can. **114** F2
Groundhog *r.* Can. **114** B2
Grover Beach U.S.A. **119** B3
Groznyy Rus. Fed. **35** D4
Grudziądz Pol. **51** D2
Grünau Namibia **98** A2
Grundarfjörður Iceland **40** [inset]
Gryazi Rus. Fed. **37** E3
Gryazovets Rus. Fed. **37** F2
Gryfice Pol. **50** D2
Gryfino Pol. **50** C2
Grytviken S. Georgia **137** E6
Guacanayabo, Golfo de *b.* Cuba **130** C2
Guadalajara Mex. **128** B2
Guadalquivir *r.* Spain **54** B2
Guadalupe *i.* Mex. **116** B4
Guadalupe, Sierra de *mts* Spain **54** B2
Guadalupe Peak U.S.A. **126** D3
Guadalupe Victoria Mex. **128** B2
Guadarrama, Sierra de *mts* Spain **54** C1
Guadeloupe *terr.* West Indies **131** D3
Guadiana *r.* Port./Spain **54** B2
Guadix Spain **54** C2
Guaíra Brazil **138** B2
Guajira, Península de la *pen.* Col. **131** C3
Guam *terr.* N. Pacific Ocean **63** D2
Guamúchil Mex. **128** B2
Guanambi Brazil **135** E4
Guanare Venez. **134** C2
Guane Cuba **130** B2
Guang'an China **75** A2
Guangchang China **75** B3
Guangdong *prov.* China **75** B3
Guangxi Zhuangzu Zizhiqu *aut. reg.* China **75** A3
Guangyuan China **74** A2
Guangzhou China **75** B3
Guanling China **75** A3
Guantánamo Cuba **131** C2
Guaporé *r.* Bol./Brazil **136** B2
Guarapuava Brazil **138** B3
Guaraqueçaba Brazil **138** C3
Guaratinguetá Brazil **139** C2
Guarda Port. **54** B1
Guarujá Brazil **139** C2
Guasave Mex. **128** B2
Guatemala *country* Central America **130** A3
Guatemala City Guat. **130** A3
Guaviare *r.* Col. **134** C2
Guayaquil Ecuador **134** B3
Guayaramerín Bol. **136** B2
Guaymas Mex. **128** A2
Guba Eth. **93** B3
Guba Dolgaya Rus. Fed. **34** E1 [?]
Gubbio Italy **53** E3
Gubkin Rus. Fed. **37** E3
Guelmine Morocco **90** A2
Guelph Can. **114** B2
Guémez Mex. **129** C2
Guéret France **52** C2
Guernsey *i.* Channel Is **47** B5
Guerrero Negro Mex. **128** A2
Guers, Lac *l.* Can. **115** D1
Guiana Highlands *reg.* Guyana/Venez. **134** C2
Guider Cameroon **94** B2
Guidonia-Montecelio Italy **56** B2

gang China **75** A3
gnicourt France **48** A3
a Moz. **99** D1
dford U.K. **47** C4
in China **75** B3
laume-Delisle, Lac *l.* Can.
4 C1
maräes Port. **54** B1
hnea *country* Africa **90** A3
hnea, Gulf of Africa **90** C4
hnea-Bissau *country* Africa
90 A3
ngamp France **52** B2
pavas France **52** B2
ratinga Brazil **138** B1
ria Venez. **134** C1
yang China **75** A3
zhou *prov.* China **75** A3
ranwala Pak. **78** B1
rat Pak. **78** B1
ovo Rus. Fed. **39** E2
ang China **74** A2
argambone Austr. **105** D2
barga India **77** B3
bene Latvia **36** C2
fport U.S.A. **124** C2
a China **73** E1
iston Uzbek. **81** D2
kevichi Rus. Fed. **39** F2
l Lake Can. **113** E2
u Uganda **95** D2
mare Botswana **96** B5
ndag Turkm. **80** C3
nmersbach Ger. **48** C2
a India **78** B2
ndagai Austr. **105** D3
ngu Dem. Rep. Congo **94** B3
aisao r. Can. **113** F2
medah Austr. **105** E2
nnison *CO* U.S.A. **119** D3
nnison *UT* U.S.A. **119** D3
nnison r. U.S.A. **120** B3
atakal India **77** B3
hungstóli Indon. **64** A1
hungtua Indon. **64** A1
azburg Ger. **50** C3
azenhausen Ger. **49** E3
ojiaba China **74** B2
rgaon India **78** D2
gueia r. Brazil **135** E3
ri, Embalse de *resr* Venez.
34 C2
rinhätä Brazil **138** C1
rupi r. Brazil **135** E3
u Sikhar *mt.* India **78** B2
au Nigeria **91** C3
shan China **69** A2
shgy Turkm. **78** A1
s'-Khrustal'nyy Rus. Fed.
7 F2
spini Italy **56** A3
stavus U.S.A. **112** B2
strow Ger. **49** F1
ersloh Ger. **49** D2

Guwahati India **79** D2
Guyana *country* S. America
134 D2
Guymon U.S.A. **127** D1
Guyra Austr. **105** E2
Guyuan China **74** A2
Guzmán Mex. **128** B1
Guzmán, Lago de *l.* Mex. **128** B1
Gwadar Pak. **78** A2
Gwalior India **79** B2
Gwanda Zimbabwe **97** B2
Gwardafuy, Gees *c.* Somalia
93 D3
Gweebarra Bay Ireland **45** B1
Gweedore Ireland **45** B1
Gweru Zimbabwe **97** B1
Gwydir r. Austr. **105** D2
Gyangzê China **79** C2
Gyaring Co *l.* China **79** C1
Gyaring Hu *l.* China **72** C2
Gydan Peninsula Rus. Fed.
34 G1
Gydanskiy Poluostrov *pen.*
Rus. Fed. *see* Gydan Peninsula
Gyigang China **66** A1
Gympie Austr. **103** E2
Gyöngyös Hungary **51** D3
Győr Hungary **51** D3
Gypsumville Can. **113** F2
Gyrfalcon Islands Can. **115** D1
Gyula Hungary **51** E3
Gyumri Armenia **81** C2
Gyzylarbat Turkm. **80** C3

H

Haapsalu Estonia **36** B2
Haarlem Neth. **48** B1
Haarstrang *ridge* Ger. **49** C2
Haast N.Z. **106** A3
Habban Yemen **82** B3
Habbaniyah, Hawr al *l.* Iraq
85 C2
Hachijô-jima *i.* Japan **71** C4
Hachinohe Japan **70** D2
Hacufera Moz. **97** C2
Hadd, Ra's al *pt* Oman **83** C2
Hadejia Nigeria **91** D3
Haderslev Denmark **41** B4
Hadyach Ukr. **39** D1
Haeju N. Korea **69** B2
Haeju-man b. N. Korea **69** B2
Haenam S. Korea **69** B3
Hafar al Bātin Saudi Arabia
82 B2
Haflong India **66** A1
Hagar Nish Plateau Eritrea **82** A3
Hagåtña Guam **63** D2
Hagen Ger. **48** C2
Hagenow Ger. **49** E1
Hagensborg Can. **112** C2
Hagerstown U.S.A. **123** E3

Hagfors Sweden **41** C3
Hagi Japan **71** B4
Ha Giang Vietnam **66** B1
Hag's Head Ireland **45** B2
Hague, Cap de la *c.* France
52 B2
Haicheng China **69** A1
Hai Duong Vietnam **66** B1
Haifa Israel **84** B2
Haikou China **75** B3
Hā'il Saudi Arabia **82** B2
Hailar China *see* Hulun Buir
Hailuoto *i.* Fin. **40** E2
Hainan *i.* China **73** D3
Hainan *prov.* China **75** A4
Haines U.S.A. **112** B2
Haines Junction Can. **112** B1
Hainich *ridge* Ger. **49** E2
Hainleite *ridge* Ger. **49** E2
Hai Phong Vietnam **66** B1
Haiti *country* West Indies
131 C3
Haiya Sudan **92** B3
Hajdúböszörmény Hungary
51 E3
Hajhir *mt.* Yemen **83** C3
Hajjah Yemen **82** B3
Hājjīābād Iran **85** D3
Hajmā' Oman **83** C3
Haka Myanmar **66** A1
Hakkâri Turkey **85** C2
Hakodate Japan **70** D2
Halab Syria *see* Aleppo
Halabān Saudi Arabia **82** B2
Halaib Sudan **92** B2
Hālaniyāt, Juzur al *is* Oman
83 C3
Halban Mongolia **72** C1
Halberstadt Ger. **49** E2
Halcon, Mount Phil. **68** B2
Halden Norway **41** C4
Haldensleben Ger. **49** E1
Haldwani India **79** B2
Hāleh Iran **83** C2
Halfmoon Bay N.Z. **106** A4
Halifax Can. **115** D2
Halifax U.K. **46** C3
Halla-san *mt.* S. Korea **69** B3
Hall Beach Can. **111** G2
Halle Belgium **48** B2
Hallein Austria **50** C3
Halle (Saale) Ger. **49** E2
Hallock U.S.A. **121** D1
Halls Creek Austr. **102** B1
Halmahera *i.* Indon. **63** C2
Halmstad Sweden **41** C4
Ham France **48** A3
Hamada Japan **71** B4
Hamadān Iran **85** C2
Hamāh Syria **84** B2
Hamamatsu Japan **71** C4
Hamar Norway **41** C3
Hamātah, Jabal *mt.* Egypt **92** B2
Hambantota Sri Lanka **77** C4

Hamburg Ger. **49** D1
Ḩamḑ, Wādī al *watercourse* Saudi Arabia **84** D2
Hamḑah Saudi Arabia **82** B3
Hämeenlinna Fin. **41** E3
Hameln Ger. **49** D1
Hamersley Range *mts* Austr. **102** A2
Hamhŭng N. Korea **69** B2
Hami China **72** C2
Hamid Sudan **92** B2
Hamilton Austr. **104** C3
Hamilton Can. **114** C2
Hamilton N.Z. **106** C2
Hamilton U.K. **44** B3
Hamilton *AL* U.S.A. **124** C2
Hamilton *MT* U.S.A. **118** D1
Hamilton *OH* U.S.A. **122** D3
Hamina Fin. **41** F3
Hamm Ger. **48** C2
Hammada du Drâa *plat.* Alg. **90** B2
Hammelburg Ger. **49** D2
Hammerdal Sweden **40** D3
Hammerfest Norway **40** F1
Hammond U.S.A. **124** B2
Hammonton U.S.A. **123** F3
Hāmūn-e Jaz Mūriān *salt marsh* Iran **83** C2
Hamun-i-Lora *dry lake* Afgh./Pak. **78** A2
Hāmūn-i-Mashkel *salt flat* Iran **83** C2
Hamun-i-Mashkel *salt flat* Pak. **78** A2
Hanak Saudi Arabia **82** A2
Hanamaki Japan **70** D3
Hanau Ger. **49** D2
Hancheng China **74** B2
Handan China **74** B2
Hangayn Nuruu *mts* Mongolia **72** C1
Hangzhou China **75** C2
Hangzhou Wan *b.* China **74** C2
Hanko Fin. **41** E4
Hanksville U.S.A. **119** D3
Hanmer Springs N.Z. **106** B3
Hanna Can. **113** D2
Hannibal U.S.A. **121** E3
Hannover Ger. **49** D1
Hannoversch Münden Ger. **49** D2
Hanöbukten *b.* Sweden **41** C4
Ha Nôi Vietnam *see* **Hanoi**
Hanoi Vietnam *see* **Ha Nôi**
Hanover S. Africa **98** B3
Hantsavichy Belarus **36** C3
Hanumana India **79** C2
Hanumangarh India **78** B2
Hanzhong China **74** A2
Haparanda Sweden **40** E2

Happy Valley - Goose Bay Can. **115** D1
Ḩaql Saudi Arabia **82** A2
Ḩaraḑh Saudi Arabia **83** B2
Haradok Belarus **36** C2
Harare Zimbabwe **97** C1
Ḩaraṣīs, Jiddat al *des.* Oman **83** C3
Har-Ayrag Mongolia **73** D1
Harbin China **73** E1
Harbour Breton Can. **115** E2
Harda India **78** B2
Hardangerfjorden *sea chan.* Norway **41** B4
Harderwijk Neth. **48** B1
Hardeveld *mts* S. Africa **98** A3
Hardin U.S.A. **118** E1
Hardisty Lake Can. **112** D1
Haren (Ems) Ger. **48** C1
Härer Eth. **93** C4
Hargeysa Somalia **93** C4
Harghita-Mădăraş, Vârful *mt.* Romania **38** C2
Hari Rūd *r.* Afgh./Iran **78** A1
Harlingen Neth. **48** B1
Harlingen U.S.A. **127** E3
Harlow U.K. **47** D4
Harlowton U.S.A. **118** E1
Harnes France **48** A2
Harney Basin U.S.A. **118** C2
Harney Lake U.S.A. **118** C2
Härnösand Sweden **41** D3
Har Nuur *l.* Mongolia **72** C1
Harper Liberia **90** B4
Harricanaw *r.* Can. **114** C1
Harrington Austr. **105** E2
Harrington Harbour Can. **115** E1
Harris *pen.* U.K. **44** A2
Harris, Lake *salt flat* Austr. **104** B2
Harris, Sound of *sea chan.* U.K. **44** A2
Harrisburg *IL* U.S.A. **122** C3
Harrisburg *PA* U.S.A. **123** E2
Harrismith S. Africa **99** C2
Harrison U.S.A. **124** B1
Harrison, Cape Can. **115** E1
Harrison Bay U.S.A. **110** B2
Harrisonburg U.S.A. **123** E3
Harrisonville U.S.A. **121** E3
Harrogate U.K. **46** C3
Hârşova Romania **38** C3
Harstad Norway **40** D2
Hartbees *watercourse* S. Africa **98** B2
Hartford U.S.A. **123** F2
Hartland Point U.K. **47** A4
Hartlepool U.K. **46** C2
Hartley Bay Can. **112** C2
Harts *r.* S. Africa **99** B2
Hartwell Reservoir U.S.A. **125** D2
Har Us Nuur *l.* Mongolia **72** C1
Harvey U.S.A. **120** C1
Harwich U.K. **47** D4

Harz *hills* Ger. **49** E2
Hasselt Belgium **48** B2
Hässleholm Sweden **41** C4
Hastings Austr. **105** D3
Hastings N.Z. **106** C2
Hastings U.K. **47** D4
Hastings *MN* U.S.A. **121** E2
Hastings *NE* U.S.A. **121** D2
Hatay Turkey *see* **Antakya**
Hatchet Lake Can. **113** E2
Hatfield Austr. **104** C2
Hatgal Mongolia **72** C1
Ha Tinh Vietnam **66** B2
Hatteras, Cape U.S.A. **125** E1
Hattiesburg U.S.A. **124** C2
Hat Yai Thai. **67** B3
Haud *reg.* Eth. **93** C4
Haugesund Norway **41** B4
Haukeligrend Norway **41** B4
Hauraki Gulf N.Z. **106** C2
Hauterive Can. **115** D2
Havana Cuba **130** B2
Havant U.K. **47** C4
Havel *r.* Ger. **49** E1
Havelberg Ger. **49** F1
Havelock N.Z. **106** B3
Havelock North N.Z. **106** C2
Haverfordwest U.K. **47** A4
Havlíčkův Brod Czech Rep. **51**
Haveysund Norway **40** F1
Havre U.S.A. **118** E1
Havre-Aubert Can. **115** D2
Havre-St-Pierre Can. **115** D1
Hawaii *i.* U.S.A. **108**
Hawaiian Islands N. Pacific Ocean **142** E3
Hawea, Lake N.Z. **106** A3
Hawera N.Z. **106** B2
Hawick U.K. **44** C3
Hawke Bay N.Z. **106** C2
Hawker Austr. **104** B2
Hawkers Gate Austr. **104** C1
Hawthorne U.S.A. **119** C3
Hay Austr. **104** C2
Hay *r.* Can. **112** D1
Hayden U.S.A. **118** C1
Hayes *r. Man.* Can. **113** F2
Hayes *r. Nunavut* Can. **111** F2
Hayotboshi tog'i *mt.* Uzbek. **81** D2
Hayrabolu Turkey **59** C2
Hay River Can. **112** D1
Hays U.S.A. **121** D3
Hays Yemen **82** B3
Haysyn Ukr. **38** D2
Haywards Heath U.K. **47** C4
Hazarajat *reg.* Afgh. **78** A1
Hazard U.S.A. **122** D3
Hazaribagh India **79** C2
Hazaribagh Range *mts* India **79** C2
Hazebrouck France **48** A2
Hazelton Can. **112** C2
Healesville Austr. **105** D3

rst Can. **114** B2
ei *prov.* China **74** B2
el Austr. **105** D1
er Springs U.S.A. **124** B1
i China **74** B2
ron Can. **115** D1
ete Strait Can. **112** B2
hi China **75** A3
he Sweden **41** C3
renveen Neth. **48** B1
rkugowaard Neth. **48** B1
rlen Neth. **48** B2
i Israel *see* Haifa
ei China **74** B2
eng China **75** B3
ang China **73** E1
le Ger. **50** B2
elberg Ger. **49** D3
bronn Ger. **49** D3
ongjiang *prov.* China **70** B1
ong Jiang *r.* China **73** E1
nola Fin. **41** F3
agsfjället *mt.* Sweden **40** C3
ena *MT* U.S.A. **124** B2
ena *MT* U.S.A. **118** D1
ensburgh U.K. **44** B2
goland *i.* Ger. **50** B2
goländer Bucht *g.* Ger. **50** B2
la Iceland **40** [inset]
evoetsluis Neth. **48** B2
in Spain **55** C2
mand *r.* Afgh. **78** A1
mbrechts Ger. **49** E2
meringhausen Namibia **98** A2
mond Neth. **48** B2
msdale U.K. **44** C1
msdale *r.* U.K. **44** C1
mstedt Ger. **49** E1
China Dong **69** B1
singborg Sweden **41** C4
singfors Fin. *see* Helsinki
singør Denmark **41** C4
sinki Fin. **41** E3
vick Head Ireland **45** C2
nel Hempstead U.K. **47** C4
nnesberget Norway **40** C2
san *prov.* China **74** B2
nderson *KY* U.S.A. **122** C3
nderson *NC* U.S.A. **125** E1
nderson *NV* U.S.A. **119** D3
nderson *TX* U.S.A. **127** F2
ndon U.K. **47** C4
ngduan Shan *mts* China **66** A1
ngelo Neth. **48** C1
ngshui China **73** D2
ngxian China **75** A3
ngyang China **75** B3
narietta Maria, Cape Can.
44 B1
ury Kater, Cape Can.
41 H2
nstedt-Ulzburg Ger. **49** D1
ntiesbaai Namibia **96** A2

Hepu China **75** A3
Herāt Afgh. **78** A1
Herbert Can. **113** E2
Hereford U.K. **47** B3
Hereford U.S.A. **127** D2
Herford Ger. **49** D1
Herma Ness *hd* U.K. **44** [inset]
Hermanus S. Africa **98** A3
Hermidale Austr. **105** D2
Hermiston U.S.A. **118** C1
Hermit Islands P.N.G. **63** D3
Hermosillo Mex. **128** A2
Hernandarias Para. **138** B3
Herne Ger. **48** C2
Herning Denmark **41** B4
Herrieden Ger. **49** E3
Hertford U.K. **47** C4
Hervey Bay Austr. **103** E2
Herzberg Ger. **49** F2
Herzogenaurach Ger. **49** E3
Heshan China **75** A3
Hess *r.* Can. **112** B1
Hesselberg *h.* Ger. **49** E3
Hessisch Lichtenau Ger. **49** D2
Hettinger U.S.A. **120** C1
Hettstedt Ger. **49** E2
Hexham U.K. **46** B2
Heyuan China **75** B3
Heywood Austr. **104** C3
Heze China **74** B2
Hezhou China **75** B3
Hiawatha U.S.A. **121** E1
Hibbing U.S.A. **121** E1
Hicks Bay N.Z. **106** C2
Hidaka-sanmyaku *mts* Japan
70 D2
Hidalgo del Parral Mex.
128 B2
Hidrolândia Brazil **138** C1
High Desert U.S.A. **118** B2
High Level Can. **112** D2
High Point U.S.A. **125** E1
High Prairie Can. **112** D2
High River Can. **112** D2
Highrock Lake Can. **113** E2
High Wycombe U.K. **47** C4
Hiiumaa *i.* Estonia **36** B2
Hijaz *reg.* Saudi Arabia **82** A2
Hikurangi *mt.* N.Z. **106** C2
Hildburghausen Ger. **49** E2
Hildesheim Ger. **49** D1
Hillah Iraq **85** C2
Hillsboro *TX* U.S.A. **127** E2
Hillston Austr. **105** D2
Hilton Head Island U.S.A.
125 D2
Hilversum Neth. **48** B1
Himalaya *mts* Asia **79** B1
Himeji Japan **71** B4
Himeville S. Africa **99** C2
Hinchinbrook Island Austr.
103 D1
Hindu Kush *mts* Afgh./Pak. **78** A1
Hinesville U.S.A. **125** D2

Hinganghat India **79** B2
Hınıs Turkey **85** C2
Hinnøya *i.* Norway **40** D2
Hinthada Myanmar **66** A2
Hinton Can. **112** D2
Hirakud Reservoir India **79** C2
Hirosaki Japan **70** D2
Hiroshima Japan **71** B4
Hirschberg Ger. **49** E2
Hirson France **53** C2
Hisar India **78** B2
Hispaniola *i.* Caribbean Sea
131 C2
Hīt Iraq **85** C2
Hitachi Japan **71** D3
Hitachinaka Japan **71** D3
Hitra *i.* Norway **40** B3
Hiva Oa *i.* Fr. Polynesia **101**
Hjälmaren *l.* Sweden **41** D4
Hjalmar Lake Can. **113** E1
Hjørring Denmark **41** C4
Hlabisa S. Africa **99** D2
Hliệ Iceland **40** [inset]
Hlobyne Ukr. **39** D2
Hlotse Lesotho **99** C2
Hlukhiv Ukr. **39** D1
Hlybokaye Belarus **36** C2
Ho Ghana **90** C4
Hoachanas Namibia **98** A1
Hobart Austr. **103** D4
Hobart U.S.A. **127** E1
Hobbs U.S.A. **127** D2
Hobro Denmark **41** B4
Hobyo Somalia **93** C4
Hoceïma, Baie d'Al *b.* Morocco
54 C2
Hồ Chí Minh City Vietnam **67** B2
Höd *reg.* Maur. **90** B3
Hodeidah Yemen **82** B3
Hódmezővásárhely Hungary
51 E3
Hodna, Chott el *salt l.* Alg. **55** D2
Hoek van Holland Neth. *see*
Hook of Holland
Hoeyang N. Korea **69** B2
Hof Ger. **49** E2
Höfn *Austurland* Iceland **40** [inset]
Höfn *Vestfirðir* Iceland **40** [inset]
Hofsjökull *ice cap* Iceland
40 [inset]
Hōfu Japan **71** B4
Hoggar *plat.* Alg. **91** C2
Högsby Sweden **41** D4
Høgste Breakulen *mt.* Norway
41 B3
Hohe Rhön *mts* Ger. **49** D2
Hohe Venn *moorland* Belgium
48 C2
Hohhot China **73** B1
Hoh Xil Shan *mts* China **79** C1
Hōi An Vietnam **67** B2
Hojai India **66** A1
Hokitika N.Z. **106** B3
Hokkaidō *i.* Japan **70** D2

Holbrook U.S.A. **126** B2
Holdrege U.S.A. **121** D2
Holguín Cuba **131** C2
Hóll Iceland **40** [inset]
Holland U.S.A. **122** C2
Hollandia *see* Jayapura
Hollum Neth. **48** B1
Holly Springs U.S.A. **124** C2
Hollywood *CA* U.S.A. **119** C4
Hollywood *FL* U.S.A. **125** D3
Holm Norway **40** C2
Holman Can. **110** F2
Holmsund Sweden **40** E3
Holoog Namibia **98** A2
Holstebro Denmark **41** B4
Holston *r.* U.S.A. **125** D1
Holyhead U.K. **46** A3
Holy Island *England* U.K. **46** C2
Holy Island *Wales* U.K. **46** A3
Holyoke U.S.A. **120** C2
Holzminden Ger. **49** D2
Homberg (Efze) Ger. **49** D2
Hombori Mali **90** B3
Homburg Ger. **48** C3
Home Bay Can. **111** H2
Homestead U.S.A. **125** D3
Homs Syria **84** B2
Homyel' Belarus **37** D3
Hendeklbpaai S. Africa **98** A3
Hondo *r.* Belize/Mex. **129** D3
Hondo U.S.A. **127** E3
Honduras *country*
  Central America **130** B3
Honefoss Norway **41** B3
Honey Lake *salt l.* U.S.A. **118** B2
Hông Gai Vietnam **66** B1
Honghu China **75** B3
Hongjiang China **75** A3
Hong Kong China **75** B3
Hong Kong *aut. reg.* China **75** B3
Hongwon N. Korea **69** B1
Hongze Hu *l.* China **74** B2
Honiara Solomon Is. **100**
Honjō Japan **70** D3
Honshū *i.* Japan **71** D3
Hood, Mount *vol.* U.S.A. **118** B1
Hood Point Austr. **105** A3
Hood River U.S.A. **118** B1
Hoogeveen Neth. **48** C1
Hoogezand-Sappemeer Neth.
  48 C1
Hook of Holland Neth. **48** B2
Hoonah U.S.A. **112** B2
Hoorn Neth. **48** B1
Hope Can. **112** C3
Hope U.S.A. **124** B2
Hopedale Can. **115** D1
Hope Mountains Can. **115** D1
Hopetoun Austr. **104** C3
Hopetown S. Africa **98** B2
Hopewell U.S.A. **123** E3
Hopewell Islands Can. **114** C1
Hopkins, Lake *salt flat* Austr.
  102 B2
Hopkinsville U.S.A. **122** C3

Horasan Turkey **85** C1
Horažďovice Czech Rep. **49** F3
Horki Belarus **37** D3
Horlivka Ukr. **39** E2
Hormak Iran **83** D2
Hormuz, Strait of Iran/Oman
  83 C2
Horn *r.* Iceland **40** [inset]
Horn, Cape Chile **137** B6
Hornell U.S.A. **123** E2
Hornepayne Can. **114** C2
Horodenka Ukr. **38** C2
Horodnya Ukr. **39** D1
Horodok *Khmel'nyts'ka Oblast'* Ukr.
  38 C2
Horodok *L'viv's'ka Oblast'* Ukr.
  38 B2
Horokhiv Ukr. **38** B1
Horse Islands Can. **115** E1
Horsham Austr. **104** C3
Horton *r.* Can. **110** D2
Hosa'ina Eth. **93** D4
Hoshab Pak. **78** A2
Hoshiarpur India **78** B1
Hotan China **79** C1
Hotazel S. Africa **98** B2
Hot Springs *AR* U.S.A. **124** B2
Hot Springs *SD* U.S.A. **120** C2
Hottah Lake Can. **112** D1
Houma China **74** B2
Houma U.S.A. **124** B3
Houston Can. **112** C2
Houston U.S.A. **127** E3
Houwater S. Africa **98** B3
Hovd Mongolia **72** C1
Hove U.K. **47** C4
Hövsgöl Nuur *l.* Mongolia **72** C1
Hövüün Mongolia **72** C1
Howa, Wadi *watercourse* Sudan
  92 A3
Howe, Cape Austr. **105** D3
Howland Island *terr.*
  N. Pacific Ocean **100**
Höxter Ger. **49** D2
Hoy *i.* U.K. **44** C1
Heyanger Norway **41** B3
Hoyerswerda Ger. **50** C2
Hpapun Myanmar **66** A1
Hradec Králové Czech Rep.
  51 D2
Hrasnica Bos.-Herz. **57** C2
Hrebinka Ukr. **39** D1
Hrodna Belarus **38** B1
Hsi-hseng Myanmar **66** A1
Hsinchu Taiwan **75** C3
Hsinying Taiwan **75** C3
Huacho Peru **134** B4
Huade China **74** B1
Huadian China **69** B1
Huai'an China **74** B2
Huaibei China **74** B2
Huaihua China **75** A3
Huainan China **74** B2
Huaiyang China **74** B2

Huaiyin China *see* Huai'an
Huajuápan de León Mex. **129**
Huaki Indon. **63** C3
Hualien Taiwan **75** C3
Huallaga *r.* Peru **134** B3
Huambo Angola **96** A1
Huancavelica Peru **134** B4
Huancayo Peru **134** B4
Huangchuan China **74** B2
Huang Hai *sea* N. Pacific Ocean
  see Yellow Sea
Huanghua China **69** B1
Huangshan China **75** B3
Huangshi China **75** B3
Huangtu Gaoyuan *plat.* China
  74 A2
Huanren China **69** B1
Huánuco Peru **134** B3
Huanuni Bol. **136** B2
Huaráz Peru **134** B3
Huarmey Peru **134** B4
Huasco Chile **136** A3
Huasco *r.* Chile **136** A3
Huatabampo Mex. **128** B2
Huatusco Mex. **129** C3
Huayuan China **75** A3
Huayxay Laos **66** B1
Hubei *prov.* China **74** B2
Hubli India **77** B3
Huddersfield U.K. **46** C3
Hudiksvall Sweden **41** D3
Hudson *r.* U.S.A. **123** F2
Hudson Bay Can. **111** G3
Hudson Bay *sea* Can. **111** G3
Hudson Strait Can. **111** H2
Huê Vietnam **66** B2
Huehuetenango Guat. **130** A3
Huehueto, Cerro *mt.* Mex.
  128 B2
Huejutla Mex. **129** C2
Huelva Spain **54** B2
Huércal-Overa Spain **55** C2
Huesca Spain **55** C1
Huéscar Spain **54** C2
Hughes Austr. **102** B3
Hugo U.S.A. **127** E2
Huhudi S. Africa **98** B2
Huib-Hoch Plateau Namibia
  98 A2
Huichang China **75** B3
Huich'ŏn N. Korea **69** B1
Huila Plateau Angola **96** A1
Huili China **66** B1
Huinan China **69** B1
Huixtla Mex. **129** C3
Huize China **75** A3
Huizhou China **75** B3
Hukuntsi Botswana **98** B1
Hulayfah Saudi Arabia **82** B2
Hulin China **73** B1
Hull Can. **114** C2
Hulun China **73** D1

n Nur l. China 73 D1
aypole Ukr. 39 E2
aitá Brazil 134 C3
ber est. U.K. 46 C3
boldt U.S.A. 124 C1
boldt r. U.S.A. 118 C2
enná Slovakia 51 E3
phreys Peak U.S.A. 126 B1
an prov. China 75 B3
chun China 69 C1
dedoara Romania 38 B2
field Ger. 49 D2
gary country Europe 51 D3
gerford Austr. 104 C1
gnam N. Korea 69 B2
He r. China 69 A1
stanton U.K. 46 D3
er Islands Austr. 103 D4
on, Lake Can./U.S.A. 122 D3
tington U.K. 47 C3
tington IN U.S.A. 122 C4
tington WV U.S.A. 122 D5
tly N.Z. 106 C2
tly U.K. 44 C2
tsville Can. 114 C2
tsville AL U.S.A. 124 C4
tsville TX U.S.A. 127 E2
on U.S.A. 121 D2
on, Lake Can./U.S.A. 122 D2
ricane U.S.A. 119 D3
avík Iceland 40 [inset]
i Romania 38 C2
i r. Croatia 57 C2
ange Zimbabwe 96 B1
nnis U.S.A. 120 C2
rgas Nuur salt l. Mongolia
C1

mița r. Romania 38 C2
ca Romania 38 C2
Romania 38 C2
dan Nigeria 90 C4

Ibagué Col. 134 B2
Ibarra Ecuador 134 B2
Ibb Yemen 82 B3
Ibbenbüren Ger. 48 C1
Ibiraçu Brazil 139 D1
Ibiza i. Spain 55 D2
Ibotirama Brazil 135 E4
Ibrā' Oman 83 C2
Ibri Oman 83 C2
Ica Peru 134 B4
İçel Turkey see Mersin
Iceland country Europe 40 [inset]
Ichinoseki Japan 70 D3
Ichnya Ukr. 39 D1
Ich'ŏn N. Korea 69 B2
Idabel U.S.A. 127 F2
Idaho state U.S.A. 118 C3
Idaho Falls U.S.A. 118 D2
Idar-Oberstein Ger. 48 C3
Idfū Egypt 92 B2
Idhān Awbārī des. Libya 91 D2
Idhān Murzūq des. Libya 91 D2
Idiofa Dem. Rep. Congo 94 B3
Idlib Syria 84 B2
Iepê Brazil 138 B2
Ieper Belgium 48 A2
Ifakara Tanz. 95 D3
Ifanadiana Madag. 97 [inset] D2
Ife Nigeria 90 C4
Ifôghas, Adrar des hills Mali
90 C3
Igan Malaysia 65 C1
Igatpuri India 78 B3
Iğdır Turkey 85 C2
Iglesias Italy 56 A3
Igloolik Can. 111 G2
Ignace Can. 114 A2
Ignalina Lith. 36 C2
Iğneada Turkey 58 C2
Igrim Rus. Fed. 34 F2
Iguaçu r. Brazil 138 B3
Iguaçu Falls Arg./Brazil 138 B3
Iguala Mex. 129 C3
Igualada Spain 55 D1
Iguape Brazil 138 C2
Iguatemi Brazil 138 B2
Iguatu Brazil 135 F3
Iguéla Gabon 94 A3
Ihbulag Mongolia 73 D2
Ihosy Madag. 97 [inset] D2
Iisalmi Fin. 40 F3
Ijebu-Ode Nigeria 90 C4
IJmuiden Neth. 48 B1
IJssel r. Neth. 48 B1
IJsselmeer l. Neth. 48 B1
Ikageng S. Africa 99 C2
Ikaria i. Greece 59 C3
Ikela Dem. Rep. Congo 94 C3
Ikhtiman Bulg. 58 B2
Iki i. Japan 71 A4
Iksan S. Korea 69 B2
Ilagan Phil. 68 B2
Īlām Iran 85 C2

Iława Pol. 51 D2
Ilazārān, Kūh-e mt. Iran 83 C2
Île-à-la-Crosse, Lac l. Can.
113 E2
Ilebo Dem. Rep. Congo 94 C3
Ileret Kenya 95 D2
Ilford U.K. 47 D4
Ilfracombe U.K. 47 A4
Ilha Grande, Baía da b. Brazil
139 D2
Ilha Grande, Represa resr Brazil
138 B2
Ilha Solteira, Represa resr Brazil
138 B2
Ílhavo Port. 54 B1
Ilhéus Brazil 135 F4
Iligan Phil. 68 B3
Iliapel Chile 136 A4
Illichivs'k Ukr. 38 D2
Illinois r. U.S.A. 122 B3
Illinois state U.S.A. 122 C3
Illintsi Ukr. 38 C2
Illizi Alg. 91 C2
Il'men', Ozero l. Rus. Fed. 37 D2
Ilmenau Ger. 49 E2
Ilo Peru 134 B4
Iloilo Phil. 68 B2
Ilorin Nigeria 90 C4
Iluka Austr. 105 E1
Ilulissat Greenland 111 I2
Imī Eth. 93 C4
Imola Italy 56 B2
Imperatriz Brazil 135 E3
Imperial U.S.A. 120 C2
Impfondo Congo 94 B2
Imphal India 66 A1
İmroz Turkey 59 C2
In Aménas Alg. 91 C2
Inari Fin. 40 F2
Inarijärvi l. Fin. 40 F2
Inawashiro-ko l. Japan 71 D3
İnce Burun pt Turkey 84 B1
Inch'ŏn S. Korea 69 B2
Incomáti r. Moz. 99 D2
Indalstø Norway 42 E1
Inda Silasē Eth. 82 B3
Independence CA U.S.A. 119 C3
Independence IA U.S.A. 121 E2
Independence KS U.S.A. 121 D3
Independence MO U.S.A. 121 E3
Independence Mountains U.S.A.
118 C2
Inderborskiy Kazakh. 80 C2
India country Asia 76 B2
Indiana U.S.A. 123 E2
Indiana state U.S.A. 122 C2
Indianapolis U.S.A. 122 C3
Indian Ocean 145
Indianola IA U.S.A. 121 E2
Indianola MS U.S.A. 124 B2
Indian Springs U.S.A. 119 C3
Indiga Rus. Fed. 34 D2
Indigirka r. Rus. Fed. 87 L2
Indija S.M. 58 B1

Indio U.S.A. **119** C4
Indonesia country Asia **63** B3
Indore India **78** B2
Indramayu, Tanjung pt Indon. **64** B2
Indre r. France **52** C2
Indus r. China/Pakistan **78** B1
Indus r. China/Pakistan **78** A2
Indus, Mouths of the Pak. **78** A2
Inebolu Turkey **84** B1
Inegöl Turkey **59** C2
Infiernillo, Presa resr Mex. **128** B3
Inglewood Austr. **105** E1
Ingolstadt Ger. **50** D3
Ingomar Austr. **104** A1
Ingraj Bazar India **79** C2
Inhambane Moz. **97** C2
Inhisbfin i. Ireland **45** A2
Inishmore i. Ireland **45** A2
Inishowen pen. Ireland **45** C1
Inland Kaikoura Range mts N.Z. **106** B3
Inn r. Europe **50** C3
Inner Mongolia aut. reg. China see **Nei Mongol Zizhiqu**
Inner Sound sea chan. U.K. **44** B2
Innisfail Austr. **103** D1
Innsbruck Austria **50** C3
Inongo Dem. Rep. Congo **94** B3
Inowrocław Pol. **51** D2
In Salah Alg. **90** C2
Insein Myanmar **66** A2
Inta Rus. Fed. **34** F2
International Falls U.S.A. **121** E1
Inukjuak Can. **114** C1
Inuvik Can. **110** C2
Inveraray U.K. **44** B3
Invercargill N.Z. **106** A4
Inverell Austr. **105** E1
Invergordon U.K. **44** B2
Invermere Can. **112** D2
Inverness U.K. **44** B2
Inverurie U.K. **44** C2
Investigator Strait Austr. **104** B3
Inya Rus. Fed. **81** F1
Inyonga Tanz. **95** D3
Inzhavino Rus. Fed. **39** F1
Ioannina Greece **59** B3
Iola U.S.A. **121** D3
Iona i. U.K. **44** A2
Ionian Islands admin. reg. Greece **59** A3
Ionian Sea Greece/Italy **59** A3
Ionioi Nisoi admin. reg. Greece see **Ionian Islands**
Ios i. Greece **59** C3
Iowa state U.S.A. **121** E2
Iowa City U.S.A. **121** E2
Ipameri Brazil **138** C1
Ipatinga Brazil **139** D1
Ipatovo Rus. Fed. **85** D1
Ipelegeng S. Africa **99** C2
Ipiales Col. **134** B2

Ipoh Malaysia **64** B1
Iporá Brazil **138** B1
Ippy C.A.R. **94** C2
Ipswich Austr. **105** E1
Ipswich U.K. **47** D3
Iqaluit Can. **111** H2
Iquique Chile **136** A3
Iquitos Peru **134** B3
Irai Brazil **138** B3
Irakleio Greece see **Iraklion**
Iraklion Greece **59** C3
Iran country Asia **85** D2
Iran, Pegunungan mts Indon. **65** C1
Īrānshahr Iran **83** D2
Irapuato Mex. **128** B2
Iraq country Asia **85** C2
Irati Brazil **138** B3
Irbid Jordan **84** B2
Irbit Rus. Fed. **34** F3
Irecê Brazil **135** E4
Ireland country Europe **45** B2
Irema Dem. Rep. Congo **94** C3
Irgiz Kazakh. **80** D2
Irigui r. Mali/Maur. **90** B3
Iringa Tanz. **95** D3
Iriri r. Brazil **135** C3
Irish Sea Ireland/U.K. **43** B3
Irkutsk Rus. Fed. **72** C1
Iron Knob Austr. **104** B2
Iron Mountain U.S.A. **122** C1
Ironwood U.S.A. **122** B1
Irosin Phil. **68** B2
Irpin' Ukr. **38** D1
Irrawaddy r. Myanmar **66** A2
Irrawaddy, Mouths of the Myanmar **67** A2
Irtysh r. Kazakh./Rus. Fed. **81** E1
Irún Spain **55** C1
Irvine U.K. **44** B3
Isabela Phil. **68** B3
Isabela, Cordillera mts Nic. **130** B3
Isafjörður Iceland **40** [inset]
Isahaya Japan **71** B4
Isar r. Ger. **53** E2
Isbister U.K. **44** [inset]
Ischia, Isola d' i. Italy **56** B2
Ise Japan **71** C4
Isernhagen Ger. **49** D1
Isère r. France **53** D2
Iseyin Nigeria **90** C4
Ishikari-wan b. Japan **70** D2
Ishim r. Kazakh./Rus. Fed. **81** E1
Ishinomaki Japan **70** D3
Ishpeming U.S.A. **122** C1
Işıklar Dağı mts Turkey **59** C2
Işıklı Turkey **59** C3
Isil'kul' Rus. Fed. **81** E1
Isipingo S. Africa **99** D2
Isiro Dem. Rep. Congo **95** C2
Iskenderun Turkey **84** B2
Iskitim Rus. Fed. **86** H3

Iskut r. Can. **112** B2
Islamabad Pak. **78** B1
Island Lagoon salt flat Austr. **104** B2
Island Lake Can. **113** F2
Islands, Bay of N.Z. **106** B2
Islay i. U.K. **44** A3
Isle of Man i. Irish Sea **46** A2
Ismoili Somoní, Qullai mt. Tajik. **81** E3
Isna Egypt **82** A2
Isola di Capo Rizzuto Italy **57** C3
Isperikh Bulg. **58** C2
Israel country Asia **84** B2
Issoire France **52** C2
İstanbul Turkey **59** C2
İstanbul Boğazı str. Turkey see **Bosporus**
Istiaia Greece **59** B3
Istres France **53** C3
Istria pen. Croatia **56** B1
Itaberaba Brazil **135** E4
Itabira Brazil **139** D1
Itabirito Brazil **139** D2
Itabuna Brazil **135** F4
Itacoatiara Brazil **134** D3
Itaí Brazil **138** C2
Itaipu, Represa de resr Brazil **138** B3
Itaituba Brazil **135** D3
Itajaí Brazil **138** C3
Itajubá Brazil **139** C2
Italy country Europe **56** B2
Itamarandiba Brazil **139** D1
Itambacuri Brazil **139** D1
Itambé, Pico de mt. Brazil **139** D1
Itanagar India **66** A1
Itanhaém Brazil **139** C2
Itanhém Brazil **139** D1
Itaobim Brazil **139** D1
Itapajipe Brazil **138** C1
Itapebi Brazil **139** E1
Itapemirim Brazil **139** D2
Itaperuna Brazil **139** D2
Itapetinga Brazil **135** E4
Itapetininga Brazil **138** C2
Itapeva Brazil **138** C2
Itapicuru Mirim Brazil **135** E3
Itapipoca Brazil **135** E3
Itapuranga Brazil **138** C1
Itararé Brazil **138** C2
Itarsi India **79** B2
Itbayat i. Phil. **68** B1
Ithaca U.S.A. **123** E2
Ith Hils ridge Ger. **49** D1
Itimbiri r. Dem. Rep. Congo **94** C2
Itinga Brazil **139** D1
Itiquira Brazil **138** B1
Itiquira r. Brazil **138** A1
Ittoqqortoormiit Greenland **111** K2
Itu Brazil **138** C2

r. Brazil **134** B3
utaba Brazil **138** C1
nbiara Brazil **138** C1
ama Brazil **138** B1
hoe Ger. **50** B2
r. Brazil **138** B2
Fin. **40** F2
ava Belarus **36** C3
hoe Austr. **104** C2
kiv Ukr. **38** C1
o-Frankivs'k Ukr. **38** B2
ovo Rus. Fed. **37** F2
sevichy Belarus **36** C3
t' Rus. Fed. **34** F2
heima Brazil **138** B2
heima r. Brazil **138** B2
uut Greenland **111** I2
a Italy **56** A1
ndi Turkey **59** C3
vik Can. **111** G2
xi Japan **71** D3
kuni Japan **71** B4
mizawa Japan **70** D2
e Belarus **36** C3
o S. Africa **99** D3
n Mex. **128** B2
al, Lago de r. Guat. **29** D3
nal Mex. **129** C2
erbash Rus. Fed. **85** C1
vsk Rus. Fed. **34** E3
ayil Turkey **59** C2
k Gölü l. Turkey **59** C2
ne Japan **71** B3
slav Ukr. **38** C1
um Ukr. **39** E2

salón r. Spain **54** C2
alpur India **79** B2
iru Austr. **102** C1
lanica Bos.-Herz. **57** C2
oatão Brazil **135** F4
oticabal Brazil **138** C2
a Spain **55** C1
areacanga Brazil **135** D3
arei Brazil **139** C2
into Brazil **139** D1
khman U.S.A. **123** F1
kson AL U.S.A. **124** C2
kson MI U.S.A. **122** C2
kson MS U.S.A. **124** B2
kson TN U.S.A. **124** C1
kson WY U.S.A. **120** A2
kson Head N.Z. **106** A3
ksonville AR U.S.A. **124** B2
ksonville FL U.S.A. **125** D3
ksonville IL U.S.A. **122** B3
ksonville NC U.S.A. **125** E2

Jacksonville TX U.S.A. **127** E2
Jacmel Haiti **131** C3
Jacobabad Pak. **78** A2
Jacobina Brazil **135** E4
Jacques Cartier, Mont mt. Can. **115** D2
Jacunda Brazil **135** E3
Jacupiranga Brazil **138** C2
Jadovnik mt. Bos.-Herz. **57** C2
Jaén Spain **54** C2
Jaffa, Cape Austr. **104** B3
Jaffna Sri Lanka **77** B4
Jagdalpur India **77** C3
Jaguariaíva Brazil **138** C2
Jahrom Iran **85** D2
Jaipur India **78** B2
Jaisalmer India **78** A2
Jakarta Indon. **64** B2
Jäkkvik Sweden **40** D2
Jakobstad Fin. **40** E3
Jalālābād Afgh. **78** B1
Jalandhar India **78** B1
Jalapa Mex. **129** C3
Jales Brazil **138** B2
Jalgaon India **78** B2
Jalingo Nigeria **97** D4
Jalna India **78** B3
Jalpa Mex. **128** B2
Jālū Libya **91** E2
Jamaica country West Indies **130** C3
Jamalpur Bangl. **79** C2
Jambi Indon. **64** B2
James r. N. Dakota/S. Dakota U.S.A. **121** D2
James r. VA U.S.A. **123** E3
James Bay Can. **111** G3
Jameson Land reg. Greenland **111** K2
Jamestown Austr. **104** B2
Jamestown ND U.S.A. **121** D1
Jamestown NY U.S.A. **123** E2
Jammu India **78** B1
Jammu and Kashmir terr. Asia **78** B1
Jamnagar India **78** B2
Jämsä Fin. **41** F3
Jamshedpur India **79** C2
Jamuna r. Bangl. **79** C2
Janakpur Nepal **79** C2
Janaúba Brazil **139** D1
Jandaq Iran **85** D2
Janesville U.S.A. **122** C2
Jan Mayen terr. Arctic Ocean **86** B2
Jansenville S. Africa **98** B3
Januária Brazil **135** E4
Japan country Asia **71** C3
Japan, Sea of N. Pacific Ocean **73** C2
Japurá r. Brazil **134** C3
Jaraguá Brazil **138** C1
Jaraguari Brazil **138** B2
Jardim Brazil **138** A2

Jargalant Mongolia **73** D1
Jarocin Pol. **51** D2
Jarosław Pol. **51** E2
Järpen Sweden **40** C3
Jartai China **74** A2
Jarú Brazil **134** C4
Jarud China see Lubei
Jarvis Island terr. S. Pacific Ocean **101**
Jāsk Iran **83** C2
Jaslo Pol. **51** E3
Jasper Can. **112** D2
Jasper IN U.S.A. **122** C3
Jasper TX U.S.A. **127** F2
Jastrzębie-Zdrój Pol. **51** D3
Jászberény Hungary **51** D3
Jataí Brazil **138** B1
Jaú Brazil **138** C2
Jaú r. Brazil **134** C3
Jaunpur India **79** C2
Java i. Indon. **64** B2
Java Sea Indon. see Jawa, Laut
Java Trench sea feature Indian Ocean **145** H6
Jawa i. Indon. see Java
Jawa, Laut sea Indon. see Java
Jawhar Somalia **93** C4
Jawor Pol. **51** D2
Jaya, Puncak mt. Indon. **63** D3
Jayapura Indon. **63** D3
Jeannin, Lac l. Can. **115** D1
Jebel, Bahr el r. Sudan/Uganda see White Nile
Jebel Abyad Plateau Sudan **92** A3
Jedburgh U.K. **44** C3
Jeddah Saudi Arabia **82** A2
Jefferson, Mount U.S.A. **119** C3
Jefferson City U.S.A. **121** E3
Jejuí Guazú r. Para. **138** A2
Jēkabpils Latvia **36** C2
Jelenia Góra Pol. **51** D2
Jelgava Latvia **36** B2
Jember Indon. **65** C2
Jena Ger. **49** E2
Jengish Chokusu mt. China/Kyrg. see Pobeda Peak
Jenin West Bank **84** B2
Jennings U.S.A. **124** B2
Jequié Brazil **135** E4
Jequitaí Brazil **139** D1
Jequitinhonha Brazil **139** D1
Jequitinhonha r. Brazil **139** E1
Jérémie Haiti **131** C3
Jerez Mex. **128** B2
Jerez de la Frontera Spain **54** B2
Jerome U.S.A. **118** D2
Jersey i. Channel Is **47** B5
Jerumenha Brazil **135** E3
Jerusalem Israel/West Bank **84** B2
Jervis Bay Territory admin. div. Austr. **105** E3
Jesenice Slovenia **56** B1
Jesi Italy **56** B2
Jessore Bangl. **79** C2

Jesup U.S.A. **125** D2
Jesús Carranza Mex. **129** C3
Jhalawar India **78** B2
Jhang Pak. **78** B1
Jhansi India **79** C2
Jharsuguda India **79** C2
Jhelum Pak. **78** B1
Jiamusi China **70** B1
Ji'an *Jiangxi* China **75** B3
Ji'an *Jilin* China **75** B3
Jiangsu *prov.* China **74** B2
Jiangxi *prov.* China **75** B3
Jiangyou China **74** A2
Jianli China **75** B3
Jianqiao China **74** B2
Jianyang *Fujian* China **75** B3
Jianyang *Sichuan* China **75** A2
Jiaohe China **69** B1
Jiaozhou China **74** C2
Jiaozuo China **74** B2
Jiaxing China **74** C2
Jiayuguan China **72** C2
Jiddah Saudi Arabia *see* Jeddah
Jiehkkevárri *mt.* Norway **40** D2
Jiexiu China **74** B2
Jihlava Czech Rep. **51** D3
Jijel Alg. **85** E2
Jijiga Eth. **93** C4
Jilf al Kabīr, Haḍabat al *plat.*
  Egypt **92** A2
Jilib Somalia **93** C4
Jilin China **69** B1
Jilin *prov.* China **74** C1
Jilin Hada Ling *mts* China **69** A1
Jima Eth. **93** B4
Jiménez *Chihuahua* Mex. **128** B2
Jiménez *Tamaulipas* Mex. **129** C2
Jinan China **74** B2
Jinchang China **72** C2
Jincheng China **74** B2
Jindabyne Austr. **105** D3
Jindřichův Hradec Czech Rep.
  50 D3
Jingdezhen China **75** B3
Jinggangshan China **75** B3
Jinghong China **66** B2
Jingning China **74** A2
Jingtai China **74** A2
Jingxi China **75** A3
Jingyu China **69** B1
Jingyuan China **74** A2
Jingzhou *Hubei* China **75** B2
Jingzhou *Hubei* China **75** B2
Jinhua China **75** B3
Jining *Nei Mongol* China **74** B1
Jining *Shandong* China **74** B2
Jinja Uganda **93** A3
Jinka Eth. **93** B4
Jinotepe Nic. **130** B3
Jinsha Jiang *r.* China *see* Yangtze
Jinshi China **75** B3
Jinzhong China **74** B2
Jinzhou China **74** C1

Jiparaná *r.* Brazil **134** C3
Jirang China **79** C1
Jírkov Czech Rep. **49** F2
Jiroft Iran **83** C2
Jishou China **75** B3
Jiu *r.* Romania **38** B2
Jiuding Shan *mt.* China **74** A2
Jiujiang China **75** B3
Jiwani Pak. **83** D2
Jixi China **70** B1
Jīzān Saudi Arabia **82** B3
Jizzax Uzbek. **81** D2
Joaçaba Brazil **138** B3
João Pessoa Brazil **135** F3
João Pinheiro Brazil **139** C1
Jodhpur India **78** B2
Joensuu Fin. **40** F3
Jõetsu Japan **71** C3
Jofane Moz. **97** C2
Jõgeva Estonia **36** C2
Johannesburg S. Africa **99** C2
John Day U.S.A. **118** C2
John Day *r.* U.S.A. **118** B1
John H. Kerr Reservoir U.S.A.
  123 E3
John o'Groats U.K. **44** C1
Johnson City U.S.A. **125** D1
Johnson's Crossing Can. **112** B1
Johnstone U.K. **44** B3
Johor Bahru Malaysia **64** B1
Jõhvi Estonia **36** C2
Joinville Brazil **138** C3
Jokkmokk Sweden **40** D2
Jökulsá á Fjöllum *r.* Iceland
  40 [inset]
Joliet U.S.A. **122** C2
Joliette Can. **114** C2
Jolo Phil. **68** B3
Joló *i.* Phil. **68** B3
Jombang Indon. **65** C2
Jos Nigeria **91** C4
José Cardel Mex. **129** C3
Joseph, Lac *l.* Can. **115** D1
Joseph Bonaparte Gulf Austr.
  102 B1
Jos Plateau Nigeria **91** C4
Jotunheimen *mts* Norway **41** B3
Jouberton S. Africa **99** C2
Juan de Fuca Strait Can./U.S.A.
  118 B1

Juan Fernández, Archipiélago
  S. Pacific Ocean **133**
Juárez Mex. **129** B2
Juàzeiro Brazil **135** E3
Juàzeiro do Norte Brazil **135**
Juba Sudan **93** B4
Jubba *r.* Somalia **93** C5
Jubbah Saudi Arabia **82** B2
Júcar *r.* Spain **55** C2
Juchitán Mex. **129** C3
Judenburg Austria **50** C3
Juigalpa Nic. **130** B3
Juist *i.* Ger. **48** C1
Juiz de Fora Brazil **139** D2
Juliaca Peru **134** B4
Jumla Nepal **79** C2
Junagadh India **78** B2
Junction U.S.A. **127** E2
Junction City U.S.A. **121** D3
Jundiaí Brazil **138** C2
Juneau U.S.A. **112** B2
Junee Austr. **105** D2
Jungfrau *mt.* Switz. **53** D2
Juniata *r.* U.S.A. **123** E2
Junsele Sweden **40** D3
Juntura U.S.A. **118** C2
Juquiá Brazil **138** C2
Jur *r.* Sudan **93** A4
Jura *mts* France/Switz. **53** D2
Jura *i.* U.K. **44** B2
Jurbarkas Lith. **36** B2
Jūrmala Latvia **36** B2
Juruá *r.* Brazil **134** B3
Juruena *r.* Brazil **134** C3
Jutaí *r.* Brazil **134** C3
Jüterbog Ger. **49** F2
Juventud, Isla de la *i.* Cuba
  130 B2
Juxian China **74** B2
Jwaneng Botswana **98** B3
Jyväskylä Fin. **41** F3

K

K2 *mt.* China/Jammu and Kashmir
  78 B1
Kabaena *i.* Indon. **65** D2
Kabalo Dem. Rep. Congo **95** C4
Kabinakagami Lake Can. **114**
Kabinda Dem. Rep. Congo **94**
Kabompo Zambia **96** B1
Kabongo Dem. Rep. Congo
  95 C3
Kābul Afgh. **78** A1
Kaburuang *i.* Indon. **68** B3
Kabwe Zambia **97** B1
Kachchh, Gulf of India **78** A2
Kachchh, Rann of *marsh* India
  78 B2
Kachug Rus. Fed. **87** J3
Kaçkar Dağı *mt.* Turkey **85** C1
Kadıköy Turkey **59** C2

190

…at atoll India **77** B3
…n Rus. Fed. **37** F3
…na Zimbabwe **97** B1
…nkani Myanmar **67** A2
…gli Sudan **93** A3
…na Nigeria **91** C3
…y Rus. Fed. **37** E2
…nerom Rus. Fed. **34** E2
…i Maur. **90** A3
…ŏng N. Korea **69** B2
…e Zambia **97** B1
…r. Zambia **96** B1
…Bandoro C.A.R. **94** B2
…Tmitskaya Rus. Fed. **39** F2
…shima Japan **71** B4
…rlyk Ukr. **38** D2
…yan r. Indon. **65** C2
…Dem. Rep. Congo **94** C4
…gi Iran **83** C2
…erusvaarat mts Fin. **40** E2
…amanmaraş Turkey **84** B2
…rak Iran **83** C2
…Kepuluan is Indon. **63** C3
…na Nigeria **90** C4
…oi N.Z. **106** B3
…ng China **74** B2
…gveld reg. S. Africa **98** B2
…oura N.Z. **106** B3
…China **75** A3
…a Indon. **63** C3
…anawa Mountains N.Z.
5 C2
…a Japan **71** C4
…i Reservoir Nigeria **90** C3
…ara Harbour N.Z. **106** B2
…na India **78** B2
…uan Tunisia **91** D1
…ia N.Z. **106** B2
…n N.Z. **106** C2
…wa N.Z. **106** C2
…atu Indon. **63** C3
…an Liaoning China **69** A1
…an Yunnan China **75** A3
…ani Fin. **40** F3
…mas S. Africa **98** B2
…mega Kenya **95** D2
…ovka Ukr. **39** D2
…ovs'ke Vodoskhovyshche
… Ukr. **39** D2
…hada India **77** C3
…ovik U.S.A. **110** C2
…bo Zambia **96** B1
…sh Rus. Fed. **39** F1
…ava Dida Kenya **95** D2
…hari Desert Africa **96** B2
…kpit Fin. **40** E3
…mare Botswana **99** C1
…maria Greece **59** B2
…mata Greece **59** B3
…mazoo U.S.A. **122** C2
…nchak Ukr. **39** D2
…n i. Indon. **65** D2
…atoa i. Indon. **65** D2
…sin Thai. **66** B2

Kalāt Afgh. **78** A1
Kalāt Iran **83** C2
Kalat Pak. **78** A2
Kalbarri Austr. **102** A2
Kalecik Turkey **84** B1
Kalema Dem. Rep. Congo
94 C4
Kalemie Dem. Rep. Congo
95 C3
Kalemyo Myanmar **66** A1
Kalevala Rus. Fed. **40** G2
Kalgoorlie Austr. **102** B3
Kaliakra, Nos pt Bulg. **58** C2
Kalima Dem. Rep. Congo
95 C3
Kalimantan reg. Indon. **65** C2
Kaliningrad Rus. Fed. **36** B3
Kalininskaya Rus. Fed. **39** E2
Kalinkavichy Belarus **36** C3
Kalispell U.S.A. **118** D1
Kalisz Pol. **51** D2
Kalitva r. Rus. Fed. **39** F2
Kalix Sweden **40** E2
Kalixälven r. Sweden **40** E2
Kalkan Turkey **59** C3
Kallavesi l. Fin. **40** F3
Kallsjön l. Sweden **40** C3
Kalmar Sweden **41** D4
Kalmarsund sea chan. Sweden
41 D4
Kalomo Zambia **96** B1
Kalone Peak Can. **112** C2
Kalpa India **79** B1
Kalpeni atoll India **77** B3
Kalpi India **79** B2
Kaluga Rus. Fed. **37** E3
Kaltenkirchen Ger. **49** D1
Kaluga Rus. Fed. **37** E3
Kalyazin Rus. Fed. **37** E2
Kalymnos i. Greece **59** C3
Kama Dem. Rep. Congo **95** C3
Kama r. Rus. Fed. **34** E3
Kamaishi Japan **70** D3
Kamanjab Namibia **96** A1
Kamarān i. Yemen **82** B3
Kamaran Pak. **78** A2
Kambala Austr. **102** B3
Kamchatka Peninsula Rus. Fed.
87 M3
Kamchiya r. Bulg. **58** C2
Kamenitsa mt. Bulg. **58** B2
Kamenjak, Rt pt Croatia **56** B2
Kamenka Rus. Fed. **39** I1
Kamen'-na-Obi Rus. Fed. **81** F1
Kamennomostskiy Rus. Fed.
39 F3
Kamenolomni Rus. Fed. **39** F2
Kamenskoye Rus. Fed. **87** N2
Kamensk-Shakhtinskiy Rus. Fed.
39 F2
Kamensk-Ural'skiy Rus. Fed.
34 F3

Kamiesberge mts S. Africa **98** A3
Kamieskroon S. Africa **98** A3
Kamilukuak Lake Can. **113** E1
Kamina Dem. Rep. Congo **95** C3
Kaminak Lake Can. **113** F1
Kamin'-Kashyrs'kyy Ukr. **38** B1
Kamloops Can. **112** C2
Kamonia Dem. Rep. Congo **94** C3
Kampala Uganda **95** D2
Kampar r. Indon. **64** B1
Kampen Neth. **48** B1
Kampene Dem. Rep. Congo
95 C3
Kamphaeng Phet Thai. **66** A2
Kâmpóng Cham Cambodia
67 B2
Kâmpóng Spœ Cambodia **67** B2
Kâmpôt Cambodia **67** B2
Kamsack Can. **113** E2
Kamsuuma Somalia **93** C4
Kam'yanets'-Podil's'kyy Ukr.
38 C2
Kam'yanka-Buz'ka Ukr. **38** B1
Kamyshevatskaya Rus. Fed.
39 E2
Kamyshin Rus. Fed. **35** D3
Kanab U.S.A. **119** D3
Kananga Dem. Rep. Congo **94** C3
Kanash Rus. Fed. **35** D3
Kanawha r. U.S.A. **123** D3
Kanazawa Japan **71** C3
Kanbalu Myanmar **66** A1
Kanchanaburi Thai. **67** A2
Kanchipuram India **77** B3
Kandahār Afgh. **78** A1
Kandalaksha Rus. Fed. **40** G2
Kandangan Indon. **65** C2
Kandhkot Pak. **78** A2
Kandi Benin **90** C3
Kandla India **78** B2
Kandos Austr. **105** D2
Kandy Sri Lanka **77** C4
Kandyagash Kazakh. **80** C2
Kanevskaya Rus. Fed. **39** E2
Kang Botswana **98** B1
Kangaatsiaq Greenland **111** I2
Kangal Turkey **84** B2
Kangān Iran **83** C2
Kangar Malaysia **64** B1
Kangaroo Island Austr. **104** B3
Kangchenjunga mt. India/Nepal
79 C2
Kangean, Kepuluan is Indon.
65 C2
Kangeq c. Greenland **111** J2
Kangersuatsiaq Greenland
111 I2
Kanggye N. Korea **69** B1
Kangiqsualujjuaq Can. **115** D1
Kangiqsujuaq Can. **111** H2
Kangirsuk Can. **111** H2
Kangmar China **79** C2
Kangnŭng S. Korea **69** B2
Kangping China **69** A1

Kangto *mt.* China/India 79 D2
Kanin, Poluostrov *pen.* Rus. Fed. 34 D2
Kanin Nos Rus. Fed. 34 D2
Kaniv Ukr. 39 D2
Kankaanpää Fin. 41 E3
Kankakee U.S.A. 122 C2
Kankan Guinea 90 B3
Kanker India 79 C2
Kano Nigeria 91 C3
Kanonpunt *pt* S. Africa 98 B3
Kanoya Japan 71 B4
Kanpur India 79 C2
Kansas *r.* U.S.A. 120 D1
Kansas *state* U.S.A. 121 D3
Kansas City U.S.A. 121 E3
Kansk Rus. Fed. 87 I3
Kantemirovka Rus. Fed. 39 E2
KaNyamazane S. Africa 99 C2
Kanye Botswana 99 C1
Kaohsiung Taiwan 75 C3
Kaokoveld *plat.* Namibia 96 A1
Kaolack Senegal 90 A3
Kaoma Zambia 95 C2
Kapanga Dem. Rep. Congo 94 C3
Kapchagay Kazakh. 81 E2
Kapchagayskoye Vodokhranilishche *resr* Kazakh. 81 E2
Kapellen Belgium 48 B2
Kapiri Mposhi Zambia 97 B1
Kapisillit Greenland 111 I2
Kapiskau *r.* Can. 114 B1
Kapit Malaysia 65 C1
Kapoe Thai. 67 A3
Kapoeta Sudan 93 B4
Kaposvár Hungary 51 C3
Kapuas *r.* Indon. 65 B2
Kapyl' Belarus 36 C2
Kara Togo 90 C4
Kara Ada *i.* Turkey 59 C3
Karabalyk Kazakh. 80 D1
Karabaur, Uval *hills* Kazakh./Uzbek. 85 D1
Kara-Bogaz-Gol, Zaliv *b.* Turkm. 80 C2
Karabük Turkey 90 D1
Karabutak Kazakh. 80 D2
Karachev Rus. Fed. 39 E2
Karachi Pak. 78 A2
Karaganda Kazakh. 81 E2
Karagayly Kazakh. 81 E2
Karaginskiy Zaliv *b.* Rus. Fed. 87 M3
Karaj Iran 85 D2
Karakelong *i.* Indon. 68 B3
Karakol Kyrg. 81 E2
Karakoram Range *mts* Asia 81 E3
Karakum, Peski *des.* Kazakh. *see* Karakum Desert
Karakum Desert Kazakh. 80 C2

Karakum Desert Turkm. *see* Karakumy, Peski
Karakumy, Peski *des.* Turkm. 80 D3
Karaman Turkey 92 B1
Karamay China 81 F2
Karamea N.Z. 106 B3
Karamea Bight *b.* N.Z. 106 B3
Karapınar Turkey 84 B2
Karasburg Namibia 98 A2
Kárášjohka Norway *see* Karasjok
Karasjok Norway 40 F2
Karasuk Rus. Fed. 81 E1
Karatau Kazakh. 81 E2
Karatau, Khrebet *mts* Kazakh. 81 D2
Karatayka Rus. Fed. 34 F2
Karatsu Japan 71 A4
Karawang Indon. 64 B2
Karbalā' Iraq 85 C2
Karcag Hungary 51 E3
Karditsa Greece 59 B3
Kärdla Estonia 36 B2
Kareeberge *mts* S. Africa 98 B3
Kareli India 79 B2
Kargil India 78 B1
Kariba Zimbabwe 97 B1
Kariba, Lake *resr* Zambia/Zimbabwe 97 B1
Karimata, Pulau-pulau *is* Indon. 64 B2
Karimata, Selat *str.* Indon. 64 B2
Karimnagar India 77 B2
Karimunjawa, Pulau-pulau *is* Indon. 65 C2
Karkinits'ka Zatoka *g.* Ukr. 39 D2
Karlivka Ukr. 39 E2
Karl Marks, Qullai *mt.* Tajik. 78 B1
Karlovac Croatia 56 C1
Karlovy Vary Czech Rep. 50 C2
Karlshamn Sweden 41 C4
Karlskrona Sweden 41 C4
Karlsruhe Ger. 49 D3
Karlstad Sweden 41 C4
Karlstadt Ger. 49 D3
Karma Belarus 37 D2
Karmey *i.* Norway 41 B4
Karnafuli Reservoir Bangl. 79 D2
Karnal India 78 B2
Karnobat Bulg. 58 C2
Karodi Pak. 78 A2
Karoi Zimbabwe 97 B1
Karonga Malawi 95 D3
Karora Eritrea 92 B3
Karpathos *i.* Greece 59 C3
Karpenisi Greece 59 B3
Karratha Austr. 104 A2
Kars Turkey 85 C1
Kārsava Latvia 36 C2
Karshi Turkm. 35 E4
Karshi Uzbek. *see* Qarshi

Karskiye Vorota, Proliv *str.* Rus. Fed. 34 E2
Karskoye More *sea* Rus. Fed. *see* Kara Sea
Karstädt Ger. 49 E1
Kartal Turkey 59 C2
Kartaly Rus. Fed. 35 F3
Karwar India 77 B3
Karystos Greece 59 B3
Kasabonika Lake Can. 114 A1
Kasama Zambia 95 D4
Kasane Botswana 96 B1
Kasangulu Dem. Rep. Congo 94 B3
Kasba Lake Can. 113 C1
Kasenga Dem. Rep. Congo 95 C4
Kasese Uganda 95 D3
Käshän Iran 85 D2
Kashary Rus. Fed. 39 F2
Kashi China 81 E3
Kashima-nada *b.* Japan 71 D3
Kashin Rus. Fed. 37 E2
Kashipur India 78 B1
Kashiralskoye Rus. Fed. 37 E3
Kashiwazaki Japan 71 C3
Käshmar Iran 80 C3
Kashmir *terr.* Asia *see* Jammu and Kashmir
Kashmor Pak. 78 A2
Kashyukulu Dem. Rep. Congo 95 C3
Kasimov Rus. Fed. 37 F3
Kaskinen Fin. 41 E3
Kasongo Dem. Rep. Congo 95 C3
Kasongo-Lunda Dem. Rep. Congo 94 B3
Kasos *i.* Greece 59 C3
Kassala Sudan 92 B3
Kassel Ger. 49 D2
Kastamonu Turkey 84 B1
Kastelli Greece 59 B3
Kastoria Greece 59 B2
Kastsyukovichy Belarus 37 E3
Kasulu Tanz. 95 D3
Kasungu Malawi 97 C1
Katahdin, Mount U.S.A. 123 G1
Katako-Kombe Dem. Rep. Congo 94 C3
Katanning Austr. 102 A3
Katchall *i.* India 67 A3
Katerini Greece 59 B2
Kate's Needle *mt.* Can./U.S.A. 112 B2
Katete Zambia 97 C1
Katha Myanmar 66 A1
Katherine *r.* Austr. 102 C1
Kathiawar *pen.* India 78 B2
Kathlehong S. Africa 99 C2
Kathmandu Nepal 79 C2
Katihar India 79 C2
Katikati N.Z. 106 C2
Katima Mulilo Namibia 96 B1
Katoomba Austr. 105 E2

owice Pol. **51** D2
trina, Jabal *mt.* Egypt **84** B3
trineholm Sweden **41** D4
tsina Nigeria **91** C3
ttegat *str.* Denmark/Sweden
1 C4
twijk aan Zee Neth. **48** B1
uai *i.* U.S.A. **108**
uhajoki Fin. **41** E3
uhasuo Fin. **40** F2
utokeino Norway **40** E2
vala Greece **59** B3
valerovo Rus. Fed. **70** C2
vala Bulg. **58** C2
vir, Dasht-e *des.* Iran **85** D2
wakawa N.Z. **103** [inset]
wanishi Japan **71** C3
wartha Lakes Can. **114** C2
wasaki Japan **71** C3
werau N.Z. **106** C2
wlin Myanmar **66** A1
wm Umbū Egypt **82** A2
xgar He *r.* China **81** E3
xya Burkina **90** E3
yan *r.* Indon. **65** C1
ycee U.S.A. **120** B2
yenta U.S.A. **126** B1
yes Mali **90** E3
ynar Kazakh. **81** E2
yseri Turkey **84** B2
zakhskiy Melkosopochnik
lain Kazakh. **81** C1
zakhskiy Zaliv *b.* Kazakh.
45 D1
zakhstan *country* Asia **80** D2
azan' Rus. Fed. **35** D3
zanlük Bulg. **84** A1
zanskaya Rus. Fed. **39** F2
zbek *mt.* Georgia/Rus. Fed.
45 D4
zerün Iran **85** D3
zincbardika Hungary **51** E3
zerce Turkey **59** B3
ady U.K. **45** C1
arney U.S.A. **121** D2
arny U.S.A. **126** B2
bkabiya Sudan **92** A3
bnekaise *mt.* Sweden **40** E2
bri Dehar Eth. **93** C4
bumen Indon. **65** B2
chika *r.* Can. **112** C2
cskemét Hungary **51** D3
dainiai Lith. **36** B2
dougou Senegal **90** E3
dzierzyn-Kozle Pol. **51** D2
ele *r.* Can. **112** C1
ele Peak Can. **112** B1
eling Taiwan *see* Chilung
ek U.S.A. **123** F2
etnamshoop Namibia **98** A2
ewatin Can. **113** F3
eftallonia *i.* Greece *see*
Cephalonia

Keflavik Iceland **40** [inset]
Kegen Kazakh. **81** E2
Keg River Can. **112** D2
Kehsi Mansam Myanmar **66** A1
Keighley U.K. **46** C3
Keila Estonia **36** M3
Keimoes S. Africa **98** B2
Keitele *l.* Fin. **40** F2
Keith Austr. **104** C3
Keith Arm *b.* Can. **112** C1
Kékes *mt.* Hungary **51** E3
Keles-Uayv, Gora *h.* Rus. Fed.
40 G2
Kelheim Ger. **50** D5
Kelkit *r.* Turkey **84** B1
Keller Lake Can. **112** C1
Kellogg U.S.A. **118** C2
Kelloselkä Fin. **40** F2
Kells Ireland **45** C2
Kelmė Lith. **36** B2
Kelowna Can. **112** D3
Kelso U.K. **44** C3
Kelso U.S.A. **118** B1
Keluang Malaysia **64** B1
Kem' Rus. Fed. **34** C2
Kemerovo Rus. Fed. **86** H3
Kemi Fin. **40** F2
Kemijärvi Fin. **40** F2
Kemijoki *r.* Fin. **40** F2
Kemmerer U.S.A. **120** A2
Kempele Fin. **40** F3
Kempsey Austr. **105** E2
Kempt, Lac *l.* Can. **114** C2
Kempten (Allgäu) Ger. **50** C3
Kempton Park S. Africa **99** C2
Kenai U.S.A. **110** B2
Kendal U.K. **46** B2
Kendari Indon. **65** C2
Kendawangan Indon. **65** C2
Kendégué Chad **91** D3
Kenema Sierra Leone **90** A4
Kenge Dem. Rep. Congo **94** B3
Kengtung Myanmar **66** A1
Kenhardt S. Africa **98** B2
Kénitra Morocco **90** B1
Kenmare Ireland **45** B3
Kenmare U.S.A. **120** C1
Kenn Ger. **48** C3
Kennett U.S.A. **121** E3
Kennewick U.S.A. **118** C1
Kenora Can. **113** F3
Kenosha U.S.A. **122** C2
Kent U.S.A. **126** D2
Kentau Kazakh. **81** D2
Kentucky *r.* U.S.A. **122** C3
Kentucky *state* U.S.A. **122** D3
Kentucky Lake U.S.A. **122** C3
Kenya *country* Africa **95** D2
Kookuk U.S.A. **121** E2
Keonjhar India **79** C2
Kerang Austr. **104** C3
Kerava Fin. **36** C1
Kerch Ukr. **39** E2

Kerema P.N.G. **63** D3
Keren Eritrea **92** B3
Kerend Iran **85** C2
Kericho Kenya **95** D3
Kerikeri N.Z. **106** B2
Kerinci, Gunung *vol.* Indon.
64 B2
Kerkyra Greece **59** A3
Kerkyra *i.* Greece *see* Corfu
Kerma Sudan **92** B3
Kermadec Islands
S. Pacific Ocean **101**
Kermān Iran **83** C1
Kermānshāh Iran **85** C2
Kermit U.S.A. **127** D2
Kern *r.* U.S.A. **119** C3
Kerpen Ger. **48** C2
Kerrville U.S.A. **127** E2
Kesagami Lake Can. **114** B1
Keşan Turkey **59** C2
Kesennuma Japan **70** D3
Keshod India **78** B2
Keswick U.K. **46** B2
Keszthely Hungary **51** D3
Ket' *r.* Rus. Fed. **86** H3
Ketapang Indon. **65** C2
Ketchikan U.S.A. **112** B2
Ketchum U.S.A. **118** D2
Kettering U.K. **47** C3
Keuruu Fin. **41** E3
Kevelaer Ger. **48** C2
Kewanee U.S.A. **122** C2
Keweenaw Bay U.S.A. **122** C1
Keweenaw Peninsula U.S.A.
122 C1
Key Largo U.S.A. **125** D3
Key West U.S.A. **125** D4
Kgotsong S. Africa **99** C2
Khabarovsk Rus. Fed. **73** F1
Khadyzhensk Rus. Fed. **84** B1
Khagrachari Bangl. **66** A1
Khairpur Pak. **78** A2
Khakhea Botswana **98** B1
Khamar-Daban, Khrebet *mts*
Rus. Fed. **72** C1
Khambhat India **78** B2
Khambhat, Gulf of India **78** B3
Khamgaon India **78** B2
Khamir Yemen **82** B3
Khamis Mushayţ Saudi Arabia
82 B3
Khammam India **77** C3
Khānābād Afgh. **78** A1
Khandwa India **78** B2
Khandyga Rus. Fed. **87** L2
Khanewal Pak. **78** B1
Khanka, Lake China/Rus. Fed.
70 B2
Khanpur Pak. **78** B2
Khantau Kazakh. **81** E2
Khantayskoye, Ozero *l.* Rus. Fed.
87 I2
Khanty-Mansiysk Rus. Fed.
34 F2

Khao Chum Thong Thai. **67** A3
Khao Laem Reservoir Thai. **67** A2
Kharabali Rus. Fed. **35** D4
Kharagpur India **79** C2
Khārān r. Iran **83** C2
Khārijah, Wāḥāt al *oasis* Egypt **92** B2
Kharkiv Ukr. **39** E2
Khar'kov Ukr. *see* Kharkiv
Kharmanli Bulg. **58** C2
Kharovsk Rus. Fed. **37** F2
Khartoum Sudan **92** B3
Khāsh Iran **83** D2
Khashm el Girba Dam Sudan **82** A3
Khasi Hills India **79** C2
Khaskovo Bulg. **58** C2
Khayamnandi S. Africa **99** C3
Khaybar Saudi Arabia **82** A2
Khayelitsha S. Africa **98** A3
Khemis Miliana Alg. **55** D2
Kherāmeh Iran **85** D3
Kherson Ukr. **39** D2
Kheta r. Rus. Fed. **87** I2
Khilok Rus. Fed. **73** I1
Khimki Rus. Fed. **37** F2
Khmel'nyts'kyy Ukr. **38** C2
Khokhol'skiy Rus. Fed. **37** F3
Kholm Afgh. **78** A1
Kholm Rus. Fed. **37** D2
Kholmsk Rus. Fed. **70** D1
Kholm-Zhirkovskiy Rus. Fed. **37** D2
Khomas Highland *hills* Namibia **98** A1
Khonj Iran **83** C2
Khon Kaen Thai. **66** B2
Khoper r. Rus. Fed. **39** F2
Khorol Ukr. **39** D2
Khorramābād Iran **85** C2
Khorramshahr Iran **85** C2
Khorugh Tajik. **81** C5
Khowst Afgh. **78** A1
Khowst Afgh. **78** A1
Khromtau Kazakh. **80** C1
Khrystynivka Ukr. **38** C2
Khūjand Tajik. **81** D2
Khulays Saudi Arabia **82** A2
Khulna Bangl. **79** C2
Khushab Pak. **78** B1
Khust Ukr. **38** B2
Khuzdar Pak. **83** D2
Khvormūj Iran **85** D3
Khvoy Iran **85** C2
Khvoynaya Rus. Fed. **37** D2
Khyber Pass Afgh./Pak. **78** B1
Kiama Austr. **105** E2
Kiambi Dem. Rep. Congo **95** C3
Kibiti Tanz. **95** D3
Kičevo Macedonia **59** B2
Kidal Mali **50** C3
Kidderminster U.K. **47** B3
Kidira Senegal **90** A3
Kidnappers, Cape N.Z. **106** C2

Kiel Ger. **50** C2
Kielce Pol. **51** E2
Kielder Water *resr* U.K. **46** B2
Kieler Bucht *b.* Ger. **41** C5
Kiev Ukr. **38** D1
Kiffa Maur. **90** A3
Kigali Rwanda **95** D3
Kigoma Tanz. **95** C3
Kihnu i. Estonia **36** B2
Kiiminki Fin. **40** F2
Kii-suidō *sea chan.* Japan **71** B4
Kikinda S.M. **58** B1
Kikondja Dem. Rep. Congo **95** C3
Kikwit Dem. Rep. Congo **94** B3
Kilchu N. Korea **69** B1
Kilembe Dem. Rep. Congo **94** B3
Kilgore U.S.A. **127** E2
Kilimanjaro *vol.* Tanz. **95** D3
Kilis Turkey **84** B2
Kiliya Ukr. **38** C2
Kilkeel U.K. **45** D1
Kilkenny Ireland **45** C2
Kilkis Greece **59** B2
Killarney Ireland **45** B2
Killeen U.S.A. **127** E2
Killybegs Ireland **45** B1
Kilmarnock U.K. **44** B3
Kilmore Austr. **105** C3
Kilosa Tanz. **95** D3
Kilrush Ireland **45** B2
Kilwa Dem. Rep. Congo **95** C3
Kilwa Masoko Tanz. **95** D3
Kimba Austr. **104** B2
Kimball U.S.A. **122** C3
Kimberley S. Africa **98** B2
Kimberley Plateau Austr. **102** B1
Kimch'aek N. Korea **69** B1
Kimch'ŏn S. Korea **69** B2
Kimmirut Can. **111** H2
Kimovsk Rus. Fed. **37** E3
Kimpese Dem. Rep. Congo **94** B3
Kimry Rus. Fed. **37** E2
Kinabalu, Gunung *mt.* Malaysia **65** C1
Kinbasket Lake Can. **112** D2
Kincardine Can. **114** B2
Kinda Dem. Rep. Congo **95** C3
Kindia Guinea **90** A3
Kindu Dem. Rep. Congo **95** C3
Kineshma Rus. Fed. **37** F2
King City U.S.A. **119** B3
Kingisepp Rus. Fed. **36** C2
King Island Austr. **103** D3
King Leopold Ranges *hills* Austr. **102** B1
Kingman U.S.A. **126** B1
Kings r. U.S.A. **119** C3
Kingscote Austr. **104** B3
King's Lynn U.K. **47** D3
Kingsmill Group *is* Kiribati **100**
King Sound *b.* Austr. **102** B1

Kings Peak U.S.A. **118** D2
Kingsport U.S.A. **125** D1
Kingston Can. **114** C2
Kingston Jamaica **131** C3
Kingston U.S.A. **123** F2
Kingston South East Austr. **104** B3
Kingston upon Hull U.K. **46** C3
Kingstown St Vincent **131** D3
Kingsville U.S.A. **127** E3
Kingswood U.K. **47** B4
Kingussie U.K. **44** B2
King William Island Can. **110** F2
King William's Town S. Africa **99** C3
Kinna Sweden **41** C4
Kinsale Ireland **45** B3
Kinshasa Dem. Rep. Congo **94** B3
Kinston U.S.A. **125** E1
Kintyre *pen.* U.K. **44** B3
Kipawa, Lac *l.* Can. **114** C2
Kireyevsk Rus. Fed. **37** E3
Kiribati *country* Pacific Ocean **101**
Kırıkkale Turkey **84** B2
Kirillov Rus. Fed. **37** E2
Kirinyaga *mt.* Kenya *see* Kenya, Mount
Kirishi Rus. Fed. **37** D2
Kiritimati *atoll* Kiribati **101**
Kırkağaç Turkey **59** C3
Kirkcaldy U.K. **44** C2
Kirkcudbright U.K. **44** B3
Kirkenes Norway **40** G2
Kirkkonummi Fin. **36** B1
Kirkland Lake Can. **114** B2
Kirksville U.S.A. **121** E2
Kirkūk Iraq **85** C2
Kirkwall U.K. **44** C1
Kirov Kaluzhskaya Oblast'
Rus. Fed. **37** D3
Kirov Kirovskaya Oblast' Rus. Fed. **34** D3
Kirovo-Chepetsk Rus. Fed. **34** E3
Kirovohrad Ukr. **39** D2
Kirovsk Rus. Fed. **40** G2
Kirovs'ke Ukr. **39** E2
Kirriemuir U.K. **44** C2
Kirsanov Rus. Fed. **39** F1
Kirthar Range *mts* Pak. **78** A2
Kiruna Sweden **40** E2
Kiryū Japan **71** C3
Kirżach Rus. Fed. **37** E2
Kisangani Dem. Rep. Congo **95** C2
Kisantu Dem. Rep. Congo **94** B3
Kisaran Indon. **64** A1
Kiselevsk Rus. Fed. **86** H3
Kishanganj India **79** C2
Kishinev Moldova *see* Chişinău
Kishkenekol' Kazakh. **81** E1

horganj Bangl. **66** A1
htwar Jammu and Kashmir
  3 B1
i Kenya **95** D3
kunfélegyháza Hungary
  1 D3
kunhalas Hungary **51** D3
lovodsk Rus. Fed. **35** D4
maayo Somalia **93** C5
oro Uganda **95** C3
sidougou Guinea **90** A4
simmee U.S.A. **125** D3
simmee, Lake U.S.A. **125** D3
sissing Lake Can. **113** E2
umu Kenya **95** D3
a Mali **90** B3
akami-gawa r. Japan **70** D3
-Kyūshū Japan **71** B4
ami Japan **70** D2
chener Can. **114** B2
ee Fin. **41** G3
oro Uganda **95** D2
mat Can. **112** C2
unda Tanz. **95** D3
wanga Can. **112** C2
we Zambia **97** B1
zingen Ger. **49** E3
ruvesi Fin. **40** F3
ülca Dağ mt. Turkey **59** C3
lyar Rus. Fed. **35** D4
llefjord Norway **40** F1
ipsvik Norway **40** D2
idno Czech Rep. **50** C2
ipeda Lith. **36** B2
ksvík Faroe Is **42** B1
math r. U.S.A. **118** B2
math Falls U.S.A. **118** B2
math Mountains U.S.A.
  18 B2
nq Malaysia **64** B1
tovy Czech Rep. **50** C2
wock U.S.A. **112** B2
ena Kleene Can. **112** C2
inbegin S. Africa **98** A2
insee S. Africa **98** A2
rksdorp S. Africa **99** C2
tnya Rus. Fed. **37** D3
navíchy Belarus **37** D3
novo Rus. Fed. **37** D3
novsk Rus. Fed. **37** D2
n Rus. Fed. **37** F2
novec mt. Czech Rep. **49** F2
teham Sweden **41** D4
ntsy Rus. Fed. **37** D3
lé Bos.-Herz. **57** C2
dzko Pol. **51** D2
sterneuburg Austria **51** D3
kze (Altmark) Ger. **49** E1
ane Lake Can. **112** B1
czbork Pol. **51** D2
kwan U.S.A. **112** B2
pro Pak. **78** A2
az'ma r. Rus. Fed. **37** F2

Klyetsk Belarus **36** C3
Knästen h. Sweden **41** C3
Knee Lake Can. **113** F2
Knetzgau Ger. **49** E3
Knin Croatia **57** C2
Knittelfeld Austria **50** C3
Knjaževac S.M. **88** B2
Knokke-Heist Belgium **48** A2
Knoxville U.S.A. **125** D1
Knysna S. Africa **98** B3
Kōbe Japan **71** C4
København Denmark see
  Copenhagen
Koblenz Ger. **48** C2
Kobroör i. Indon. **63** C3
Kobryn Belarus **36** B3
Kočani Macedonia **58** B2
Kocasu r. Turkey **59** C2
Koch Bihar India **79** C2
Kōchi Japan **71** B4
Kochubey Rus. Fed. **35** D4
Kodarma India **79** C2
Kodiak Island U.S.A. **110** B3
Kodok Sudan **93** B4
Kodyma Ukr. **38** C2
Kodzhaele mt. Bulg./Greece
  59 C2
Koës Namibia **98** A2
Koffiefontein S. Africa **98** C2
Koforidua Ghana **90** B4
Kōfu Japan **71** C3
Kogaluk r. Can. **115** D1
Kohat Pak. **78** B1
Kohima India **66** A1
Kohila-Järve Estonia **36** C2
Kokand Uzbek. see Qo'qon
Kokkola Fin. **40** E3
Kokomo U.S.A. **122** C2
Kokpekti Kazakh. **81** F2
Kokshetau Kazakh. **81** D1
Koksoak r. Can. **115** D1
Kokstad S. Africa **99** C3
Koktokay China see Fuyun
Kolaka Indon. **65** D2
Kola Peninsula Rus. Fed. **34** C2
Kolari Fin. **40** E2
Kolda Senegal **90** A3
Kolding Denmark **41** B4
Koléa Alg. **55** D2
Kolguyev, Ostrov i. Rus. Fed.
  34 D2
Kolhapur India **77** B3
Kolkasrags pt Latvia **36** B2
Kolkata India **79** C2
Kolmanskop Namibia **98** A2
Köln Ger. see Cologne
Kołobrzeg Pol. **51** D2
Kolokani Mali **90** B3
Kolomna Rus. Fed. **37** D2
Kolomyya Ukr. **38** C2
Kolonedale Indon. **65** D2
Kolonkwaneng Botswana **98** B2
Kolpashevo Rus. Fed. **86** H3
Kolpny Rus. Fed. **37** E3

Kol'skiy Poluostrov pen.
  Rus. Fed. see Kola Peninsula
Koluli Eritrea **82** B3
Kolwezi Dem. Rep. Congo **95** C4
Kolymskaya Nizmennost' low-
  land Rus. Fed. **87** N2
Kolymskiy, Khrebet mts
  Rus. Fed. **87** N2
Komaki Japan **71** C3
Komandorskiye Ostrova is
  Rus. Fed. **87** N3
Komárno Slovakia **51** D3
Komati r. Swaziland **99** D2
Komatsu Japan **71** C3
Kominternivs'k Ukr. **38** D2
Komiža Croatia **57** C2
Komotini Greece **59** C2
Komsberg mts S. Africa **98** B3
Komsomolets, Ostrov i.
  Rus. Fed. **87** I1
Komsomol'sk Rus. Fed. **37** F2
Komsomol'sk Ukr. **39** D2
Komsomol'sk-na-Amure
  Rus. Fed. **73** F1
Konakovo Rus. Fed. **37** E2
Kondagaon India **79** C2
Kondoa Tanz. **95** D3
Kondopoga Rus. Fed. **34** C2
Kondrovo Rus. Fed. **37** E3
Kong Christian IX Land reg.
  Greenland **111** J2
Kong Frederik VI Kyst
  coastal area Greenland **111** J2
Kongju S. Korea **69** B2
Kongolo Dem. Rep. Congo **95** C3
Kongsberg Norway **41** B4
Kongsvinger Norway **41** C3
Kongur Shan mt. China **81** E3
Königswinter Ger. **48** C2
Königs Wusterhausen Ger.
  49 F1
Konin Pol. **51** D2
Konjic Bos.-Herz. **57** C2
Konkiep watercourse Namibia
  98 A2
Konotop Ukr. **39** D1
Konstantinovsk Rus. Fed. **39** F2
Konstanz Ger. **50** B3
Kontagora Nigeria **91** C3
Kon Tum Vietnam **67** B2
Kon Tum, Cao Nguyên plat.
  Vietnam **67** B2
Konya Turkey **84** B2
Konz Ger. **48** C3
Kooskia U.S.A. **118** C1
Kootenay Lake Can. **112** D3
Kópasker Iceland **40** [inset]
Koper Slovenia **56** B1
Koprivnica Croatia **57** C1
Korablino Rus. Fed. **37** F3
Koraput India **77** C3
Korbach Ger. **49** D2
Korçë Albania **59** B2
Korčula Croatia **57** C2

Korčula i. Croatia 57 C2
Korea, North country Asia 69 B1
Korea, South country Asia 69 B2
Korea Bay g. China/N. Korea 69 A2
Korea Strait Japan/S. Korea 69 B3
Korenovsk Rus. Fed. 39 E2
Korets' Ukr. 38 C1
Körfez Turkey 59 C2
Korhogo Côte d'Ivoire 90 B4
Korinthos Greece see Corinth
Kōris-hegy h. Hungary 51 D3
Kōriyama Japan 71 D3
Korkuteli Turkey 84 B2
Korla China 81 F2
Körmend Hungary 51 D3
Koroc r. Can. 115 D1
Korocha Rus. Fed. 39 E1
Korogwe Tanz. 95 D1
Koror Palau 63 C2
Korosten' Ukr. 38 C1
Korostyshiv Ukr. 38 C1
Koro Toro Chad 91 D3
Korsakov Rus. Fed. 70 D1
Korser Denmark 50 C1
Korsun'-Shevchenkivs'kyy Ukr. 39 D2
Kortrijk Belgium 48 A2
Koryakskiy Khrebet mts Rus. Fed. 87 N2
Koryazhma Rus. Fed. 34 D2
Koryukivka Ukr. 39 D1
Kos Greece 59 C3
Kos i. Greece 59 C3
Kościan Pol. 51 D2
Kosciuszko, Mount Austr. 105 D3
Kosh-Agach Rus. Fed. 81 F2
Košice Slovakia 51 E3
Kosōng N. Korea 69 B2
Kosovo prov. S.M. 58 B2
Kosovska Mitrovica S.M. 58 B2
Kosrae atoll Micronesia 100
Kossou, Lac de l. Côte d'Ivoire 90 B4
Kostanay Kazakh. 80 D1
Koster S. Africa 99 C2
Kosti Sudan 93 B3
Kostomuksha Rus. Fed. 40 G3
Kostopil' Ukr. 38 C1
Kostroma Rus. Fed. 37 F2
Kostroma r. Rus. Fed. 37 F2
Kostrzyn Pol. 50 C2
Koszalin Pol. 51 D2
Kőszeg Hungary 51 D3
Kota India 78 B2
Kotaagung Indon. 64 B2
Kotabaru Indon. 65 C2
Kota Belud Malaysia 65 C1
Kota Bharu Malaysia 64 B1
Kotabumi Indon. 64 B2
Kota Kinabalu Malaysia 65 C1

Kota Samarahan Malaysia 65 C1
Kotel'nich Rus. Fed. 34 D3
Kotel'nyy, Ostrov i. Rus. Fed. 87 L1
Köthen (Anhalt) Ger. 49 E2
Kotka Fin. 41 F3
Kottas Rus. Fed. 34 D2
Kotlik U.S.A. 110 B2
Kotor Varoš Bos.-Herz. 57 C2
Kotovsk Rus. Fed. 37 F3
Kotovs'k Ukr. 38 C2
Kotzebue U.S.A. 110 B2
Kotzebue Sound sea chan. U.S.A. 110 B2
Kötzting Ger. 49 F3
Koudougou Burkina 90 B3
Koufonisi i. S. Africa 98 B3
Koulamoutou Gabon 94 B3
Koulikoro Mali 90 B3
Koundâra Guinea 90 A3
Kourou Fr. Guiana 135 D2
Koutiala Mali 90 B3
Kouvola Fin. 41 F3
Kovdor Rus. Fed. 40 G2
Kovel' Ukr. 38 B1
Kovrov Rus. Fed. 37 F2
Kowhitirangi N.Z. 106 B3
Koyda Rus. Fed. 34 D2
Koyukuk r. U.S.A. 110 B2
Kozani Greece 59 B2
Kozelets' Ukr. 38 D1
Kozel'sk Rus. Fed. 37 E3
Kozyatyn Ukr. 38 C2
Krabi Thai. 67 A3
Kra Buri Thai. 67 A2
Krâchéh Cambodia 67 B2
Kragerø Norway 41 B4
Kraggenburg Neth. 48 B1
Kragujevac S.M. 58 B2
Krakatau i. Indon. 64 B2
Kraków Pol. 51 D2
Kramators'k Ukr. 39 E2
Kramfors Sweden 40 D3
Krasino Rus. Fed. 34 E1
Krāslava Latvia 36 C2
Krasnaya Gora Rus. Fed. 37 D3
Krasnaya Gorbatka Rus. Fed. 37 F2
Krasnoarmeysk Rus. Fed. 35 D3
Krasnoarmiys'k Ukr. 39 E2
Krasnodar Rus. Fed. 39 E2
Krasnodon Ukr. 39 E2
Krasnogvardeyskoye Belgorodskaya Oblast' Rus. Fed. 39 E1
Krasnogvardeyskoye Stavropol'skiy Kray Rus. Fed. 39 F2
Krasnohrad Ukr. 39 E2
Krasnohvardiys'ke Ukr. 39 D2
Krasnokamsk Rus. Fed. 34 E3
Krasnoperekops'k Ukr. 39 D2
Krasnoufimsk Rus. Fed. 34 E3
Krasnoyarsk Rus. Fed. 87 I3

Krasnoye-na-Volge Rus. Fed. 37 F2
Krasnyy Rus. Fed. 37 D3
Krasnyy Kholm Rus. Fed. 37 E2
Krasnyy Luch Ukr. 35 C4
Krasnyy Sulin Rus. Fed. 39 F2
Krasyliv Ukr. 38 C2
Krefeld Ger. 48 C2
Kremenchuk Ukr. 39 D2
Kremenchuts'ka Vodoskhovyshche resr Ukr. 39 D2
Kreminna Ukr. 39 E2
Krems an der Donau Austria 51 D3
Kresttsy Rus. Fed. 37 D2
Kretinga Lith. 36 B2
Kreuztal Ger. 48 C2
Kribi Cameroon 94 B2
Krikellos Greece 59 B3
Kril'on, Mys c. Rus. Fed. 70 D1
Krishna r. India 77 C3
Krishnanagar India 79 C2
Kristiansand Norway 41 B4
Kristianstad Sweden 41 C4
Kristiansund Norway 40 B3
Kristinehamn Sweden 41 C4
Kriti i. Greece see Crete
Križevci Croatia 57 C1
Krk i. Croatia 56 B1
Krokom Sweden 40 C3
Krolevets' Ukr. 39 D1
Kronach Ger. 49 E2
Kröng Kaôh Kŏng Cambodia 67 B2
Kronprins Frederik Bjerge nunataks Greenland 111 J2
Kroonstad S. Africa 99 C2
Kropotkin Rus. Fed. 39 F2
Krosno Pol. 51 E3
Krui Indon. 64 B2
Krujë Albania 58 A2
Krumovgrad Bulg. 59 C2
Krung Thep Thai. see Bangkok
Krupki Belarus 37 D3
Kruševac S.M. 58 B2
Kruše Hory mts Czech Rep. 49 F2
Kruzof Island U.S.A. 112 B2
Krychaw Belarus 37 D3
Krymsk Rus. Fed. 39 E3
Krytiko Pelagos sea Greece 59 C3
Kryvyy Rih Ukr. 39 D2
Ksabi Alg. 90 B2
Ksar Chellala Alg. 55 D2
Ksar el Boukhari Alg. 55 D2
Kshenskiy Rus. Fed. 37 E3
Kū', Jabal al h. Saudi Arabia 82 B2
Kuala Belait Brunei 65 C1
Kuala Kerai Malaysia 64 B1
Kuala Lipis Malaysia 64 B1
Kuala Lumpur Malaysia 64 B1

lapembuang Indon.
6 C2
ula Terengganu Malaysia
5 B1
alatungal Indon. 64 B2
ndian China 69 A1
artan Malaysia 64 B1
aruk Can. 111 G2
enskoye, Ozero l. Rus. Fed.
7 E2
rat Bulg. 58 C2
la Indon. 65 C1
hing Malaysia 65 C1
ovë Albania 59 A2
lat Malaysia 65 C1
luktuk Can. 110 E2
mo Fin. 40 F3
rān, Kūh-e mt. Iran 83 C2
seb watercourse Namibia
8 A1
to Angola 96 A1
raniemi Fin. 40 F2
zing N. Korea 69 B2
les Albania 58 B2
a Turkey 59 C3
a Kangri mt. Bhutan/China
1 C2
ndy Kazakh. 80 C2
diga Latvia 36 B2
ebaki Rus. Fed. 37 F2
mbach Ger. 49 E2
ob Tajik. 81 D3
sary Kazakh. 80 C2
unda Rus. Fed. 81 E1
s. Fed. 81 E1
luuk Greenland 111 J2
nagaya Japan 71 C3
namoto Japan 71 B4
nanovo Macedonia 58 B2
nasi Ghana 90 B4
nba Cameroon 94 A2
nertau Rus. Fed. 35 E3
ka S. Korea 69 B2
nla Sweden 41 D3
no Nigeria 91 D3
non Range mts Myanmar
4 A1
nylzhenskiy Rus. Fed. 39 F2
bashir, Ostrov i. Rus. Fed.
1 E2
eene r. Angola/Namibia 96 A1
ngei Alatau mts Kazakh./Kyrg.
1 E3
gsbacka Sweden 41 C4
nga Dem. Rep. Congo 94 B2
agur Rus. Fed. 34 D2
hing Myanmar 66 A1
slun Shan mts China 79 B1
aming China 75 A3
nsan S. Korea 69 B2
aunurra Austr. 102 B1

Künzelsau Ger. 49 D3
Kuopio Fin. 40 F3
Kupa r. Croatia/Slovenia 56 C1
Kupang Indon. 63 C3
Kupiškis Lith. 36 B2
Kupreanof Island U.S.A. 112 B2
Kup"yans'k Ukr. 39 E2
Kuqa China 81 C2
Kurashiki Japan 71 B4
Kurayoshi Japan 71 B3
Kurchatov Rus. Fed. 37 E3
Kürdzhali Bulg. 58 C2
Kure Japan 71 B4
Kuressaare Estonia 36 B2
Kurgan Rus. Fed. 35 F3
Kurganinsk Rus. Fed. 39 F3
Kurikka Fin. 41 E3
Kuril Islands Rus. Fed. 87 L3
Kuril'sk Rus. Fed. 87 L3
Kurmuk Sudan 93 B3
Kurnool India 77 B3
Kuroiso Japan 71 C3
Kurri Kurri Austr. 105 E2
Kursk Rus. Fed. 37 E3
Kuruman S. Africa 98 B2
Kuruman watercourse S. Africa
98 B2
Kurume Japan 71 B4
Kurumkan Rus. Fed. 87 J3
Kurunegala Sri Lanka 77 C4
Kuşadası Turkey 59 C3
Kuşadası Körfezi b. Turkey
59 C3
Kus Gölü l. Turkey 59 C2
Kushchevskaya Rus. Fed. 39 E2
Kushiro Japan 70 D2
Kushmurun Kazakh. 80 C1
Kushtia Bangl. 79 C2
Kuskokwim r. U.S.A. 87 P2
Kuskokwim Mountains U.S.A.
110 B2
Kussharo-ko l. Japan 70 D2
Kütahya Turkey 59 C3
K'ut'aisi Georgia 85 C1
Kutno Pol. 51 D2
Kutu Dem. Rep. Congo 94 B3
Kuujjua r. Can. 110 E2
Kuujjuaq Can. 115 D1
Kuujjuarapik Can. 114 C1
Kuusamo Fin. 40 F2
Kuvango Angola 96 A1
Kuvshinovo Rus. Fed. 37 D2
Kuwait country Asia 83 B2
Kuwait Kuwait 83 B2
Kuybyshev Ukr. 39 E2
Kuybyshevskoye
Vodokhranilishche resr
Rus. Fed. 35 D3
Kuytun China 81 E2
Kuznetsk Rus. Fed. 35 D3
Kuznetsovs'k Ukr. 38 C1
Kvalsund Norway 40 F1
KwaMashu S. Africa 99 D2
Kwandang Indon. 65 D1

Kwangju S. Korea 69 B2
Kwanmo-bong mt. N. Korea
69 B1
Kwanobuhle S. Africa 99 C3
Kwanonzame S. Africa 98 B3
Kwatinidubu S. Africa 99 C3
Kwazulu-Natal prov. S. Africa
99 D2
Kwekwe Zimbabwe 97 B1
Kwenge r. Dem. Rep. Congo 94 B3
Kwidzyn Pol. 51 D2
Kwilu r. Angola/Dem. Rep. Congo
94 B3
Kwoka mt. Indon. 63 C3
Kyabram Austr. 105 D3
Kyaikto Myanmar 66 A2
Kyakhta Rus. Fed. 72 D1
Kyancutta Austr. 104 B2
Kyaukpadaung Myanmar 66 A1
Kyaukpyu Myanmar 66 A2
Kybartai Lith. 36 B3
Kyeintali Myanmar 66 A2
Kyelang India 78 B1
Kyiv Ukr. see Kiev
Kyklades is Greece see Cyclades
Kyle Can. 113 E2
Kyle of Lochalsh U.K. 44 B2
Kyll r. Ger. 48 C3
Kyllini mt. Greece 59 B3
Kymi Greece 59 B3
Kyneton Austr. 104 C3
Kyoga, Lake Uganda 95 D2
Kyogle Austr. 105 E1
Kyonggi-man b. S. Korea 69 B2
Kyŏngju S. Korea 69 B2
Kyōto Japan 71 C4
Kypshak, Ozero salt l. Kazakh.
81 D1
Kyrgyzstan country Asia 81 E2
Kyritz Ger. 49 F1
Kyrönjoki r. Fin. 40 E3
Kythira i. Greece 59 B3
Kythnos i. Greece 59 B3
Kyūshū i. Japan 71 B4
Kyustendil Bulg. 58 B2
Kyiv's'ke Vodoskhovyshche resr
Ukr. 38 D1
Kyzyl Rus. Fed. 72 C1
Kyzylkum Desert Kazakh./Uzbek.
80 D2
Kyzyl-Mazhalyk Rus. Fed. 81 G1
Kyzylorda Kazakh. 81 D2

L

La Angostura, Presa de resr
Mex. 129 C3
Laascaanood Somalia 93 C4
La Asunción Venez. 134 C1
Laâyoune Western Sahara 90 A2
Laba r. Rus. Fed. 39 F2
La Babia Mex. 128 B2

La Banda Arg. **136** B3
La Baule-Escoublac France **52** B2
Labé Guinea **90** A3
Laberge, Lake Can. **112** B1
La Biche, Lac *l.* Can. **113** D2
Labinsk Rus. Fed. **39** F3
Labouheyre France **52** B3
Labrador *reg.* Can. **115** D1
Labrador City Can. **115** D1
Labrador Sea Can./Greenland **111** I2
Lábrea Brazil **134** C3
Labuan Malaysia **65** C1
Labuhanbajo Indon. **65** D2
Labuhanbilik Indon. **64** B1
Labuna Indon. **63** C3
Labutta Myanmar **66** A2
Labytnangi Rus. Fed. **34** F2
Laç Albania **58** A2
La Capelle France **53** C2
Laccadive Islands India **77** B3
Lac du Bonnet Can. **113** F2
La Ceiba Hond. **130** B3
Lachlan *r.* Austr. **105** C2
Lachute Can. **123** F1
La Ciotat France **53** D3
Lac La Biche Can. **113** D2
Lac-Mégantic Can. **115** C2
Lacombe Can. **112** D2
La Concepción Panama **130** B4
Laconia U.S.A. **123** F2
La Crosse U.S.A. **122** B2
La Cruz Mex. **128** B2
La Cuesta Mex. **128** B2
Ladakh Range *mts* India **79** B1
Ladismith S. Africa **98** B3
Ladoga, Lake Rus. Fed. **37** D1
Ladozhskoye Ozero *l.* Rus. Fed.
see Ladoga, Lake
Ladysmith S. Africa **99** C2
Lae P.N.G. **63** D3
Læsø *i.* Denmark **41** C4
La Fayette U.S.A. **125** C2
Lafayette *IN* U.S.A. **122** C2
Lafayette *LA* U.S.A. **124** B2
Lafia Nigeria **91** C4
La Flèche France **52** B2
Laforge Can. **115** C1
Läft Iran **83** C2
La Galite *i.* Tunisia **56** A3
Lagan' Rus. Fed. **35** D4
Laghouat Alg. **90** C1
Lagoa Santa Brazil **139** D1
Lagos Nigeria **90** C4
Lagos Port. **54** B2
La Grande U.S.A. **118** C1
La Grande 2, Réservoir *resr* Can.
114 C1
La Grande 3, Réservoir *resr* Can.
114 C1
La Grande 4, Réservoir *resr* Can.
115 C1
Lagrange Austr. **102** B1

La Grange U.S.A. **125** C2
La Gran Sabana *plat.* Venez.
134 C2
Laguna Brazil **136** D3
Laguna, Picacho de la *mt.* Mex.
128 A2
La Habana Cuba see Havana
Lahad Datu Malaysia **65** C1
Lahat Indon. **64** B2
Lahij Yemen **82** B3
Lāhījān Iran **85** C2
Lahore Pak. **78** B1
Lahri Pak. **78** A2
Lahti Fin. **41** F3
Laï Chad **91** D4
Laidley Austr. **105** E1
Laingsburg S. Africa **98** B3
Lainioälven *r.* Sweden **40** E2
Lairg U.K. **44** B1
Laives Italy **56** B1
Laiwu China **74** B2
Laiyang China **74** B2
Laizhou China **74** B2
Laizhou Wan *b.* China **74** B2
Lajamanu Austr. **102** C1
Lajes Brazil **136** C3
La Junta Mex. **128** B2
La Junta U.S.A. **120** C3
Lake Cargelligo Austr. **105** D2
Lake Charles U.S.A. **124** B2
Lake City *FL* U.S.A. **125** D2
Lake City *SC* U.S.A. **125** E2
Lake Havasu City U.S.A.
126 B2
Lakeland U.S.A. **125** D3
Lake Louise Can. **112** C2
Lake Oswego U.S.A. **118** B1
Lake Paringa N.Z. **106** A3
Lake Providence U.S.A. **124** B2
Lakes Entrance Austr. **105** D3
Lakeview U.S.A. **118** B2
Lakewood *CO* U.S.A. **120** B3
Lakewood *NJ* U.S.A. **123** F2
Lake Worth U.S.A. **125** D3
Lakhpat India **78** A2
Lakki Pak. **78** B1
Lakonikos Kolpos *b.* Greece
59 B3
Laksely Norway **40** E1
La Libertad Guat. **129** C3
Lalín Spain **54** B1
Lalitpur India **79** B2
La Louvière Belgium **48** B2
La Maddalena Italy **56** A2
Lamag Malaysia **65** C1
La Manche *str.* France/U.K. see
English Channel
Lamar U.S.A. **120** C3
Lamard Iran **83** C2
La Marmora, Punta *mt.* Italy
56 A3
La Martre, Lac *l.* Can. **112** D1
Lambaréné Gabon **94** B3

Lambert's Bay S. Africa **98** A3⊟
La Merced Peru **134** B4
Lameroo Austr. **104** C3
Lamesa U.S.A. **127** C2
Lamia Greece **59** B3
Lamoni U.S.A. **121** E2
Lampang Thai. **66** A2
Lampasas U.S.A. **127** E2
Lamphun Thai. **66** A2
Lamu Kenya **95** E3
Lanbi Kyun *i.* Myanmar **67** A2
Lancang Jiang *r.* China see
Mekong
Lancaster U.K. **46** B2
Lancaster *CA* U.S.A. **119** C3
Lancaster *OH* U.S.A. **122** D3
Lancaster *PA* U.S.A. **123** E2
Lancaster *SC* U.S.A. **125** D2
Lancaster Sound *str.* Can.
111 G2
Landau in der Pfalz Ger. **48** D3
Landeck Austria **50** C3
Land's End *pt* U.K. **47** A4
Landshut Ger. **50** C3
Landskrona Sweden **41** C4
Lanett U.S.A. **125** C2
Langberg *mts* S. Africa **98** B3
Langdon U.S.A. **121** D1
Langeland *i.* Denmark **41** C4
Langen Ger. **49** D1
Langeoog Ger. **48** C1
Langeoog *i.* Ger. **48** C1
Langgöns Ger. **49** D2
Langjökull *ice cap* Iceland
40 [inset]
Langogne France **53** C3
Langon France **52** B3
Langres France **53** D2
Langsa Indon. **64** A1
Lang Son Vietnam **66** B1
Linkäran Azer. **85** C2
Lannion France **52** B2
Lansing U.S.A. **122** D2
Lanxi China **75** B3
Lanya Sudan **93** B4
Lanzarote *i.* Canary Is **90** A2
Lanzhou China **74** A2
Laoag Phil. **68** B1
Lao Cai Vietnam **66** B1
Laohekou China **74** B2
Lao Ling *mts* China **69** B1
Laon France **53** C2
Laos *country* Asia **66** B2
Laotougou China **69** B1
Lapa Brazil **138** C3
La Palma *i.* Canary Is **90** A2
La Palma Panama **130** C4
La Paz Bol. **136** B2
La Paz Hond. **129** D3
La Paz Mex. **128** A2
La Pedrera Col. **134** C3
La Pérouse Strait
Japan/Rus. Fed. **70** D1

a Pesca Mex. **129** C2
a Piedad Mex. **128** B2
a Plata Arg. **137** C4
a Plata, Rio de *sea chan.*
Arg./Uru. **137** C4
a Quiaca Arg. **136** B3
a Potherie, Lac *l.* Can. **115** C1
appeenranta Fin. **41** F3
appersdorf Ger. **49** F3
appland *reg.* Europe **40** D2
apseki Turkey **59** C2
aptev Sea Rus. Fed. **87** K1
apteyekh, More *sea* Rus. Fed.
see Laptev Sea
apua Fin. **40** E3
a Quiaca Arg. **136** B3
ar Iran **83** C2
arache Morocco **90** B1
aramie U.S.A. **120** B2
aramie Mountains U.S.A.
120 B2
aranda Turkey *see* Karaman
arantuka Indon. **65** D2
arat *i.* Indon. **63** C3
arba Alg. **55** D2
aredo Spain **54** D1
aredo U.S.A. **127** E3
args U.K. **44** B3
a Rioja Arg. **136** B3
arisa Greece **59** B3
arkana Pak. **78** A2
arnaca Cyprus **84** B2
arne U.K. **45** D1
a Rochelle France **52** B2
a Roche-sur-Yon France **52** B2
a Roda Spain **55** C2
a Romana Dom. Rep. **131** D3
a Ronge Can. **110** E3
a Ronge, Lac *l.* Can. **110** F3
arrimah Austr. **102** C1
arsen Ice Shelf Antarctica
107 K3
arvik Norway **41** C4
a Cruces U.S.A. **126** C2
a Serena Chile **136** A3
a Herag. **137** B4
ahio Myanmar **66** A1
ahkar Gãh Afgh. **78** A1
a Sila *reg.* Italy **57** C3
a Lomitas Arg. **136** B3
a Nieves Mex. **128** C2
as Palmas de Gran Canaria
anary is **90** A2
a Spezia Italy **56** A2
as Plumas Arg. **137** B5
st Mountain Lake Can. **113** E2
tovo *i.* Croatia **57** C2
Tres Virgenes, Volcán *vol.*
ex. **128** A2
as Tunas Cuba **131** C2
Varas *Chihuahua* Mex.
28 B2
as Varas *Nayarit* Mex. **128** B2
egas *NM* U.S.A. **126** C1

Las Vegas *NV* U.S.A. **119** C3
Latakia Syria **84** B2
La Teste-de-Buch France **52** B3
Latina Italy **56** B2
La Tuque Can. **115** C2
Latvia *country* Europe **36** B2
Lauchhammer Ger. **49** F2
Lauf an der Pegnitz Ger. **49** E3
Launceston Austr. **103** D4
Launceston U.K. **47** A4
Laura Austr. **103** D1
Laurel *MS* U.S.A. **124** C2
Laurel *MT* U.S.A. **118** E1
Lauria Italy **57** C2
Laurinburg U.S.A. **125** E2
Lausanne Switz. **53** D2
Laut *i.* Indon. **65** C2
Lautersbach (Hessen) Ger.
49 D2
Laut Kecil, Kepulauan *is* Indon.
65 C2
Lauwersmeer *l.* Neth. **48** C1
Laval France **52** B2
Lavras Brazil **139** D2
Lawrence U.S.A. **121** D3
Lawrenceburg U.S.A. **124** C1
Lawton U.S.A. **127** E2
Lawz, Jabal al *mt.* Saudi Arabia
82 A2
Laxå Sweden **41** C4
Lazarevac S.M. **58** B2
Lázaro Cárdenas *Baja California*
Mex. **128** A1
Lázaro Cárdenas *Michoacán* Mex.
128 B3
Leader Can. **113** E2
Leadville U.S.A. **120** B3
Leaf Rapids Can. **113** E2
Leavenworth U.S.A. **121** E3
Lebach Ger. **48** C3
Lebanon *country* Asia **84** B2
Lebanon *MO* U.S.A. **121** E3
Lebanon *NH* U.S.A. **123** F2
Lebanon *OR* U.S.A. **118** B2
Lebanon *PA* U.S.A. **123** E2
Lebedyan' Rus. Fed. **37** E3
Lebedyn Ukr. **39** D1
Lebork Pol. **51** D2
Lebowakgomo S. Africa **99** C1
Lebrija Spain **54** B2
Lebu Chile **137** A4
Le Bugue France **52** C3
Le Catelet France **48** A2
Lecce Italy **57** C2
Lecco Italy **56** A1
Lechaing China **121** E3
Lechaina Greece **59** B3
Lechang China **75** B3
Ledesma Spain **54** B1
Leduc Can. **112** D2
Leech Lake U.S.A. **121** E1
Leeds U.K. **46** C3
Leer (Ostfriesland) Ger. **48** C1
Leesburg U.S.A. **125** D3

Leesville U.S.A. **124** B2
Leeton Austr. **105** D2
Leeu-Gamka S. Africa **98** B3
Leeuwarden Neth. **48** B1
Leeuwin, Cape Austr. **102** A3
Leeward Islands Caribbean Sea
131 D3
Lefkada Greece **59** B3
Lefkada *i.* Greece **59** B3
Lefkosia Cyprus *see* Nicosia
Legaspi Phil. **68** B2
Legnago Italy **56** B1
Legnica Pol. **51** D2
Leh India **79** B1
Le Havre France **52** C2
Lehututu Botswana **98** B1
Leiah Pak. **78** B1
Leibnitz Austria **51** D3
Leicester U.K. **47** C3
Leicht *r.* Austr. **103** C1
Leiden Neth. **48** B1
Leie *r.* Belgium **48** A2
Leigh Creek Austr. **104** B2
Leikanger Norway **41** B3
Leimen Ger. **49** D3
Leine *r.* Ger. **49** D1
Leinster *reg.* Ireland **45** C2
Leipzig Ger. **49** F2
Leiranger Norway **40** C2
Leiria Port. **54** B2
Leirvik Norway **41** B4
Leixlip Ireland **45** C2
Leiyang China **75** B3
Leizhou China **75** B3
Leizhou Bandao *pen.* China
75 A3
Lelystad Neth. **48** B1
Le Maire, Estrecho de *sea chan.*
Arg. **137** B6
Léman, Lac *l.* France/Switz. *see*
Geneva, Lake
Le Mans France **52** C2
Le Mars U.S.A. **121** D2
Leme Brazil **138** C2
Lemesos Cyprus *see* Limassol
Lemieux Islands Can. **111** H2
Lemmon U.S.A. **120** C2
Lemoore U.S.A. **119** C3
Le Moyne, Lac *l.* Can. **115** D1
Le Murge *hills* Italy **57** C2
Lena *r.* Rus. Fed. **87** K2
Lendery Rus. Fed. **40** G3
Lengerich Ger. **48** C1
Lengshuijiang China **75** B3
Lengshuitan China **75** B3
Lenine Ukr. **39** E2
Leningradskaya Rus. Fed. **39** E2
Leninskiy Rus. Fed. **37** E3
Lensk Rus. Fed. **87** J2
Lenti Italy **56** C3
Léo Burkina **90** B3
Leoben Austria **50** D3
León Mex. **128** B2
León Nic. **130** B3

León Spain **54** B1
Leonardville Namibia **98** A1
Leonora Austr. **102** B2
Lephalale S. Africa **99** C1
Lephepe Botswana **99** C1
Leping China **75** B3
Le Puy-en-Velay France **52** C3
Lerala Botswana **99** C1
Lérida Spain *see* Lleida
Lérida Col. **134** B3
Lerma Spain **54** E1
Leros *i.* Greece **59** C3
Le Roy, Lac *l.* Can. **114** C1
Lerum Sweden **41** C4
Lerwick U.K. **44** [inset]
Lesbos *i.* Greece **59** C3
Les Cayes Haiti **131** C3
Leshan China **72** C3
Leshukonskoye Rus. Fed. **34** D2
Leskovac S.M. **58** B2
Lesosibirsk Rus. Fed. **87** I3
Lesotho *country* Africa **99** C2
Lesozavodsk Rus. Fed. **70** B1
Les Sables-d'Olonne France
52 B2
Lesser Antilles *is* Caribbean Sea
131 D3
Lesser Caucasus *mts* Asia **85** C1
Lesser Slave Lake Can. **112** D2
Lesvos *i.* Greece *see* Lesbos
Leszno Pol. **51** D2
Letchworth U.K. **47** C4
Lethbridge Can. **113** D3
Lethem Guyana **134** F3
Leticia Col. **134** C3
Letlhakeng Botswana **99** C1
Letsok-aw Kyun *i.* Myanmar
67 A2
Letsopa S. Africa **99** C2
Leucate, Étang de *l.* France
52 C3
Leuser, Gunung *mt.* Indon. **64** A1
Leuven Belgium **48** B3
Levadeia Greece **59** B3
Levelland U.S.A. **127** C2
Lévêque, Cape Austr. **102** B1
Leverkusen Ger. **48** C2
Levice Slovakia **51** D3
Levin N.Z. **106** C3
Lewis, Isle of *i.* U.K. **44** A1
Lewisburg U.S.A. **123** D3
Lewis Range *mts* U.S.A. **118** D1
Lewiston *ID* U.S.A. **118** C1
Lewiston *ME* U.S.A. **123** F2
Lewistown U.S.A. **118** E1
Lexington *KY* U.S.A. **122** D3
Lexington *NE* U.S.A. **122** D2
Lexington *VA* U.S.A. **123** E3
Leyte *i.* Phil. **68** B2
Lezhë Albania **58** A2
Lezhnevo Rus. Fed. **37** F2
L'gov Rus. Fed. **37** E3
Lhagoi Kangri *mt.* China **79** C2
Lhasa China **79** D2
Lhazê China **79** C2

Lhokseumawe Indon. **64** A1
Liancheaol Rocks *i.*
N. Pacific Ocean **69** C2
Lianjiang China **75** B3
Lianshan China **74** B1
Lianyungang China **74** B2
Lianzhou China **75** B3
Liaocheng China **74** B2
Liaodong Bandao *pen.* China
74 C1
Liaodong Wan *b.* China **74** C1
Liao He *r.* China **69** A1
Liaoning *prov.* China **74** C1
Liaoyang China **74** C1
Liaoyuan China **69** B1
Libby U.S.A. **118** C1
Libenge Dem. Rep. Congo **94** B2
Liberal U.S.A. **120** C3
Liberec Czech Rep. **50** D2
Liberia *country* Africa **90** B4
Liberia Costa Rica **130** B3
Libourne France **52** B3
Libreville Gabon **94** A2
Libya *country* Africa **91** D2
Libyan Desert Egypt/Libya **91** E2
Libyan Plateau Egypt **92** A1
Licata Italy **56** B3
Lichinga Moz. **97** C1
Lichtenburg S. Africa **99** C2
Lichtenfels Ger. **49** E2
Lida Belarus **36** C3
Lidköping Sweden **41** C4
Liebenwalde Ger. **49** F1
Liebig, Mount Austr. **102** C2
Liechtenstein *country* Europe
53 D2
Liège Belgium **48** B2
Lieksa Fin. **40** G3
Lienz Austria **50** C3
Liepāja Latvia **42** B2
Liévin France **48** A2
Liezen Austria **50** C3
Liffey *r.* Ireland **45** C2
Lifford Ireland **45** C1
Lightning Ridge Austr. **105** D1
Ligonha *r.* Moz. **97** C1
Ligurian Sea France/Italy **56** A2
Likasi Dem. Rep. Congo **95** C4
Likhoslavl' Rus. Fed. **37** E2
Liku Indon. **64** B1
Lilla Edet Sweden **41** C4
Lille France **52** C1
Lille Bælt *sea chan.* Denmark *see*
Little Belt
Lillehammer Norway **41** C3
Lillestrøm Norway **41** C4
Lilongwe Malawi **97** C1
Lima Peru **134** B4
Lima U.S.A. **122** D2
Limassol Cyprus **84** B2
Limavady U.K. **45** C1
Limay *r.* Arg. **137** B4
Limbach-Oberfrohna Ger. **49** F2
Limbaži Latvia **36** B2

Limbe Cameroon **94** A2
Limburg an der Lahn Ger. **48**
Lime Acres S. Africa **98** B2
Limeira Brazil **138** C2
Limerick Ireland **45** B2
Limfjorden *sea chan.* Denmark
41 B4
Limnos *i.* Greece **59** C3
Limoges France **52** C2
Limon U.S.A. **120** C3
Limoux France **52** C3
Limpopo *prov.* S. Africa **99** C1
Limpopo *r.* S. Africa/Zimbabwe
99 D2
Linares Chile **137** A4
Linares Mex. **129** C2
Linares Spain **54** C2
Lincang China **66** B1
Lincoln U.K. **46** C3
Lincoln *IL* U.S.A. **122** C2
Lincoln *NE* U.S.A. **121** D2
Linden Guyana **135** D2
Lindi *r.* Dem. Rep. Congo **95** C
Lindi Tanz. **95** D3
Lindisfarne *i.* U.K. *see* Holy Isl
Lindsay Can. **123** E2
Line Islands Kiribati **143** E4
Linfen China **74** B2
Lingayen Phil. **68** B2
Lingelihle S. Africa **99** C3
Lingen (Ems) Ger. **48** C1
Lingga, Kepulauan *is* Indon.
64 B2
Lingshui China **75** A4
Linguère Senegal **90** A3
Linhares Brazil **139** D1
Linhe China **74** A1
Linköping Sweden **41** D4
Linkou China **70** B1
Linnhe, Loch *inlet* U.K. **44** B2
Linqing China **74** B2
Lins Brazil **138** C2
Linton U.S.A. **120** C1
Linxi China **74** B1
Linxia China **74** A2
Linyi *Shandong* China **74** B2
Linyi *Shandong* China **74** B2
Linying China **74** B2
Linz Austria **50** C3
Lion, Golfe du *g.* France **53** C
Lipari Italy **56** B3
Lipari, Isole *is* Italy **56** B3
Lipetsk Rus. Fed. **37** E3
Lipin Bor Rus. Fed. **37** E1
Lipova Romania **38** B2
Lippstadt Ger. **49** D2
Lipu China **75** B3
Lisala Dem. Rep. Congo **94** C2
Lisboa Port. *see* Lisbon
Lisbon Port. **54** B2
Lisburn U.K. **45** C1
Liscannor Bay Ireland **45** B2
Lisieux France **52** C2
Liskeard U.K. **47** A4

li Rus. Fed. **37** E3
ore Austr. **105** E1
owel Ireland **45** B2
ng *Guangxi* China **75** A3
ng *Sichuan* China **72** C2
afield *IL* U.S.A. **122** C3
afield *MN* U.S.A. **121** E1
gow Austr. **105** E2
no, Akra *pt* Greece **59** B4
uania *country* Europe **36** B2
měřice Czech Rep. **50** C2
e Abaco *i.* Bahamas **131** C2
e Andaman *i.* India **67** A2
e Belt *sea chan.* Denmark
 45 D2
e Falls U.S.A. **121** D1
efield U.S.A. **127** D2
ehampton U.K. **47** C4
e Karoo *plat.* S. Africa **98** B3
e Minch *sea chan.* U.K. **44** A2
e Missouri *r.* U.S.A. **120** C1
e Nicobar *i.* India **67** A3
e Rock U.S.A. **124** B2
achang China **75** B2
zhou China **75** A3
nt Latvia **36** C2
rmore, Mount U.S.A.
 116 D2
rpool Can. **115** D2
rpool U.K. **46** B3
rpool Range *mts* Austr.
 95 D2
ngston *MT* U.S.A. **118** D1
ngston *TX* U.S.A. **127** F2
ngston, Lake U.S.A. **127** E2
ngstone Zambia **96** B1
e Bos.-Herz. **57** C2
y Rus. Fed. **37** E3
nia U.S.A. **122** D2
e Tanz. **95** D3
erd Point U.K. **47** A5
ljana Slovenia **56** B1
ngan *r.* Sweden **41** D3
ngby Sweden **41** C4
sdal Sweden **41** D3
snan *r.* Sweden **41** D3
sdelo U.K. **47** B4
sdovery U.K. **47** B4
sdrindod Wells U.K. **47** B3
sdudno U.K. **46** B3
melli U.K. **47** A4
sgefni U.K. **46** A3
no Estacado *plain* U.S.A.
 127 D2
sos *reg.* Col./Venez. **134** C2
da Spain **55** D1
a Spain **55** C2
dio Spain **54** D1
st George, Mount Can. **112** C2
dyd Lake Can. **113** E2
sdminster Can. **113** D2
sdaillaco, Volcán *vol.* Chile
 136 B3

Lobatse Botswana **99** C2
Lobito Angola **96** A1
Lochboisdale U.K. **44** A2
Lochgilphead U.K. **44** B2
Lochinver U.K. **44** B1
Lochmaddy U.K. **44** A2
Lochnagar *mt.* U.K. **44** C2
Lock Austr. **104** B2
Lockerbie U.K. **44** C3
Lockport U.S.A. **123** E2
Lodeynoye Pole Rus. Fed. **34** C2
Løding Norway **40** C2
Lodwar Kenya **95** D2
Łódź Pol. **51** D2
Loei Thai. **66** B2
Loeriesfontein S. Africa **98** A3
Lofoten *is* Norway **40** C2
Logan U.S.A. **118** D2
Logan, Mount Can. **112** A1
Logansport U.S.A. **122** C2
Logatec Slovenia **56** B1
Logroño Spain **55** C1
Löhne Ger. **49** D1
Lohne (Oldenburg) Ger. **49** D1
Loikaw Myanmar **66** A2
Loi Lan *mt.* Myanmar/Thai.
 66 A2
Loire *r.* France **52** B2
Loja Ecuador **134** B3
Loja Spain **54** C2
Lokan tekojärvi *l.* Fin. **40** F2
Lokeren Belgium **48** B2
Lokichar Kenya **95** D2
Loknya Rus. Fed. **37** D2
Lokoja Nigeria **91** C4
Lokot' Rus. Fed. **37** D3
Loks Land *i.* Can. **111** H2
Lolland *i.* Denmark **41** C5
Lolwane S. Africa **98** B2
Lom Bulg. **58** B2
Lomami *r.* Dem. Rep. Congo
 95 C2
Lomas de Zamora Arg. **137** C4
Lombok *i.* Indon. **65** C2
Lombok, Selat *sea chan.* Indon.
 65 C2
Lomé Togo **90** C4
Lomela *r.* Dem. Rep. Congo
 94 C3
Lomme France **48** A2
Lommel Belgium **48** B2
Lomond, Loch *l.* U.K. **44** B2
Lomonosov Rus. Fed. **36** C2
Lompobattang, Gunung *mt.*
 Indon. **65** C2
Lompoc U.S.A. **119** B2
Lom Sak Thai. **66** B2
Łomża Pol. **51** E2
London Can. **114** B2
London U.K. **47** C4
London U.S.A. **122** D3
Londonderry U.K. **45** C1
Londonderry, Cape Austr.
 102 B1

Londrina Brazil **138** B2
Longa, Proliv *sea chan.* Rus. Fed.
 87 N2
Long Akah Malaysia **65** C1
Long Bay U.S.A. **125** E2
Long Beach U.S.A. **119** C4
Longford Ireland **45** C2
Longiram Indon. **65** C2
Long Island Bahamas **131** C2
Long Island Can. **114** C1
Long Island P.N.G. **63** D3
Long Island U.S.A. **123** F2
Longlac Can. **114** B2
Longmont U.S.A. **120** B2
Long Point Can. **123** D2
Long Range Mountains Can.
 115 E2
Longreach Austr. **103** D2
Longtown U.K. **46** B2
Longuyon France **53** D2
Longview *TX* U.S.A. **127** F2
Longview *WA* U.S.A. **118** B1
Longxi China **74** A2
Longxi Shan *mt.* China **75** B3
Long Xuyên Vietnam **67** B2
Longyan China **75** B3
Longyearbyen Svalbard **86** D1
Lons-le-Saunier France **50** B3
Lookout, Cape U.S.A. **125** E2
Loop Head Ireland **45** B2
Lop Buri Thai. **67** B2
Lopez Phil. **68** B2
Lop Nur *salt flat* China **72** C2
Lopori *r.* Dem. Rep. Congo
 94 B2
Lora del Río Spain **54** B2
Lorain U.S.A. **122** D2
Loralai Pak. **78** A1
Lorca Spain **55** C2
Lord Howe Island Austr. **103** E3
Lordsburg U.S.A. **126** C2
Lorena Brazil **139** C2
Loreto Bol. **136** B2
Loreto Mex. **128** A2
Lorient France **52** B2
Lorn, Firth of *est.* U.K. **44** B2
Lorne Austr. **104** C3
Los Alamos U.S.A. **126** C1
Los Aldamas Mex. **127** E3
Los Ángeles Chile **137** A4
Los Angeles U.S.A. **119** C4
Los Banos U.S.A. **119** B3
Los Blancos Arg. **136** B3
Losevo Rus. Fed. **39** F1
Lošinj *i.* Croatia **56** B2
Los Mochis Mex. **128** B2
Losombo Dem. Rep. Congo
 94 B2
Los Roques, Islas *is* Venez.
 131 D3
Lossiemouth U.K. **44** C2
Los Teques Venez. **134** C1
Los Vilos Chile **136** A4
Lot *r.* France **52** C3

Loth U.K. **44** C1
Lotikipi Plain Kenya **95** D2
Loto Dem. Rep. Congo **94** C3
Louangnamtha Laos **66** B1
Louangphabang Laos **66** B2
Loubomo Congo **94** B3
Loudéac France **52** B2
Loudi China **75** B3
Louga Senegal **90** A3
Loughborough U.K. **47** C3
Louisburgh Ireland **45** B2
Louisiade Archipelago *is* P.N.G. **103** E1
Louisiana *state* U.S.A. **124** B2
Louisville *KY* U.S.A. **122** C3
Louisville *MS* U.S.A. **124** C2
Loukhi Rus. Fed. **40** G2
Louny Czech Rep. **49** F2
Lourdes France **52** B3
Lousã Port. **54** B1
Louth Austr. **105** D2
Louth U.K. **46** C3
Louvet' r. Rus. Fed. **37** D2
Lovech Bulg. **58** B2
Loveland U.S.A. **120** B2
Lovelock U.S.A. **118** C2
Lovington U.S.A. **127** F2
Lowa Dem. Rep. Congo **95** C3
Lowell U.S.A. **123** F2
Lower Arrow Lake Can. **112** D3
Lower Hutt N.Z. **106** B3
Lower Lough Erne *l.* U.K. **45** C1
Lowestoft U.K. **47** D3
Lowicz Pol. **51** D2
Lowville U.S.A. **123** E2
Loxton Austr. **104** C2
Loyauté, Îles *is* New Caledonia **100**
Loyew Belarus **37** D3
Løypskardtinden *mt.* Norway **40** C2
Loznica S.M. **58** A2
Lozova Ukr. **39** E2
Luacano Angola **96** B1
Lu'an China **74** B2
Luanda Angola **96** B1
Luangwa *r.* Zambia **97** C1
Luanshya Zambia **97** B1
Luarca Spain **54** B1
Luau Angola **96** B1
Lubango Angola **96** A1
Lubao Dem. Rep. Congo **95** C3
Lubartów Pol. **51** E2
Lübbecke Ger. **49** D1
Lübben Ger. **49** F2
Lübbenau Ger. **49** F2
Lubbock U.S.A. **127** C2
Lübeck Ger. **49** E1
Lubei China **74** C1
Lubin Pol. **51** D2
Lublin Pol. **51** E2
Lubny Ukr. **39** D1
Lubudi Dem. Rep. Congo **95** C3

Lubuklinggau Indon. **64** B2
Lubumbashi Dem. Rep. Congo **95** C4
Lubungu Zambia **96** B1
Lubutu Dem. Rep. Congo **95** C3
Lucala Angola **96** A1
Lucan Ireland **45** C2
Lucapa Angola **94** C3
Luce Bay U.K. **44** B3
Lucélia Brazil **138** B2
Lucena Phil. **68** B2
Lucena Spain **54** C2
Lučenec Slovakia **51** D3
Lucera Italy **56** C2
Lucerne Switz. *see* Luzern
Lüchow Ger. **49** E1
Lucira Angola **96** A1
Luckau Ger. **49** F2
Luckenwalde Ger. **49** F1
Luckhoff S. Africa **98** B2
Lucknow India **79** C2
Lucusse Angola **96** B1
Lüderitz Namibia **98** A2
Ludhiana India **78** B1
Ludlow U.K. **47** B3
Ludlow U.S.A. **119** C4
Ludogorie *reg.* Bulg. **58** C2
Ludvika Sweden **41** D3
Ludwigsburg Ger. **50** B2
Ludwigsfelde Ger. **49** F1
Ludwigshafen am Rhein Ger. **49** D3
Ludwigslust Ger. **49** E1
Ludza Latvia **36** C2
Luebo Dem. Rep. Congo **94** C3
Luena Angola **96** A1
Lüeyang China **74** A2
Lufeng China **75** B3
Lufkin U.S.A. **127** F2
Luga Rus. Fed. **36** C2
Luga *r.* Rus. Fed. **36** C2
Lugano Switz. **53** D1
Lugenda *r.* Moz. **97** C1
Lugo Spain **54** B1
Lugoj Romania **58** B1
Luhans'k Ukr. **39** E2
Luhombero Tanz. **95** D3
Luhyny Ukr. **38** C1
Luiana Angola **96** B1
Luilaka *r.* Dem. Rep. Congo **94** C3
Luiro *r.* Fin. **40** F2
Lukavac Bos.-Herz. **57** C2
Lukenie *r.* Dem. Rep. Congo **94** B3
Lukeville U.S.A. **126** B2
Lukh *r.* Rus. Fed. **37** F2
Lukhovitsy Rus. Fed. **37** E3
Łuków Pol. **51** E2
Lukulu Zambia **96** B1
Luleå Sweden **40** E2
Luleälven *r.* Sweden **40** E2
Lüleburgaz Turkey **58** C2
Lüliang Shan *mts* China **74** B2
Lumajang Indon. **65** C2

Lumajangdong Co *salt l.* China **79** C1
Lumbala Kaquengue Angola **96** B1
Lumbala N'guimbo Angola **96** B1
Lumberton U.S.A. **125** E2
Lumbis Indon. **65** C1
Lumphät Cambodia **67** B2
Lumsden Can. **113** E2
Lumsden N.Z. **106** A4
Lund Sweden **41** C4
Lundazi Zambia **97** C1
Lundy *i.* U.K. **47** A4
Lüneburg Ger. **49** E1
Lüneburger Heide *reg.* Ger. **49** E1
Lunéville France **53** D2
Lunga *r.* Zambia **96** B1
Lungnaquilla Mountain *h.* Ireland **45** C2
Lungwebungu *r.* Zambia **96** B1
Luni *r.* India **78** B2
Luninyets Belarus **36** C3
Lunsar Sierra Leone **90** A4
Luntai China **81** F2
Luoding China **75** B3
Luohe China **74** B2
Luoyang China **74** B2
Lupanshui China **75** A3
Lupeni Romania **38** B2
Lupilichi Moz. **97** C1
Lúrio Moz. **97** D1
Lurio *r.* Moz. **97** D1
Lusaka Zambia **97** B1
Lusambo Dem. Rep. Congo **94** C3
Lushnjë Albania **59** A2
Lusk U.S.A. **120** C2
Lut, Dasht-e *des.* Iran **80** C3
Lutherstadt Wittenberg Ger. **49** F2
Luton U.K. **47** C4
Łutselk'e Can. **113** D1
Luts'k Ukr. **38** C1
Lutzputs S. Africa **98** B2
Lutzville S. Africa **98** A3
Luuq Somalia **93** C4
Luverne U.S.A. **121** D2
Luvua *r.* Dem. Rep. Congo **95** C3
Luwero Uganda **95** D2
Luwuk Indon. **65** D2
Luxembourg *country* Europe **48** C3
Luxembourg Lux. **48** C3
Luxolweni S. Africa **99** C3
Luxor Egypt **92** B2
Luza Rus. Fed. **34** D3
Luziânia Brazil **138** C1
Luzon *i.* Phil. **68** B2
Luzon Strait Phil. **68** B1
L'viv Ukr. **38** B2
L'vov Ukr. *see* L'viv

khavichy Belarus **36** C3
ksele Sweden **40** D3
nburg S. Africa **99** D2
l'chytsy Belarus **36** C3
oyel' Belarus **36** C3
e Bay U.K. **47** B4
brough U.S.A. **123** C3
n Lake Can. **113** E2
a Lake Can. **113** E1
n France **53** C2
zna Belarus **37** D2
'va Rus. Fed. **34** E3
ychans'k Ukr. **39** E2
am St Anne's U.K. **46** B3
han' Belarus **36** C3
bertsy Rus. Fed. **37** E2
beshiv Ukr. **38** C1
bim Rus. Fed. **37** F2
botyn Ukr. **39** E2
bytino Rus. Fed. **37** D3
dinovo Rus. Fed. **37** D3

ân Jordan **84** B2
ardu Estonia **36** C2
as r. Neth. **48** B2
aseik Belgium **48** B2
asin Phil. **68** D2
astricht Neth. **48** B2
balane Moz. **97** C2
baruma Guyana **134** D2
bote Moz. **97** C2
bule Botswana **98** B2
butsane Botswana **98** B1
caé Brazil **139** D2
caloge Moz. **97** C1
cao China **73** D3
capá Brazil **135** D2
carani Brazil **139** D1
cassar Strait Indon. see
akassar, Selat
cclesfield U.K. **46** B3
cdonald, Lake salt flat Austr.
02 B2
cdonnell Ranges mts Austr.
02 C2
cDowell Lake Can. **114** A1
cedo de Cavaleiros Port.
54 B1
cedon mt. Austr. **104** C3
cedonia country Europe **58** B2
celió Brazil **135** F3
cerata Italy **56** E2
cfarlane, Lake salt flat Austr.
04 B2
cgillicuddy's Reeks mts
eland **45** B3
ch Pak. **78** A2
chaila Moz. **97** C2
chakos Kenya **95** D3
chala Ecuador **134** B3

Machanga Moz. **97** C2
Machault France **48** B3
Macheng China **74** B2
Machias U.S.A. **123** G2
Machiques Venez. **134** B1
Machu Picchu Peru **134** B4
Macia Moz. **99** D2
Macka Romania **38** C2
Macintyre r. Austr. **105** E1
Mackay Austr. **103** D2
Mackay, Lake salt flat Austr.
102 B2
Mackenzie Can. **113** D1
Mackenzie r. Can. **112** C2
Mackenzie r. Can. **112** B1
Mackenzie Bay Can. **110** C2
Mackenzie King Island Can.
110 E1
Mackenzie Mountains Can.
112 B1
Macksville Austr. **105** E2
Maclean Austr. **105** E1
MacLeod, Lake imp. l. Austr.
102 A2
Macomb U.S.A. **122** B2
Macomer Italy **56** A2
Mâcon France **53** C2
Macon GA U.S.A. **125** D2
Macon MO U.S.A. **121** E3
Macquarie r. Austr. **105** D2
Macquarie Island
S. Pacific Ocean **100**
Macquarie Marshes Austr. **105** D2
Macroom Ireland **45** B3
Macumba watercourse Austr.
104 C1
Macuspana Mex. **129** C3
Macuzari, Presa resr Mex.
128 B2
Madadeni S. Africa **99** D2
Madagascar country Africa
97 [inset] D2
Madanga Niger **91** D2
Madan Bulg. **59** B2
Madang P.N.G. **63** D3
Madeira r. Brazil **134** D3
Madeira terr. N. Atlantic Ocean
90 A1
Madeleine, Îles de la is Can.
115 D2
Madera Mex. **128** B2
Madgaon India **77** B3
Madingou Congo **94** B3
Madison IN U.S.A. **122** C3
Madison WI U.S.A. **122** C2
Madison WV U.S.A. **122** D3
Madisonville U.S.A. **122** C3
Madiun Indon. **65** C2
Mado Gashi Kenya **95** D2
Madol China **72** C2
Madona Latvia **36** C2
Madrakah Saudi Arabia **82** A2
Madras India see Chennai

Madras U.S.A. **118** B2
Madre, Laguna lag. Mex.
129 C2
Madre de Dios r. Peru **134** C4
Madre del Sur, Sierra mts Mex.
129 B3
Madre Occidental, Sierra mts
Mex. **128** B2
Madre Oriental, Sierra mts Mex.
129 B2
Madrid Spain **54** C1
Madridejos Spain **54** C2
Madura i. Indon. **65** C2
Madura, Selat sea chan. Indon.
65 C2
Madurai India **77** B4
Maebashi Japan **71** C3
Mae Hong Son Thai. **66** A2
Mae Sai Thai. **66** A1
Mafeteng Lesotho **99** C2
Mafia Island Tanz. **95** D3
Mafikeng S. Africa **99** C2
Mafinga Tanz. **95** D3
Mafra Brazil **138** C3
Magadan Rus. Fed. **87** M3
Magangue Col. **131** C4
Magdalena r. Col. **132**
Magdalena Mex. **128** A1
Magdalena U.S.A. **126** C2
Magdalena, Bahía b. Mex.
128 A2
Magdeburg Ger. **49** E1
Magellan, Strait of Chile **137** A6
Magherafelt U.K. **45** C1
Magnitogorsk Rus. Fed. **35** E3
Magnolia U.S.A. **124** B2
Magpie, Lac l. Can. **115** D1
Magta' Lahjar Maur. **90** A3
Maguarinho, Cabo c. Brazil
135 E3
Magude Moz. **99** D2
Magwe Myanmar **66** A1
Mahābād Iran **85** C2
Mahajanga Madag. **97** [inset] D1
Mahakam r. Indon. **65** C2
Mahalapye Botswana **99** C1
Mahanadi r. India **79** C2
Mahanoro Madag. **97** [inset] D1
Maha Sarakham Thai. **67** B2
Mahavavy r. Madag. **97** [inset] D1
Mahbubnagar India **77** B3
Mahd adh Dhahab Saudi Arabia
82 B2
Mahdia Alg. **55** D2
Mahdia Guyana **134** D2
Mahesana India **78** B2
Mahia Peninsula N.Z. **106** C2
Mahilyow Belarus **37** D3
Mahón Spain **55** D2
Mahony Lake Can. **112** C1
Mahuva India **78** B2
Maidstone U.K. **47** D4
Maiduguri Nigeria **91** D3
Main r. Ger. **49** D2

Mai-Ndombe, Lac *l.*
Dem. Rep. Congo **94** B3
Main-Donau-Kanal *canal* Ger.
49 E3
Maine *state* U.S.A. **123** G1
Maingkwan Myanmar **66** A1
Mainland *i.* Scotland U.K. **44** C1
Mainland *i.* Scotland U.K.
44 (inset)
Maintirano Madag. **97** [inset] D1
Mainz Ger. **49** D2
Maiquetía Venez. **131** D1
Maitland *N.S.W.* Austr. **105** E2
Maitland S.A. Austr. **104** B2
Maíz, Islas del *is* Nic. **130** B3
Maizuru Japan **71** C3
Maja Jezercë *mt.* Albania **58** A2
Majene Indon. **65** C2
Majorca *i.* Spain **55** D2
Majuro *atoll* Marshall Is **100**
Makabana Congo **94** B3
Makale Indon. **65** C2
Makanchi Kazakh. **81** F2
Makarska Croatia **57** C2
Makassar Indon. **65** C2
Makassar, Selat *str.* Indon. **65** C2
Makat Kazakh. **80** C2
Makatini Flats *lowland* S. Africa
99 D2
Makeni Sierra Leone **90** A4
Makgadikgadi *salt pan* Botswana
96 B2
Makhachkala Rus. Fed. **35** D4
Makhado S. Africa **99** C1
Makhambet Kazakh. **80** C2
Makhazine, Barrage El *dam*
Morocco **54** B3
Makindu Kenya **95** B3
Makinsk Kazakh. **81** E1
Makiyivka Ukr. **39** E2
Makkah Saudi Arabia *see* Mecca
Makkovik Can. **115** E1
Mako Hungary **51** E3
Makokou Gabon **94** B2
Makongolosi Tanz. **95** D3
Makopong Botswana **98** B2
Makran *reg.* Iran/Pak. **83** D2
Makran Coast Range *mts* Pak.
78 A2
Maksatikha Rus. Fed. **37** E2
Mākū Iran **85** C2
Makum India **66** A1
Makurazaki Japan **71** B4
Makurdi Nigeria **91** C4
Malā Sweden **40** D2
Malabo Equat. Guinea **94** A2
Malacca, Strait of
Indon./Malaysia **64** A1
Malad City U.S.A. **118** D2
Maladzyechna Belarus **36** C3
Málaga Spain **54** C2
Malaita *i.* Solomon Is **100**
Malakal Sudan **93** B4
Malakula *i.* Vanuatu **100**

Malamala Indon. **65** C2
Malang Indon. **65** C2
Malanje Angola **94** B3
Mälaren *l.* Sweden **41** D4
Malatya Turkey **84** B2
Malawi *country* Africa **97** C1
Malawi, Lake Africa *see*
Nyasa, Lake
Malaya Vishera Rus. Fed. **37** D2
Malaybalay Phil. **68** B3
Malāyer Iran **85** C2
Malaysia *country* Asia **64** B1
Malbork Pol. **51** D2
Malchin Ger. **49** F1
Malden Island Kiribati **101**
Maldives *country* Indian Ocean
77 B4
Male Maldives **77** B4
Maleas, Akra *pt* Greece **59** B3
Male Atoll Maldives **77** B4
Malé Karpaty *hills* Slovakia **51** D3
Malheur Lake U.S.A. **118** C2
Mali *country* Africa **90** B3
Malili Indon. **65** D2
Malindi Kenya **95** E3
Malin Head Ireland **45** C1
Malkara Turkey **59** C2
Mal'kavichy Belarus **36** C3
Mallacoota Austr. **105** D3
Mallacoota Inlet *b.* Austr. **105** D3
Mallaig U.K. **44** B2
Mallery Lake Can. **113** F1
Mallorca *i.* Spain *see* Majorca
Mallow Ireland **45** B2
Malmberget Sweden **40** E2
Malmédy Belgium **48** C2
Malmesbury S. Africa **98** A3
Malmö Sweden **41** C4
Malong China **75** A3
Måløy Norway **41** B3
Maloyaroslavets Rus. Fed. **37** E2
Maloy Borisovo Rus. Fed. **37** E2
Malta *country* Europe **91** F1
Malta Latvia **36** C2
Malta U.S.A. **118** E1
Maltahöhe Namibia **98** A1
Malton U.K. **46** C2
Maluku *is* Indon. *see* Moluccas
Maluku, Laut *sea* Indon. **65** C2
Maluti Mountains Lesotho **99** C2
Malvern U.S.A. **124** B2
Malyn Ukr. **38** C1
Malyy Anyuy *r.* Rus. Fed. **87** N2
Malyy Lyakhovskiy, Ostrov *i.*
Rus. Fed. **87** L2
Mambéré *r.* C.A.R. **94** B2
Mamelodi S. Africa **99** C2
Mamoré *r.* Bol./Brazil **136** B2
Mamou Guinea **90** A3
Mamuju Indon. **65** C2
Man Côte d'Ivoire **90** B4
Manacapuru Brazil **134** C3
Manacor Spain **55** D2

Manado Indon. **63** C2
Managua Nic. **130** B3
Manakara Madag. **97** [inset] D1
Manākhah Yemen **82** B3
Manama Bahrain **83** C2
Manam Island P.N.G. **63** D3
Mananara Avaratra Madag.
97 [inset] D1
Mananjary Madag. **97** [inset] D1
Manantali, Lac de *l.* Mali **90** A3
Manas Hu *l.* China **81** F2
Manatuto East Timor **63** C3
Man-aung Kyun *i.* Myanmar
66 A2
Manaus Brazil **134** C3
Manavgat Turkey **84** B2
Manchester U.K. **46** B3
Manchester U.S.A. **123** F2
Mandabe Madag. **97** [inset] D1
Mandal Norway **41** B4
Mandalay Myanmar **66** A1
Mandalgovi Mongolia **72** D1
Mandan U.S.A. **120** C1
Mandla India **79** C2
Mandritsara Madag. **97** [inset]
Mandsaur India **78** B2
Mandurah Austr. **102** A3
Mandya India **77** B3
Manevychi Ukr. **38** C1
Manfredonia Italy **57** C2
Mangai Dem. Rep. Congo **94** B3
Mangakino N.Z. **106** C2
Mangalia Romania **38** C3
Mangalore India **77** B3
Mangaung S. Africa **99** C2
Manggar Indon. **64** B2
Mangnai China **72** C2
Mangochi Malawi **97** C1
Mangystau Kazakh. **80** C2
Manhattan U.S.A. **121** D3
Manhica Moz. **97** C2
Manhuaçu Brazil **139** D2
Mania *r.* Madag. **97** [inset] D1
Maniago Italy **56** B1
Manicoré Brazil **134** C3
Manicouagan *r.* Can. **115** D2
Manicouagan, Petit Lac *l.* Can.
115 D1
Manicouagan, Réservoir *resr*
Can. **115** D1
Manīfah Saudi Arabia **83** B2
Manila Phil. **68** B2
Manilla Austr. **105** E2
Manisa Turkey **59** C3
Manistee U.S.A. **122** C2
Manitoba *prov.* Can. **113** F2
Manitoba, Lake Can. **113** F2
Manitou Islands U.S.A. **122** C2
Manitoulin Island Can. **114** B2
Manitowoc U.S.A. **122** C2
Manizales Col. **134** B2
Mankato U.S.A. **121** E2
Mankono Côte d'Ivoire **90** B4
Mankota Can. **118** E1

nmad India 78 B2
nnar, Gulf of India/Sri Lanka
 F2
nnheim Ger. 49 D3
nning Can. 112 D2
nnville Can. 113 D2
nokwari Indon. 63 C3
nono Dem. Rep. Congo 95 C3
nosque France 53 D3
nouane, Lac l. Can. 115 C1
nresa Spain 55 D1
nsa Zambia 97 B1
nsel Island Can. 111 G2
nsel'kya ridge Fin./Rus. Fed.
 F2
nsfield Austr. 105 D3
nsfield U.K. 46 C3
nsfield LA U.S.A. 124 B2
nsfield OH U.S.A. 122 D2
nta Ecuador 134 A3
ntes-la-Jolie France 52 C2
ntiqueira, Serra de mts Brazil
 39 C2
ntova Italy see Mantua
ntua Italy 56 B1
nui l. Indon. 65 D2
nukau N.Z. 106 B2
nus Island P.N.G. 63 D3
ny U.S.A. 124 B2
nych-Gudilo, Ozero l.
Rus. Fed. 35 D4
nyoni Tanz. 95 D3
nzanares Spain 54 C2
nzanillo Mex. 128 B3
nzhouli China 73 D1
nzini Swaziland 99 D2
o Chad 91 D3
oks, Pegunungan mts Indon.
53 D3
okeng S. Africa 99 C2
okoi Shan mt. China 69 A1
ooming China 75 B3
pai Moz. 97 C2
pane Indon. 65 D2
pastepec Mex. 129 C3
pimi, Bolsón de des. Mex.
28 B2
pin l. Phil. 68 A3
apinhane Moz. 97 C2
puto Moz. 97 C2
puto r. Moz./S. Africa 99 D2
quan he r. China 79 C2
quela do Zombo Angola
94 B3
quoketa U.S.A. 121 E2
raazul Brazil 134 C3
raba Brazil 135 E3
racá, Ilha de i. Brazil 135 D2
racaibo Venez. 134 B1
racaibo, Lake Venez. 134 B2
racaju Brazil 138 A2
racaju, Serra de hills Brazil
138 A2
racay Venez. 134 C1

Marädah Libya 91 B2
Maradi Niger 91 C3
Marägheh Iran 85 C2
Marajó, Baía de est. Brazil
 135 E3
Marajó, Ilha de i. Brazil 135 D3
Maräkï Iran 83 C2
Marand Iran 85 C2
Maranoa r. Austr. 105 D1
Marañón r. Peru 134 B3
Marathon Can. 114 B2
Marathon U.S.A. 125 D4
Marbella Spain 54 C2
Marble Bar Austr. 102 A2
Marburg S. Africa 99 D3
Marburg an der Lahn Ger. 49 D2
Marche-en-Famenne Belgium
 48 B2
Mar Chiquita, Lago l. Arg.
 136 B4
Marchtrenk Austria 53 E2
Marcoing France 48 A2
Marcy, Mount U.S.A. 123 F2
Mardan Pak. 78 B1
Mar del Plata Arg. 137 C4
Mardin Turkey 85 C2
Maree, Loch l. U.K. 44 B2
Marettimo, Isola i. Italy 56 B3
Marevo Rus. Fed. 37 D2
Marfa U.S.A. 126 D2
Margaret River Austr. 102 A3
Margarita, Isla de i. Venez.
 131 D3
Margate U.K. 47 D4
Margherita Peak
 Dem. Rep. Congo/Uganda
 95 C2
Märgow, Dasht-e des. Afgh.
 78 A1
Marhanets' Ukr. 39 D2
María Elena Chile 136 B3
Mariana Trench sea feature
 N. Pacific Ocean 142 C4
Marianna AR U.S.A. 124 B2
Marianna FL U.S.A. 125 C2
Mariánské Láznĕ Czech Rep.
 50 C3
Marias, Islas is Mex. 128 B2
Mariato, Punta pt Panama 134 A2
Ma'rib Yemen 82 B3
Maribor Slovenia 56 C1
Maridi watercourse Sudan 93 A4
Marie Byrd Land reg. Antarctica
 107 I2
Mariehamn Fin. 41 D3
Mariental Namibia 98 A1
Mariestad Sweden 41 C4
Marietta GA U.S.A. 125 D2
Marietta OH U.S.A. 122 D3
Marignane France 53 D3
Mari, Mys pt Rus. Fed. 87 L3
Marijampolė Lith. 36 B3
Marília Brazil 138 C2
Marín Spain 54 B1

Mar"ina Horka Belarus 36 C3
Maringá Brazil 138 B2
Marinha Grande Port. 54 B2
Marion IN U.S.A. 122 C2
Marion OH U.S.A. 122 D2
Marion, Lake U.S.A. 125 D2
Marion Bay Austr. 104 B3
Mariscal Estigarribia Para.
 136 B3
Mariupol' Ukr. 39 E2
Marka Somalia 93 C4
Marken S. Africa 99 C1
Markermeer l. Neth. 48 B1
Markha r. Rus. Fed. 87 J2
Markivka Ukr. 39 E2
Marksville U.S.A. 124 B2
Marktheidenfeld Ger. 49 D3
Marktredwitz Ger. 49 F2
Marle France 48 A3
Marlin U.S.A. 127 E2
Marmande France 52 C3
Marmara, Sea of g. Turkey
 59 C2
Marmara Denizi g. Turkey see
 Marmara, Sea of
Marmaris Turkey 59 C3
Marne r. France 48 A3
Marne-la-Vallée France 52 C2
Maroantsetra Madag.
 97 [inset] D1
Maromokotro mt. Madag.
 97 [inset] D1
Marondera Zimbabwe 97 C1
Maroni r. Fr. Guiana 135 D2
Maroua Cameroon 94 D1
Marovoay Madag. 97 [inset] D1
Marquesas Islands Fr. Polynesia
 101
Marquette U.S.A. 122 C1
Marquion France 48 A2
Marra, Jebel mt. Sudan 93 A3
Marrakech Morocco 90 B1
Marra Plateau Sudan 93 A3
Marree Austr. 104 B1
Marresale Rus. Fed. 34 F2
Marrupa Moz. 97 C1
Marsá al'Alam Egypt 92 B2
Marsabit Kenya 95 D2
Marsala Italy 56 B3
Marsá Matrūḥ Egypt 92 A1
Marsberg Ger. 49 D2
Marsden Austr. 105 D2
Marseille France 53 D3
Marshall MN U.S.A. 121 D2
Marshall MO U.S.A. 121 E3
Marshall TX U.S.A. 127 E2
Marshall Islands country
 N. Pacific Ocean 100
Marshalltown U.S.A. 121 E2
Marshfield U.S.A. 122 B2
Marsh Harbour Bahamas 125 E3
Marsh Island U.S.A. 124 B3
Märsta Sweden 36 A2

Martapura *Kalimantan Selatan* Indon. **65** C2

Martapura *Sumatera Selatan* Indon. **64** B2

Martha's Vineyard *i.* U.S.A. **123** F2

Martigny Switz. **53** D2

Martin Slovakia **51** D3

Martin U.S.A. **120** C2

Martínez Mex. **129** C2

Martinique *terr.* West Indies **131** D3

Martinsburg U.S.A. **123** E3

Marton N.Z. **106** C3

Martos Spain **54** C2

Martuk Kazakh. **80** C1

Mary Turkm. **80** D3

Maryborough Austr. **103** E2

Marydale S. Africa **98** B2

Maryland *state* U.S.A. **123** E3

Marysville U.S.A. **121** D3

Maryville *MO* U.S.A. **121** E2

Maryville *TN* U.S.A. **125** D1

Masai Steppe *plain* Tanz. **95** D3

Masaka Uganda **95** D3

Masamba Indon. **65** D2

Masan S. Korea **69** B2

Masasi Tanz. **95** D4

Masbate Phil. **68** B2

Masbate *i.* Phil. **68** B2

Mascara Alg. **55** D2

Maseru Lesotho **99** C2

Mashhad Iran **80** C3

Masibambane S. Africa **99** C3

Masilah, Wādi al *watercourse* Yemen **83** C3

Masilo S. Africa **99** C2

Masindi Uganda **95** D2

Maşīraḩ, Jazīrat *i.* Oman **83** C2

Maşīraḩ, Khalīj *b.* Oman **83** C2

Masjed Soleymān Iran **85** C2

Mask, Lough *l.* Ireland **45** B2

Masoala, Tanjona *c.* Madag. **97** [inset] E1

Mason City U.S.A. **121** E2

Masqaţ Oman *see* Muscat

Massa Italy **56** B2

Massachusetts *state* U.S.A. **123** F2

Massachusetts Bay U.S.A. **123** F2

Massango Angola **94** B3

Massawa Eritrea **90** B3

Massena U.S.A. **123** F2

Masset Can. **112** B2

Massif Central *mts* France **52** C2

Massillon U.S.A. **122** D2

Massina Mali **90** B3

Massinga Moz. **97** C3

Massingir Moz. **99** D1

Mastābah Saudi Arabia **82** A2

Masterton N.Z. **106** C3

Mastung Pak. **78** A2

Mastūrah Saudi Arabia **82** A2

Masty Belarus **36** B3

Masuda Japan **71** B4

Masvingo Zimbabwe **97** C2

Matadi Dem. Rep. Congo **94** B3

Matagalpa Nic. **130** B3

Matagami Can. **114** C2

Matagami, Lac *l.* Can. **114** C2

Matagorda Island U.S.A. **127** E3

Matala Angola **96** A1

Matam Senegal **90** A3

Matamoros *Coahuila* Mex. **128** B2

Matamoros *Tamaulipas* Mex. **129** C2

Matandu *r.* Tanz. **95** D3

Matane Can. **115** D2

Matanzas Cuba **130** B2

Mataram Indon. **65** C2

Mataranka Austr. **102** C1

Mataró Spain **55** D1

Mataura N.Z. **106** A4

Matā'utu Wallis and Futuna Is **101**

Matawai N.Z. **106** C2

Mategua Bol. **136** B2

Matehuala Mex. **129** B2

Matera Italy **57** C2

Mathis U.S.A. **127** E3

Mathura India **79** B2

Mati Phil. **68** B3

Matias Romero Mex. **130** A3

Matlock U.K. **46** C3

Mato Grosso, Planalto do *plat.* Brazil **138** B1

Matola Moz. **99** D2

Matsue Japan **71** B3

Matsumae Japan **70** D2

Matsusaka Japan **71** C4

Matsu Tao *i.* Taiwan **75** C3

Matsuyama Japan **71** B4

Mattagami *r.* Can. **114** B1

Matterhorn *mt.* Italy/Switz. **53** D2

Mattoon U.S.A. **122** C3

Maturín Venez. **134** C2

Matwabeng S. Africa **99** C2

Maubeuge France **48** A2

Maūī *i.* U.S.A. **108**

Maumee *r.* U.S.A. **122** D2

Maumere Indon. **65** D2

Maun Botswana **96** B1

Maunatlala Botswana **99** C1

Maurice, Lake *salt flat* Austr. **102** C2

Mauritania *country* Africa **90** A3

Mauritius *country* Indian Ocean **89**

Mawāw, Khashm *h.* Saudi Arabia **82** B2

Mawanga Dem. Rep. Congo **94** B3

Mawkmai Myanmar **66** A1

Mawlaik Myanmar **66** A1

Mawlamyaing Myanmar **66** A2

Mawqaq Saudi Arabia **82** B2

Mawza Yemen **82** B3

Maxia, Punta *mt.* Italy **56** A3

Maya *r.* Rus. Fed. **87** K2

Mayaguana *i.* Bahamas **131** C2

Mayamey Iran **85** D2

Maybole U.K. **44** B3

Mayenne France **52** B2

Mayerthorpe Can. **112** D2

Maykop Rus. Fed. **39** F3

Maymaq Can. **112** B1

Mayoko Congo **94** B3

Mayotte *terr.* Africa **97** D1

Mayskiy Rus. Fed. **87** K3

Maysville U.S.A. **122** D3

Mayumba Gabon **94** B3

Mazagão Brazil **135** D3

Mazamet France **52** C3

Mazar China **78** B1

Mazara del Vallo Italy **56** B3

Mazār-e Sharīf Afgh. **78** A1

Mazatán Mex. **128** A2

Mazatenango Guat. **130** A3

Mazatlán Mex. **128** B2

Mažeikiai Lith. **36** B2

Mazunga Zimbabwe **97** B2

Mazyr Belarus **36** C3

Mbabane Swaziland **99** D2

Mbaïki C.A.R. **94** B2

Mbala Zambia **95** D3

Mbale Uganda **95** D2

Mbalmayo Cameroon **94** B2

Mbandaka Dem. Rep. Congo **94** B3

M'banza Congo Angola **94** B3

Mbeya Tanz. **95** D3

Mbinga Tanz. **95** D4

Mbomo Congo **94** B2

Mbouda Cameroon **94** B2

Mbour Senegal **90** A3

Mbuji-Mayi Dem. Rep. Congo **94** C3

McAlester U.S.A. **127** E2

McAllen U.S.A. **127** E3

McBride Can. **112** C2

McCall U.S.A. **118** C2

McClintock Channel Can. **110** F2

McClure Strait Can. **110** E2

McComb U.S.A. **124** B2

McConaughy, Lake U.S.A. **120** C2

McCook U.S.A. **120** C2

McDermitt U.S.A. **118** C2

McDonald Peak U.S.A. **118** D1

McGrath U.S.A. **110** B2

McGuire, Mount U.S.A. **118** D1

M'Chounèche Alg. **55** E3

McKinley, Mount U.S.A. **110** B2

McLennan Can. **112** D2

McLeod Lake Can. **112** C2

McMinnville *OR* U.S.A. **118** B1
McMinnville *TN* U.S.A. **125** C1
McPherson U.S.A. **121** D3
McTavish Arm *b.* Can. **112** D1
Mdantsane S. Africa **99** C3
Mead, Lake *resr* U.S.A. **119** D3
Meadow Lake Can. **113** E2
Meadville U.S.A. **123** D2
Meaken-dake *vol.* Japan **70** D2
Mealy Mountains Can. **115** E1
Meander River Can. **112** D2
Meaux France **48** A3
Mecca Saudi Arabia **82** A2
Mechelen Belgium **48** B2
Mechernich Ger. **48** C2
Meckenheim Ger. **48** C2
Mecklenburger Bucht *b.* Ger. **41** C5
Meda Port. **54** B1
Medan Indon. **64** A1
Medanosa, Punta *pt* Arg. **137** B5
Medawachchiya Sri Lanka **77** C4
Médéa Alg. **55** D2
Medellín Col. **134** B2
Medenine Tunisia **91** D1
Medford U.S.A. **118** B2
Medgidia Romania **38** C3
Mediaș Romania **38** B2
Medicine Bow Mountains U.S.A. **120** B2
Medicine Bow Peak U.S.A. **120** B2
Medicine Hat Can. **113** D2
Medicine Lodge U.S.A. **121** D3
Medina Brazil **139** D1
Medina Saudi Arabia **82** A2
Medinaceli Spain **54** C1
Medina del Campo Spain **54** C1
Medina de Rioseco Spain **54** B1
Mediterranean Sea **55** C2
Medjedel Alg. **55** D2
Medley Can. **113** D2
Mednogorsk Rus. Fed. **35** E3
Medvezh'i, Ostrova *is* Rus. Fed. **87** M2
Medvezh'yegorsk Rus. Fed. **34** C2
Meekatharra Austr. **102** A2
Meeker U.S.A. **120** B2
Meerut India **79** B2
Megalopoli Greece **59** B3
Meghasani *mt.* India **79** C2
Megisti *i.* Greece **59** C3
Mehamn Norway **40** F1
Meharry, Mount Austr. **102** A2
Mehrān *watercourse* Iran **83** C2
Meia Ponte *r.* Brazil **138** C1
Meiganga Cameroon **94** B2
Meihekou China **69** B1
Meiktila Myanmar **66** A1
Meiningen Ger. **49** E2
Meißen Ger. **49** F2
Meizhou China **75** B3
Mek'elē Eth. **93** B3
Mekerrhane, Sebkha *salt pan* Alg. **90** C2
Meknès Morocco **90** B1
Mekong *r.* Asia **67** B2
Mekong *r.* China **66** B1
Mekong, Mouths of the Vietnam **67** B3
Melaka Malaysia **64** B1
Melanesia *is* Pacific Ocean **142** D5
Melbourne Austr. **105** C3
Melbourne U.S.A. **125** D3
Mele, Capo *c.* Italy **56** A2
Melenki Rus. Fed. **37** F2
Mélèzes, Rivière aux *r.* Can. **115** C1
Mélfi Chad **91** D3
Melfi Italy **56** C2
Melfort Can. **113** E2
Melilla N. Africa **54** C2
Melitopol' Ukr. **39** E2
Melle Ger. **49** D1
Mellerud Sweden **41** C4
Mellrichstadt Ger. **49** E2
Mellum *i.* Ger. **48** D1
Melo Uru. **136** C4
Melton Mowbray U.K. **47** C3
Melun France **52** C2
Melville Can. **110** F3
Melville, Cape Austr. **103** D1
Melville, Lake Can. **115** E1
Melville Island Austr. **102** C1
Melville Island Can. **110** E1
Melville Peninsula Can. **111** G2
Memboro Indon. **65** C2
Memmingen Ger. **50** C3
Memphis *tourist site* Egypt **84** B3
Memphis *TN* U.S.A. **124** B1
Memphis *TX* U.S.A. **127** D2
Mena Ukr. **39** D1
Mena U.S.A. **124** B2
Ménaka Mali **90** C3
Mènam Khong *r.* Asia *see* **Mekong**
Mende France **53** C3
Mendefera Eritrea **92** B3
Mendī Eth. **95** D2
Mendip Hills U.K. **47** B4
Mendoza Arg. **137** B4
Menemen Turkey **59** C3
Menggala Indon. **64** B2
Mengzi China **75** A3
Menindee Austr. **104** C2
Menindee, Lake Austr. **104** C2
Meningie Austr. **104** B3
Menominee U.S.A. **122** C1
Menongue Angola **96** A1
Menorca *i.* Spain *see* **Minorca**
Mentawai, Kepulauan *is* Indon. **64** A2
Mentok Indon. **64** B2
Menzies Austr. **102** B2
Meppel Neth. **48** C1
Meppen Ger. **48** C1
Mepuze Moz. **99** D1
Meqheleng S. Africa **99** C2
Merano Italy **56** B1
Merauke Indon. **63** D3
Merbein Austr. **104** C2
Merced U.S.A. **119** B3
Mercedes Arg. **136** C3
Mercy, Cape Can. **111** H2
Meredith, Lake U.S.A. **127** D1
Merefa Ukr. **39** E2
Merga Oasis Sudan **92** A3
Mergui Archipelago *is* Myanmar **67** A2
Meriç *r.* Greece/Turkey **59** C2
Mérida Mex. **129** D2
Mérida Spain **54** B2
Mérida Venez. **134** B2
Meridian U.S.A. **124** C2
Mérignac France **52** B3
Merimbula Austr. **105** D3
Mérouana Alg. **55** E2
Merowe Sudan **92** B3
Merredin Austr. **102** A3
Merrick *h.* U.K. **44** B3
Merrillville U.S.A. **122** C2
Merrygoen Austr. **105** D2
Mersch Lux. **48** C3
Merseburg (Saale) Ger. **49** E2
Mersin Turkey **84** B2
Mersing Malaysia **64** B1
Mers-les-Bains France **47** D4
Merta India **78** B2
Merthyr Tydfil U.K. **47** B4
Mértola Port. **54** B2
Mertvyy Kultuk, Sor *dry lake* Kazakh. **80** C2
Meru *vol.* Tanz. **95** D3
Merzig Ger. **48** C3
Mesa U.S.A. **126** B2
Mesagne Italy **57** C2
Meschede Ger. **49** D2
Meshchovsk Rus. Fed. **37** E3
Meshkovskaya Rus. Fed. **39** F2
Mesimeri Greece **59** B2
Mesolongi Greece **59** B3
Messalo *r.* Moz. **97** D1
Messina Italy **56** C3
Messina, Stretta di *str.* Italy **57** C3
Messiniakos Kolpos *b.* Greece **59** B3
Meta *r.* Col./Venez. **134** C2
Metán Arg. **136** B3
Methoni Greece **59** B3
Metković Croatia **57** C2
Metu Eth. **93** B4
Metz France **53** D2
Meuse *r.* Belgium/France **48** B2
Mexia U.S.A. **127** E2
Mexicali Mex. **128** A1
Mexico *country* Central America **128** B2
Mexico U.S.A. **121** E3
Mexico, Gulf of Mex./U.S.A. **130** A2

Mexico City Mex. **129** C3
Meymaneh Afgh. **78** A1
Mezen' Rus. Fed. **34** D2
Mezen' r. Rus. Fed. **34** D2
Mezhdusharskiy, Ostrov i. Rus. Fed. **34** E1
Mezőtúr Hungary **80** A3
Mfuwe Zambia **97** C1
Mhow India **78** B2
Miahuatlán Mex. **129** C3
Miajadas Spain **54** B3
Miami FL U.S.A. **125** D3
Miami OK U.S.A. **127** F1
Miami Beach U.S.A. **125** D3
Miandowāb Iran **85** C2
Miandrivazo Madag. **97** [inset] D1
Miañeh Iran **85** C2
Mianwali Pak. **78** B1
Mianyang China **75** A3
Miarinarivo Madag. **97** [inset] D1
Miass Rus. Fed. **35** F3
Mica Creek Can. **114** C2
Michalovce Slovakia **51** E3
Michigan state U.S.A. **122** C1
Michigan, Lake U.S.A. **122** C2
Michigan City U.S.A. **122** C2
Michipicoten Island Can. **114** B2
Michipicoten River Can. **114** B2
Michurinsk Rus. Fed. **37** F3
Micronesia is Pacific Ocean **142** D4
Micronesia, Federated States of country N. Pacific Ocean **63** D2
Middelburg Neth. **48** A2
Middelburg E. Cape S. Africa **99** C3
Middle Alkali Lake U.S.A. **118** B2
Middle Andaman i. India **67** A2
Middle Loup r. U.S.A. **120** D2
Middlesboro U.S.A. **122** D3
Middlesbrough U.K. **46** C2
Middletown NY U.S.A. **123** F2
Middletown OH U.S.A. **122** D3
Midi Yemen **82** B3
Midland Can. **114** C2
Midland TX U.S.A. **127** D2
Midleton Ireland **45** B3
Miðvágur Faroe Is **42** B1
Midzhur mt. Bulg./S.M. **58** B2
Mielec Pol. **51** E2
Miercurea-Ciuc Romania **38** C2
Mieres Spain **54** B1
Mieste Ger. **49** E1
Migriggyangzham Co l. China **79** D1
Miguel Alemán, Presa resr Mex. **129** C3
Miguel Auza Mex. **128** B2
Miguel Hidalgo, Presa resr Mex. **128** B2
Migyaunglaung Myanmar **67** A2
Mikhaylov Rus. Fed. **37** E3
Mikhaylovka Rus. Fed. **70** B2

Mikhaylovskiy Rus. Fed. **81** E1
Mikkeli Fin. **41** F3
Mikuni-sanmyaku mts Japan **71** C3
Mila Alg. **55** E2
Miladhunmadulu Atoll Maldives **77** B4
Milan Italy **56** A1
Milano Italy see Milan
Milas Turkey **59** C3
Milbank U.S.A. **121** D1
Mildenhall U.K. **47** D3
Mildura Austr. **104** C2
Mile China **75** A3
Miles City U.S.A. **120** B1
Milford UT U.S.A. **119** D3
Milford Haven U.K. **47** A4
Milford Sound N.Z. **106** A3
Miliana Alg. **55** D2
Milk, Wadi el watercourse Sudan **92** B3
Milk River Can. **113** D3
Millau France **52** C3
Milledgeville U.S.A. **125** D2
Mille Lacs lakes U.S.A. **121** E1
Mille Lacs, Lac des l. Can. **114** A2
Miller U.S.A. **121** D2
Millerovo Rus. Fed. **39** F2
Millers Creek Austr. **104** B2
Millicent Austr. **104** C3
Millmerran Austr. **105** E1
Mills Lake Can. **112** D1
Milos i. Greece **59** C3
Miloslavskoye Rus. Fed. **37** E3
Milove Ukr. **39** F2
Milparinka Austr. **104** C1
Milton N.Z. **106** A4
Milton Keynes U.K. **47** C3
Milwaukee U.S.A. **122** C2
Milwaukee Deep sea feature Caribbean Sea **144** B4
Mimizan France **52** B3
Mimongo Gabon **94** B3
Mīnāb Iran **83** C2
Minahasa, Semenanjung pen. Indon. **65** D1
Mina Jebel Ali U.A.E. **83** C2
Minas Uru. **134** C4
Minas Indon. **64** B1
Minas Novas Brazil **139** D1
Minatitlán Mex. **129** C3
Minbu Myanmar **66** A1
Mindanao i. Phil. **68** B3
Minden Ger. **49** D1
Minden LA U.S.A. **124** B2
Mindoro i. Phil. **68** B2
Mindoro Strait Phil. **68** A2
Minehead U.K. **47** B4
Mineiros Brazil **138** B1
Mineral Wells U.S.A. **127** E2
Minfeng China **79** C1

Minga Dem. Rep. Congo **95** C4
Mingäçevir Azer. **85** C1
Mingan Can. **115** D1
Mingary Austr. **104** C2
Mingguang China **74** B2
Mingin Myanmar **66** A1
Mingoyo Tanz. **95** D4
Minhe China **74** A2
Minicoy atoll India **77** B4
Minilya Austr. **102** A2
Minipi Lake Can. **115** D1
Minna Nigeria **91** C4
Minneapolis U.S.A. **121** E2
Minnedosa Can. **113** F2
Minnesota r. U.S.A. **121** E2
Minnesota state U.S.A. **121** E1
Miño r. Port./Spain **54** B1
Minorca i. Spain **55** D1
Minot U.S.A. **120** C1
Minsk Belarus **36** C3
Minsk Belarus 36 C3
Minto, Lac l. Can. **114** C1
Minutang India **66** A1
Minxian China **74** A2
Miracéma Brazil **139** D1
Miramichi Can. **115** D2
Mirampelou, Kolpos b. Greece **59** C3
Miranda Brazil **138** A2
Miranda r. Brazil **138** A1
Miranda de Ebro Spain **54** C1
Mirandela Port. **54** B1
Mirandópolis Brazil **138** B2
Mirbāṭ Oman **83** C3
Miri Malaysia **65** C1
Mirim, Lagoa l. Brazil **137** C4
Mirjāveh Iran **83** D2
Mirnyy Rus. Fed. **87** J2
Mirpur Khas Pak. **78** A2
Mirtoö Pelagos sea Greece **59** B3
Miryang S. Korea **69** B2
Mirzapur India **79** C2
Mishan China **70** B1
Miskitos, Cayos is Nic. **130** B3
Miskolc Hungary **51** E3
Misoöl i. Indon. **63** C3
Miṣrātah Libya **91** D1
Missinaibi r. Can. **114** B1
Missinaibi Lake Can. **114** B2
Mission Can. **112** C3
Missisa Lake Can. **114** B1
Mississippi r. U.S.A. **124** C3
Mississippi state U.S.A. **124** C2
Mississippi Delta U.S.A. **124** C3
Missoula U.S.A. **118** D1
Missouri r. U.S.A. **121** E3
Missouri state U.S.A. **121** E3
Mistanipisipou, Rivière r. Can. **115** D1
Mistassini, Lac l. Can. **114** C1
Mistastin Lake Can. **115** D1
Mistelbach Austria **51** D3
Mistinibi, Lac l. Can. **115** D1
Mitchell Austr. **103** D2
Mitchell r. Austr. **103** D1

shell U.S.A. **121** D2
chelstown Ireland **45** B2
ni Pak. **78** A2
e Japan **71** D3
le Tanz. **95** D3
agong Austr. **105** E2
a Col. **134** B2
amba, Chaîne des *mts*
em. Rep. Congo **95** C4
umba, Monts *mts*
em. Rep. Congo **95** C3
ric Gabon **94** B2
ake-jima *i.* Japan **71** C4
ako Japan **70** D3
dah Libya **91** D1
en Head Ireland **45** B2
hhir"ya Ukr. **38** B2
iby Sweden **41** D4
sa *i.* Norway **41** C4
dá Boleslav Czech Rep.
C2
denovac S.M. **58** B2
wa Pol. **51** E2
ngisi S. Africa **99** C3
niv Ukr. **38** C1
abatho S. Africa **99** C2
athethe Botswana **99** C2
Norway **42** E1
ab U.S.A. **119** E3
a Moz. **99** D2
ba Dem. Rep. Congo **95** C3
bayi-Mbongo
em. Rep. Congo **94** C2
perly U.S.A. **121** E3
pile U.S.A. **124** C2
pile Bay U.S.A. **124** C2
cbridge U.S.A. **120** C1
cambique Moz. **97** D1
c Châu Vietnam **66** B1
cha Yemen **82** B3
chudi Botswana **99** C1
simboa da Praia Moz. **97** D1
ckmühl Ger. **49** D3
coa Col. **134** B2
coca Brazil **138** C2
ctezuma *Chihuahua* Mex.
B1
ctezuma *Sonora* Mex. **128** B2
cuba Moz. **97** C1
cane France **53** D2
cdder *r.* S. Africa **98** B2
cdena Italy **56** B2
cdesto U.S.A. **119** B3
cdimolle S. Africa **99** C1
ce Austr. **105** D3
cers Ger. **48** C2
ffat U.K. **44** C2
cgadishu Somalia **93** C4
cgakwena *r.* S. Africa **99** C1
cgaung Myanmar **66** A1

Mogi-Mirim Brazil **138** C2
Mogocha Rus. Fed. **87** J3
Mogok Myanmar **66** A1
Mohács Hungary **51** D3
Mohale's Hoek Lesotho **99** C3
Mohammadia Alg. **55** D2
Mohawk *r.* U.S.A. **123** F2
Mohoro Tanz. **95** D3
Mohyliv Podil's'kyy Ukr. **38** C2
Moijabana Botswana **99** C1
Moineşti Romania **38** C2
Mo i Rana Norway **40** C2
Moissac France **52** C3
Mojave U.S.A. **119** C3
Mojave Desert U.S.A. **119** C3
Mojiang China **66** B1
Moji das Cruzes Brazil **139** C2
Mokau N.Z. **106** B2
Mokhotlong Lesotho **99** C2
Mokopane S. Africa **99** C1
Mokp'o S. Korea **69** B3
Molango Mex. **129** C2
Molde Norway **40** B3
Moldova *country* Europe **38** C2
Moldoveanu, Vârful *mt.* Romania **38** B2
Moldovei Centrale, Podişul *plat.* Moldova **38** C2
Molepolole Botswana **99** C1
Molfetta Italy **57** C2
Möllenbeck Ger. **48** F1
Mollendo Peru **134** B4
Molong Austr. **105** D2
Molopo *watercourse* Botswana/S. Africa **98** B2
Moloundou Cameroon **94** B2
Moluccas *is* Indon. **93** C3
Molucca Sea Indon. *see* Maluku, Laut
Momba Austr. **104** C2
Mombasa Kenya **95** D3
Mombuca, Serra da *hills* Brazil **138** B1
Momi, Ra's *pt* Yemen **83** C3
Men *i.* Denmark **41** C4
Monaco *country* Europe **53** D3
Monadhliath Mountains U.K. **44** B2
Monaghan Ireland **45** C1
Monastyrshchina Rus. Fed. **37** D3
Monastyryshche Ukr. **38** C2
Monbetsu Japan **70** D2
Moncalieri Italy **56** A1
Monchegorsk Rus. Fed. **40** G2
Mönchengladbach Ger. **48** C2
Monclova Mex. **128** B2
Moncouche, Lac *l.* Can. **123** F1
Moncton Can. **115** D2
Mondlo S. Africa **99** D2
Mondovì Italy **56** A2
Monemvasia Greece **59** B3
Moneron, Ostrov *i.* Rus. Fed. **70** D1

Monfalcone Italy **56** B1
Monforte Spain **54** B1
Mongolia *country* Asia **72** C1
Mongu Zambia **96** B1
Monitor Range *mts* U.S.A. **119** C3
Mono Lake U.S.A. **119** C3
Monopoli Italy **57** C2
Monroe *LA* U.S.A. **124** B2
Monroeville U.S.A. **124** C2
Monrovia Liberia **90** A4
Mons Belgium **48** A2
Montalto *mt.* Italy **57** C3
Montana Bulg. **58** B2
Montana *state* U.S.A. **116** C2
Montargis France **52** C2
Montauban France **52** C3
Montauk Point U.S.A. **123** F2
Mont-aux-Sources *mt.* Lesotho **99** C2
Montbard France **53** C2
Mont Blanc *mt.* France/Italy **53** D2
Mont-de-Marsan France **52** B3
Monte Alegre Brazil **135** D3
Monte-Carlo Monaco **53** D3
Monte Caseros Arg. **136** C4
Montego Bay Jamaica **130** C3
Montélimar France **53** C3
Montemorelos Mex. **129** C2
Montendre France **52** B2
Montenegro *aut. rep.* S.M. *see* Crna Gora
Montepuez Moz. **97** C1
Monterey U.S.A. **119** B3
Monterey Bay U.S.A. **119** B3
Montería Col. **134** B2
Montero Bol. **136** B2
Monterrey Mex. **129** B2
Monte Santo Brazil **135** F4
Monte Santu, Capo di *c.* Italy **56** A2
Montes Claros Brazil **139** D1
Montevideo Uru. **137** C4
Montevideo U.S.A. **121** D2
Montgomery U.S.A. **125** C2
Monthey Switz. **53** D2
Monticello *AR* U.S.A. **124** B2
Monticello *UT* U.S.A. **119** E3
Montilla Spain **54** C2
Mont-Laurier Can. **114** C2
Montluçon France **52** C2
Montmagny Can. **115** C2
Montpelier *ID* U.S.A. **118** D2
Montpellier *VT* U.S.A. **123** F2
Montpellier France **53** C3
Montréal Can. **114** C2
Montreal Lake Can. **113** E2
Montreal Lake *l.* Can. **113** E2
Montreux Switz. **53** D2
Montrose U.K. **44** C2
Montrose U.S.A. **120** B3
Montserrat *terr.* West Indies **131** D3

Monywa Myanmar 66 A1
Monza Italy 56 A1
Monzón Spain 55 D1
Mookane Botswana 99 C1
Moonie Austr. 105 E1
Moonie r. Austr. 105 D1
Moora, Lake salt flat Austr. 102 A2
Moorhead U.S.A. 121 D1
Moose r. Can. 114 B1
Moosehead Lake U.S.A. 123 G1
Moose Jaw Can. 110 E3
Moose Lake U.S.A. 121 E1
Moosonee Can. 114 B1
Mootwingee Austr. 104 C2
M'Ooukal Alg. 55 F2
Mopti Mali 90 B3
Moquegua Peru 134 B4
Mora Sweden 41 C3
Mora U.S.A. 121 E1
Moradabad India 79 B2
Moramanga Madag. 97 [inset] D1
Morava r. Europe 58 A1
Moray Firth b. U.K. 44 B2
Morbi India 78 B2
Mordaga China 73 E1
Morden Can. 113 F3
Morecambe U.K. 46 B2
Morecambe Bay U.K. 46 B2
Moree Austr. 105 D1
Morehead City U.S.A. 125 E2
Morelia Mex. 129 B3
Morella Spain 55 C1
Morena, Sierra mts Spain 54 B2
Moreni Romania 33 D2
Moresby, Mount Can. 112 B2
Moresby Island Can. 112 B2
Moreton Island Austr. 105 E1
Morgan City U.S.A. 124 D3
Morganton U.S.A. 125 D1
Morgantown U.S.A. 123 E3
Morges Switz. 53 D2
Morice Lake Can. 112 C2
Morioka Japan 70 D3
Morisset Austr. 105 E2
Morlaix France 52 B2
Mornington Island Austr. 103 C1
Morocco country Africa 90 B1
Morogoro Tanz. 95 D3
Moro Gulf Phil. 68 B3
Morokweng S. Africa 98 B2
Morombe Madag. 97 [inset] D2
Mörön Mongolia 72 C1
Morondava Madag. 97 [inset] D2
Moroni Comoros 97 D1
Morotai i. Indon. 63 C2
Moroto Uganda 95 D2
Morozovsk Rus. Fed. 39 F2
Morpeth U.K. 46 C2
Morrinhos Brazil 138 C1
Morris Can. 113 F3
Morris U.S.A. 121 D1
Morristown U.S.A. 125 D1

Morshanka Rus. Fed. 37 F3
Mortlake Austr. 104 C3
Moruya Austr. 105 E3
Morvern reg. U.K. 44 B2
Morwell Austr. 105 D3
Mosbach Ger. 49 D3
Moscow Rus. Fed. 37 E2
Moscow U.S.A. 118 C1
Mosel r. Ger. 48 C2
Moselle r. France 53 D2
Moses Lake U.S.A. 118 C1
Mosfellsbær Iceland 40 [inset]
Mosgiel N.Z. 106 B4
Moshi Tanz. 95 D3
Mosjøen Norway 40 C2
Mosquitos, Golfo de los b. Panama 130 B4
Moss Norway 41 C4
Mossel Bay S. Africa 98 B3
Mossendjo Congo 94 B3
Mossgiel Austr. 104 C2
Mossman Austr. 103 D1
Mossoró Brazil 135 F3
Moss Vale Austr. 105 E2
Most Czech Rep. 50 C2
Mostaganem Alg. 90 C1
Mostar Bos.-Herz. 57 C2
Mostardas Brazil 136 C4
Mostovskoy Rus. Fed. 39 F3
Mosul Iraq 85 C2
Motala Sweden 41 D4
Motherwell U.K. 44 C3
Motokwe Botswana 98 B1
Motril Spain 54 C2
Motru Romania 38 D3
Mottama, Gulf of Myanmar 66 A2
Motul Mex. 129 D2
Moudros Greece 59 C3
Mouila Gabon 94 B3
Moulamein Austr. 104 C2
Moulins France 53 C2
Moultrie U.S.A. 125 D2
Moultrie, Lake U.S.A. 125 E2
Mound City U.S.A. 122 C3
Moundou Chad 91 D4
Mountain Grove U.S.A. 121 E3
Mountain Home AR U.S.A. 124 B1
Mountain Home ID U.S.A. 118 C2
Mount Barker Austr. 104 B3
Mount Desert Island U.S.A. 123 D2
Mount Fletcher S. Africa 99 C3
Mount Frere S. Africa 99 C3
Mount Gambier Austr. 104 C3
Mount Hagen P.N.G. 63 D3
Mount Hope Austr. 105 D2
Mount Isa Austr. 103 C2
Mount Magnet Austr. 102 A2
Mount Manara Austr. 104 C2
Mount Maunganui N.Z. 106 C2

Mount Pleasant IA U.S.A. 121
Mount Pleasant MI U.S.A. 122 D2
Mount Pleasant TX U.S.A. 127 F2
Mount Shasta U.S.A. 118 B2
Mount Vernon IL U.S.A. 122 C3
Mount Vernon OH U.S.A. 122 D2
Mount Vernon WA U.S.A. 118 B1
Moura Austr. 103 D2
Mourdi, Dépression du depr. Chad 91 E3
Mourne Mountains U.K. 45 C1
Mouscron Belgium 48 A2
Moussoro Chad 91 D3
Moutong Indon. 65 D1
Mouydir, Monts du plat. Alg. 90 C2
Moy r. Ireland 45 B1
Moyale Eth. 93 B4
Moyeni Lesotho 99 C3
Mo'ynoq Uzbek. 80 C2
Mozambique country Africa 97 C2
Mozambique Channel Africa 97 D2
Mozhaysk Rus. Fed. 37 E2
Mpanda Tanz. 95 D3
Mpika Zambia 97 C1
Mporokoso Zambia 95 D3
Mpumalanga prov. S. Africa 99 C2
Mrauk-U Myanmar 66 A1
Mrkonjić-Grad Bos.-Herz. 58 A1
Mshinskaya Rus. Fed. 36 C2
M'Sila Alg. 55 D2
Msta r. Rus. Fed. 37 D2
Mstinskiy Most Rus. Fed. 37 D
Mstsislaw Belarus 37 D3
Mtsensk Rus. Fed. 37 E3
Mtwara Tanz. 95 E4
Muanda Dem. Rep. Congo 94 B3
Muang Hinboun Laos 75 A4
Muang Khôngxédôn Laos 67 B2
Muang Ngoy Laos 66 B1
Muang Pakbeng Laos 66 B2
Muang Sing Laos 66 B1
Muar Malaysia 64 B1
Muarabungo Indon. 64 B2
Muaralaung Indon. 65 C2
Muarasiberut Indon. 64 A2
Muarateweh Indon. 65 C2
Mubende Uganda 95 D2
Mubi Nigeria 91 D3
Muchkapskiy Rus. Fed. 39 F1
Mucuri Brazil 139 E1
Mucuri r. Brazil 139 E1
Mudanjiang China 70 A2
Mudan Jiang r. China 70 A1
Mudanya Turkey 59 C2
Mudgee Austr. 105 D2
Mueda Moz. 97 C1
Mufulira Zambia 97 B1

rfumbwe Zambia **96** B1
agla Turkey **59** C3
hammad Qol Sudan **92** B2
hlhausen (Thüringen) Ger.
49 E2
ine Bheag Ireland **45** C2
nite Moz. **97** C1
kacheve Ukr. **38** B2
kalla Yemen **83** B3
kdahan Thai. **66** B2
kinbudln Austr. **102** A3
komuko Indon. **64** B2
lanje, Mount Malawi **97** C1
lde r. Ger. **49** F2
lepê Mex. **128** A2
leshoe U.S.A. **127** D2
lhacén mt. Spain **54** C2
lheim an der Ruhr Ger. **48** C2
lhouse France **53** D2
ling China **70** B2
ling He r. China **70** B1
li i. U.K. **44** B2
llaley Austr. **105** D2
llen U.S.A. **120** C2
ller, Pegunungan mts Indon.
5 C2
llingar Ireland **45** C2
ll of Galloway c. U.K. **44** B3
ll of Kintyre hd U.K. **44** B3
ll of Oa hd U.K. **44** A3
lobezi Zambia **96** B1
ltan Pak. **78** B1
mbaí India **77** B3
mbwa Zambia **96** B1
mba i. Indon. **65** D2
na Mex. **129** D2
nchberg Ger. **49** E2
nchen Ger. see Munich
ndrabilla Austr. **102** B3
ngbere Dem. Rep. Congo
5 C2
nger India **79** C2
ngeranie Austr. **104** B1
ngindi Austr. **105** D1
nich Ger. **50** C3
niz Freire Brazil **139** D2
inster Niedersachsen Ger.
48 C2
inster reg. Ireland **45** C2
insterland reg. Ger. **48** C2
wong Nhie Vietnam **66** B1
ionio Fin. **40** E2
ionioälven r. Fin./Sweden
40 E2
qdisho Somalia see
Mogadishu
ar r. Austria **51** D3
ramvya Burundi **95** C3
arati r. Turkey **85** B2
arfat Turkey **59** C2
rchison watercourse Austr.
02 A2

Murcia Spain **55** C2
Mureşul r. Romania **38** B2
Muret France **52** C3
Murfreesboro U.S.A. **125** C1
Murghab r. Afgh. **78** A1
Murghob Tajik. **81** E3
Muriaé Brazil **139** D2
Muriege Angola **94** C3
Müritz l. Ger. **49** F1
Murmansk Rus. Fed. **40** G2
Murom Rus. Fed. **37** F2
Muroran Japan **70** D2
Muros Spain **54** B1
Muroto Japan **71** B4
Murphy U.S.A. **125** C1
Murra Murra Austr. **105** D1
Murray r. Austr. **105** B3
Murray r. Can. **112** C2
Murray U.S.A. **122** C3
Murray, Lake U.S.A. **125** D2
Murray Bridge Austr. **104** B3
Murraysburg S. Africa **98** B3
Murrayville Austr. **104** C3
Murrumbidgee r. Austr. **104** C2
Murrupula Moz. **97** C1
Murrurundi Austr. **105** E2
Murska Sobota Slovenia **57** C1
Murupara N.Z. **106** C2
Mururoa atoll Fr. Polynesia **101**
Murwara India **79** C2
Murwillumbah Austr. **105** E1
Murzechirla Turkm. **35** F5
Murzūq Libya **91** D2
Muş Turkey **85** C2
Musala mt. Bulg. **58** B2
Musan N. Korea **69** B1
Musaymir Yemen **82** B3
Muscat Oman **83** C2
Muscatine U.S.A. **121** E2
Musgrave Ranges mts Austr.
102 C2
Mushie Dem. Rep. Congo
94 B3
Musina S. Africa **99** D1
Muskogee U.S.A. **127** E1
Muskwa r. Can. **112** C2
Muslimbagh Pak. **78** A1
Musoma Tanz. **95** D3
Musselburgh U.K. **44** C3
Mustjala Estonia **36** B2
Muswellbrook Austr. **105** E2
Mūṭ Egypt **92** A2
Mutare Zimbabwe **97** C1
Mutsu Japan **70** D2
Mutuali Moz. **97** C1
Muurola Fin. **40** F2
Mu Us Shamo des. China
74 A2
Muyezerskiy Rus. Fed. **40** G3
Muyinga Burundi **95** C3
Muzaffargarh Pak. **78** B1
Muzaffarpur India **79** C2
Muzamane Moz. **99** D1
Múzquiz Mex. **128** B2

Muztag mt. China **79** C1
Muz Tag mt. China **79** C1
Mwanza Tanz. **95** D3
Mweka Dem. Rep. Congo **94** C3
Mwenda Zambia **95** C3
Mwene-Ditu Dem. Rep. Congo
94 C3
Mwenezi Zimbabwe **97** C2
Mweru, Lake
Dem. Rep. Congo/Zambia **95** C3
Mwimba Dem. Rep. Congo
94 C3
Mwinilunga Zambia **96** B1
Myadzyel Belarus **36** C3
Myanmar country Asia **66** A1
Myaungmya Myanmar **66** A2
Myeik Myanmar **67** A2
Myingyan Myanmar **66** A1
Myitkyina Myanmar **66** A1
Mykolayiv Ukr. **39** D2
Mykonos Greece **59** C3
Mykonos i. Greece **59** C3
Mymensingh Bangl. **79** D2
Myŏnggan N. Korea **69** B1
Myory Belarus **36** C2
Mýrdalsjökull ice cap Iceland
40 [inset]
Myrhorod Ukr. **39** D2
Myronivka Ukr. **38** D2
Myrtle Beach U.S.A. **125** E2
Myshkin Rus. Fed. **37** E2
Mysore India **77** B3
My Tho Vietnam **67** B2
Mytilini Greece **59** C3
Mytishchi Rus. Fed. **37** E2
Mzimba Malawi **97** C1
Mzuzu Malawi **97** C1

N

Naas Ireland **45** C2
Nababeep S. Africa **98** A2
Naberezhnyye Chelny Rus. Fed.
35 E3
Nabire Indon. **63** D3
Naboomspruit S. Africa **99** C1
Nacala Moz. **97** D1
Nachuge India **67** A2
Nacogdoches U.S.A. **127** F2
Nadiad India **78** B2
Nador Morocco **54** C2
Nadvirna Ukr. **38** B2
Nadym Rus. Fed. **34** G2
Næstved Denmark **41** C4
Nafpaktos Greece **59** B3
Nafplio Greece **59** B3
Naga Phil. **68** B2
Nagagami r. Can. **114** B1
Nagano Japan **71** C3
Nagaoka Japan **71** C3
Nagaon India **79** D2
Nagar Parkar Pak. **78** B2
Nagasaki Japan **71** A4

Nagaur India 78 B2
Nagercoil India 77 B4
Nag' Ḥammādī Egypt 82 A2
Nagina India 78 B2
Nagoya Japan 71 C3
Nagpur India 78 B2
Naggu China 79 D1
Nagykanizsa Hungary 51 D3
Nahanni Butte Can. 112 C1
Nahˈävand Iran 85 C2
Nahrendorf Ger. 49 E1
Nain Can. 115 D1
Nāˈīn Iran 85 C2
Nairn U.K. 44 C2
Nairobi Kenya 95 D3
Naivasha Kenya 95 D3
Najafābād Iran 85 D2
Najd reg. Saudi Arabia 82 B2
Najin N. Korea 69 C1
Najrān Saudi Arabia 82 B3
Nakatsugawa Japan 71 C3
Nakfa Eritrea 82 A3
Nakhodka Rus. Fed. 70 B2
Nakhon Pathom Thai. 67 B2
Nakhon Ratchasima Thai. 67 B2
Nakhon Sawan Thai. 67 B2
Nakhon Si Thammarat Thai. 67 A3
Nakina Can. 114 B1
Nakonde Zambia 95 D3
Nakskov Denmark 41 C5
Nakuru Kenya 95 D3
Nakusp Can. 112 D2
Naľchik Rus. Fed. 35 D4
Nālūt Libya 91 D1
Namahadi S. Africa 99 C2
Namakzar-e Shadad salt flat Iran 83 C1
Namangan Uzbek. 81 E2
Namaqualand reg. S. Africa 98 A2
Nambour Austr. 103 E2
Nambucca Heads Austr. 105 E2
Nam Co salt l. China 79 D1
Nam Định Vietnam 66 B1
Namib Desert Namibia 96 A2
Namibe Angola 96 A1
Namibia country Africa 98 A3
Namjagbarwa Feng mt. China 76 D2
Namoi r. Austr. 105 D2
Nampa U.S.A. 118 C2
Nampala Mali 90 B3
Nampˈo N. Korea 69 B2
Nampula Moz. 97 C1
Namrup India 66 A1
Namsang Myanmar 66 A1
Namsos Norway 40 C3
Namtu Myanmar 66 A1
Namur Belgium 48 B2
Namwala Zambia 96 B1
Namwˈon S. Korea 69 B2
Namya Ra Myanmar 66 A1
Nan Thai. 66 B2
Nanaimo Can. 112 C3

Nananib Plateau Namibia 98 A1
Nanao Japan 71 C3
Nanchang Jiangxi China 75 B3
Nanchang Jiangxi China 75 B3
Nanchong China 74 A2
Nancy France 53 D2
Nanda Devi mt. India 79 C1
Nandan China 75 A3
Nanded India 77 B3
Nandurbar India 78 B2
Nandyal India 77 B3
Nanga Eboko Cameroon 94 B2
Nangahpinoh Indon. 65 C2
Nanga Parbat mt.
  Jammu and Kashmir 78 B1
Nangatayap Indon. 65 C2
Nangong China 74 B2
Nangulangwa Tanz. 95 D3
Nanjing China 74 B2
Nanking China see Nanjing
Nankova Angola 96 A1
Nan Ling mts China 75 B3
Nanning China 75 A3
Nanortalik Greenland 111 I2
Nanpan Jiang r. China 75 A3
Nanpara India 79 C2
Nanping China 75 B3
Nansei-shotō is Japan see
  Ryukyu Islands
Nantes France 52 B2
Nantong China 74 C2
Nantucket Island U.S.A.
  123 G2
Nanxiong China 75 B3
Nanyang China 74 B2
Nanzhang China 74 B2
Nao, Cabo de la c. Spain 55 D2
Naococane, Lac l. Can. 115 C1
Napa U.S.A. 119 B3
Napaktulik Lake Can. 113 D1
Napasoq Greenland 111 I2
Napier N.Z. 106 C2
Naples Italy 56 B2
Naples U.S.A. 125 D3
Napo r. Ecuador 134 B3
Napoli Italy see Naples
Nara Mali 90 B3
Naracoorte Austr. 104 C3
Naranjos Mex. 129 C2
Narathiwat Thai. 67 B3
Narbonne France 52 C3
Nares Strait Can./Greenland
  111 H1
Narib Namibia 98 A1
Narimanov Rus. Fed. 35 D4
Narmada r. India 78 B2
Narnaul India 78 B2
Narni Italy 56 B2
Narodychi Ukr. 38 C1
Naro-Fominsk Rus. Fed. 37 E2
Narooma Austr. 105 E3
Narrabri Austr. 105 D2

Narrandera Austr. 105 D2
Narromine Austr. 105 D2
Narva Estonia 36 C2
Narva Bay Estonia/Rus. Fed.
  36 C2
Narvik Norway 40 D2
Narvskoye Vodokhranilishche
  resr Estonia/Rus. Fed. 36 C2
Narˈyan-Mar Rus. Fed. 34 E2
Naryn Kyrg. 81 E2
Nashik India 78 B2
Nashua U.S.A. 123 F2
Nashville U.S.A. 124 C1
Nasir Sudan 93 B4
Nass r. Can. 112 C2
Nassau Bahamas 131 C2
Nasser, Lake resr Egypt 92 B2
Nässjö Sweden 41 C4
Nastapoca r. Can. 114 C1
Nastapoka Islands Can. 114 C1
Nata Botswana 96 B2
Natal Brazil 135 F3
Natal prov. S. Africa see
  Kwazulu-Natal
Natashquan Can. 115 D2
Natashquan r. Can. 115 D1
Natchez U.S.A. 124 B2
Natchitoches U.S.A. 124 B2
Natitingou Benin 90 C3
Natividade Brazil 135 E4
Natori Japan 70 D3
Natuashish Can. 115 D1
Natuna, Kepulauan is Indon.
  64 B1
Natuna Besar i. Indon. 64 B1
Nauchas Namibia 98 A1
Nauen Ger. 49 F1
Naujoji Akmenė Lith. 36 B2
Naumburg (Saale) Ger. 49 E2
Nauru country S. Pacific Ocean
  100
Naustdal Norway 42 E1
Navahrudak Belarus 36 C3
Navalmoral de la Mata Spain
  54 B2
Navan Ireland 45 C2
Navapolatsk Belarus 36 C2
Navarin, Mys c. Rus. Fed. 87 N1
Navarino, Isla i. Chile 137 B6
Navashino Rus. Fed. 37 F2
Naver r. U.K. 44 B1
Navlya Rus. Fed. 37 D3
Năvodari Romania 38 C3
Navoiy Uzbek. 81 D2
Navojoa Mex. 128 B2
Navolato Mex. 128 B2
Nawabshah Pak. 78 A2
Nawnghkio Myanmar 66 A1
Nawngleng Myanmar 66 A1
Naxçıvan Azer. 85 C2
Naxos i. Greece 59 C3
Nayoro Japan 70 D2
Nazareth Israel 84 B2
Nazas Mex. 128 B2

...tas r. Mex. **128** B2
...tca Peru **134** B4
...zilli Turkey **59** C1
...crêt Eth. **93** B4
...ojwa Oman **83** C2
...helenge Zambia **95** C3
...ojane Botswana **98** B1
...alatando Angola **94** B3
...élé C.A.R. **94** C2
...endé Gabon **94** B3
...amena Chad **91** D3
...ola Zambia **97** B1
...agh, Lough *l.* U.K. **45** C1
...ale, Lake *salt flat* Austr. **32** C2
...ath U.K. **47** B4
...oine Creek *r.* Austr. **105** D1
...blina, Pico da *mt.* Brazil **34** C2
...braska *state* U.S.A. **120** C2
...braska City U.S.A. **121** D2
...brodi, Monti *mts* Italy **56** B3
...cochea Arg. **137** C4
...dlouc, Lac *l.* Can. **115** C1
...droma Alg. **55** C2
...edles U.S.A. **119** D4
...emuch India **78** B2
...ftekamsk Rus. Fed. **35** E3
...fteyuganisk Rus. Fed. **34** G2
...gage Angola **94** B3
...gêlê Eth. **93** B4
...gra, Punta *pt* Peru **134** A3
...gra, Cape Myanmar **67** A2
...gro *r.* Arg. **137** B5
...gro *r.* Brazil **138** A1
...gro *r.* S. America **134** D3
...gro *r.* Uru. **136** C4
...gro, Cabo *c.* Morocco **54** B2
...gros *i.* Phil. **68** B3
...hbandan Iran **83** D1
...he China **73** E1
...hjiang China **75** A3
...I Mongol Dizhiqu *aut. reg.* China **74** A1
...iva Col. **134** B2
...iganilini Lake Can. **113** F2
...idovo Rus. Fed. **37** D2
...kore India **77** B3
...lson Can. **112** D3
...lson *r.* Can. **113** F2
...lson N.Z. **106** B3
...lson, Cape Austr. **104** C3
...lson Bay Austr. **105** E2
...lson Reservoir U.S.A. **118** E1
...lspruit S. Africa **99** D2
...ma Maur. **90** B3
...man Rus. Fed. **36** B2
...mda *r.* Rus. Fed. **37** H2
...mours France **52** C2
...muro Japan **70** F2
...myriv Ukr. **38** C2
...nagh Ireland **45** B2

Nene *r.* U.K. **47** D3
Nenjiang China **73** E1
Neosho U.S.A. **121** E3
Nepal *country* Asia **79** C2
Nepalganj Nepal **79** C2
Nephi U.S.A. **119** D3
Nephin *h.* Ireland **45** B1
Nephin Beg Range *hills* Ireland **45** B1
Nepisiguit *r.* Can. **115** D2
Nepomuk Czech Rep. **49** F3
Nérac France **52** C3
Nerang Austr. **105** E1
Nerchinsk Rus. Fed. **73** D1
Nerekhta Rus. Fed. **37** F2
Neris *r.* Lith. **36** B3
Nerl' *r.* Rus. Fed. **37** E2
Nerópolis Brazil **138** C1
Neryungri Rus. Fed. **87** K3
Ness, Loch *l.* U.K. **44** B2
Ness City U.S.A. **120** D3
Nestos *r.* Greece **59** B2
Netherlands *country* Europe **48** B1
Netherlands Antilles *terr.* West Indies **131** D3
Neubrandenburg Ger. **49** F1
Neuchâtel Switz. **53** D2
Neuenhagen Berlin Ger. **49** F1
Neufchâteau Belgium **48** B3
Neufchâteau France **53** D2
Neuhof Ger. **49** D2
Neumarkt in der Oberpfalz Ger. **49** E3
Neumünster Ger. **50** B2
Neunkirchen Ger. **48** C3
Nequén Arg. **137** B5
Neuquen *r.* Arg. **137** B4
Neuruppin Ger. **49** F1
Neuss Ger. **48** C2
Neustadt am Rübenberge Ger. **49** D1
Neustadt an der Aisch Ger. **49** E3
Neustadt an der Weinstraße Ger. **48** D3
Neustrelitz Ger. **49** F1
Neutraubling Ger. **49** F3
Neuwied Ger. **48** C2
Nevada U.S.A. **121** E3
Nevada *state* U.S.A. **119** C3
Nevada, Sierra *mts* Spain **54** C2
Nevada, Sierra *mts* U.S.A. **119** B2
Nevel' Rus. Fed. **36** C2
Nevers France **52** C2
Nevertire Austr. **105** D2
Nevesinje Bos.-Herz. **57** C2
Nevinnomyssk Rus. Fed. **35** D4
New Albany U.S.A. **122** C3
New Amsterdam Guyana **135** D2
Newark *NJ* U.S.A. **123** F2
Newark *OH* U.S.A. **122** D2
Newark-on-Trent U.K. **46** C3

New Bedford U.S.A. **123** F2
New Bern U.S.A. **125** E1
Newberry U.S.A. **125** D2
New Boston U.S.A. **127** F2
New Braunfels U.S.A. **127** E3
Newbridge Ireland **45** C2
New Britain *i.* P.N.G. **142** D5
New Brunswick *prov.* Can. **115** D2
Newbury U.K. **47** C4
New Caledonia *terr.* S. Pacific Ocean **100**
Newcastle Austr. **105** E2
Newcastle S. Africa **99** C2
Newcastle U.K. **45** D1
New Castle U.S.A. **123** D2
Newcastle U.S.A. **120** C2
Newcastle-under-Lyme U.K. **46** B3
Newcastle upon Tyne U.K. **46** C2
Newcastle West Ireland **45** B2
New Delhi India **78** B2
New England Range *mts* Austr. **105** E2
Newfoundland *i.* Can. **115** E2
Newfoundland and Labrador *prov.* Can. **115** E1
New Glasgow Can. **115** D2
New Guinea *i.* Indon./P.N.G. **63** D3
New Halfa Sudan **82** A3
New Hampshire *state* U.S.A. **123** F2
New Haven U.S.A. **123** F2
New Hazelton Can. **112** C2
New Iberia U.S.A. **124** B2
New Ireland *i.* P.N.G. **100**
New Jersey *state* U.S.A. **123** F3
New Liskeard Can. **114** C2
Newman Austr. **102** A2
New Mexico *state* U.S.A. **126** C2
New Orleans U.S.A. **124** B3
New Philadelphia U.S.A. **122** D2
New Plymouth N.Z. **106** B2
Newport *England* U.K. **47** C4
Newport *Wales* U.K. **47** B4
Newport *AR* U.S.A. **124** B1
Newport *OR* U.S.A. **118** B2
Newport *RI* U.S.A. **123** F2
Newport *VT* U.S.A. **123** F2
Newport *WA* U.S.A. **118** C1
Newport News U.S.A. **123** E3
New Providence *i.* Bahamas **125** E3
Newquay U.K. **47** A4
New Roads U.S.A. **124** B2
New Ross Ireland **45** C2
Newry U.K. **45** C1
New Siberia Islands Rus. Fed. **87** L1
New South Wales *state* Austr. **105** D2
Newton *IA* U.S.A. **121** E2

Newton KS U.S.A. 121 D3
Newton Abbot U.K. 47 B4
Newton Stewart U.K. 44 B3
Newtown Ireland 45 B2
Newtown U.K. 47 B3
Newtownabbey U.K. 45 D1
Newtownards U.K. 45 D1
New Ulm Ger. 121 C2
New York U.S.A. 123 E2
New York state U.S.A. 123 E2
New Zealand country Oceania 106
Neya Rus. Fed. 37 F2
Neya r. Rus. Fed. 37 F2
Neyrīz Iran 85 D3
Neyshābūr Iran 80 C3
Nezahualcóyotl Mex. 129 C3
Nezahualcóyotl, Presa resr Mex. 129 C3
Ngabang Indon. 65 B1
Nganglong Kangri mt. China 79 C1
Nganglong Kangri mts China 79 C1
Ngangzê Co salt l. China 79 C1
Ngao Thai. 66 A2
Ngaoundéré Cameroon 94 B2
Ngaruawahia N.Z. 106 C2
Ngo Congo 94 B3
Ngoc Linh mt. Vietnam 66 D2
Ngoring Hu l. China 72 C2
Ngourti Niger 91 D3
Nguigmi Niger 91 D3
Ngulu atoll Micronesia 63 D2
Nguru Nigeria 91 D3
Ngwelezana S. Africa 99 D2
Nhamalabué Moz. 97 C1
Nha Trang Vietnam 67 B2
Nhill Austr. 104 C3
Nhlangano Swaziland 99 D2
Nhulunbuy Austr. 103 C1
Niagara Falls Can. 123 E2
Niamey Niger 90 C3
Niangara Dem. Rep. Congo 95 C2
Niangay, Lac l. Mali 90 B3
Nias i. Indon. 64 A1
Nicaragua country Central America 130 B3
Nicaragua, Lake Nic. 130 B3
Nice France 52 D3
Nicobar Islands India 77 D4
Nicosia Cyprus 84 B2
Nicoya, Golfo de b. Costa Rica 130 B4
Nidžica Pol. 51 E2
Niebüll Ger. 50 B2
Niederaula Ger. 49 D2
Niefang Equat. Guinea 94 B2
Niemegk Ger. 49 F1
Nienburg (Weser) Ger. 49 D1

Nieuw Nickerie Suriname 135 D2
Nieuwoudtville S. Africa 98 A3
Nieuwpoort Belgium 48 A2
Niğde Turkey 84 B2
Niger country Africa 91 D3
Niger, Mouths of the Nigeria 91 C4
Nigeria country Africa 91 C4
Nighthawk Lake Can. 114 B2
Nigrita Greece 59 B2
Niigata Japan 71 C3
Niihama Japan 71 B4
Nii-jima i. Japan 71 C4
Niitsu Japan 71 C3
Nijmegen Neth. 48 B2
Nijverdal Neth. 48 C1
Nikel' Rus. Fed. 40 G2
Nikol'skoye Rus. Fed. 87 N3
Nikopol' Ukr. 39 D2
Nikshahr Iran 83 D2
Nikšić S.M. 58 A2
Nile r. Africa 92 B1
Niles U.S.A. 122 C2
Nîmes France 53 C3
Nimmitabel Austr. 105 D3
Nimule Sudan 93 B4
Nindigully Austr. 105 D1
Nine Degree Channel India 77 B4
Ninety Mile Beach Austr. 105 D3
Ninety Mile Beach N.Z. 106 B1
Ningbo China 75 B3
Ningde China 75 B3
Ninghai China 75 C3
Ninging India 66 A1
Ningjing Shan mts China 72 C2
Ningxia Huizu Zizhiqu aut. reg. China 74 A2
Ningyang China 74 B2
Ninh Binh Vietnam 66 B1
Ninh Hoa Vietnam 67 B2
Ninohe Japan 70 D2
Niobrara r. U.S.A. 121 D2
Niono Mali 90 B3
Nioro Mali 90 B3
Niort France 52 B2
Nipigon Can. 114 B2
Nipigon, Lake Can. 114 B2
Nipishish Lake Can. 115 D1
Nipissing, Lake Can. 114 C2
Nipton U.S.A. 119 C3
Niquelândia Brazil 135 E4
Nirmal India 77 B3
Niš S.M. 58 B2
Nišava r. S.M. 58 B2
Nishino-omote Japan 71 B4
Niterói Brazil 139 D2
Nith r. U.K. 44 C3
Nitra Slovakia 51 D3
Niue terr. S. Pacific Ocean 101
Nivala Fin. 40 E3
Nivelles Belgium 48 B2
Nizamabad India 77 B3
Nizhnekamsk Rus. Fed. 35 E3

Nizhnevartovsk Rus. Fed. 86 H
Nizhniy Novgorod Rus. Fed. 35 D3
Nizhniy Odes Rus. Fed. 34 E2
Nizhniy Tagil Rus. Fed. 34 E3
Nizhyn Ukr. 39 D1
Njazidja i. Comoros 97 C1
Njombe Tanz. 95 D3
Nkongsamba Cameroon 94 A2
Nkwenkwezi S. Africa 99 C3
Nobeoka Japan 71 B4
Noccundra Austr. 104 C1
Nogales Mex. 128 A1
Nogales U.S.A. 126 B2
Nogent-le-Rotrou France 52 C
Noginsk Rus. Fed. 37 E2
Nohfelden Ger. 48 C3
Noirmoutier, Île de i. France 52 B2
Noirmoutier-en-l'Île France 52 B2
Noisseville France 48 C3
Nojima-zaki c. Japan 71 C4
Nokha India 78 B2
Nokia Fin. 41 E3
Nok Kundi Pak. 78 A2
Nola C.A.R. 94 B2
Nomonde S. Africa 99 C3
Nong Khai Thai. 66 B2
Nonning Austr. 104 B2
Nonoava Mex. 128 B2
Nonsan S. Korea 69 D2
Nonthaburi Thai. 67 B2
Nonzwakazi S. Africa 98 B3
Noranda Can. 123 E1
Nordaustlandet i. Svalbard 86
Norden Ger. 48 C1
Nordenham Ger. 49 D1
Nordenshel'da, Arkhipelag is Rus. Fed. 87 I1
Norderney Ger. 48 C1
Norderney i. Ger. 48 C1
Norderstedt Ger. 49 E1
Nordfjordeid Norway 41 B3
Nordhausen Ger. 49 E2
Nordholz Ger. 49 D1
Nordhorn Ger. 48 C1
Nordkapp c. Norway see North Cape
Nordli Norway 40 D3
Nordmaling Sweden 40 D3
Norðoyar i. Faroe Is 42 B1
Nore r. Ireland 45 C2
Norfolk NE U.S.A. 121 D2
Norfolk VA U.S.A. 123 E3
Norfolk Island terr. S. Pacific Ocean 100
Noril'sk Rus. Fed. 86 H2
Norkyung China 79 C2
Norman r. U.S.A. 127 E1
Normandes, Îles is English Cha see Channel Islands
Normandy reg. France 52 B2
Normanton Austr. 103 D1
Norman Wells Can. 112 C1

orrköping Sweden 41 D4
orrtälje Sweden 41 D4
orseman Austr. 102 B3
orsjö Sweden 40 D3
orthallerton U.K. 46 C2
orthampton Austr. 102 A2
orthampton U.K. 47 C3
orth Andaman i. India 87 A2
orth Battleford Can. 110 E3
orth Bay Can. 114 C2
orth Belcher Islands Can. 114 C1
orth Berwick U.K. 44 C2
orth Cape Norway 40 F1
orth Cape N.Z. 106 B1
orth Caribou Lake Can. 114 A1
orth Carolina state U.S.A. 125 E1
orth Channel lake channel Can. 114 B2
orth Channel U.K. 45 C1
orth Cowichan Can. 112 C3
orth Dakota state U.S.A. 120 C1
orth Downs hills U.K. 47 C4
ortheim Ger. 49 D2
orthern Cape prov. S. Africa 98 A2
orthern Indian Lake Can. 113 F2
orthern Ireland prov. U.K. 45 C1
orthern Mariana Islands terr. N. Pacific Ocean 63 D1
orthern Territory admin. div. Austr. 102 C1
orthfield U.S.A. 121 E2
orth Foreland c. U.K. 47 D4
orth Frisian Islands Ger. 50 B2
orth Geomagnetic Pole 146 J2
orth Island N.Z. 106 B2
orth Korea country Asia 69 B1
orth Knife Lake Can. 113 F2
orth Lakhimpur India 66 A1
orth Magnetic Pole Can. 146 K1
orth Nahanni r. Can. 112 C1
orth Platte U.S.A. 120 C2
orth Platte r. U.S.A. 120 C2
orth Pole Arctic Ocean 146 C1
orth Ronaldsay i. U.K. 44 C1
orth Sea Europe 42 D2
orth Spirit Lake Can. 114 A1
orth Stradbroke Island Austr. 105 E1
orth Taranaki Bight b. N.Z. 106 B2
orth Twin Island Can. 114 C1
orth Tyne r. U.K. 46 B2
orth Uist i. U.K. 44 A2
orthumberland Strait Can. 115 D2

North West prov. S. Africa 98 C2
North West Cape Austr. 102 A2
North West River Can. 115 E1
Northwest Territories admin. div. Can. 110 E2
North York Moors moorland U.K. 46 C2
Norton U.S.A. 122 D3
Norton Zimbabwe 97 C1
Norton Sound sea chan. U.S.A. 110 B2
Norwalk U.S.A. 122 D2
Norway country Europe 41 C3
Norwegian Sea N. Atlantic Ocean 40 B2
Norwich U.K. 47 D3
Norwich CT U.S.A. 123 F2
Noshiro Japan 70 D2
Nosivka Ukr. 39 D1
Nosop watercourse Africa 98 B2
Nosratābād Iran 83 C2
Nossen Ger. 49 F2
Noteć r. Pol. 51 D2
Noto-hantō pen. Japan 71 C3
Notre Dame, Monts mts Can. 115 D2
Notre Dame Bay Can. 115 E2
Nottaway r. Can. 114 C1
Nottingham U.K. 46 C3
Nouâdhibou Maur. 90 A2
Nouakchott Maur. 90 A3
Nouâmghâr Maur. 90 A3
Nouméa New Caledonia 100
Nouna Burkina 90 B3
Nova Esperança Brazil 138 B2
Nova Friburgo Brazil 139 D2
Nova Gradiška Croatia 57 C1
Nova Granada Brazil 138 C2
Nova Iguaçu Brazil 139 D2
Nova Kakhovka Ukr. 39 D2
Nova Lima Brazil 139 D1
Nova Londrina Brazil 138 B2
Nova Odesa Ukr. 39 D2
Nova Paraiso Brazil 134 C2
Nova Scotia prov. Can. 115 D2
Nova Venécia Brazil 139 D1
Novaya Sibir', Ostrov i. Rus. Fed. 87 L1
Novaya Zemlya is Rus. Fed. 34 E1
Nové Zámky Slovakia 51 D3
Novhorod-Sivers'kyy Ukr. 39 D1
Novi Ligure Italy 56 A2
Novi Pazar S. Serb. 58 B2
Novi Sad Serb. 58 A1
Novoaleksandrovsk Rus. Fed. 39 F2
Novoanninskiy Rus. Fed. 39 F1
Novo Aripuanã Brazil 134 C3
Novoazovs'k Ukr. 39 E2
Novocherkassk Rus. Fed. 39 F2
Novodvinsk Rus. Fed. 34 D2
Novo Hamburgo Brazil 136 C3

Novohrad-Volyns'kyy Ukr. 38 C1
Novokhopersk Rus. Fed. 37 F3
Novokubansk Rus. Fed. 39 F2
Novokuznetsk Rus. Fed. 81 F1
Novo Mesto Slovenia 50 D3
Novomikhaylovskiy Rus. Fed. 39 E3
Novomoskovsk Rus. Fed. 37 E3
Novomoskovs'k Ukr. 39 E2
Novomyrhorod Ukr. 39 D2
Novonikolayevskiy Rus. Fed. 39 F1
Novooleksiyivka Ukr. 39 D2
Novopokrovskaya Rus. Fed. 39 F2
Novopskov Ukr. 39 E2
Novorossiysk Rus. Fed. 39 E3
Novorzhev Rus. Fed. 36 C2
Novosergiyevka Rus. Fed. 35 E3
Novoshakhtinsk Rus. Fed. 39 E2
Novosibirsk Rus. Fed. 86 H3
Novosibirskiye Ostrova is Rus. Fed. see New Siberia Islands
Novosokol'niki Rus. Fed. 37 D2
Novotroyits'ke Ukr. 39 D2
Novoukrayinka Ukr. 39 D2
Novovolyns'k Ukr. 38 B1
Novozybkov Rus. Fed. 37 D3
Novy Jičín Czech Rep. 51 D3
Novyy Bor Rus. Fed. 34 E2
Novyy Oskol Rus. Fed. 39 E1
Novyy Port Rus. Fed. 34 G2
Novyy Urengoy Rus. Fed. 34 G2
Nowogard Pol. 50 D2
Nowra Austr. 105 E2
Now Shahr Iran 85 D2
Nowshera Pak. 78 B1
Nowy Sącz Pol. 51 E3
Nowy Targ Pol. 51 E3
Noyabr'sk Rus. Fed. 35 G2
Noyon France 52 C2
Nsanje Malawi 97 C1
Nu'aym reg. Oman 83 C2
Nubian Desert Sudan 92 B2
Nudo Coropuna mt. Peru 134 B4
Nueltin Lake Can. 113 F1
Nueva Lubecka Arg. 137 A5
Nueva Rosita Mex. 129 C2
Nuevo Casas Grandes Mex. 128 B1
Nuevo Laredo Mex. 129 C2
Nugaal watercourse Somalia 93 C4
Nuits-St-Georges France 53 C2
Nu Jiang r. China/Myanmar see Salween
Nu Jiang r. China/Myanmar see Salween
Nuku'alofa Tonga 101
Nuku Hiva i. Fr. Polynesia 101
Nukus Uzbek. 80 C2
Nullagine Austr. 102 B2
Nullarbor Plain Austr. 102 B3

Numan Nigeria **91** D4
Numazu Japan **71** C3
Numedal val. Norway **41** B3
Numfoor i. Indon. **93** C3
Numurkah Austr. **105** D3
Nunap Isua c. Greenland *see*
   Farewell, Cape
Nunavik *reg.* Can. **111** H3
Nunavut *admin. div.* Can. **110** G2
Nuneaton U.K. **47** C3
Nunivak Island U.S.A. **87** O3
Nuoro Italy **56** A2
Nuqrah Saudi Arabia **82** B2
Nuremberg Ger. **49** E3
Nuriootpa Austr. **104** B2
Nurmes Fin. **40** F3
Nürnberg Ger. *see* Nuremberg
Nu Shan *mts* China **66** A1
Nushki Pak. **78** A2
Nuuk Greenland **111** I2
Nuussuaq Greenland **111** I2
Nuussuaq *pen.* Greenland **111** I2
Nuwaybi' al Muzayyinah Egypt
   84 B3
Nuweveldberge *mts* S. Africa
   98 B3
Nyagan' Rus. Fed. **34** G3
Nyaingêntanglha Feng *mt.* China
   79 D1
Nyaingêntanglha Shan *mts* China
   79 D1
Nyala Sudan **93** A3
Nyandoma Rus. Fed. **34** D2
Nyanga *r.* Gabon **94** B3
Nyasa, Lake Africa **97** C1
Nyborg Denmark **41** C4
Nybro Sweden **41** C4
Nybro Sweden **41** D4
Nyeri Kenya **95** D3
Nyima China **79** C1
Nyingchi China **72** C3
Nyíregyháza Hungary **51** E3
Nykøbing Denmark **41** C5
Nyköping Sweden **41** D4
Nymagee Austr. **105** C2
Nynäshamn Sweden **41** D4
Nyngan Austr. **105** D2
Nyoman *r.* Belarus/Lith. **36** B3
Nýřany Czech Rep. **49** F3
Nyrob Rus. Fed. **34** E2
Nyssa U.S.A. **118** C2
Nyunzu Dem. Rep. Congo **95** C3
Nyzhn'ohirs'kyy Ukr. **39** D2
Nzega Tanz. **95** D3
Nzérékoré Guinea **90** B4
N'zeto Angola **95** B4

O

Oahe, Lake U.S.A. **120** C2
Oahu *i.* U.S.A. **108**
Oakbank Austr. **104** C2

Oakey Austr. **105** E1
Oak Harbor U.S.A. **118** B1
Oak Hill U.S.A. **122** D3
Oakland U.S.A. **119** B3
Oakover *r.* Austr. **102** B2
Oak Ridge U.S.A. **125** D1
Oamaru N.Z. **106** B4
Oas Phil. **68** B2
Oaxaca Mex. **129** C3
Ob' *r.* Rus. Fed. **34** F2
Obala Cameroon **94** B2
Oban U.K. **44** B2
O Barco Spain **54** B1
Oberá Arg. **138** A3
Oberon Austr. **105** D2
Oberpfälzer Wald *mts* Ger. **49** F3
Obi *i.* Indon. **93** C3
Óbidos Brazil **135** D3
Obihiro Japan **70** D2
Obluch'ye Rus. Fed. **73** E1
Obninsk Rus. Fed. **37** E2
Obo C.A.R. **95** C2
Obock Djibouti **93** C3
Obouya Congo **94** B3
Oboyan' Rus. Fed. **37** E3
Obregón, Presa *resr* Mex.
   128 B2
Obshchiy Syrt *hills* Rus. Fed.
   35 E3
Obskaya Guba *sea chan.*
   Rus. Fed. **34** G2
Obuasi Ghana **90** B4
Obukhiv Ukr. **38** D1
Ob"yachevo Rus. Fed. **34** D2
Ocala U.S.A. **125** D3
Ocampo Mex. **128** B2
Ocaña Spain **54** C2
Occidental, Cordillera *mts* Col.
   134 B2
Occidental, Cordillera *mts* Peru
   134 B4
Ocean City U.S.A. **123** E3
Ocean Falls Can. **112** C2
Oceanside U.S.A. **119** C4
Ochakiv Ukr. **39** D2
Ocher Rus. Fed. **34** E3
Ochsenfurt Ger. **49** E3
Oconee *r.* U.S.A. **125** D2
Ocussi *enclave* East Timor
   63 C3
Oda, Jebel *mt.* Sudan **92** B3
Ôdate Japan **71** C3
Odawara Japan **71** C3
Odda Norway **41** B3
Ôdemiş Turkey **59** C3
Odense Denmark **41** C4
Odenwald *reg.* Ger. **49** D3
Oderbucht *b.* Ger. **50** C2
Odesa Ukr. **36** D2
Odessa U.S.A. **127** D2
Odienné Côte d'Ivoire **90** B4
Odra *r.* Ger./Pol. **51** D3
Oeiras Brazil **135** D3

Oelde Ger. **48** D2
Oelrichs U.S.A. **120** C2
Oelsnitz Ger. **49** F2
Oenkerk Neth. **48** B1
Ofanto *r.* Italy **57** C2
Offenbach am Main Ger. **49** D2
Offenburg Ger. **50** B3
Ogaden *reg.* Eth. **93** C4
Ôga-hantô *pen.* Japan **70** C3
Ôgaki Japan **71** C3
Ogbomosho Nigeria **90** C4
Ogden U.S.A. **118** D2
Ogilvie *r.* Can. **110** C2
Ogilvie Mountains Can. **110** C3
Oglethorpe, Mount U.S.A.
   125 D2
Ogoki *r.* Can. **114** B1
Ogoki Reservoir Can. **114** B1
Ogre Latvia **36** B2
Ogulin Croatia **56** C1
Ohio *r.* U.S.A. **123** C3
Ohio *state* U.S.A. **122** D2
Ohrdruf Ger. **49** E2
Ohrid Macedonia **59** B2
Oiapoque Brazil **135** D3
Oil City U.S.A. **123** E2
Oise *r.* France **48** A3
Ôita Japan **71** C4
Ojinaga Mex. **128** B2
Ojos del Salado, Nevado *mt.*
   Arg./Chile **136** B3
Oka *r.* Rus. Fed. **37** F2
Okahandja Namibia **96** A2
Okanagan Lake Can. **112** B3
Okanogan U.S.A. **118** C1
Okanogan *r.* U.S.A. **118** C1
Okara Pak. **78** B1
Okavango *r.* Botswana/Namibia
   96 B1
Okavango Delta *swamp*
   Botswana **96** B1
Okayama Japan **71** B4
Okazaki Japan **71** C4
Okeechobee, Lake U.S.A.
   125 D3
Okefenokee Swamp U.S.A.
   125 D2
Okehampton U.K. **47** A4
Okha Rus. Fed. **87** L3
Okhotka *r.* Rus. Fed. **87** L3
Okhotsk Rus. Fed. **87** L3
Okhotsk, Sea of Japan/Rus. Fed.
   87 L4
Okhtyrka Ukr. **39** D1
Okinawa *i.* Japan **71** B3
Oki-shotô *is* Japan **71** B3
Oklahoma *state* U.S.A. **127** E1
Oklahoma City U.S.A. **127** E1
Okmulgee U.S.A. **127** E1
Oko, Wadi *watercourse* Sudan
   82 A2
Okovskiy Les *for.* Rus. Fed.
   37 D3

yo Congo **94** B3
fjord Norway **40** E1
win Myanmar **66** A2
yabr'skiy *Arkhangel'skaya
blast'* Rus. Fed. **34** D2
yabr'skiy *Kamchatskaya
blast'* Rus. Fed. **87** M3
yabr'skiy *Respublika
Bashkortostan* Rus. Fed. **35** E3
yabr'skoye Rus. Fed. **34** F2
yabr'skoy Revolyutsii, Ostrov
Rus. Fed. **87** I1
lovka Rus. Fed. **37** D2
ushiri-tô *i.* Japan **70** C2
fsvik Iceland **40** [inset]
nd *l.* Sweden **41** D4
ry Austr. **104** C2
varria Arg. **137** B4
ernhau Ger. **49** F2
ia Italy **56** A2
enburg Ger. **49** D1
enburg in Holstein Ger.
0 C2
enzaal Neth. **48** C1
0 A4
s Head of Kinsale *hd* Ireland
5 B3
cs Can. **112** D2
Wives Lake Can. **113** E2
a U.S.A. **123** E2
ecko Pol. **51** E2
kminsk Rus. Fed. **87** K2
aksandriya Ukr. **39** D2
en Norway **42** E2
enegorsk Rus. Fed. **40** G2
enek Rus. Fed. **37** D2
anino Rus. Fed. **37** D2
evs'k Ukr. **38** C1
são Port. **54** B2
fants *r.* Moz./S. Africa **99** D1
fants *r.* S. Africa **98** A3
fantshoek S. Africa **98** B2
anda Brazil **135** F3
va Spain **55** C2
enza Spain **54** B2
ague Chile **136** B3
ney U.S.A. **122** C3
a U.S.A. **122** C3
omouc Czech Rep. **51** D3
engapo Phil. **68** B2
oron-Ste-Marie France **52** B3
at Spain **55** D1
ovyannaya Rus. Fed. **73** D1
be Ger. **48** C2
r. Romania **38** B3
lu Turkey **59** B3
ympia *tourist site* Greece **59** B3
ympia U.S.A. **118** B1
ympus, Mount Greece **59** B3
ympus, Mount U.S.A. **118** B1
yutorskiy, Mys *c.* Rus. Fed.
87 N3

Omagh U.K. **45** C1
Omaha U.S.A. **121** D2
Oman *country* Asia **83** C2
Oman, Gulf of Asia **83** C2
Omaruru Namibia **96** A2
Omatako *watercourse* Namibia
96 B1
Omdurman Sudan **92** B3
Ometepec Mex. **129** C3
Om Hajër Eritrea **82** A3
Omineca Mountains Can.
112 C2
Ōmiya Japan **71** C3
Ommen Neth. **48** C1
Omolon *r.* Rus. Fed. **87** M2
Omsk Rus. Fed. **81** E1
Omulchukchan Rus. Fed. **87** M2
Omu, Vârful *mt.* Romania **38** C2
Onancock U.S.A. **123** E3
Onaping Lake Can. **122** D1
Oncócua Angola **96** A1
Onderstedorings S. Africa **98** B3
Ondjiva Angola **96** A1
Onega Rus. Fed. **34** C2
Onega *r.* Rus. Fed. **34** C2
Onega, Lake Rus. Fed. **34** C2
Oneida Lake U.S.A. **123** E2
O'Neill U.S.A. **121** D2
Oneşti Romania **38** C2
Onezhskoye Ozero *l.* Rus. Fed.
see Onega, Lake
Ongjin N. Korea **69** B2
Ongole India **77** C3
Onilahy *r.* Madag. **97** [inset] D2
Onitsha Nigeria **91** C4
Onseepkans S. Africa **98** B3
Onslow Austr. **102** A2
Onslow Bay U.S.A. **125** E2
Ontario *prov.* Can. **114** A1
Ontario U.S.A. **118** C2
Ontario, Lake Can./U.S.A.
123 E2
Oodnadatta Austr. **104** B1
Oostende Belgium *see* Ostend
Oosterhout Neth. **48** B2
Oosterschelde *est.* Neth. **48** A2
Oost-Vlieland Neth. **48** B1
Ootsa Lake Can. **112** C2
Opataca, Lac *l.* Can. **114** C1
Opava Czech Rep. **51** D3
Opelika U.S.A. **125** C2
Opelousas U.S.A. **124** B2
Opinaca, Réservoir *resr* Can.
114 C1
Opiscotéo, Lac *l.* Can. **115** D1
Opochka Rus. Fed. **36** C2
Opole Pol. **51** D2
Oporto Port. **54** B1
Opotiki N.Z. **106** C2
Oppdal Norway **41** B3
Opunake N.Z. **106** C2
Opuwo Namibia **96** A1
Oradea Romania **38** B2
Oran Alg. **90** B1

Orán Arg. **136** B3
Ōrang N. Korea **69** B1
Orange Austr. **105** D2
Orange France **53** C3
Orange *r.* Namibia/S. Africa **98** A2
Orange U.S.A. **127** F2
Orangeburg U.S.A. **125** D2
Orangeville Can. **123** D2
Orange Walk Belize **129** D3
Oranienburg Ger. **49** F1
Oranjemund Namibia **98** A2
Orapa Botswana **96** B3
Orăştie Romania **38** B2
Orbetello Italy **56** B2
Orbost Austr. **105** D3
Ord, Mount Austr. **102** B1
Ordes Spain **54** B1
Ordos China **74** D2
Ordu Turkey **84** B1
Ordzhonikidze Ukr. **39** D2
Örebro Sweden **41** D4
Oregon *state* U.S.A. **118** B2
Oregon City U.S.A. **118** B1
Orel Rus. Fed. **37** E3
Orem U.S.A. **118** D2
Orenburg Rus. Fed. **35** E3
Orepuki N.Z. **106** A4
Øresund *str.* Denmark/Sweden
41 C4
Orford Ness *hd* U.K. **47** D3
Orhaneli Turkey **59** C3
Orhangazi Turkey **59** C2
Orhon Gol *r.* Mongolia **87** J3
Oriental, Cordillera *mts* Bol.
136 B2
Oriental, Cordillera *mts* Col.
134 B2
Oriental, Cordillera *mts* Peru
134 B4
Orihuela Spain **55** C2
Orikhiv Ukr. **39** E2
Orillia Can. **114** C2
Orinoco *r.* Col./Venez. **134** C2
Orinoco Delta Venez. **134** C2
Orissaare Estonia **36** B2
Oristano Italy **56** A3
Orivesi *l.* Fin. **40** F3
Oriximiná Brazil **135** D3
Orizaba Mex. **129** C3
Orizaba, Pico de *vol.* Mex.
129 C3
Orkanger Norway **40** B3
Örkelljunga Sweden **41** C4
Orkla *r.* Norway **40** B3
Orkney Islands *Scotland* U.K.
44 C1
Orlando U.S.A. **125** D3
Orléans France **52** C2
Ormara Pak. **78** A2
Ormoc Phil. **68** B2
Ormskirk U.K. **46** B3
Örnsköldsvik Sweden **40** D3
Orodara Burkina **90** B3
Orofino U.S.A. **118** C2

Oroquieta Phil. **68** B3
Orosei, Golfo di *b.* Italy **56** A2
Orosháza Hungary **51** E3
Oroville U.S.A. **119** B3
Orsha Belarus **37** D2
Orsk Rus. Fed. **35** E3
Ørsta Norway **41** B3
Ortegal, Cabo *c.* Spain **54** B1
Orthez France **52** B3
Ortigueira Spain **54** B1
Ortonville U.S.A. **121** D1
Orulgan, Khrebet *mts* Rus. Fed. **87** K2
Orūmīyeh, Daryācheh-ye *salt l.* Iran *see* Urmia, Lake
Oruro Bol. **136** B2
Orvieto Italy **56** B2
Osage *r.* U.S.A. **121** E3
Ōsaka Japan **71** C4
Oschersleben (Bode) Ger. **49** E1
Oschiri Italy **56** A2
Osetr *r.* Rus. Fed. **37** E3
Osh Kyrg. **81** E2
Ōshakati Namibia **96** A3
Oshawa Can. **114** D2
Ō-shima *i.* Japan **70** C2
Ō-shima *i.* Japan **71** C4
Oshkosh U.S.A. **122** C2
Oshnovīyeh Iran **85** C2
Oshogbo Nigeria **90** C4
Oshwe Dem. Rep. Congo **94** B3
Osijek Croatia **57** C1
Osilinka *r.* Can. **112** C3
Osimo Italy **56** B2
Osizweni S. Africa **99** D2
Oskaloosa U.S.A. **121** E2
Oskarshamn Sweden **41** D4
Oskol *r.* Rus. Fed. **37** E3
Oslo Norway **41** C4
Oslofjorden *sea chan.* Norway **41** C4
Osmancık Turkey **84** B1
Osmaniye Turkey **84** B1
Osnabrück Ger. **48** D1
Osorno Chile **137** A5
Osorno Spain **54** C1
Osoyoos Can. **112** D3
Oseyri Norway **42** E1
Oss Neth. **48** B2
Ossa, Mount Austr. **103** D4
Ostashkov Rus. Fed. **37** D2
Oste *r.* Ger. **49** D1
Ostend Belgium **48** A2
Osterburg (Altmark) Ger. **49** E1
Österdalälven *l.* Sweden **41** C3
Osterholz-Scharmbeck Ger. **49** D1
Osterode am Harz Ger. **49** E2
Östersund Sweden **40** C3
Ostfriesland *reg.* Ger. **48** C1
Östhammar Sweden **41** D3
Ostrava Czech Rep. **51** D3
Ostróda Pol. **51** D2
Ostrogozhsk Rus. Fed. **37** E3

Ostrołęka Pol. **51** E2
Ostrov Czech Rep. **49** F2
Ostrov Rus. Fed. **36** C2
Ostrowiec Świętokrzyski Pol. **51** E2
Ostrów Mazowiecka Pol. **51** E2
Ostrów Wielkopolski Pol. **51** D2
Osüm *r.* Bulg. **58** B2
Ōsumi-kaikyō *sea chan.* Japan **71** B4
Ōsumi-shotō *is* Japan **71** B4
Osuna Spain **54** B2
Oswego U.S.A. **123** D2
Oswestry U.K. **46** B3
Otago Peninsula N.Z. **106** B4
Otaki N.Z. **106** C3
Otaru Japan **70** C2
Otavi Namibia **96** A1
Othello U.S.A. **118** C1
Otjiwarongo Namibia **96** A2
Otoro, Jebel *mt.* Sudan **93** B3
Otra *r.* Norway **41** B4
Otranto, Strait of Albania/Italy **59** A2
Ōtsu Japan **71** C3
Otta Norway **41** B3
Ottawa Can. **114** C2
Ottawa *r.* Can. **114** C2
Ottawa IL U.S.A. **122** C2
Ottawa KS U.S.A. **121** D3
Ottawa Islands Can. **114** F3
Ottignies Belgium **48** B2
Ottumwa U.S.A. **121** E2
Otway, Cape Austr. **104** C3
Ouachita *r.* U.S.A. **124** B2
Ouachita, Lake U.S.A. **124** B2
Ouachita Mountains U.S.A. **124** B2
Ouadda C.A.R. **94** C2
Ouaddaï *reg.* Chad **91** D3
Ouagadougou Burkina **90** B3
Ouahigouya Burkina **90** B3
Oualâta Maur. **90** B3
Ouarâne *reg.* Maur. **90** B3
Ouargla Alg. **91** C1
Ouarzazate Morocco **90** B1
Oudenaarde Belgium **48** A2
Oudtshoorn S. Africa **98** B3
Oued Tlélat Alg. **55** C2
Ouessant, Île d' *i.* France **52** A2
Ouesso Congo **94** B3
Ouistreham France **47** C5
Oujda Morocco **90** B1
Oulad Farès Alg. **55** D2
Oulu Fin. **40** F2
Oulujärvi *l.* Fin. **40** F3
Oulx Italy **56** A1
Oum-Chalouba Chad **91** E3
Oum-Hadjer Chad **91** D3
Ounianga Kébir Chad **91** E3
Oupeye Belgium **48** B2
Our *r.* Lux. **48** C3
Ourense Spain **54** B1
Ourinhos Brazil **139** C3

Ouro Preto Brazil **139** D2
Ourthe *r.* Belgium **48** B2
Ouse *r.* U.K. **46** C3
Outardes *r.* Can. **115** D2
Outardes Quatre, Réservoir *resr* Can. **115** D1
Outer Hebrides *is* U.K. **44** A2
Outjo Namibia **96** A2
Outokumpu Fin. **40** F3
Ouyen Austr. **104** C3
Ovar Port. **54** B1
Överkalix Sweden **40** E2
Overton U.S.A. **119** D3
Övertorneå Sweden **40** E2
Oviedo Spain **54** B1
Øvruch Ukr. **38** C1
Owando Congo **94** B3
Owase Japan **71** C4
Owatonna U.S.A. **121** E2
Owensboro U.S.A. **122** C3
Owens Lake U.S.A. **119** C3
Owen Sound Can. **114** C2
Owerri Nigeria **91** C4
Owyhee U.S.A. **118** C2
Owyhee *r.* U.S.A. **118** C2
Oxelösund Sweden **36** A2
Oxford N.Z. **106** B3
Oxford U.K. **47** C4
Oxford OH U.S.A. **122** C4
Oxford Lake Can. **113** F2
Oxley Austr. **104** C2
Oxnard U.S.A. **119** C4
Oyama Japan **71** C3
Oyem Gabon **94** B2
Oyen Can. **113** D2
Oyonnax France **52** D2
Ozark U.S.A. **125** C2
Ozark Plateau U.S.A. **121** E3
Ozarks, Lake of the U.S.A. **121** E3
Ozernovskiy Rus. Fed. **87** M3
Ozery Rus. Fed. **37** E3
Ozinki Rus. Fed. **35** D3

Paamiut Greenland **111** O3
Paarl S. Africa **98** A3
Pabianice Pol. **51** D2
Pabna Bangl. **79** C2
Pab Range *mts* Pak. **78** A2
Pachino Italy **56** C3
Pachuca Mex. **129** C2
Pacific Ocean **142**
Padang Indon. **64** B2
Padang-Chaloung Indon. **64** B2
Padangsidimpuan Indon. **64** A1
Paderborn Ger. **49** D2
Padova Italy *see* Padua
Padre Island U.S.A. **127** E3
Padua Italy **56** B1
Paducah KY U.S.A. **122** C3

218

ucah *TX* U.S.A. **127** D2
gam N. Korea **69** B1
ngnyŏng-do *i.* S. Korea **69** A2
roa N.Z. **106** C2
ss Cyprus *see* Paphos
  Croatia **56** C2
dian Phil. **68** B3
ai Selatan *i.* Indon. **64** B2
ai Utara *i.* Indon. **64** B2
an *i.* N. Mariana Is **63** D1
atan Indon. **65** C1
e U.S.A. **126** B1
egiai Lith. **36** B2
ala Springs U.S.A. **120** B3
de Estonia **36** C2
änne *i.* Fin. **41** F3
kū Co *i.* China **79** C2
nted Desert U.S.A. **126** B1
aley U.K. **44** B3
ala Sweden **40** E2
istan *country* Asia **78** A2
okku Myanmar **66** A1
ts Hungary **51** D3
wash Lake Can. **114** A1
xan Laos **66** B2
xé Laos **67** B2
a Chad **91** D4
abuhanratu, Teluk *b.* Indon.
  64 B2
aikastro Greece **59** C3
aiochora Greece **59** B3
amakoloi Botswana **98** B5
amós Spain **55** D1
ana Rus. Fed. **87** M3
angkaraya Indon. **65** C2
anpur India **78** B2
apye Botswana **99** C1
atka Rus. Fed. **87** M2
atka U.S.A. **125** D3
aw Myanmar **67** A2
awan *i.* Phil. **68** A3
diski Estonia **36** B2
ekh Rus. Fed. **37** F2
embang Indon. **64** B2
encia Spain **54** C1
enque Mex. **129** C3
ermo Italy **56** B2
estine U.S.A. **127** E2
etwa Myanmar **66** A1
d India **78** B2
ikino Rus. Fed. **36** C2
x Strait India/Sri Lanka **77** B4
liser, Îles *is* Fr. Polynesia **101**
ma del Rio Spain **54** B2
ma de Mallorca Spain **55** D2
mas **135** E4
meira Brazil **138** C3

Palmer U.S.A. **110** C2
Palmer Land *reg.* Antarctica
  107 K3
Palmerston North N.Z. **106** C3
Palmi Italy **57** C3
Palmira Col. **134** B2
Palmyra Atoll *terr.*
  N. Pacific Ocean **101**
Palopo Indon. **65** D2
Palos, Cabo de *c.* Spain **55** C2
Palú Indon. Fin. **40** F3
Palu Indon. **65** C2
Palyavaam *r.* Rus. Fed. **87** N2
Pamiers France **52** C3
Pamir *mts* Asia **81** F1
Pamlico Sound *sea chan.* U.S.A.
  125 E1
Pampas *reg.* Arg. **137** B4
Pamplona Col. **134** B2
Pamplona Spain **55** C1
Pamukova Turkey **59** D2
Panaitan *i.* Indon. **64** B2
Panaji India **77** B3
Panama *country* Central America
  130 B4
Panama, Gulf of Panama **130** C4
Panama Canal Panama **130** C4
Panama City Panama **130** C4
Panama City U.S.A. **125** C2
Panamint Range *mts* U.S.A.
  119 C3
Panarik Indon. **64** B1
Panay *i.* Phil. **68** B2
Pančevo S.M. **58** B2
Panda Moz. **99** D1
Panevėžys Lith. **36** B2
Pangkalanbuun Indon. **65** C2
Pangkalpinang Indon. **64** B2
Pangnirtung Can. **111** K2
Pangody Rus. Fed. **34** H2
Panipat India **78** B2
Panjgur Pak. **78** A2
Pan Ling *mts* China **69** B1
Panna India **79** C2
Pannawonica Austr. **102** A2
Panorama Brazil **138** B2
Panshi China **69** B1
Pantanal *reg.* Brazil **136** C2
Pánuco Mex. **129** C3
Panzhihua China **66** B1
Paola Italy **57** C3
Pápa Hungary **51** D3
Papakura N.Z. **106** B2
Papantla Mex. **129** C2
Papeete Fr. Polynesia **101**
Papenburg Ger. **48** C1
Paphos Cyprus **84** F2
Papua, Gulf of P.N.G. **63** D3
Papua New Guinea *country*
  Oceania **63** D3
Pará *r.* Rus. Fed. **37** F3
Paraburdoo Austr. **102** A2
Paracatu Brazil **138** C1
Paracatu *r.* Brazil **139** C1

Parachilna Austr. **104** B2
Paraćin S.M. **58** B2
Pará de Minas Brazil **139** D1
Paradise U.S.A. **119** B3
Paragould U.S.A. **124** B1
Paraguai *r.* Brazil **135** D4
Paraguay *r.* Arg./Para. **136** C3
Paraguay *country* S. America
  136 C3
Parakou Benin **90** C4
Paramaribo Suriname **135** D2
Paraná Arg. **136** B4
Paraná *r.* S. America **138** B2
Paranaguá Brazil **138** C3
Paranaíba Brazil **138** B1
Paranaíba *r.* Brazil **138** B2
Paranapanema *r.* Brazil **138** B2
Paranapiacaba, Serra *mts* Brazil
  138 B2
Paranavaí Brazil **138** B2
Parapararaumu N.Z. **106** B3
Parati Brazil **139** D2
Paraúna Brazil **138** B1
Paray-le-Monial France **53** C2
Parbhani India **77** B3
Parchim Ger. **49** E1
Pardo *r.* Bahia Brazil **139** E1
Pardo *r. Mato Grosso do Sul* Brazil
  138 B2
Pardo *r. São Paulo* Brazil **138** C2
Pardubice Czech Rep. **51** D2
Parecis, Serra dos *hills* Brazil
  134 C4
Parent, Lac *l.* Can. **114** C2
Parepare Indon. **65** C2
Parfino Rus. Fed. **37** D2
Parga Greece **59** B3
Pargas Fin. **36** B1
Parima, Serra *mts* Brazil **134** C3
Parintins Brazil **135** D3
Paris France **52** C2
Paris *TN* U.S.A. **124** C1
Paris *TX* U.S.A. **127** E2
Parkano Fin. **41** E3
Parker U.S.A. **126** B2
Parkersburg U.S.A. **122** D3
Parkes Austr. **105** D2
Park Rapids U.S.A. **121** D1
Parma Italy **56** B2
Parnaíba Brazil **135** E3
Parnassos *mt.* Greece **59** B3
Parnassus N.Z. **106** B3
Parnon *mts* Greece **59** B3
Pärnu Estonia **36** B2
Paroo *watercourse* Austr. **104** C2
Propamisus *mts* Afgh. **78** A1
Paros *i.* Greece **59** C3
Parras Mex. **128** B2
Parry Channel Can. **108**
Parry Islands Can. **110** E1
Parry Sound Can. **114** D2
Parsons U.S.A. **121** D3
Parthenay France **52** B2
Partry Mountains Ireland **45** B2

219

Paru r. Brazil 135 D3
Pasadena U.S.A. 119 C4
Pascagoula U.S.A. 124 C2
Paçani Romania 38 C2
Pasco U.S.A. 118 C1
Pasewalk Ger. 50 C2
Pasfield Lake Can. 113 E2
Pasni Pak. 78 A2
Paso Rio Mayo Arg. 137 A5
Paso Robles U.S.A. 119 B3
Passau Ger. 50 C3
Passo Fundo Brazil 136 C3
Passos Brazil 139 C2
Pastavy Belarus 36 C3
Pastaza r. Peru 134 B3
Pasto Col. 134 B2
Pasuruan Indon. 65 C2
Pasvalys Lith. 36 B2
Patagonia reg. Arg. 137 A6
Patan Nepal 79 C2
Patea N.Z. 106 B2
Paterson U.S.A. 123 F2
Pathfinder Reservoir U.S.A.
120 B2
Pati Indon. 65 C2
Patmos i. Greece 59 C3
Patna India 79 C2
Patnos Turkey 85 C2
Pato Branco Brazil 138 B3
Patos, Lagoa dos l. Brazil
136 C3
Patos de Minas Brazil 139 C1
Patquía Arg. 136 B4
Patras Greece 59 B3
Patrocínio Brazil 138 C1
Pattani Thai. 67 B3
Pattaya Thai. 67 B2
Patterson, Mount Can. 112 B1
Pattullo, Mount Can. 112 C2
Patuakhali Bangl. xx. 128 B3
Pau France 52 B3
Pauillac France 52 B2
Paulo Afonso Brazil 135 F3
Paulpietersburg S. Africa 99 D2
Pauls Valley U.S.A. 127 E2
Paungde Myanmar 66 A2
Pavão Brazil 139 D1
Pavia Italy 56 A1
Pāvilosta Latvia 36 B2
Pavlikeni Bulg. 58 C2
Pavlodar Kazakh. 81 E1
Pavlohrad Ukr. 39 E2
Pavlovo Rus. Fed. 37 F2
Pavlovsk Rus. Fed. 39 F1
Pavlovskaya Rus. Fed. 39 E2
Payakumbuh Indon. 64 B2
Payette U.S.A. 118 C2
Payette r. U.S.A. 118 C2
Payne, Lac l. Can. 114 C1
Paysandú Uru. 136 C4
Pazardzhik Bulg. 58 B2
Pazin Croatia 56 B1
Peace r. Can. 112 D2
Peace River Can. 112 D2

Peale, Mount U.S.A. 119 E3
Pearl r. U.S.A. 124 C2
Pearsall U.S.A. 127 E3
Pebane Moz. 97 C1
Peć SR 58 B2
Peçanha Brazil 139 D1
Pechora Rus. Fed. 34 E2
Pechora r. Rus. Fed. 34 E2
Pechory Rus. Fed. 36 C2
Pecos U.S.A. 127 D2
Pecos r. U.S.A. 127 D3
Pécs Hungary 51 D3
Pedra Azul Brazil 139 D1
Pedregulho Brazil 138 C2
Pedreiras Brazil 135 E3
Pedro, Point Sri Lanka 77 C4
Pedro Afonso Brazil 135 E3
Pedro Gomes Brazil 138 B1
Pedro Juan Caballero Para.
136 C3
Peebles U.K. 44 C3
Pee Dee r. U.S.A. 125 E2
Peel r. Can. 110 D2
Peel Isle of Man 46 A2
Pegasus Bay N.Z. 106 B3
Pegu Myanmar 66 A2
Pegu Yoma mts Myanmar 66 A2
Peine Ger. 49 E1
Peipus, Lake Estonia/Rus. Fed.
36 C2
Peixe r. Brazil 138 B2
Peixoto de Azevedo Brazil
136 C2
Pekalongan Indon. 65 B2
Pekan Malaysia 64 B1
Pekanbaru Indon. 64 B1
Peking China see Beijing
Pelee Island Can. 114 B2
Peleng i. Indon. 65 D2
Pelkosenniemi Fin. 40 F2
Pelleluhu Islands P.N.G. 63 D3
Pello Fin. 40 E2
Pelly r. Can. 112 B1
Pelly Mountains Can. 112 B1
Pelotas Brazil 136 C4
Pelotas, Rio das r. Brazil 136 C3
Pemadumcook Lake U.S.A.
123 G1
Pematangsiantar Indon. 64 A1
Pemba Moz. 97 D1
Pemba Zambia 96 B1
Pemba Island Tanz. 95 D3
Pemberton Can. 112 C2
Pembina r. Can. 121 D1
Pembroke Can. 114 C2
Pembroke U.K. 47 A4
Peña Nevada, Cerro mt. Mex.
129 C2
Penápolis Brazil 138 B2
Peñarroya mt. Spain 55 D1
Peñarroya-Pueblonuevo Spain
54 B2
Peñas, Cabo de c. Spain 54 B1

Penas, Golfo de g. Chile 137 A6
Pendleton U.S.A. 118 C1
Pend Oreille Lake U.S.A. 118 C1
Penglai China 74 C2
Pengshui China 75 A3
Peniculik U.K. 44 C3
Peninsular Malaysia Malaysia
64 B1
Pennines hills U.K. 46 B2
Pennsylvania state U.S.A.
123 E2
Penobscot r. U.S.A. 123 G2
Penola Austr. 104 C3
Penong Austr. 102 C3
Penrhyn atoll Cook Is 101
Penrith U.K. 46 B2
Pensacola U.S.A. 124 C2
Pensacola Mountains Antarctica
107 K1
Pensiangan Malaysia 65 C1
Penticton Can. 112 D3
Pentland Firth sea chan. U.K.
44 C1
Penza Rus. Fed. 35 D3
Penzance U.K. 47 A4
Peoria U.S.A. 122 C2
Percy Isles Austr. 103 E2
Pereira Col. 134 B2
Pereira Barreto Brazil 138 B2
Peremyshlyany Ukr. 38 B2
Pereslavl'-Zalesskiy Rus. Fed.
37 E2
Pereyaslav-Khmel'nyts'kyy Ukr.
39 D1
Pergamino Arg. 137 B4
Perhonjoki r. Fin. 40 E3
Perico Arg. 136 B3
Pericos Mex. 128 B2
Périgueux France 52 C2
Perito Moreno Arg. 137 A5
Perleberg Ger. 49 E1
Perm' Rus. Fed. 34 E3
Pernatty Lagoon salt flat Austr.
104 B2
Pernik Bulg. 84 A1
Péronne France 52 C2
Perote Mex. 129 C3
Perpignan France 52 C3
Perry FL U.S.A. 125 D2
Perry GA U.S.A. 125 D2
Perry OK U.S.A. 127 D1
Perryville U.S.A. 121 F3
Pershotravens'k Ukr. 39 E2
Persian Gulf Asia see The Gulf
Perth Austr. 102 A3
Perth U.K. 44 C2
Pertusato, Capo c. France 56 B
Peru country S. America 134 B
Perugia Italy 56 B2
Péruwelz Belgium 48 A2
Pervomays'k Ukr. 38 D2
Pervomays'ke Ukr. 39 D2
Pervomayskiy Rus. Fed. 37 F3
Pervomays'kyy Ukr. 39 E2

aro Italy **56** B2
cara Italy **56** B2
cara r. Italy **56** B2
chanokopskoye Rus. Fed.
 F2
nawar Pak. **78** B1
nkopi Albania **58** B2
nica Slovenia **56** C1
sac France **51** C5
covo Rus. Fed. **37** E2
atlán Mex. **128** B3
nwell Lake U.S.A. **122** C2
rborough Austr. **104** B2
rborough Can. **114** C2
rborough U.K. **47** C3
rhead U.K. **44** D2
rmann Ranges mts Austr.
 B2
r Pond Lake Can. **113** E2
rsburg AK U.S.A. **112** B2
rsburg VA U.S.A. **123** E3
rshagen Ger. **49** D1
t Mecatina r. Can. **115** E1
x Mex. **129** D2
oskey U.S.A. **122** C1
a tourist site Jordan **84** B2
a Velikogo, Zaliv b. Rus. Fed.
rich Bulg. **59** B2
olinia Brazil **135** E3
opavlovsk Kazakh. **81** D1
opavlovsk-Kamchatskiy
s. Fed. **87** M3
oşani Romania **38** B2
ovskoye Rus. Fed. **37** F3
ozavodsk Rus. Fed. **34** C2
usburg S. Africa **99** C2
usville S. Africa **98** B3
ukhovo Rus. Fed. **35** F3
ushki Rus. Fed. **37** E2
resula Indon. **64** A1
ok Rus. Fed. **87** N2
zheim Ger. **50** B3
ngstadt Ger. **49** D3
hameng S. Africa **99** C2
alaborwa S. Africa **99** D1
olodi India **78** B2
ng Hoei, San Khao mts Thai.
 B2
ngnga Thai. **67** A3
n Rang Vietnam **67** B2
n Thiêt Vietnam **67** B2
atthalung Thai. **67** B3
yao Thai. **66** A2
lps Lake Can. **113** E2
nix City U.S.A. **125** C2
t Buri Thai. **67** A2
chit Thai. **66** B2
adelphia U.S.A. **123** E3
p U.S.A. **120** C2
ippeville Belgium **48** B2
ippines country Asia **68** B3
ippine Sea N. Pacific Ocean

Philip Smith Mountains U.S.A.
 110 C2
Phillip Island Austr. **105** D3
Phillipsburg U.S.A. **121** D3
Phirltona S. Africa **99** C2
Phitsanulok Thai. **66** B2
Phnom Penh Cambodia **67** B2
Phoenix U.S.A. **126** B2
Phoenix Islands Kiribati **101**
Phôngsali Laos **66** B1
Phrae Thai. **66** B2
Phuket Thai. **67** A3
Phumĭ Sâmraông Cambodia
 67 B2
Phyu Myanmar **66** A2
Piacenza Italy **56** A1
Pianosa, Isola i. Italy **53** E3
Piatra Neamţ Romania **38** C2
Piauí r. Brazil **135** E3
Pibor r. Sudan **93** B4
Pibor Post Sudan **93** B4
Picayune U.S.A. **124** C2
Pichanal Arg. **136** B3
Pichilingue Mex. **128** A2
Pickle Lake Can. **114** A1
Picos Brazil **135** E3
Pico Truncado Arg. **137** B5
Picton Can. **105** E2
Picton N.Z. **106** B3
Piedras Negras Mex. **129** B2
Pieksämäki Fin. **41** F3
Pielinen l. Fin. **40** F3
Pierre U.S.A. **120** C2
Pierrelatte France **53** C3
Pietermaritzburg S. Africa **99** D2
Pietersburg S. Africa see
 Polokwane
Pietrosa mt. Romania **38** B2
Pigeon Lake Can. **112** D2
Pigüé Arg. **137** B4
Pijijiapan Mex. **129** C3
Pikes Peak U.S.A. **120** C3
Piketberg S. Africa **98** A3
Pikeville U.S.A. **122** D3
Pila Pol. **51** D2
Pilar Arg. **137** C4
Pilar Para. **136** C1
Pilliga Austr. **105** D2
Pilões, Serra dos mts Brazil
 138 C1
Pimenta Bueno Brazil **134** C4
Pinamar Arg. **137** C4
Pınarbaşı Turkey **51** C1
Pinar del Rio Cuba **130** B2
Pińczów Pol. **51** E2
Pindaré r. Brazil **135** E3
Pindos mts Greece see
 Pindus Mountains
Pindus Mountains Greece **59** B3
Pine Bluff U.S.A. **124** B2
Pine Creek Austr. **102** C1
Pinedale U.S.A. **120** B2
Pinega Rus. Fed. **34** D2
Pinehouse Lake Can. **113** E2

Pineios r. Greece **59** B3
Pine Point Can. **112** D1
Pine Ridge U.S.A. **120** C2
Pinetown S. Africa **99** D2
Pingdingshan China **74** B2
Pingliang China **74** A2
P'ingtung Taiwan **75** C3
Pingxiang Guangxi China **75** A3
Pingxiang Jiangxi China **75** B3
Pinheiro Brazil **135** E3
Pinneberg Ger. **49** D1
Pinotepa Nacional Mex. **129** C3
Pinsk Belarus **36** C3
Pioche U.S.A. **119** D3
Pionki Pol. **51** E2
Piotrków Trybunalski Pol. **51** D2
Pipestone U.S.A. **121** D2
Pipmuacan, Réservoir resr Can.
 115 C2
Piquiri r. Brazil **138** B2
Piracanjuba Brazil **138** C1
Piracicaba Brazil **138** C2
Piraçununga Brazil **138** C2
Piraeus Greece **59** B3
Piraí do Sul Brazil **138** C2
Pirajuí Brazil **138** C2
Piranhas Brazil **138** B1
Piranhas r. Brazil **135** F3
Pirapora Brazil **139** D1
Pires do Rio Brazil **138** C1
Piripiri Brazil **135** E3
Pirmasens Ger. **48** C3
Pirna Ger. **49** F2
Pisa Italy **56** B2
Pisagua Chile **136** A2
Pisco Peru **134** B4
Pisek Czech Rep. **50** C3
Pishin Iran **83** D2
Pisté Mex. **129** D2
Pisticci Italy **57** C2
Pistoia Italy **56** B2
Pisuerga r. Spain **54** C1
Pit r. U.S.A. **118** B2
Pitanga Brazil **138** B2
Pitcairn Islands terr.
 S. Pacific Ocean **101**
Piteå Sweden **40** E2
Piteälven r. Sweden **40** E2
Piteşti Romania **38** B3
Pithoragarh India **79** C2
Pitlochry U.K. **44** C2
Pitt Island Can. **112** C2
Pittsburg U.S.A. **121** E3
Pittsburgh U.S.A. **123** E2
Pittsfield U.S.A. **123** F2
Piumhí Brazil **139** C2
Piura Peru **134** A3
Pivdennyy Buh r. Ukr. **38** D2
Placerville U.S.A. **119** B3
Plainview U.S.A. **127** D2
Planaltina Brazil **138** C1
Plaquemine U.S.A. **124** B2
Plasencia Spain **54** B1
Plasy Czech Rep. **49** F3

Platte r. U.S.A. **121** D2
Plattsburgh U.S.A. **123** F2
Plau Ger. **49** F1
Plauen Ger. **49** F2
Plauer See l. Ger. **49** F1
Plavsk Rus. Fed. **37** E3
Plây Cu Vietnam **67** B2
Playgreen Lake Can. **113** F2
Plaza Huincul Arg. **137** B4
Pleaux France **52** C2
Pledger Lake Can. **114** B1
Plenty, Bay of b. N.Z. **106** C2
Plesetsk Rus. Fed. **34** D2
Plétipi, Lac l. Can. **115** C3
Plettenberg Ger. **48** C2
Plettenberg Bay S. Africa **98** B3
Pleven Bulg. **58** B2
Ploče Croatia **57** C2
Płock Pol. **51** D2
Pločno mt. Bos.-Herz. **57** C2
Ploemeur France **52** B2
Ploiești Romania **38** C3
Ploskoye Rus. Fed. **37** F2
Plouzané France **52** B2
Plovdiv Bulg. **58** B2
Plungė Lith. **36** B2
Plyeshchanitsy Belarus **36** C3
Plymouth Montserrat **131** D3
Plymouth U.K. **47** A4
Plyussa Rus. Fed. **36** C2
Plzeň Czech Rep. **50** C3
Pô Burkina **90** B3
Po r. Italy **56** B1
Pobeda Peak China/Kyrg. **81** F2
Pocahontas U.S.A. **124** B1
Pocatello U.S.A. **118** D2
Pochayiv Ukr. **38** C1
Pochep Rus. Fed. **37** D3
Pochinok Rus. Fed. **37** D3
Pochutla Mex. **129** C3
Pocomoke City U.S.A. **123** E3
Poços de Caldas Brazil **139** C2
Podbořany Czech Rep. **49** F2
Poděbrady Rus. Fed. **37** D2
Podgorenskiy Rus. Fed. **39** E1
Podgorica Serb. **58** A2
Podkamennaya Tunguska r.
Rus. Fed. **87** I2
Podol'sk Rus. Fed. **37** E2
Podařaddere S. Africa **98** A2
Pogar Rus. Fed. **37** D3
Pogradec Albania **59** B2
P'ohang S. Korea **69** B2
Pohnpei atoll Micronesia **100**
Poiana Mare Romania **38** B3
Poim Rus. Fed. **37** F3
Pointe-Noire Congo **94** B3
Point Lake Can. **113** D1
Poitiers France **52** C2
Pokaran India **78** B2
Pokhara Nepal **79** C2
Pokrovsk Rus. Fed. **87** K2

Pokrovskoye Rus. Fed. **39** E3
Polacca U.S.A. **126** B1
Pola de Lena Spain **54** B1
Poland country Europe **51** D2
Polatsk Belarus **36** C2
Pol-e Khomrī Afgh. **78** A1
Police Pol. **50** C2
Policoro Italy **57** C2
Polillo Islands Phil. **68** B2
Polis'ke Ukr. **38** C1
Pollino, Monte mt. Italy **57** C3
Polohy Ukr. **39** E2
Polokwane S. Africa **99** C1
Polonne Ukr. **38** C1
Polson U.S.A. **118** D1
Poltava Ukr. **39** D2
Poltavka Rus. Fed. **70** B2
Poltavskaya Rus. Fed. **39** E2
Põlva Estonia **36** C2
Polyarnyy Rus. Fed. **40** G2
Polyarnyye Zori Rus. Fed. **40** G2
Polygyros Greece **59** B2
Polykastro Greece **84** A1
Polynesia is Pacific Ocean
142 E5
Pomezia Italy **56** B2
Pomokaira reg. Fin. **40** F2
Pomorie Bulg. **58** C2
Pomorska, Zatoka b. Pol. **50** C2
Pompéu Brazil **139** D1
Ponca City U.S.A. **127** E1
Ponce Puerto Rico **131** D3
Pondicherry India **77** B3
Pond Inlet Can. **112** G1
Ponferrada Spain **54** B1
Pongo watercourse Sudan **93** A4
Pongola r. S. Africa **99** D2
Ponta Grossa Brazil **138** B3
Pontalina Brazil **138** C1
Pont-à-Mousson France **53** D2
Ponta Porã Brazil **138** A2
Pontarlier France **53** D2
Pontchartrain, Lake U.S.A.
124 B2
Pontes-e-Lacerda Brazil **134** D4
Pontevedra Spain **54** B1
Pontiac Il. U.S.A. **122** C2
Pontiac MI U.S.A. **122** D2
Pontianak Indon. **64** B2
Pontivy France **52** B2
Pontoetoe Suriname **135** C3
Pontoise France **43** D4
Ponton Can. **113** F2
Pontypool U.K. **47** B4
Ponziane, Isole is Italy **56** B2
Poochera Austr. **104** A2
Poole U.K. **47** C4
Poona India see Pune
Pooncarie Austr. **104** C2
Poopó, Lago de l. Bol. **136** B2
Popayán Col. **134** B2
Popiltah Austr. **104** C2
Poplar r. Can. **113** F2
Poplar Bluff U.S.A. **121** E3

Popocatépetl, Volcán vol. Mex.
129 C3
Popokabaka Dem. Rep. Congo
94 B3
Popovo Bulg. **58** C2
Poprad Slovakia **51** E3
Porangatu Brazil **135** E4
Porbandar India **78** A2
Pori Fin. **41** E3
Porirua N.Z. **106** B3
Porkhov Rus. Fed. **36** C2
Poronaysk Rus. Fed. **73** F1
Poros Greece **59** B3
Porsgrunn Norway **41** B4
Portadown U.K. **45** C1
Portaferry U.K. **45** D1
Portage U.S.A. **122** C2
Portage la Prairie Can. **113** F3
Port Alberni Can. **112** C3
Portalegre Port. **54** B2
Portales U.S.A. **127** D2
Port Alice Can. **112** C2
Port Angeles U.S.A. **118** B1
Port Arthur U.S.A. **127** F3
Port Askaig U.K. **44** A3
Port Augusta Austr. **104** B2
Port-au-Prince Haiti **131** C3
Port aux Choix Can. **115** E1
Port Blair India **67** A2
Port Campbell Austr. **104** C3
Port Chalmers N.Z. **106** C4
Port Charlotte U.S.A. **125** D3
Port-de-Paix Haiti **131** C3
Port Edward Can. **112** B2
Porteirinha Brazil **139** D1
Port Elgin Can. **114** B2
Port Elizabeth S. Africa **99** C3
Port Ellen U.K. **44** A3
Port Erin Isle of Man **46** A2
Port Fairy Austr. **104** C3
Port Fitzroy N.Z. **106** C2
Port-Gentil Gabon **94** A3
Port Harcourt Nigeria **91** C4
Port Hardy Can. **112** C2
Port Hedland Austr. **102** A2
Porthmadog U.K. **46** A3
Port Hope Simpson Can. **115** E2
Port Huron U.S.A. **122** D2
Portimão Port. **54** B2
Portland N.S.W. Austr. **105** D2
Portland Vic. Austr. **104** C3
Portland ME U.S.A. **123** F2
Portland OR U.S.A. **118** B1
Portland Canal inlet Can. **112** B2
Portlaoise Ireland **45** C2
Port Lavaca U.S.A. **127** E3
Port Lincoln Austr. **104** B2
Port Louis Mauritius **89**
Port Macquarie Austr. **105** E2
Port McNeill Can. **112** C2
Port-Menier Can. **115** D2
Port Moresby P.N.G. **63** D3
Port Ness U.K. **44** A1
Port Nolloth S. Africa **98** A2

Port. see Oporto
Alegre Brazil **136** C4
Esperidião Brazil **134** D4
oferraio Italy **56** B2
Franco Brazil **135** E3
of Spain Trin. and Tob.
D3
ogruaro Italy **56** B1
Murtinho Brazil **136** C3
Nacional Brazil **138** E4
Novo Benin **90** C4
Primavera, Represa *resr*
zil **138** B2
Santana Brazil **135** D3
Seguro Brazil **139** E1
Tolle Italy **56** B2
Torres Italy **56** A2
Vecchio France **53** D3
Phillip Bay Austr. **104** C3
Pirie Austr. **104** B2
ee U.K. **44** A2
ush U.K. **45** C1
Said Egypt **92** B1
Shepstone S. Africa **99** D3
smouth U.K. **47** C4
smouth *NH* U.S.A. **123** F2
smouth *OH* U.S.A. **122** D3
smouth *VA* U.S.A. **123** E3
stewart U.K. **45** C1
St Joe U.S.A. **125** C3
St Johns S. Africa **99** C3
Sudan Sudan **92** A2
Sulphur U.S.A. **124** C3
Talbot U.K. **47** B4
ugal *country* Europe **54** B2
Vendres France **53** D3
Vila Vanuatu **100**
oo Fin. **41** F3
adas Arg. **136** C3
ekhon'ye Rus. Fed. **37** E2
o Fin. **40** F2
Indon. **65** D2
o Brazil **135** E4
eck Ger. **49** E2
U.S.A. **127** D2
e-de-la-Baleine Can. *see*
ajjuarapik
nasburg S. Africa **98** B2
au U.S.A. **127** F1
nza Italy **57** C2
Georgia **85** C1
kum Nigeria **91** D3
mac, South Branch *r.* U.S.A.
E3
si Bol. **136** B2
tan Phil. **68** B2
ero del Llano Mex. **126** D3
dam Ger. **49** F1
dam U.S.A. **123** F2
town U.S.A. **123** E2
sville U.S.A. **123** E2
h Cove Can. **115** E2

Poughkeepsie U.S.A. **123** F2
Pouso Alegre Brazil **139** C2
Poŭthisǎt Cambodia **67** B2
Povlen *mt.* S.M. **58** A2
Póvoa de Varzim Port. **54** B1
Povorino Rus. Fed. **39** F1
Powell U.S.A. **120** B2
Powell, Lake *resr* U.S.A. **119** D3
Powell River Can. **112** C3
Pozorén Brazil **138** B1
Poza Rica Mex. **129** C2
Požega Croatia **57** C1
Požega S.M. **58** B2
Pozm Tiāb Iran **83** D2
Poznań Pol. **51** C2
Pozoblanco Spain **54** C2
Pozzuoli Italy **56** B2
Prabumulih Indon. **64** B2
Prachatice Czech Rep. **50** C3
Prachuap Khiri Khan Thai. **67** A2
Prado Brazil **139** E1
Prague Czech Rep. **50** C2
Praha Czech Rep. *see* Prague
Praia Cape Verde **88**
Prairie Dog Town Fork *r.* U.S.A. **127** D2
Prairie du Chien U.S.A. **122** B2
Prata Italy **53** E3
Prato Italy **53** E3
Pratt U.S.A. **121** D3
Praya Indon. **65** C2
Preäh Vihear Cambodia **67** B2
Prechistoye Rus. Fed. **37** F2
Preili Latvia **36** C2
Premer Austr. **105** D2
Premnitz Ger. **49** F1
Prenzlau Ger. **49** F1
Preparis Island Cocos Is **67** A2
Preparis North Channel Cocos Is **67** A2
Preparis South Channel Cocos Is **67** A2
Přerov Czech Rep. **51** D3
Prescott U.S.A. **126** B2
Presidencia Roque Sáenz Peña Arg. **136** B3
Presidente Dutra Brazil **135** E3
Presidente Epitácio Brazil **138** B2
Presidente Prudente Brazil **138** B2
Presidio U.S.A. **126** D3
Prešov Slovakia **51** E3
Presque Isle U.S.A. **123** G1
Přeštice Czech Rep. **49** F3
Preston U.K. **46** B3
Preto *r.* Brazil **139** D1
Pretoria S. Africa **99** C2
Preveza Greece **59** B3
Prey Vêng Cambodia **67** B2
Priboj S.M. **58** A2
Price U.S.A. **119** D3
Prienai Lith. **36** B3
Prieska S. Africa **98** B2

Prievidza Slovakia **51** D3
Prijedor Bos.-Herz. **57** C2
Prikaspiyskaya Nizmennost' *lowland* Kazakh./Rus. Fed. see Caspian Lowland
Prilep Macedonia **59** B2
Primorsko-Akhtarsk Rus. Fed. **39** E2
Primrose Lake Can. **113** E2
Prince Albert Can. **110** E3
Prince Albert Peninsula Can. **110** E2
Prince Alfred, Cape Can. **110** D2
Prince Charles Island Can. **111** G2
Prince Charles Mountains Antarctica **107** E2
Prince Edward Island *prov.* Can. **115** D2
Prince George Can. **112** C2
Prince of Wales Island Can. **110** F2
Prince of Wales Island U.S.A. **112** B2
Prince Patrick Island Can. **110** E1
Prince Rupert Can. **112** B2
Princess Charlotte Bay Austr. **103** D1
Princess Royal Island Can. **112** C2
Príncipe *i.* São Tomé and Príncipe **94** A2
Priozersk Rus. Fed. **41** G3
Pripet *r.* Belarus see Prypyats'
Pripet Marshes Belarus/Ukr. **36** B3
Priština S.M. **58** B2
Pritzwalk Ger. **49** F1
Privolzhsk Rus. Fed. **37** F2
Prizren S.M. **58** B2
Professor van Blommestein Meer *resr* Suriname **135** D2
Progreso Mex. **129** D2
Prokhladnyy Rus. Fed. **85** C1
Prokop'je Rus. Fed. **89** F2
Proletarsk Rus. Fed. **39** F2
Prophet *r.* Can. **110** D3
Prophet River Can. **112** C2
Proserpine Austr. **103** D2
Protvino Rus. Fed. **37** E3
Provence *reg.* France **53** D3
Providence U.S.A. **123** F2
Providencia, Isla de *i.* Caribbean Sea **130** B3
Provideniya Rus. Fed. **87** O2
Provo U.S.A. **118** D2
Provost Can. **113** D2
Prudentópolis Brazil **138** B3
Prudhoe Bay U.S.A. **110** C2
Prüm Ger. **48** C2
Pruszków Pol. **51** E2
Prut *r.* Europe **38** C2

Pryluky Ukr. **39** D1
Prymors'k Ukr. **39** E2
Pryor U.S.A. **127** E1
Pryp'yats' r. Belarus **36** C3
Przemyśl Pol. **51** E3
Psara i. Greece **59** C3
Pshekha r. Rus. Fed. **39** E3
Pskov Rus. Fed. **36** C2
Pskov, Lake Estonia/Rus. Fed. **36** C2
Ptolemaïda Greece **59** B2
Ptuj Slovenia **57** C1
Pucallpa Peru **134** B3
Pucheng China **75** B3
Puchezh Rus. Fed. **37** F2
Puch'ŏn S. Korea **69** B1
Pudasjärvi Fin. **40** F2
Pudong China **74** C2
Puebla Mex. **129** C3
Pueblo U.S.A. **127** E3
Puente-Genil Spain **54** C2
Puerto Ángel Mex. **129** C3
Puerto Armuelles Panama **130** B4
Puerto Ayacucho Venez. **134** C2
Puerto Barrios Guat. **129** D3
Puerto Cabezas Nic. **130** B3
Puerto Carreño Venez. **134** C2
Puerto Cortés Mex. **128** A2
Puerto Escondido Mex. **129** C3
Puerto Frey Bol. **134** B2
Puerto Inírida Col. **134** C2
Puerto Isabel Bol. **136** C2
Puerto Libertad Mex. **128** A2
Puerto Limón Costa Rica **130** B3
Puertollano Spain **54** C2
Puerto Madryn Arg. **137** B6
Puerto Maldonado Peru **134** C4
Puerto Montt Chile **137** A5
Puerto Natales Chile **137** A6
Puerto Peñasco Mex. **128** A1
Puerto Princesa Phil. **68** A3
Puerto Rico Arg. **138** A3
Puerto Rico terr. West Indies **131** D3
Puerto Rico Trench sea feature Caribbean Sea **144** B4
Puerto San José Guat. **130** A3
Puerto Vallarta Mex. **128** B2
Pukaki, Lake N.Z. **106** B3
Pukatawagan Can. **113** C2
Pukchin N. Korea **69** B1
Pukch'ŏng N. Korea **69** B1
Pukekohe N.Z. **106** B2
Puksubaek-san mt. N. Korea **69** B1
Pula Croatia **56** B2
Pulkkila Fin. **40** F3
Pullman U.S.A. **118** C1
Pulog, Mount Phil. **68** B2
Puná, Isla i. Ecuador **134** A3
Punakaiki N.Z. **106** B3

Pune India **77** B3
P'ungsan N. Korea **69** B1
Púngué r. Moz. **97** C1
Punta Alta Arg. **137** B4
Punta Arenas Chile **137** A6
Punta del Este Uru. **137** C4
Punta Gorda Belize **129** D3
Puntarenas Costa Rica **130** B3
Punto Fijo Venez. **134** B1
Pur r. Rus. Fed. **34** G2
Puri India **79** C3
Purmerend Neth. **48** B1
Puruliya India **79** C2
Purus r. Peru **134** C3
Puryŏng N. Korea **69** B1
Pusan S. Korea **69** B2
Pustoshka Rus. Fed. **36** C2
Putao Myanmar **66** A1
Putian China **75** B3
Puting, Tanjung pt Indon. **65** C2
Putrajaya Malaysia **64** B1
Puttgarden Ger. **50** C2
Putumayo r. Col. **134** B3
Putusibau Indon. **65** C1
Putyvl' Ukr. **39** D1
Puvurnituq Can. **114** C1
Puyang China **74** B2
Pwllheli U.K. **46** A3
Pyapon Myanmar **66** A2
Pyasina r. Rus. Fed. **86** H2
Pyatigorsk Rus. Fed. **35** D4
P'yatykhatky Ukr. **39** D2
Pyè Myanmar **66** A2
Pyetrykaw Belarus **36** C3
Pyhäjärvi l. Fin. **41** F3
Pyhäjoki r. Fin. **40** F3
Pyhäsalmi Fin. **40** F3
Pyinmana Myanmar **66** A2
Pyŏksŏng N. Korea **69** B2
P'yŏngsan N. Korea **69** B2
P'yŏngyang N. Korea **69** B2
P'yŏngyang N. Korea **69** B2
Pyramid Lake U.S.A. **118** C2
Pyramids of Giza tourist site Egypt **84** B3
Pyrenees mts Europe **55** D1
Pyrgos Greece **59** B3
Pyryatyn Ukr. **39** D1
Pyrzyce Pol. **50** C2
Pytalovo Rus. Fed. **36** C2
Pyxaria mt. Greece **59** B3

Q

Qaanaaq Greenland see **Thule**
Qacha's Nek Lesotho **99** C3
Qādub Yemen **83** C3
Qagan Nur China **69** A1
Qaidam Pendi basin China **72** C2
Qalansīyah Yemen **83** C3

Qal'at Bīshah Saudi Arabia **82** B2
Qamanirjuaq Lake Can. **113** F1
Qamar, Ghubbat al b. Yemen **83** C3
Qarshi Uzbek. **81** D3
Qaryat al Ulyā Saudi Arabia **83** B2
Qasigiannguit Greenland **111**
Qassimiut Greenland **111** I2
Qatar country Asia **83** C2
Qattara Depression Egypt **92** A2
Qausuittuq Can. see **Resolute**
Qazax Azer. **85** C1
Qazimämmäd Azer. **85** C1
Qazvīn Iran **85** C2
Qeqertarsuaq i. Greenland **111** I2
Qeqertarsuatsiaat Greenland **111** I2
Qeqertarsuup Tunua b. Greenland **111** I2
Qeshm Iran **83** C2
Qianjiang Chongqing China **75** A3
Qian Shan mts China **69** A1
Qiemo China **81** F3
Qijiang China **75** A3
Qijiaojing China **72** C2
Qikiqtarjuaq Can. **111** H2
Qilian Shan mts China **72** C2
Qillak i. Greenland **111** J2
Qimusseriarsuaq b. Greenland **111** H1
Qinā Egypt **92** B2
Qingdao China **74** C2
Qinghai prov. China **79** D1
Qinghai Hu salt l. China **72** C2
Qinghai Nanshan mts China **72** C2
Qingyuan Guangdong China **75** B3
Qingyuan Liaoning China **69** A1
Qingzang Gaoyuan plat. China see **Tibet, Plateau of**
Qingzhou China **74** B2
Qinhuangdao China **74** B2
Qin Ling mts China **74** A2
Qinzhou China **75** A3
Qionghai China **75** B4
Qionglai Shan mts China **74** A2
Qiqihar China **73** E1
Qitaihe China **70** E1
Qixian China **74** B2
Qogir Feng mt. China/Jammu and Kashmir see **K2**
Qom Iran **85** C2
Qomolangma Feng mt. China/Nepal see **Everest, Mount**
Qo'ng'irot Uzbek. **80** C2
Qo'qon Uzbek. **81** C2
Qoraqalpog'iston Uzbek. **80**

224

kenbrück Ger. **48** C1
ng Ngai Vietnam **67** B2
ng Tri Vietnam **66** B2
nzhou *Fujian* China **75** B3
nzhou *Guangxi* China **75** B3
rtu Sant'Elena Italy **56** A3
rtzsite U.S.A. **126** B2
s Azer. **95** C2
anbeyan Austr. **105** D3
bec Can. **115** C2
bec *prov.* Can. **114** C1
dlinburg Ger. **49** E2
en Charlotte Can. **112** B2
en Charlotte Islands Can. 2 B2
en Charlotte Sound a *chan.* Can. **112** C2
en Charlotte Strait Can. 2 C2
en Elizabeth Islands Can. 0 E1
en Maud Gulf Can. **110** F2
en Maud Land *reg.* Antarctica 7 C2
en Maud Mountains antarctica **107** I1
ensland *state* Austr. **103** D2
enstown Austr. **103** D4
enstown N.Z. **106** A4
enstown S. Africa **99** C3
mlimane Moz. **97** C1
mado U.S.A. **126** C2
erétaro Mex. **129** B2
erfurt Ger. **49** E2
snel Can. **112** C2
snel Lake Can. **112** C2
tta Pak. **78** A1
zaltenango Guat. **29** C3
zon City Phil. **68** B2
bala Angola **96** A1
odo Col. **134** B2
beron France **52** B2
mes Arg. **137** C4
on India **77** B4
pie Austr. **103** D2
pué Chile **137** A4
mbole Angola **94** B3
mper France **52** B2
mperlé France **52** B2
ncy *IL* U.S.A. **122** B3
ncy *MA* U.S.A. **123** F2
nto Spain **55** C1
onga Moz. **95** E4
rindi Austr. **105** E2
tapa Angola **94** B4
to Ecuador **134** B3
xadá Brazil **135** F3
ng China **75** B3
nar He *r.* China **79** D1
bich *r.* Can. **113** F1
rn Austr. **104** B2

Qurayat Oman **83** C2
Qürghonteppa Tajik. **81** D3
Quzhou China **75** B3

R

Raab *r.* Austria **51** D3
Raahe Fin. **40** E3
Raalte Neth. **48** C1
Raas i. Indon. **65** C2
Raba Indon. **65** C2
Rabat Morocco **90** B1
Rābigh Saudi Arabia **82** A2
Race, Cape Can. **115** E2
Rach Gia Vietnam **67** B3
Racine U.S.A. **122** C2
Radā' Yemen **82** B3
Rădăuți Romania **38** C2
Radcliff U.S.A. **122** C3
Radebeul Ger. **49** F2
Radhanpur India **78** B2
Radisson Can. **114** C1
Radom Pol. **51** E2
Radomsko Pol. **51** D2
Radomyshl' Ukr. **38** C1
Radoviš Macedonia **57** D2
Radviliškis Lith. **36** B2
Radwá, Jabal *mt.* Saudi Arabia **82** A2
Radyvyliv Ukr. **38** C1
Rae Bareli India **79** C2
Rae-Edzo Can. **112** D1
Rae Lakes Can. **112** D1
Raetihi N.Z. **106** C2
Rafaela Arg. **136** B4
Rafaï C.A.R. **94** C2
Raffā' Saudi Arabia **82** B2
Rafsanjān Iran **85** D2
Ragusa Italy **56** B3
Raha Indon. **65** D2
Rahachow Belarus **39** D3
Rahimyar Khan Pak. **78** B2
Raichur India **77** B3
Raigarh India **79** C2
Rainbow Lake Can. **112** D2
Rainier, Mount *vol.* U.S.A. **118** B1
Rainy Lake Can./U.S.A. **113** F3
Rainy River Can. **113** F3
Raipur India **79** C2
Raisio Fin. **41** E3
Rajahmundry India **77** C3
Rajang *r.* Malaysia **65** C1
Rajanpur Pak. **78** B2
Rajapalaiyam India **77** B4
Rajasthan Canal India **78** B2
Rajkot India **78** B2
Rajshahi Bangl. **79** C2
Rakaia *r.* N.Z. **106** B3
Rakhiv Ukr. **38** B2
Rakitnoye Rus. Fed. **39** E1
Rakovník Czech Rep. **49** F2

Rakvere Estonia **36** C2
Raleigh U.S.A. **125** E1
Rambutyo Island P.N.G. **63** D3
Ramgarh India **78** B2
Rämhormoz Iran **85** C2
Rāmnicu Sărat Romania **38** C2
Rāmnicu Vâlcea Romania **38** B2
Ramon' Rus. Fed. **37** E3
Ramotswa Botswana **99** C1
Rampur India **79** B2
Ramree Island Myanmar **66** A2
Ramsey Isle of Man **46** A2
Ramsgate U.K. **47** D4
Ramsing India **66** A1
Ranaghat India **79** C2
Ranau Malaysia **65** C1
Rancagua Chile **137** A4
Ranchi India **79** C2
Randers Denmark **41** C4
Rangiora N.Z. **106** B3
Rangitaiki *r.* N.Z. **106** C2
Rangoon Myanmar **66** A2
Rangpur Bangl. **79** C2
Rankin Inlet Can. **113** F1
Rankin's Springs Austr. **105** D2
Rannoch Moor *moorland* U.K. **44** B2
Ranong Thai. **67** A3
Ransiki Indon. **63** C3
Rantaupanjang Indon. **65** C2
Rantauprapat Indon. **64** A1
Rantepao Indon. **65** C2
Ranua Fin. **40** F2
Ranyah, Wādī *watercourse* Saudi Arabia **82** B2
Rapa i. Fr. Polynesia **101**
Rapid City U.S.A. **120** C2
Rapla Estonia **36** B2
Rapur India **78** A2
Rasa, Punta *pt* Arg. **137** B5
Ra's al Khaymah U.A.E. **83** C2
Ras Dejen *mt.* Eth. **93** B3
Raseiniai Lith. **36** B2
Ra's Ghārib Egypt **84** B3
Rasht Iran **85** C2
Ras Koh *mt.* Pak. **78** A2
Rasony Belarus **36** C2
Rasskazovo Rus. Fed. **37** F3
Rastede Ger. **49** D1
Rätan Sweden **41** C3
Ratangarh India **78** B2
Rat Buri Thai. **67** A2
Rathedaung Myanmar **66** A1
Rathenow Ger. **49** F1
Rathlin Island U.K. **45** C1
Ratlam India **78** B2
Ratnagiri India **77** B3
Ratnapura Sri Lanka **77** C4
Ratne Ukr. **38** B1
Raton U.S.A. **126** D1
Rattray Head U.K. **44** D2
Ratzeburg Ger. **49** E1
Raufarhöfn Iceland **40** [inset]

Raukumara Range *mts* N.Z. **106** C2
Rauma Fin. **41** E3
Raurkela India **79** C3
Ravalli U.S.A. **118** D1
Ravānsar Iran **85** C2
Ravenna Italy **56** B2
Ravensburg Ger. **50** B3
Ravi *r.* Pak. **78** B1
Rawalpindi Pak. **78** B1
Rawicz Pol. **51** D2
Rawlinna Austr. **102** B3
Rawlins U.S.A. **120** B2
Rawson Arg. **137** B5
Raydah Yemen **82** B3
Rayevskiy Rus. Fed. **35** E3
Raymond Can. **118** D1
Raymond Terrace Austr. **105** E2
Raymondville U.S.A. **127** E3
Rayón Mex. **129** C2
Rayong Thai. **67** B2
Rayyis Saudi Arabia **82** A2
Raz, Pointe du *pt* France **52** B2
Razāzah, Buḩayrat ar *l.* Iraq **85** C2
Razgrad Bulg. **58** C2
Razim, Lacul *lag.* Romania **38** C3
Ré, Île de *i.* France **52** B2
Reading U.K. **47** C4
Reading U.S.A. **123** D2
Rebiana Sand Sea *des.* Libya **91** E2
Rebun-tō *i.* Japan **70** D1
Recherche, Archipelago of the *is* Austr. **102** B3
Rechytsa Belarus **37** D3
Recife Brazil **135** F3
Recklinghausen Ger. **48** C2
Reconquista Arg. **136** C3
Red *r.* U.S.A. **127** E2
Red Bay Can. **115** E1
Red Bluff U.S.A. **118** B2
Redcar U.K. **46** C2
Red Cliffs Austr. **104** C2
Red Deer Can. **112** D2
Red Deer *r.* Can. **110** E3
Red Deer Lake Can. **113** E2
Redding U.S.A. **118** B2
Redditch U.K. **47** C3
Redfield U.S.A. **121** D2
Red Lake Can. **114** A1
Red Lakes U.S.A. **121** E1
Redmond U.S.A. **118** B2
Red Oak U.S.A. **121** D2
Red Sea Africa/Asia **82** A2
Redstone *r.* Can. **112** C1
Reduzum Neth. **48** B1
Red Wing U.S.A. **121** E2
Redwood Falls U.S.A. **121** D2
Ree, Lough *l.* Ireland **45** C2
Reedsport U.S.A. **118** B2
Reefton N.Z. **106** B3
Regen Ger. **49** F3
Regência Brazil **139** D1
Regensburg Ger. **49** F3
Regenstauf Ger. **49** F3
Reggane Alg. **90** C2
Reggio di Calabria Italy **57** C3
Reggio nell'Emilia Italy **56** B2
Reghin Romania **38** B2
Regina Can. **110** F3
Rehoboth Namibia **98** A1
Reichenbach Ger. **49** F2
Reidsville U.S.A. **125** E1
Reigate U.K. **47** C4
Reims France **53** C2
Reina Adelaida, Archipiélago de la *is* Chile **137** A6
Reinbek Ger. **49** E1
Reindeer *r.* Can. **113** E2
Reindeer Island Can. **113** F2
Reindeer Lake Can. **113** E2
Reine Norway **40** C2
Reinsfeld Ger. **48** C3
Reitz S. Africa **99** C2
Reivilo S. Africa **98** B2
Reliance Can. **113** E1
Relizane Alg. **55** D2
Remeshk Iran **83** C2
Remiremont France **53** D2
Remscheid Ger. **48** C2
Rendsburg Ger. **50** B2
Renfrew Can. **123** E1
Rengat Indon. **64** B2
Reni Ukr. **38** C2
Renmark Austr. **104** C2
Rennes France **52** B2
Rennie Lake Can. **113** E1
Reno *r.* Italy **56** B2
Reno U.S.A. **119** C3
Renukut India **79** C2
Renwick N.Z. **106** B3
Reo Indon. **65** D2
Republican *r.* U.S.A. **120** D3
Repulse Bay Can. **111** G2
Requena Peru **134** B3
Requena Spain **55** C2
Resistencia Arg. **136** C3
Reşiţa Romania **38** B2
Resolute Can. **110** F2
Resolution Island Can. **111** H2
Rethel France **53** C2
Rethymno Greece **59** B3
Réunion *terr.* Indian Ocean **89**
Reus Spain **55** D1
Reutlingen Ger. **50** B3
Revelstoke Can. **112** D2
Revillagigedo, Islas *is* Mex. **128** A3
Revillagigedo Island U.S.A. **112** B2
Rewa India **79** C2
Rexburg U.S.A. **118** D2
Reykjanestá *pt* Iceland **40** [inset]
Reykjavík Iceland **40** [inset]
Reynosa Mex. **129** C2
Rēzekne Latvia **36** C2
Rhein *r.* Ger. *see* Rhine
Rheine Ger. **48** C1
Rhin *r.* France *see* Rhine
Rhine *r.* France **50** B3
Rhine *r.* Ger. **48** C2
Rhinelander U.S.A. **122** C1
Rhinluch *marsh* Ger. **49** F1
Rhode Island *state* U.S.A. **123**
Rhodes Greece **59** C3
Rhodes *i.* Greece **59** C3
Rhodope Mountains Bulg./Greece **58** B2
Rhône *r.* France/Switz. **53** C3
Rhoufi Alg. **55** E2
Rhyl U.K. **46** B3
Riau, Kepulauan *is* Indon. **64**
Ribadeo Spain **54** B1
Ribas do Rio Pardo Brazil **138** B2
Ribauè Moz. **97** C1
Ribécourt-Dreslincourt France **48** A3
Ribeira *r.* Brazil **138** C2
Ribeirão Preto Brazil **138** C2
Riberalta Bol. **136** B2
Rîbniţa Moldova **38** C2
Ribnitz-Damgarten Ger. **50** C1
Rice Lake U.S.A. **122** B1
Richards Bay S. Africa **99** D2
Richardson Mountains Can. **110** C2
Richfield U.S.A. **119** D3
Richland U.S.A. **118** C1
Richmond *N.S.W.* Austr. **105** E1
Richmond *Qld* Austr. **103** D2
Richmond N.Z. **106** B3
Richmond U.K. **46** C2
Richmond *IN* U.S.A. **122** D3
Richmond *KY* U.S.A. **122** D3
Richmond *VA* U.S.A. **123** E3
Rideau Lakes Can. **114** C2
Ridgecrest U.S.A. **119** C3
Riesa Ger. **49** F2
Rietberg Ger. **49** D2
Rieti Italy **56** B2
Rifle U.S.A. **120** B3
Riga Latvia **36** B2
Riga, Gulf of Estonia/Latvia **41** E4
Rīgān Iran **83** C2
Rigolet Can. **115** E1
Riihimäki Fin. **41** E3
Rijeka Croatia **56** B1
Riley U.S.A. **118** C2
Rimah, Wādī al *watercourse* Saudi Arabia **82** B2
Rimavská Sobota Slovakia **51**
Rimini Italy **56** B2
Rimouski Can. **115** D2
Ringebu Norway **41** B3
Ringkøbing Denmark **41** B4
Ringvassøya *i.* Norway **40** D2
Rinteln Ger. **49** D1
Riobamba Ecuador **134** B3
Rio Branco Brazil **134** C4

Brilhante Brazil **138** B2
Claro Brazil **138** C2
Colorado Arg. **137** B4
Cuarto Arg. **137** B4
de Janeiro Brazil **139** D2
do Sul Brazil **138** C3
Gallegos Arg. **137** B6
Grande Arg. **137** B6
Grande Brazil **136** C4
Grande Mex. **128** B2
Grande r. Mex./U.S.A. **128** C2
Grande City U.S.A. **127** E3
acha Col. **134** B1
Lagartos Mex. **129** D2
n France **53** C2
Mulatos Bol. **136** B2
Negro Brazil **138** C3
Pardo de Minas Brazil
9 D1
Rancho U.S.A. **126** C1
Tigre Ecuador **134** B3
Verde Brazil **138** B1
Verde Mex. **129** C2
Verde de Mato Grosso Brazil
8 B1
xy Ukr. **38** D1
oll Spain **55** D1
on U.K. **46** C2
airi-tō i. Japan **70** D1
er Norway **41** B4
hie's Africa **98** B2
hie's Archipelago is India
A2
ville U.S.A. **118** C1
del Garda Italy **56** B1
as Nic. **130** B3
ara Ukr. **136** C4
erina reg. Austr. **105** C2
ersdale S. Africa **98** B3
rside U.S.A. **119** C4
erton U.S.A. **120** B2
rview Can. **115** D2
ière-du-Loup Can. **115** D2
ie Ukr. **38** C1
aka N.Z. **106** B3
dh Saudi Arabia **82** B2
o Turkey **85** C1
nao China **74** B2
ne France **53** C2
noke U.S.A. **123** E3
noke r. U.S.A. **125** E1
noke Rapids U.S.A. **125** E1
r Austr. **104** B3
el Ger. **49** F1
ertsfors Sweden **40** E3
ertsport Liberia **90** A4
erval Can. **115** C2
inson Range hills Austr.
2 A2
invale Austr. **104** C2
alin Can. **113** E2
son, Mount Can. **112** D2
ca Busambra mt. Italy **56** B3
ha Uru. **137** C4

Rochdale U.K. **46** B3
Rochefort Belgium **48** B2
Rochefort France **52** B2
Rochester MN U.S.A. **121** E2
Rochester NY U.S.A. **123** E2
Rockford U.S.A. **122** C2
Rockhampton Austr. **103** E2
Rock Hill U.S.A. **125** D2
Rockingham Austr. **102** A3
Rock Springs MT U.S.A. **120** B1
Rocksprings U.S.A. **127** D3
Rock Springs WY U.S.A. **120** B2
Rocky Ford U.S.A. **120** C3
Rocky Mount U.S.A. **125** E1
Rocky Mountains Can./U.S.A.
116 C2
Rocroi France **48** B3
Rødbyhavn Denmark **50** C2
Rodez France **52** C3
Roding Ger. **49** F3
Rodniki Rus. Fed. **37** F2
Rodos Greece see Rhodes
Rodos i. Greece see Rhodes
Roebourne Austr. **102** A2
Roebuck Bay Austr. **102** B1
Roermond Neth. **48** B2
Roeselare Belgium **48** A2
Roggeveldberge esc. S. Africa
98 B3
Rognan Norway **40** D2
Rogue r. U.S.A. **118** B2
Rokan r. Indon. **64** B1
Rokiškis Lith. **41** D5
Rokycany Czech Rep. **49** F3
Rokytne Ukr. **38** C1
Rolla U.S.A. **121** E3
Roma Austr. **103** D2
Roma Italy see Rome
Romain, Cape U.S.A. **125** E2
Roman Romania **38** C2
Romania country Europe **38** B2
Roman-Kosh mt. Ukr. **39** D3
Romanovka Respublika Buryatiya
Rus. Fed. **73** D1
Romanovka Saratovskaya Oblast'
Rus. Fed. **39** F1
Romblon Phil. **68** B2
Rome Italy **56** B2
Rome GA U.S.A. **125** C2
Romilly-sur-Seine France **53** C2
Romny Ukr. **39** D1
Romorantin-Lanthenay France
52 C2
Romsey U.K. **47** C4
Roncador, Serra do hills Brazil
135 D4
Ronda Spain **54** B2
Rondonópolis Brazil **138** B1
Rondu Jammu and Kashmir
78 B1
Rong'an China **75** A3
Rongjiang China **75** A3
Rongklang Range mts Myanmar
66 A1

Rønne Denmark **41** C4
Ronne Ice Shelf Antarctica
107 K2
Ronse Belgium **48** A2
Roorkee India **79** B2
Roosendaal Neth. **48** B2
Roosevelt U.S.A. **118** E2
Roosevelt, Mount Can. **112** C2
Roosevelt Island Antarctica
107 I2
Roraima, Mount Guyana **134** C2
Røros Norway **41** C3
Rosario Arg. **137** B4
Rosario Baja California Mex.
128 A1
Rosario Sinaloa Mex. **128** B2
Rosario Sonora Mex. **128** B2
Rosário Oeste Brazil **135** D4
Rosarito Mex. **128** A2
Rosarno Italy **57** C3
Roscoff France **52** B2
Roscommon Ireland **45** B2
Roseau Dominica **131** D3
Roseau U.S.A. **121** D1
Roseburg U.S.A. **118** B2
Rosenberg U.S.A. **127** E3
Rosendal Norway **42** E2
Rosengarten Ger. **49** D1
Rosenheim Ger. **50** C3
Rosetown Can. **113** E2
Roshchino Rus. Fed. **36** C1
Rosh Pinah Namibia **98** A2
Roşiori de Vede Romania **38** C3
Roskilde Denmark **41** C4
Roslavl' Rus. Fed. **37** D3
Rossano Italy **57** C3
Rossan Point Ireland **45** B1
Ross Ice Shelf Antarctica **107** H1
Rossignol, Lake Can. **115** D2
Rosslare Ireland **45** C2
Rosso Maur. **90** A3
Ross-on-Wye U.K. **47** B4
Rossosh' Rus. Fed. **39** E1
Ross River Can. **112** B1
Rossvatnet l. Norway **40** C2
Rostäq Iran **85** D3
Rostock Ger. **50** C2
Rostov Rus. Fed. **37** E2
Rostov-na-Donu Rus. Fed. **39** E2
Rosvik Sweden **40** E2
Roswell U.S.A. **126** D2
Rota i. N. Mariana Is **63** D2
Rote i. Indon. **63** C3
Rotenburg (Wümme) Ger. **49** D1
Roth Ger. **49** E3
Rothenburg ob der Tauber Ger.
49 E3
Rotherham U.K. **46** C3
Rothesay U.K. **44** B3
Roto Austr. **105** D2
Rotondo, Monte mt. France
53 D3
Rotorua N.Z. **106** C2
Rotorua, Lake N.Z. **106** C2

Rottenmann Austria 50 C3
Rotterdam Neth. 48 B2
Rottweil Ger. 50 B3
Rotuma i. Fiji 100
Roubaix France 53 C1
Rouen France 52 C2
Round Mountain Austr. 105 E2
Round Pond l. Can. 115 E2
Round Rock U.S.A. 127 E2
Roundup U.S.A. 118 E1
Rousay i. U.K. 44 C1
Rouyn-Noranda Can. 114 C2
Rovaniemi Fin. 40 F2
Roven'ki Rus. Fed. 39 E2
Roven'ky Ukr. 39 E2
Rovereto Italy 56 B1
Rovigo Italy 56 B1
Roxas Phil. 68 B2
Roxas Phil. 68 B2
Roxas Phil. 68 B2
Roxas Phil. 68 B3
Roxby Downs Austr. 104 B2
Roy U.S.A. 126 D1
Royale, Isle i. U.S.A. 122 C1
Royan France 52 B2
Roye France 48 A3
Rozdil'na Ukr. 38 D2
Rozdol'ne Ukr. 39 D2
Rtishchevo Rus. Fed. 35 D3
Ruapehu, Mount vol. N.Z. 106 C2
Ruapuke Island N.Z. 106 A4
Rub' al Khālī des. Saudi Arabia 82 B3

Rubtsovsk Rus. Fed. 81 F1
Ruby U.S.A. 110 B2
Ruby Mountains U.S.A. 118 C2
Rudnya Rus. Fed. 37 D3
Rudnyy Kazakh. 80 D1
Rudolstadt Ger. 49 E2
Rufiji r. Tanz. 95 D3
Rufino Arg. 137 B4
Rugby U.K. 47 C3
Rugby U.S.A. 120 C1
Rügen i. Ger. 50 C2
Ruhnu i. Estonia 36 B2
Ruhr r. Ger. 48 C2
Rui'an China 75 C3
Ruidoso U.S.A. 126 C2
Ruiz Mex. 128 B2
Rukwa, Lake Tanz. 95 D3
Rum i. U.K. 44 A2
Ruma S.M. 58 A1
Rumāh Saudi Arabia 82 B2
Rumbek Sudan 93 A4
Runanga N.Z. 106 B3
Runcorn U.K. 46 B3
Rundu Namibia 96 A1
Ruoqiang China 81 F3
Rupert r. Can. 114 C1
Rupert Bay Can. 114 C1
Rusape Zimbabwe 97 C1
Ruse Bulg. 58 C2

Rushville U.S.A. 120 C2
Rushworth Austr. 105 D3
Russell N.Z. 106 B2
Russell N.Z. 106 B2
Russellville AL U.S.A. 124 C2
Russellville AR U.S.A. 124 B1
Rüsselsheim Ger. 49 D2
Russian Federation country Asia/Europe 86 G2
Ruston U.S.A. 124 B2
Ruteng Indon. 65 D2
Ruvuma r. Moz./Tanz. 95 E4
Ruweis U.A.E. 83 C2
Ruzayevka Kazakh. 81 D1
Ruzayevka Rus. Fed. 35 D3
Rwanda country Africa 95 C3
Ryazan' Rus. Fed. 37 E3
Ryazhsk Rus. Fed. 37 F3
Rybachiy, Poluostrov pen. Rus. Fed. 40 G2
Rybinsk Rus. Fed. 37 E2
Rybinskoye Vodokhranilishche resr Rus. Fed. 37 E2
Rybnik Pol. 51 D2
Rybnoye Rus. Fed. 37 E3
Ryl'sk Rus. Fed. 37 D3
Ryōtsu Japan 70 C3
Ryukyu Islands Japan 73 B3
Rzeszów Pol. 51 E2
Rzhaksa Rus. Fed. 37 F3
Rzhev Rus. Fed. 37 D2

S

Saale r. Ger. 49 E2
Saalfeld Ger. 49 E2
Saarbrücken Ger. 48 C3
Saaremaa i. Estonia 36 B2
Saarenkylä Fin. 40 F2
Saarijärvi Fin. 40 F3
Saarlouis Ger. 48 C3
Sab' Ābār Syria 84 B2
Sabadell Spain 55 D1
Sabah state Malaysia 65 C1
Sabalana i. Indon. 65 C2
Sabará Brazil 139 D1
Sabhā Libya 91 D2
Sabinas Mex. 129 B2
Sabinas Hidalgo Mex. 129 B2
Sable, Cape Can. 115 D2
Sable, Cape U.S.A. 125 D3
Sable Island Can. 115 E2
Sabugal Port. 54 B1
Şabyā Saudi Arabia 82 B3
Sabzevār Iran 80 C3
Sachigo Lake Can. 114 A1
Sach'on S. Korea 69 B3
Sachs Harbour Can. 110 D2
Sacramento U.S.A. 119 B3
Sacramento Mountains U.S.A. 126 C2
Sacramento Valley U.S.A. 118 B2
Sada S. Africa 99 C3

Şa'dah Yemen 82 B3
Sadoga-shima i. Japan 70 C3
Sa Dragonera i. Spain 55 D2
Säffle Sweden 41 C4
Safford U.S.A. 126 C2
Saffron Walden U.K. 47 D3
Safi Morocco 90 B1
Safonovo Smolenskaya Oblast' Rus. Fed. 37 D2
Safrā' as Sark esc. Saudi Arabia 82 B2
Saga China 79 C2
Saga Japan 71 B4
Sagaing Myanmar 66 A1
Sagamihara Japan 71 C3
Sagar India 79 B2
Saginaw U.S.A. 122 D2
Saginaw Bay U.S.A. 122 D2
Saguenay r. Can. 123 C1
Sagunto Spain 55 C2
Sahagún Spain 54 B1
Sahara des. Africa 90 C3
Saharan Atlas mts Alg. see Atlas Saharien
Saharanpur India 79 B2
Saharsa India 79 C2
Sahel reg. Africa 90 B3
Sāhiwal Pak. 78 B1
Şahūq reg. Saudi Arabia 82 B2
Saïda Morocco 55 C2
Saidpur Bangl. 79 C2
Saigon Vietnam see Hồ Chí Minh City
Saiha India 66 A1
Saihan Tal China 74 B1
Saiki Japan 71 B4
Saimaa l. Fin. 41 F3
St Abb's Head U.K. 44 C3
St Albans U.K. 47 C4
St Alban's Head U.K. 47 B4
St Aldhelm's Head U.K. see St Alban's Head
St Andrews U.K. 44 C2
St Anthony Can. 115 E1
St Anthony U.S.A. 118 D2
St Arnaud Austr. 104 C3
St-Augustin Can. 115 E1
St Augustin r. Can. 115 E1
St Augustine U.S.A. 125 D3
St Austell U.K. 47 A4
St-Avertin France 52 C2
St-Avold France 48 C3
St Bees Head U.K. 46 B2
St Bride's Bay U.K. 47 A4
St-Brieuc France 52 B2
St Catharines Can. 114 C2
St Catherine's Point U.K. 47 C4
St Charles U.S.A. 122 C3
St Clair, Lake Can./U.S.A. 114 B2
St Cloud U.S.A. 121 E1
St Croix r. U.S.A. 123 B2
St David's Head U.K. 47 A4
St-Denis Réunion 89

228

izier France 53 C2
grève France 53 D2
lias Mountains Can. 110 C2
Marguerite r. Can. 115 D1
te Rose du Lac Can. 113 F2
tes France 52 B2
tienne France 53 C2
lorent France 56 A2
lour France 52 C2
rancis U.S.A. 120 C3
saudens France 52 C3
George U.S.A. 119 D3
George Island U.S.A. 125 D3
Georges Can. 115 C2
George's Grenada 131 D3
George's Channel Ireland/U.K.
 48 B1
otthard Pass Switz. 53 D2
elena i. S. Atlantic Ocean 89
elena and Dependencies
 r. S. Atlantic Ocean
elena Bay b. S. Africa 98 A3
elens U.K. 46 B3
elens, Mount vol. U.S.A.
 B B1
elier Channel Is 47 B5
lubert Belgium 48 B2
lyacinthe Can. 123 F1
gnace U.S.A. 122 D1
gnace Island Can. 114 B2
ves U.K. 47 A4
ames, Cape Can. 112 B2
Jean, Lac l. Can. 115 C2
Jean-sur-Richelieu Can.
 4 C2
érôme Can. 123 F1
oe r. U.S.A. 118 C1
at John Can. 111 H3
John r. U.S.A. 123 G1
John's Antigua 123 D3
John's Can. 115 E2
ohns U.S.A. 126 C2
ohnsbury U.S.A. 123 F2
oseph U.S.A. 121 E3
oseph, Lake Can. 114 A1
oseph Island Can. 114 B2
unien France 52 C2
ilda is U.K. 42 B2
Kitts and Nevis country
 est Indies 131 D3
Laurent, Golfe du g. Can. see
 Lawrence, Gulf of
aurent-du-Maroni Fr. Guiana
 55 D2
awrence inlet Can. 115 D2
awrence, Gulf of Can.
 5 D2
awrence Island U.S.A.
 B A2
ô France 52 B2
ouis Senegal 90 A3
ouis U.S.A. 121 E3
ouis r. U.S.A. 121 E1

St Lucia country West Indies
 131 D3
St Lucia Estuary S. Africa 99 D2
St-Malo France 52 B2
St-Malo, Golfe de g. France
 52 B2
St-Martin i. West Indies 131 D3
St Martin, Cape S. Africa
 98 A3
St Matthias is P.N.G.
 63 D3
St-Nazaire France 52 B2
St-Omer France 52 C1
St Paul U.S.A. 121 E2
St Peter U.S.A. 121 E2
St Peter Port Channel Is 47 B5
St Petersburg Rus. Fed. 37 D2
St Petersburg U.S.A. 125 D3
St-Pierre St Pierre and Miquelon
 115 E2
St Pierre and Miquelon terr.
 N. America 115 E2
St-Pierre-d'Oléron France 52 B2
St-Quentin France 53 C2
St-Siméon Can. 115 D2
St Thomas Can. 114 B2
St-Tropez France 53 D3
St-Tropez, Cap de c. France
 53 D3
St Vincent, Gulf Austr. 104 B3
St Vincent and the Grenadines
 country West Indies 131 D3
St-Vith Belgium 48 C2
Saipan i. N. Mariana Is 63 D1
Sajama, Nevado mt. Bol. 136 B2
Sak watercourse S. Africa 98 B2
Sakai Japan 71 C4
Sakaide Japan 71 B4
Sakākah Saudi Arabia 82 B2
Sakakawea, Lake U.S.A. 120 C1
Sakarya Turkey see Adapazarı
Sakarya r. Turkey 59 D2
Sakata Japan 70 C3
Sakchu N. Korea 69 B1
Sakhalin i. Rus. Fed. 70 D1
Sakhile S. Africa 99 C2
Şäki Azer. 85 C1
Šakiai Lith. 36 D2
Sakishima-shotō is Japan 73 E3
Sakon Nakhon Thai. 66 B2
Sakrivier S. Africa 98 B3
Sakura Japan 71 D3
Saky Ukr. 39 D2
Sal r. Rus. Fed. 39 F2
Salaberry-de-Valleyfield Can.
 114 C2
Salacgrīva Latvia 36 B2
Sala Consilina Italy 56 C2
Salada, Laguna l. Mex. 126 A2
Salado r. Arg. 136 B4
Salado r. Mex. 129 C2
Salal Chad 91 D3
Şalālah Oman 83 C3
Salamanca Mex. 129 B2

Salamanca Spain 54 B1
Salavan Laos 67 B2
Salawati i. Indon. 63 C3
Salayar i. Indon. 65 D2
Salbris France 52 C2
Šalčininkai Lith. 36 C3
Saldanha S. Africa 98 A3
Saldus Latvia 36 B2
Sale Austr. 105 D3
Salekhard Rus. Fed. 34 F2
Salem India 77 B3
Salem MO U.S.A. 121 E3
Salem OR U.S.A. 118 B2
Salen U.K. 44 B2
Salerno Italy 56 B2
Salford U.K. 46 B3
Salgado r. Brazil 135 F3
Salgótarján Hungary 51 D3
Salgueiro Brazil 135 F3
Salida U.S.A. 120 B3
Salihli Turkey 59 C3
Salihorsk Belarus 36 C3
Salimo Moz. 97 C1
Salina U.S.A. 121 D3
Salina, Isola i. Italy 56 B3
Salina Cruz Mex. 129 C3
Salinas Brazil 139 D1
Salinas Mex. 128 B2
Salinas U.S.A. 119 B3
Salinas, Cap de see c. Spain
 55 D2
Salinópolis Brazil 135 E3
Salisbury U.K. 47 C4
Salisbury MD U.S.A. 123 E3
Salisbury NC U.S.A. 125 D1
Salisbury Plain U.K. 47 B4
Salluit Can. 111 G2
Salmãs Iran 85 C2
Salmon U.S.A. 118 D1
Salmon r. U.S.A. 118 C1
Salmon Arm Can. 112 D2
Salmon River Mountains U.S.A.
 118 C2
Salmtal Ger. 48 C3
Salo Fin. 41 E3
Sal'sk Rus. Fed. 39 F2
Salt watercourse S. Africa 98 B3
Salt r. U.S.A. 126 B2
Salta Arg. 136 B3
Saltillo Mex. 129 B2
Salt Lake City U.S.A. 118 D2
Salto Brazil 138 C2
Salto Uru. 136 C4
Salto del Guairá Para. 138 B2
Salton Sea salt l. U.S.A. 119 C4
Salvador Brazil 135 F4
Salwah Saudi Arabia 83 C2
Salween r. China/Myanmar 66 A1
Salween r. China/Myanmar 72 C3
Salyan Azer. 85 C2
Salzburg Austria 50 C3
Salzgitter Ger. 49 E1
Salzkotten Ger. 49 D2
Salzwedel Ger. 49 E1

Samani Japan **70** D2
Samar *i.* Phil. **68** B2
Samara Rus. Fed. **35** E3
Samarinda Indon. **65** C2
Samarqand Uzbek. **81** D3
Sāmarrā' Iraq **85** C2
Şamaxı Azer. **85** C1
Samba Dem. Rep. Congo **95** C3
Sambaliung *mts* Indon. **65** C1
Sambalpur India **79** C2
Sambar, Tanjung *pt* Indon. **65** C2
Sambas Indon. **64** B1
Sambava Madag. **97** [inset] E1
Sambir Ukr. **38** B2
Samborombón, Bahía *b.* Arg.
  137 C4
Samch'ŏk S. Korea **69** B2
Samdi Dag *mt.* Turkey **85** C2
Same Tanz. **95** D3
Samīrah Saudi Arabia **82** B2
Samoa *country* S. Pacific Ocean
  101
Samos *i.* Greece **59** C3
Samothraki Greece **59** C2
Samothraki *i.* Greece **59** C2
Sampit Indon. **65** C2
Sampwe Dem. Rep. Congo **95** C3
Samsun Turkey **84** B1
Samtredia Georgia **85** C1
Samui, Ko *i.* Thai. **67** B3
San Mali **90** B3
Şan'ā' Yemen **82** B3
San S. Pacific Ocean **133**
Sanandaj Iran **85** C2
San Andrés, Isla de *i.*
  Caribbean Sea **130** B3
San Andres Mountains U.S.A.
  126 C2
San Andrés Tuxtla Mex. **129** C3
San Angelo U.S.A. **127** C2
San Antonio U.S.A. **127** E3
San Antonio, Mount U.S.A.
  119 C4
San Antonio Abad Spain **55** D2
San Antonio Oeste Arg. **137** B5
San Benedetto del Tronto Italy
  56 B2
San Benedicto, Isla *i.* Mex.
  128 A3
San Bernardino U.S.A. **119** C4
San Bernardino Mountains
  U.S.A. **119** C4
San Blas, Cape U.S.A. **125** C3
San Borja Bol. **136** B2
San Buenaventura Mex. **128** B2
San Carlos Phil. **68** B2
San Carlos de Bariloche Arg.
  137 A5
San Clemente Island U.S.A.
  119 C4
San Cristóbal Venez. **134** B2

San Cristóbal de las Casas Mex.
  129 C3
Sancti Spíritus Cuba **130** C2
Sandakan Malaysia **65** C1
Sandane Norway **41** B3
Sandakski Bulg. **59** B2
Sanday *i.* U.K. **44** C1
Sanderson U.S.A. **127** D2
Sandia Peru **134** C4
San Diego U.S.A. **119** C4
Sandikli Turkey **84** B2
Sandnes Norway **41** B4
Sandnessjøen Norway **40** C2
Sandoa Dem. Rep. Congo **94** C3
Sandomierz Pol. **51** E2
Sandoy *i.* Faroe Is **42** B1
Sandpoint U.S.A. **118** C1
Sandu China **75** B3
Sandur Faroe Is **42** B1
Sandusky U.S.A. **122** D2
Sandveld *mts* S. Africa **98** A3
Sandvika Norway **41** C4
Sandviken Sweden **41** D3
Sandwich Bay Can. **115** E1
Sandy Cape Austr. **103** E2
Sandy Lake Can. **114** A1
Sandy Lake *I.* Can. **114** A1
San Estanislao Para. **138** A2
San Felipe *Baja California* Mex.
  128 A1
San Felipe *Guanajuato* Mex.
  129 B2
San Felipe Venez. **134** C1
San Félix Chile **133**
San Fernando *Baja California* Mex.
  128 A2
San Fernando *Tamaulipas* Mex.
  129 C2
San Fernando Phil. **68** B2
San Fernando Phil. **68** B2
San Fernando Spain **54** B2
San Fernando Trin. and Tob.
  131 D3
San Fernando de Apure Venez.
  134 C2
Sanford *FL* U.S.A. **125** D3
San Francisco Arg. **136** B4
San Francisco U.S.A. **119** B3
San Francisco Javier Spain
  55 D2
San Gavino Monreale Italy
  56 A3
Sangerhausen Ger. **49** E2
Sanggau Indon. **65** C1
Sangha *r.* Congo **94** B3
San Giovanni in Fiore Italy
  57 C3
Sangir *i.* Indon. **68** B3
Sangir, Kepulauan *is* Indon.
  63 C2
Sangju S. Korea **69** B2
Sangkulirang Indon. **65** C1
Sangli India **77** B3
Sangmélima Cameroon **94** B2

Sango Zimbabwe **97** C2
Sangre de Cristo Range *mts*
  U.S.A. **120** B3
San Hipólito, Punta *pt* Mex.
  128 A2
Sanikiluaq Can. **114** C1
Sanjiang China **75** A3
San Joaquin *r.* U.S.A. **119** B3
San Jorge, Golfo de *g.* Arg.
  137 B5
San José Costa Rica **130** B4
San Jose Phil. **68** B2
San Jose Phil. **68** B2
San Jose U.S.A. **119** B3
San José, Isla *i.* Mex. **128** A2
San José de Buenavista Phil
  68 B2
San José de Comondú Mex.
  128 A2
San José del Cabo Mex. **128** B3
San José del Guaviare Col.
  134 B2
San Juan Arg. **136** B4
San Juan *r.* Costa Rica/Nic.
  130 B3
San Juan Puerto Rico **131** D3
San Juan *r.* U.S.A. **119** D3
San Juan Bautista Spain **55**
San Juan Islands U.S.A. **118**
San Juan Mountains U.S.A.
  120 B3
San Julián Arg. **137** B5
Sankh *r.* India **79** C2
Sankt Gallen Switz. **53** D2
Sankt Moritz Switz. **53** D2
Sankt-Peterburg Rus. Fed. *se*
  St Petersburg
Sankt Veit an der Glan Austri
  50 C3
Sankt Wendel Ger. **48** C3
Şanlıurfa Turkey **84** B2
San Lorenzo Mex. **126** C3
Sanlúcar de Barrameda Spai
  54 B2
San Lucas Mex. **128** B2
San Luis Arg. **137** B4
San Luis de la Paz Mex. **129**
San Luisito Mex. **126** B2
San Luis Obispo U.S.A. **119** B
San Luis Potosí Mex. **129** B2
San Luis Río Colorado Mex.
  128 A1
San Marcos U.S.A. **127** E3
San Marino *country* Europe
  56 B2
San Marino San Marino **56** B2
San Martín de los Andes Arg
  137 A5
San Mateo, Golfo *g.* Arg. **137**
Sanmenxia China **74** B2
San Miguel El Salvador **130** B
San Miguel de Tucumán Arg.
  136 B3
Sanming China **75** B3

n Nicolás de los Arroyos Arg.
   37 B4
n Nicolás Island U.S.A.
   19 C4
nnieshof S. Africa 99 C2
nok Pol. 51 E3
n Pablo Phil. 68 B2
n Pedro Arg. 136 B3
n Pedro Mex. 128 A2
n Pedro watercourse U.S.A.
   26 B2
n Pedro, Sierra de mts Spain
   54 B2
n Pedro de las Colonias Mex.
   28 B2
n Pedro Sula Hond. 130 B3
n Pietro, Isola di i. Italy 56 A3
n Quintín, Cabo c. Mex.
   28 A1
n Rafael Arg. 137 B4
n Remo Italy 56 A2
n Salvador El Salvador 130 B3
n Salvador de Jujuy Arg.
   36 B3
n Severo Italy 56 C2
njski Most Bos.-Herz. 57 C2
nta Ana El Salvador 130 B3
nta Ana Mex. 128 A1
nta Ana U.S.A. 124 C4
nta Bárbara Mex. 128 B2
nta Bárbara U.S.A. 124 C4
nta Bárbara, Serra de hills
   razil 138 B2
nta Clara Cuba 130 C2
nta Clara U.S.A. 119 C3
nta Croce, Capo c. Italy 56 C3
nta Cruz r. Arg. 137 B6
nta Cruz Bol. 136 B2
nta Cruz U.S.A. 119 B3
nta Cruz Barillas Guat.
   30 B3
nta Cruz Cabrália Brazil
   39 E1
nta Cruz de Tenerife Canary Is
   0 A2
nta Cruz Island U.S.A. 119 C4
nta Cruz Islands Solomon Is
   00
nta Fé Arg. 136 B4
nta Fe U.S.A. 126 C1
nta Helena de Goiás Brazil
   38 B1
nta Luisa, Serra de hills Brazil
   38 B1
nta Maria Brazil 136 C3
nta Maria r. Mex. 128 B1
nta Maria U.S.A. 119 B3
nta Maria, Cabo de c. Moz.
   9 D2
nta Maria, Cabo de c. Port.
   4 B2
nta Maria das Barreiras Brazil
   35 E3
nta Maria di Leuca, Capo c.

Italy 57 C3
Santa Marta Col. 134 B1
Santa Monica U.S.A. 119 C4
Santander Spain 54 C1
Sant'Antíoco Italy 56 A3
Sant'Antíoco, Isola di i. Italy
   56 A3
Santarém Brazil 135 D3
Santarém Port. 54 B2
Santa Rita do Araguaia Brazil
   138 B1
Santa Rosa Arg. 137 B4
Santa Rosa CA U.S.A. 119 B3
Santa Rosa NM U.S.A. 126 C2
Santa Rosa de Copán Hond.
   130 B3
Santa Rosa Island U.S.A. 119 B4
Santa Rosalía Mex. 128 A2
Santiago Brazil 136 C3
Santiago Chile 137 A4
Santiago Dom. Rep. 131 C3
Santiago Mex. 128 B2
Santiago Panama 130 B4
Santiago Phil. 68 B2
Santiago de Compostela Spain
   54 B1
Santiago Ixcuintla Mex. 128 B2
Sant Jordi, Golf de g. Spain
   55 D1
Santo André Brazil 139 C2
Santo Angelo Brazil 136 C3
Santo Antônio de Jesus Brazil
   135 F4
Santo Antônio do Içá Brazil
   134 C3
Santo Domingo Dom. Rep.
   131 D3
Santo Domingo Pueblo U.S.A.
   126 C1
Santorini i. Greece see Thira
Santos Brazil 139 C2
San Valentin, Cerro mt. Chile
   137 A5
San Vicente El Salvador 130 B3
San Vicente Mex. 128 A1
San Vincenzo Italy 56 B2
San Vito, Capo c. Italy 56 B3
Sanya China 75 A4
São Bernardo do Campo Brazil
   139 C2
São Borja Brazil 136 C3
São Carlos Brazil 138 C2
São Félix Mato Grosso Brazil
   135 D4
São Félix Pará Brazil 135 D3
São Fidélis Brazil 139 D2
São Francisco Brazil 139 D1
São Francisco r. Brazil 135 E4
São Francisco, Ilha de i. Brazil
   138 C3
São Francisco do Sul Brazil
   138 C3
São Gabriel Brazil 136 C4
São Gonçalo Brazil 139 D2

São João da Barra Brazil 139 D2
São João da Boa Vista Brazil
   139 C2
São João da Madeira Port.
   54 B1
São Joaquim da Barra Brazil
   138 C2
São José do Rio Preto Brazil
   138 C2
São José dos Campos Brazil
   139 C2
São José dos Pinhais Brazil
   138 C3
São Lourenço, Pantanal de
   marsh Brazil 138 A1
São Luís Brazil 135 E3
São Manuel Brazil 138 C2
São Mateus Brazil 139 E1
São Paulo Brazil 139 C2
São Raimundo Nonato Brazil
   135 E3
São Romão Brazil 139 C1
São Sebastião, Ilha do i. Brazil
   139 C2
São Sebastião do Paraíso Brazil
   138 C2
São Simão Brazil 138 B1
São Simão, Barragem de resr
   Brazil 138 B1
São Tomé São Tomé and Príncipe
   94 A2
São Tomé i.
   São Tomé and Príncipe 94 A2
São Tomé, Cabo de c. Brazil
   139 D2
São Tomé and Príncipe country
   Africa 94 A2
São Vicente Brazil 139 C2
São Vicente, Cabo de c. Port.
   54 B2
Sapporo Japan 70 D2
Sappez Iran 85 C2
Sarāb Iran 85 C2
Sara Buri Thai. 67 B2
Sarai Rus. Fed. 37 F3
Sarajevo Bos.-Herz. 57 C2
Saranac Lake U.S.A. 123 F2
Sarandē Albania 59 B3
Sarangani Islands Phil. 68 B3
Saransk Rus. Fed. 35 D3
Sarapul Rus. Fed. 35 E3
Sarasota U.S.A. 125 D3
Sarata Ukr. 38 C2
Saratoga Springs U.S.A. 123 F2
Saratok Malaysia 65 C1
Saratov Rus. Fed. 35 D3
Saravan Iran 83 D2
Sarawak state Malaysia 65 C1
Sarayköy Turkey 59 C3
Sardarshahr India 78 B2
Sardegna i. Italy see Sardinia
Sardinia i. Italy 56 A2
Sarektjåkkå mt. Sweden 40 D2
Sar-e Pol Afgh. 78 A1

Sargasso Sea N. Atlantic Ocean 144 B4
Sargodha Pak. 78 B1
Sarh Chad 91 D4
Sarhad reg. Iran 83 D2
Sārī Iran 85 D2
Sarigöl Turkey 59 C3
Sarıkamış Turkey 85 C1
Sarikei Malaysia 65 C1
Sarir Tibesti des. Libya 91 D2
Sariwŏn N. Korea 69 B2
Sariyer Turkey 59 C2
Sarkand Kazakh. 81 E2
Şarköy Turkey 59 C2
Sármi Indon. 63 D3
Sarnia Can. 122 D2
Sarny Ukr. 38 C1
Saronikos Kolpos g. Greece 59 B3
Saros Körfezi b. Turkey 59 C2
Sarova Rus. Fed. 35 D3
Sarrebourg France 53 D2
Sarria Spain 54 B1
Sarrión Spain 55 C1
Sártène France 53 D3
Sárvár Hungary 51 D3
Sarykamyshskoye Ozero salt l. Turkm./Uzbek. 80 C2
Saryozek Kazakh. 81 E2
Saryshagan Kazakh. 81 E2
Sarysu watercourse Kazakh. 86 G3
Sary-Tash Kyrg. 81 E3
Sasaram India 79 C2
Sasebo Japan 71 A4
Saskatchewan prov. Can. 113 E2
Saskatchewan r. Can. 113 E2
Saskatoon Can. 110 E3
Sasolburg S. Africa 99 C2
Sasovo Rus. Fed. 37 F3
Sassandra Côte d'Ivoire 90 B4
Sassari Italy 56 A2
Sassnitz Ger. 50 C2
Satadougou Mali 90 A3
Satara S. Africa 99 D1
Satna India 79 C2
Satpura Range mts India 78 B2
Satu Mare Romania 38 B2
Satun Thai. 67 B3
Saucillo Mex. 128 B2
Sauda Norway 41 B4
Sauðárkrókur Iceland 40 [inset]
Saudi Arabia country Asia 82 B2
Saulieu France 53 C2
Sault Sainte Marie Can. 114 B2
Sault Sainte Marie U.S.A. 122 C1
Saumalkol' Kazakh. 81 D1
Saumakki Indon. 63 C3
Saumur France 52 B2
Saurimo Angola 94 C3
Sava r. Europe 58 C2
Savaiʻi i. Samoa 101

Savala r. Rus. Fed. 37 F3
Savannah GA U.S.A. 125 D2
Savannah TN U.S.A. 124 C1
Savannah r. U.S.A. 125 D2
Savannakhét Laos 66 B2
Savant Lake Can. 114 A1
Savaştepe Turkey 59 C3
Savona Italy 56 A2
Savonlinna Fin. 41 F3
Savu i. Indon. 65 D3
Savu Sea Indon. see Sawu, Laut
Sawai Madhopur India 78 B2
Sawankhalok Thai. 66 A2
Swatch Range mts U.S.A. 120 B3
Sawhāj Egypt 92 B2
Sawtell Austr. 105 E2
Sawu, Laut sea Indon. 65 D2
Sayhūt Yemen 83 C3
Saynshand Mongolia 73 D2
Sayre U.S.A. 123 E2
Sayula Jalisco Mex. 128 B3
Sayula Veracruz Mex. 129 C3
Scafell Pike h. U.K. 46 B2
Scalea Italy 57 C3
Scapa Flow inlet U.K. 44 C1
Scarborough U.K. 46 C2
Scarborough Trin. and Tob. 131 D3
Scarborough U.K. 46 C2
Scarborough Shoal sea feature S. China Sea 68 A2
Scarinish U.K. 44 A2
Scarpanto i. Greece see Karpathos
Schaffhausen Switz. 53 D2
Schagen Neth. 48 B1
Scharendijke Neth. 48 A2
Scheeßel Ger. 49 D1
Schefferville Can. 115 D1
Schell Creek Range mts U.S.A. 119 D3
Schenectady U.S.A. 123 F2
Scheßlitz Ger. 49 E3
Schiermonnikoog i. Neth. 48 C1
Schio Italy 56 B1
Schleiz Ger. 49 E2
Schleswig Ger. 50 B2
Schloss Holte-Stukenbrock Ger. 49 D2
Schlüchtern Ger. 49 D2
Schmallenberg Ger. 49 D2
Schneverdingen Ger. 49 D1
Schönebeck (Elbe) Ger. 49 E1
Schöningen Ger. 49 E1
Schouten Islands P.N.G. 63 D3
Schwabach Ger. 49 E3
Schwäbische Alb mts Ger. 50 B3
Schwandorf Ger. 49 F3
Schwaner, Pegunungan mts Indon. 65 C2
Schwarzenbek Ger. 49 E1
Schwarzenberg Ger. 49 F2
Schwarzrand mts Namibia 98 A2

Schwarzwald mts Ger. see Black Forest
Schwaz Austria 50 C3
Schwedt an der Oder Ger. 50 C2
Schweinfurt Ger. 49 E2
Schwerin Ger. 49 E1
Schweriner See i. Ger. 49 E1
Schwyz Switz. 53 D2
Sciacca Italy 56 B3
Scilly, Isles of U.K. 43 B4
Scioto r. U.S.A. 122 D3
Scobey U.S.A. 120 E1
Scone Austr. 105 E2
Scotia Sea S. Atlantic Ocean 107 A4
Scotland admin. div. U.K. 44 C2
Scott, Cape Can. 112 C2
Scottburgh S. Africa 99 D3
Scott City U.S.A. 120 C3
Scottsbluff U.S.A. 120 C2
Scottsboro U.S.A. 125 C2
Scourie U.K. 44 B1
Scranton U.S.A. 123 E2
Scunthorpe U.K. 46 C3
Seal r. Can. 113 F2
Seal, Cape S. Africa 98 B3
Sea Lake Austr. 104 C3
Searcy U.S.A. 124 B1
Seascale U.K. 46 B2
Seattle U.S.A. 118 B1
Sebago Lake U.S.A. 123 F2
Sebastián Vizcaíno, Bahía b. Mex. 128 A2
Sebeş Romania 38 B2
Sebeşi i. Indon. 64 B2
Sebezh Rus. Fed. 36 C2
Sebring U.S.A. 125 D3
Sechelt Can. 112 C3
Secunderabad India 77 B3
Sedalia U.S.A. 121 E3
Sedan France 53 C2
Seddon N.Z. 106 B3
Sedona U.S.A. 126 B2
Seehausen (Altmark) Ger. 49 E1
Seeheim Namibia 98 A2
Sées France 52 C2
Seesen Ger. 49 E2
Seevetal Ger. 49 E1
Segamat Malaysia 64 B1
Segovia Spain 54 C1
Séguédine Niger 91 D2
Séguéla Côte d'Ivoire 90 B4
Seguin U.S.A. 127 E3
Segura r. Spain 55 C2
Segura, Sierra de mts Spain 54 C2
Sehithwa Botswana 96 B3
Seinäjoki Fin. 40 E3
Seine r. France 52 C2
Seine, Baie de b. France 52 B2
Sekondi Ghana 90 B4

aru i. Indon. 63 C3
atan, Tanjung pt Indon. 65 C2
awik U.S.A. 110 B2
by U.K. 46 C3
ebi-Phikwe Botswana 96 B2
astat France 53 D2
oss Iceland 40 [inset]
babi Maur. 90 A3
gman U.S.A. 126 B1
ma Oasis Sudan 92 A2
nguë, Lac de l. Mali 90 B3
tharovo Rus. Fed. 37 D2
ord Norway 41 B4
kirk Can. 113 F2
kirk Mountains Can. 112 D2
ma AL U.S.A. 124 C2
ma CJ U.S.A. 119 C3
tso Rus. Fed. 37 D3
va reg. Brazil 134 B3
way r. U.S.A. 118 C1
wyn Lake Can. 113 E1
wyn Mountains Can. 112 B1
wyn Range hills Austr. 103 C2
narang Indon. 65 C2
natan Malaysia 65 B1
menivka Ukr. 39 D1
neru, Gunung vol. Indon.
  5 C2
minoe U.S.A. 127 D2
minole, Lake U.S.A. 125 D2
nipalatinsk Kazakh. 81 F1
mnän Iran 85 D2
mporna Malaysia 65 C1
na Madureira Brazil 134 C3
nanga Zambia 96 D1
ndai Kagoshima Japan 71 B4
ndai Miyagi Japan 70 D3
negal country Africa 90 A3
négal r. Maur./Senegal 90 A3
nftenberg Ger. 49 G2
nhor do Bonfim Brazil
  35 E4
ngallia Italy 56 B2
nj Croatia 56 B2
nja i. Norway 40 D2
nlis France 52 C2
mnonorom Cambodia 67 B2
nmar Sudan 93 B3
nneterre Can. 114 C2
nqu r. Lesotho 99 C5
ns France 53 C2
nta S.M. 58 B1
ntinel Peak Can. 112 C2
nul India 79 B2
oul S. Korea 69 B2
opetiba, Baía de b. Brazil
  39 D2
olk r. P.N.G. 63 D3
pinang Indon. 65 C1

Sept-Îles Can. 115 D1
Seram i. Indon. 63 C3
Seram, Laut sea Indon. 63 C3
Serang Indon. 64 B2
Serbia aut. rep. S.M. see Srbija
Serbia and Montenegro country
  Europe 58 B2
Seremban Malaysia 64 B1
Serengeti Plain Tanz. 95 D3
Sergiyev Posad Rus. Fed. 37 E2
Seria Brunei 65 C1
Sérifos i. Greece 59 B3
Serik Turkey 84 B2
Serov Rus. Fed. 34 F3
Serowe Botswana 99 C1
Serpa Port. 54 B2
Serpukhov Rus. Fed. 37 E3
Serra da Mesa, Represa resr
  Brazil 135 E4
Serre r. France 48 A3
Serres Greece 59 B2
Sêrro Brazil 139 D1
Sertãozinho Brazil 138 C2
Sertolovo Rus. Fed. 37 D1
Seruyan r. Indon. 65 C2
Sesfontein Namibia 96 A1
Sessa Aurunca Italy 56 B2
Sestri Levante Italy 56 A2
Sestroretsk Rus. Fed. 36 C1
Sète France 53 C3
Sete Lagoas Brazil 139 D1
Setermoen Norway 40 D2
Setesdal val. Norway 41 B4
Sétif Alg. 91 C1
Seto-naikai sea Japan 71 B4
Settle U.K. 46 B2
Setúbal Port. 54 B2
Setúbal, Baía de b. Port. 54 B2
Seul, Lac l. Can. 114 A1
Sevan Armenia 35 D4
Sevan, Lake Armenia 80 D2
Sevastopol' Ukr. 39 D3
Seven Islands Bay Can. 115 D1
Sévérac-le-Château France
  52 C3
Severn r. Can. 114 B1
Severn S. Africa 98 B2
Severn r. U.K. 47 B4
Severnaya Dvina r. Rus. Fed.
  34 D2
Severnaya Zemlya is Rus. Fed.
  87 I1
Severnyy Nenetskiy Avtonomnyy
  Okrug Rus. Fed. 34 D2
Severnyy Respublika Komi
  Rus. Fed. 34 F2
Severodvinsk Rus. Fed. 34 C2
Severomorsk Rus. Fed. 40 C2
Severskaya Rus. Fed. 39 E3
Sevier r. U.S.A. 119 D3
Sevier Lake U.S.A. 119 D3
Sevilla Spain see Seville
Seville Spain 54 B2
Seward U.S.A. 110 C2

Seward Peninsula U.S.A.
  110 B2
Sextín r. Mex. 128 B2
Seyakha Rus. Fed. 34 G1
Seychelles country Indian Ocean
  89
Seyðisfjörður Iceland 40 [inset]
Seym r. Rus. Fed./Ukr. 39 D1
Seymchan Rus. Fed. 87 M2
Seymour Austr. 105 D3
Seymour IN U.S.A. 122 C3
Seymour TX U.S.A. 127 E2
Sézanne France 52 C2
Sfakia Greece 59 B3
Sfântu Gheorghe Romania 38 C2
Sfax Tunisia 91 D1
's-Gravenhage Neth. see
  The Hague
Sgurr Alasdair h. U.K. 44 A2
Shaanxi prov. China 74 A2
Shabel'sk Rus. Fed. 39 E2
Shache China 81 E3
Shackleton Range mts Antarctica
  107 A1
Shaftesbury U.K. 47 B4
Shageluk U.S.A. 110 B2
Shahdol India 79 C2
Shah Fuladi mt. Afgh. 78 A1
Shahjahanpur India 79 B2
Shahr-e Kord Iran 85 D2
Shahrezā Iran 85 D2
Shahrisabz Uzbek. 81 D3
Shakhovskaya Rus. Fed. 37 E2
Shakhty Rus. Fed. 39 F2
Shakhun'ya Rus. Fed. 37 F2
Shakotan-misaki c. Japan 70 D2
Shalkar Kazakh. 80 C2
Shaluli Shan mts China 72 C2
Shamattawa Can. 113 F2
Shamrock U.S.A. 127 D1
Shandan China 72 C2
Shandong prov. China 74 B2
Shandong Bandao pen. China
  74 C2
Shangani r. Zimbabwe 97 B1
Shanghai China 74 C2
Shanghai mun. China 74 C2
Shanghang China 75 B3
Shangluo China 74 A2
Shangrao China 75 B3
Shangzhou China see Shangluo
Shannon r. Ireland 45 B2
Shannon, Mouth of the Ireland
  45 B2
Shantou China 75 B3
Shanxi prov. China 74 B2
Shaoguan China 75 B3
Shaowu China 75 B3
Shaoxing China 75 C2
Shaoyang China 75 B3
Shaqrā' Saudi Arabia 92 C2
Sharhorod Ukr. 38 C2
Sharjah U.A.E. 83 D2
Sharkawshchyna Belarus 36 C2

Shark Bay Austr. **102** A2
Sharm ash Shaykh Egypt **82** A2
Shar'ya Rus. Fed. **34** D3
Shashe r. Botswana/Zimbabwe **97** B2
Shashemenē Eth. **93** B4
Shasta, Mount vol. U.S.A. **118** B2
Shasta Lake U.S.A. **118** B2
Shatsk Rus. Fed. **37** F3
Shatura Rus. Fed. **37** E2
Shaunavon Can. **122** C2
Shawano U.S.A. **122** C2
Shawnee U.S.A. **127** E1
Shay Gap Austr. **102** B2
Shchekino Rus. Fed. **37** E3
Shchelkovo Rus. Fed. **37** E2
Shchigry Rus. Fed. **37** E3
Shchors Ukr. **39** D1
Shchuchyn Belarus **36** B3
Shebekino Rus. Fed. **39** E1
Sheberghān Afgh. **78** A1
Sheboygan U.S.A. **122** C2
Shebsh r. Rus. Fed. **39** E3
Sheelin, Lough l. Ireland **45** C2
Sheffield U.K. **46** C3
Sheksna Rus. Fed. **37** E2
Sheksninskoye
   Vodokhranilishche resr
   Rus. Fed. **37** E2
Shelagskiy, Mys pt Rus. Fed. **87** N2
Shelburne Can. **115** D2
Shelby U.S.A. **118** D1
Shelbyville IN U.S.A. **122** C3
Shelbyville TN U.S.A. **125** C1
Shelikhova, Zaliv g. Rus. Fed. **87** M2
Shellbrook Can. **113** E2
Shelton U.S.A. **118** B1
Shenandoah r. U.S.A. **123** D3
Shendam Nigeria **94** A2
Shendi Sudan **82** A3
Shenyang China **74** C1
Shenzhen China **75** B3
Shepetivka Ukr. **38** C1
Shepparton Austr. **105** D3
Sheppey, Isle of i. U.K. **47** D4
Sherbrooke N.S. Can. **115** D2
Sherbrooke Que. Can. **115** C2
Shereiq Sudan **92** B3
Sheridan U.S.A. **120** B2
Sherman U.S.A. **127** E2
's-Hertogenbosch Neth. **48** B2
Shetland Islands Scotland U.K. **44** [inset]
Shetpe Kazakh. **80** C2
Sheyenne r. U.S.A. **121** D1
Shibām Yemen **83** B3
Shibetsu Japan **70** D2
Shiel, Loch l. U.K. **44** B2
Shihezi China **81** F2
Shijiazhuang China **74** B2
Shikarpur Pak. **78** A2
Shikoku i. Japan **71** B4

Shikotsu-ko l. Japan **70** D2
Shiliguri India **79** C2
Shillong India **79** D2
Shilovo Rus. Fed. **37** F3
Shimbiris mt. Somalia **93** C3
Shimla India **79** B1
Shimoga India **77** B3
Shimonoseki Japan **71** B4
Shin, Loch l. U.K. **44** B1
Shindand Afgh. **78** A1
Shingū Japan **71** C4
Shingwedzi S. Africa **99** D1
Shingwedzi r. S. Africa **99** D1
Shinyanga Tanz. **95** D3
Shiono-misaki c. Japan **71** C4
Shiprock U.S.A. **126** C1
Shiquan China **74** A2
Shīrāz Iran **85** D3
Shiretoko-misaki c. Japan **70** D2
Shiriya-zaki c. Japan **70** D2
Shiv India **78** B2
Shiyan China **74** B2
Shizuishan China **74** A2
Shizuoka Japan **71** C4
Shklow Belarus **37** D3
Shkodër Albania **59** C2
Shoshone U.S.A. **119** C3
Shoshone Mountains U.S.A. **119** C3
Shoshong Botswana **99** C1
Shostka Ukr. **39** D1
Showak Sudan **82** A3
Show Low U.S.A. **126** B2
Shpola Ukr. **39** D2
Shreveport U.S.A. **124** B2
Shrewsbury U.K. **47** B3
Shu'ab, Ra's pt Yemen **83** C3
Shuangjiang China **66** A1
Shuangliao China **69** A1
Shuangyang China **69** B1
Shuangyashan China **70** B1
Shubarkuduk Kazakh. **80** C2
Shubrā al Khaymah Egypt **92** B1
Shumba Zimbabwe **99** C1
Shumen Bulg. **58** C2
Shumilina Belarus **36** C2
Shumyachi Rus. Fed. **37** D3
Shungnak U.S.A. **110** B2
Shuqrah Yemen **82** B3
Shushtar Iran **85** C2
Shuswap Lake Can. **112** C2
Shuya Rus. Fed. **37** F2
Shuyskoye Rus. Fed. **37** F2
Shwebo Myanmar **66** A1
Shymkent Kazakh. **81** D2
Shyroke Ukr. **39** D2
Sia Indon. **63** C3
Siahan Range mts Pak. **78** A2
Sialkot Pak. **78** B1
Siargao i. Phil. **68** B3

Šiauliai Lith. **36** B2
Šibenik Croatia **57** C2
Siberia reg. Rus. Fed. **87** J2
Siberut i. Indon. **64** A2
Sibi Pak. **78** A2
Sibiu Romania **38** B2
Sibolga Indon. **64** A1
Sibsagar India **66** A1
Sibu Malaysia **65** C1
Sibut C.A.R. **94** B2
Sibuyan i. Phil. **68** B2
Sibuyan Sea Phil. **68** B2
Sicamous Can. **112** D2
Sichon Thai. **67** A3
Sichuan prov. China **74** A2
Sichuan Pendi basin China **75** A3
Sicié, Cap c. France **53** D3
Sicilia i. Italy see Sicily
Sicilian Channel Italy/Tunisia **56** B3
Sicily i. Italy **56** B3
Sicuani Peru **134** B4
Siddhapur India **78** B2
Sideros, Akra pt Greece **59** C3
Sidi Aïssa Alg. **55** D2
Sidi Ali Alg. **55** D2
Sidi Bel Abbès Alg. **90** B1
Sidikalang Indon. **64** A1
Sidi Okba Alg. **55** C3
Sidlaw Hills U.K. **44** C2
Sidmouth U.K. **47** B4
Sidney Can. **118** B1
Sidney MT U.S.A. **120** C1
Sidney NE U.S.A. **120** C2
Sidney OH U.S.A. **122** C2
Sidney Lanier, Lake U.S.A. **125** D2
Sidoan Indon. **65** D1
Sidon Lebanon **84** B2
Sidrolândia Brazil **138** B2
Siedlce Pol. **51** E2
Siegen Ger. **48** D2
Siĕmréab Cambodia **67** B2
Siena Italy **56** B2
Sieradz Pol. **51** D2
Sierra Grande Arg. **137** B5
Sierra Leone country Africa **90** A4
Sierra Vista U.S.A. **126** B2
Sierre Switz. **53** D2
Sifnos i. Greece **59** B3
Sig Alg. **55** C2
Siggiup Nunaa pen. Greenland **111** I2
Sighetu Marmaţiei Romania **38** B2
Sighişoara Romania **38** B2
Siglufjörður Iceland **40** [inset]
Sigmaringen Ger. **50** B3
Signy-l'Abbaye France **48** B3
Sigüenza Spain **54** C1
Siguiri Guinea **90** B3
Sigulda Latvia **36** B2

anoukville Cambodia 67 B2
njärvi Fin. 40 F3
ke Turkey 85 C2
har India 78 B2
asso Mali 90 B3
aston U.S.A. 121 F3
note-Alin' mts Rus. Fed.
D B2
inos i. Greece 59 C3
o Mex. 128 B2
har India 66 A1
ltitzniz, Ozero salt l. Kazakh.
l E1
arhi Nepal 79 C2
ke Turkey 84 B2
ng Co salt l. China 79 C1
stra Bulg. 58 C2
r. Sweden 41 C3
amäe Estonia 36 C2
bela S. Africa 99 D2
tê Lith. 36 B2
an Turkey 85 C2
ver City U.S.A. 126 C2
erton U.S.A. 120 B3
av Turkey 59 C3
au Dağları mts Turkey 59 C3
ba Dem. Rep. Congo 94 C2
ce, Lake Can. 123 E2
eulue i. Indon. 64 A1
aferopol' Ukr. 39 D3
aleu Silvaniei Romania 38 B2
onhouse Can. 113 E2
pson Desert Austr. 103 C1
arishamn Sweden 41 C4
abang Indon. 64 A1
anju N. Korea 69 B2
bo Myanmar 66 A1
celejo Col. 134 B2
dor Rus. Fed. 34 F2
es Port. 54 B2
es, Cabo de c. Port. 54 B2
ga Sudan 82 A3
gahi India 79 C2
gapore Asia 64 B1
gapore country Asia 64 B1
garaja Indon. 65 C2
gida Tanz. 95 D3
gkang Indon. 65 C2
gkawang Indon. 64 B1
gkil Indon. 64 A1
gleton Austr. 105 E2
iscola Italy 56 A2
j Croatia 57 C2
jal Indon. 65 C2
kat Sudan 92 B3
kiang aut. reg. China see
  Xinjiang Uygur Zizhiqu
op Turkey 84 B1
p'o N. Korea 69 B1
sheim Ger. 49 D3
tang Indon. 65 C1

Sint Anthonis Neth. 48 B2
Sint Maarten i. Neth. Antilles 131 D3
Sint-Niklaas Belgium 48 B2
Sinton U.S.A. 127 E3
Sinŭiju N. Korea 69 A1
Siófok Hungary 51 D3
Sion Switz. 53 D2
Sioux Center U.S.A. 121 D2
Sioux City U.S.A. 121 D2
Sioux Falls U.S.A. 121 D2
Sioux Lookout Can. 114 A1
Siping China 69 A1
Sipiwesk Lake Can. 113 F2
Sipura i. Indon. 64 A2
Sira r. Norway 41 B4
Sir Edward Pellew Group is
Austr. 103 C1
Siri Kit Dam Thai. 66 B2
Sir James MacBrien, Mount
Can. 112 C1
Sirjan Iran 85 D3
Sırnak Turkey 85 C2
Sirsa India 78 B2
Sirte Libya 91 D1
Sirte, Gulf of Libya 91 D1
Širvintos Lith. 36 C2
Sisal Mex. 129 C2
Sishen S. Africa 98 B2
Sisian Armenia 85 C2
Sisipuk Lake Can. 113 E2
Sisŏphŏn Cambodia 67 B2
Sisteron France 53 D3
Sitapur India 79 C2
Siteki Swaziland 99 D2
Sitka U.S.A. 112 B2
Sittard Neth. 48 B2
Sittwe Myanmar 66 A1
Situbondo Indon. 65 C2
Sivas Turkey 84 B2
Siverek Turkey 84 B2
Sivrihisar Turkey 84 B2
Siwah Egypt 92 A2
Siwah, Wāḥāt oasis Egypt 84 A3
Siwalik Range mts India/Nepal
78 B1
Siwa Oasis Egypt see
  Siwah, Wāḥāt
Six-Fours-les-Plages France
53 D3
Siyabuswa S. Africa 99 C2
Skadovs'k Ukr. 39 D2
Skagen Denmark 41 C4
Skagerrak str. Denmark/Norway
41 B4
Skagit r. U.S.A. 118 B1
Skagway U.S.A. 112 B2
Skarżysko-Kamienna Pol. 51 E2
Skeena r. Can. 112 C2
Skeena Mountains Can. 112 C2
Skegness U.K. 46 D3
Skellefteå Sweden 40 E3
Skellefteälven r. Sweden 40 E3
Skerries Ireland 45 C2

Skiathos i. Greece 59 B3
Skibbereen Ireland 45 B3
Skiðadals-jökull glacier Iceland
40 [inset]
Skiddaw h. U.K. 46 B2
Skien Norway 41 B4
Skierniewice Pol. 51 E2
Skikda Alg. 91 C1
Skjervøy Norway 40 E1
Skodje Norway 42 E1
Skopelos i. Greece 59 B3
Skopin Rus. Fed. 37 E3
Skopje Macedonia 58 B2
Skövde Sweden 41 C4
Skowhegan U.S.A. 123 G2
Skrunda Latvia 36 B2
Skukum, Mount Can. 112 B1
Skukuza S. Africa 99 D1
Skuodas Lith. 36 B2
Skye i. U.K. 44 A2
Skyros i. Greece 59 B3
Skyros i. Greece 59 B3
Slagelse Denmark 41 C4
Slaney r. Ireland 45 C2
Slantsy Rus. Fed. 36 C2
Slatina Croatia 57 C1
Slatina Romania 38 B3
Slave r. Can. 113 D1
Slave Coast Africa 90 C4
Slave Lake Can. 112 D2
Slavgorod Rus. Fed. 81 E1
Slavonski Brod Croatia 57 C1
Slavuta Ukr. 38 C1
Slavutych Ukr. 38 D1
Slavyanka Rus. Fed. 70 B2
Slavyansk-na-Kubani Rus. Fed.
39 E2
Sławno Pol. 51 D2
Slea Head Ireland 45 A2
Sleeper Islands Can. 114 C1
Slieve Donard h. U.K. 45 C1
Sligo Ireland 45 B1
Sligo Bay Ireland 45 B1
Slite Sweden 41 D4
Sliven Bulg. 58 C2
Slobozia Romania 38 C3
Slonim Belarus 36 C3
Sloten Neth. 48 B1
Slough U.K. 47 C4
Slovakia country Europe 51 D3
Slovenia country Europe 56 B1
Slov"yans'k Ukr. 39 E2
Sluch r. Ukr. 38 C1
Słupsk Pol. 51 D2
Slutsk Belarus 36 C3
Slyne Head Ireland 45 A2
Smallwood Reservoir Can.
115 D1
Smalyavichy Belarus 36 C3
Smarhon' Belarus 36 C3
Smeaton Can. 113 E2
Smederevo S.M. 58 B2
Smederevska Palanka S.M.
58 B2

Smila Ukr. **39** D2
Smithers Can. **112** C2
Smithfield U.S.A. **125** E1
Smith Mountain Lake U.S.A. **123** E3
Smoky Hills U.S.A. **121** D3
Smøla i. Norway **40** B3
Smolensk Rus. Fed. **37** D3
Smolyan Bulg. **58** B2
Smooth Rock Falls Can. **114** B2
Smyrna Turkey *see* Izmir
Snæfell *mt.* Iceland **40** [inset]
Snaefell h. Isle of Man **46** A2
Snake r. U.S.A. **118** C1
Snake River Plain U.S.A. **118** D2
Sneek Neth. **48** B1
Sneeuberge *mts* S. Africa **98** B3
Snežnik *mt.* Slovenia **56** B1
Snihurivka Ukr. **39** D2
Snøhetta *mt.* Norway **41** B3
Snowbird Lake Can. **113** E1
Snowdon *mt.* U.K. **46** A3
Snowdrift r. Can. **113** D1
Snow Lake Can. **113** E2
Snowtown Austr. **104** B2
Snowy r. Austr. **105** D3
Snowy Mountains Austr. **105** D3
Snyder U.S.A. **127** D2
Soalala Madag. **97** [inset] D1
Sobat r. Sudan **93** B4
Sobernheim Ger. **48** C3
Sobinka Rus. Fed. **37** F3
Sobradinho, Barragem de resr Brazil **135** E4
Sobral Brazil **135** E3
Sochi Rus. Fed. **39** E3
Söch'ŏn S. Korea **69** B5
Society Islands Fr. Polynesia **143** E6
Socorro U.S.A. **126** C2
Socorro, Isla i. Mex. **128** A3
Socotra i. Yemen **83** C3
Soc Trăng Vietnam **67** B3
Socuéllamos Spain **54** C2
Sodankylä Fin. **40** F2
Soda Springs U.S.A. **118** D2
Söderhamn Sweden **41** D3
Södertälje Sweden **41** D4
Sodiri Sudan **92** A3
Sodo Eth. **93** B4
Soest Ger. **48** D2
Sofia Bulg. **58** B2
Sofiya Bulg. *see* Sofia
Sofporog Rus. Fed. **40** G2
Sōfu-gan i. Japan **71** D5
Sog China **72** C2
Sognefjorden *inlet* Norway **41** B3
Soignies Belgium **48** C4
Soissons France **53** C2
Sokal' Ukr. **38** D1
Söke Turkey **59** C3
Sokhumi Georgia **85** C1

Sokodé Togo **90** C4
Sokol Rus. Fed. **37** F2
Sokolov Czech Rep. **49** F2
Sokoto Nigeria **91** C3
Sokyryany Ukr. **38** C2
Solapur India **77** B3
Soledad U.S.A. **119** B3
Solihull U.K. **47** C3
Solikamsk Rus. Fed. **34** E3
Sol'-Iletsk Rus. Fed. **35** E3
Solingen Ger. **48** C2
Sollefteå Sweden **40** D3
Sollentuna Sweden **41** D4
Solling *hills* Ger. **49** D2
Solnechnogorsk Rus. Fed. **37** E2
Solok Indon. **64** B2
Solomon Islands *country* S. Pacific Ocean **142** D7
Solomon Sea S. Pacific Ocean **142** D7
Solothurn Switz. **53** D2
Soltau Ger. **49** D2
Sol'tsy Rus. Fed. **37** D2
Solway Firth *est.* U.K. **44** C3
Solwezi Zambia **96** B1
Soma Turkey **59** C3
Somalia *country* Africa **93** C4
Sombo Angola **94** C3
Sombor S.M. **58** A1
Sombrerete Mex. **128** B2
Somerset U.S.A. **122** D3
Somerset Island Can. **110** F2
Somerset West S. Africa **98** A3
Sömmerda Ger. **49** E2
Son r. India **79** C2
Sønderborg Denmark **41** B5
Sondershausen Ger. **49** E2
Sông Đa r. Vietnam *see* Black River
Songea Tanz. **95** D4
Sŏnggan N. Korea **69** B4
Songhua Hu resr China **69** B3
Songkhla Thai. **67** B3
Sŏngnam S. Korea **69** B5
Songnim N. Korea **69** B5
Songo Angola **94** B3
Songo Moz. **97** C1
Sonkovo Rus. Fed. **37** E2
Son La Vietnam **66** B1
Sonmiani Pak. **78** A2
Sonneberg Ger. **49** E2
Sonora r. Mex. **128** A2
Sonora CA U.S.A. **119** B3
Sonora TX U.S.A. **127** D2
Sopo *watercourse* Sudan **93** A4
Sopron Hungary **51** D3
Sora Italy **56** B2
Sorel Can. **114** C2
Sorell Austr. **103** C3
Soria Spain **54** C1
Soroca Moldova **38** C2
Sorocaba Brazil **138** C2
Sorol *atoll* Micronesia **63** D2

Sorong Indon. **63** C3
Soroti Uganda **95** D2
Sørøya i. Norway **40** E1
Sorsele Sweden **40** D2
Sorsogon Phil. **68** B2
Sortavala Rus. Fed. **41** G3
Sortland Norway **40** D2
Sŏsan S. Korea **69** B2
Soshanguve S. Africa **99** C2
Sosna r. Rus. Fed. **37** E3
Sosnogorsk Rus. Fed. **34** E2
Sosnovka *Tambovskaya Oblast'* Rus. Fed. **37** F3
Sosnovyy Bor Rus. Fed. **36** C2
Sosnowiec Pol. **51** D2
Sosyka r. Rus. Fed. **39** E2
Soto la Marina Mex. **129** C2
Souanké Congo **94** B2
Souguear Alg. **55** D2
Souillac France **52** C4
Sŏul S. Korea *see* Seoul
Soulac-sur-Mer France **52** B2
Sour el Ghozlane Alg. **55** D2
Souris r. Can. **120** D1
Sousa Brazil **135** F3
Sousse Tunisia **91** D1
South Africa, Republic of *country* Africa **98** B3
Southampton U.K. **47** C4
Southampton, Cape Can. **113** G1
Southampton Island Can. **113** F1
South Andaman i. India **67** A2
South Australia *state* Austr. **104** A2
South Bend U.S.A. **122** C2
South Carolina *state* U.S.A. **125** D2
South China Sea N. Pacific Ocean **62** B2
South Dakota *state* U.S.A. **120** C2
South Downs *hills* U.K. **47** C4
Southend-on-Sea U.K. **47** D4
Southern Alps *mts* N.Z. **106** B3
Southern Cross Austr. **102** A3
Southern Indian Lake Can. **113** F2
Southern Ocean **107** A3/G3
Southern Pines U.S.A. **125** E1
Southern Uplands *hills* U.K. **44** B3
South Geomagnetic Pole Antarctica **107** F1
South Georgia i. S. Atlantic Ocean **137** E6
South Georgia and South Sandwich Islands *terr.* S. Atlantic Ocean **133**
South Henik Lake Can. **113** F1
South Island N.Z. **106** B3
South Korea *country* Asia **69** B3

th Lake Tahoe U.S.A. **119** B3
th **Magnetic Pole** Antarctica **7** G3
th **Orkney Islands**
Atlantic Ocean **107** A3
th **Platte** r. U.S.A. **120** C2
th **Pole** Antarctica **107**
thport U.K. **46** B3
thport U.S.A. **125** E2
th **Ronaldsay** i. U.K. **44** C1
th **Saskatchewan** r. Can. **3** E2
th **Seal** r. Can. **113** F2
th **Shetland Islands**
tarctica **107** A3
th **Shields** U.K. **46** C2
th **Taranaki Bight** b. N.Z. **6** B2
th **Twin Island** Can. **114** C1
th **Uist** i. U.K. **44** A2
th **West Rocks** Austr. **105** E2
thwold U.K. **47** D3
erato Italy **57** C3
etsk Rus. Fed. **36** B2
oetskiy *Khanty-Mansiyskiy tonomnyy Okrug* Rus. Fed. **4** F2
yets'kyy Ukr. **39** D2
weto S. Africa **99** C2
a-misaki c. Japan **70** D1
h r. Europe **38** D1
opol Bulg. **58** C2
ain *country* Europe **54** C1
alding U.K. **46** C3
anish Fork U.S.A. **118** D2
arks U.S.A. **119** C3
arta U.S.A. **122** B2
artanburg U.S.A. **125** D2
arti Greece **59** B3
artivento, Capo c. Italy **57** C3
as-Demensk Rus. Fed. **37** D3
as-Klepiki Rus. Fed. **37** F2
assk-Dal'niy Rus. Fed. **70** B2
atha, Akra *pt* Greece **59** B3
earfish U.S.A. **120** C2
encer U.S.A. **121** D2
encer **Gulf** *est.* Austr. **104** B2
ennymoor U.K. **46** C2
enser **Mountains** N.Z. **106** B3
essart *reg.* Ger. **49** D3
ey r. U.K. **44** C2
eyer Ger. **49** D3
ekeroog i. Ger. **48** C1
ukenisse Neth. **48** B2
rit **River** Can. **112** D2
tsbergen i. Svalbard **82** D5
ttal an der Drau Austria **0** C3
it Croatia **57** C2
lit **Lake** Can. **113** F2
lit **Lake** i. Can. **113** F2
okane U.S.A. **118** C1
eleto Italy **53** E3
ooner U.S.A. **122** B1

Spree r. Ger. **50** C2
Springbok S. Africa **98** A2
Springdale Can. **115** E2
Springdale U.S.A. **124** B1
Springe Ger. **49** D1
Springer U.S.A. **126** D1
Springerville U.S.A. **126** C2
Springfield *CO* U.S.A. **120** C3
Springfield *IL* U.S.A. **122** C3
Springfield *MA* U.S.A. **123** F2
Springfield *MO* U.S.A. **121** D3
Springfield *OH* U.S.A. **122** D3
Springfield *OR* U.S.A. **118** B2
Springfontein S. Africa **99** C3
Spring Hill U.S.A. **125** D3
Springs Junction N.Z. **106** B3
Spurn Head U.K. **46** D3
Squamish Can. **112** C3
Squillace, Golfo di *g.* Italy **57** C3
Srbija *aut. rep.* S.M. **58** B2
Srebrenica Bos.-Herz. **57** C2
Sredets Bulg. **58** C2
Sredinnyy Khrebet *mts* Rus. Fed. **87** M3
Sredne-Russkaya Vozvyshennost' *hills* Rus. Fed. *see* Central Russian Upland
Srednogorie Bulg. **58** B2
Sretensk Rus. Fed. **73** D1
Sri Aman Malaysia **65** C1
Sri Jayewardenepura Kotte Sri Lanka **77** B4
Srikakulam India **77** C3
Sri Lanka *country* Asia **77** C4
Srinagar India **78** B1
Sri Pada *mt.* Sri Lanka **77** C4
Stade Ger. **49** D1
Stadensen Ger. **49** E1
Stadskanaal Neth. **48** C1
Stadtallendorf Ger. **49** D2
Stadthagen Ger. **49** D1
Staffelstein Ger. **49** E2
Stafford U.K. **46** B3
Staines U.K. **47** C4
Stakhanov Ukr. **39** E2
Stalingrad Rus. Fed. *see* Volgograd
Stalowa Wola Pol. **51** E2
Stamford U.K. **47** C3
Stamford *CT* U.S.A. **123** F2
Stamford *TX* U.S.A. **127** E2
Stampriet Namibia **98** A1
Standish U.S.A. **122** D2
Stanger S. Africa **99** D2
Staňkov Czech Rep. **49** F3
Stanley Falkland Is **137** C6
Stanley U.S.A. **120** C1
Stanovoy Nagor'ye *mts* Rus. Fed. **87** J3
Stanovoy Khrebet *mts* Rus. Fed. **87** K3
Stanthorpe Austr. **105** E1
Starachowice Pol. **51** E2

Stara Planina *mts* Bulg./S.M. *see* Balkan Mountains
Staraya Russa Rus. Fed. **37** D2
Staraya Toropa Rus. Fed. **37** D2
Stara Zagora Bulg. **58** C2
Stargard Szczeciński Pol. **51** D2
Starkville U.S.A. **124** C2
Starobil's'k Ukr. **39** E2
Starodub Rus. Fed. **37** D3
Starogard Gdański Pol. **51** D2
Starokostyantyniv Ukr. **38** C2
Starominskaya Rus. Fed. **39** E2
Staroshcherbinovskaya Rus. Fed. **39** E2
Starotitarovskaya Rus. Fed. **39** E2
Start Point U.K. **47** B4
Staryya Darohi Belarus **36** C3
Staryy Oskol Rus. Fed. **37** E3
Staßfurt Ger. **49** E2
State College U.S.A. **123** E2
Statesboro U.S.A. **125** D2
Statesville U.S.A. **125** D1
Stavanger Norway **41** B4
Stavropol' Rus. Fed. **35** D4
Stavropol'skaya Vozvyshennost' *hills* Rus. Fed. **35** D4
Stawell Austr. **104** C3
Steamboat Springs U.S.A. **120** B2
Steen River Can. **112** D2
Steens Mountain U.S.A. **118** C2
Steenwijk Neth. **48** C1
Stefansson Island Can. **110** E2
Steigerwald *mts* Ger. **49** E3
Steinbach Can. **113** F3
Steinfurt Ger. **48** C1
Steinhausen Namibia **96** A2
Steinkjer Norway **40** C3
Steinkort S. Africa **98** A2
Stella S. Africa **98** B2
Stendal Ger. **49** E1
Stephenville Can. **115** E2
Stephenville U.S.A. **127** E2
Sterling S. Africa **98** B3
Sterling *CO* U.S.A. **120** C2
Sterlitamak Rus. Fed. **35** E3
Steubenville U.S.A. **123** D2
Stevenage U.K. **47** C4
Stevenson Lake Can. **113** F2
Stevens Village U.S.A. **110** C2
Stewart Can. **112** C2
Stewart r. Can. **112** B1
Stewart Island N.Z. **106** A4
Steyr Austria **50** C3
Steytlerville S. Africa **98** B3
Stikine r. Can. **112** B2
Stikine Plateau Can. **112** B2
Stilbaai S. Africa **98** B3
Stillwater U.S.A. **127** E1
Štip Macedonia **59** D2
Stirling U.K. **44** C2
Stjørdalshalsen Norway **40** C3
Stockholm Sweden **41** D4

Stockport U.K. **46** B3
Stockton U.S.A. **119** B3
Stockton-on-Tees U.K. **46** C2
Stod Czech Rep. **49** F3
Stœng Trêng Cambodia **67** B2
Stoke-on-Trent U.K. **46** B3
Stol *mt.* S.M. **58** B2
Stolberg (Rheinland) Ger. **48** C2
Stolbovoy Rus. Fed. **34** E1
Stolin Belarus **36** C3
Stollberg Ger. **49** F2
Stolzenau Ger. **49** D1
Stonehaven U.K. **44** C2
Stony Rapids Can. **110** E3
Storavan *l.* Sweden **40** D2
Store Bælt *sea chan.* Denmark *see* Great Belt
Støren Norway **40** C3
Storkerson Peninsula Can. **110** E2
Storm Lake U.S.A. **121** D2
Stornoway U.K. **44** A1
Storozhevsk Rus. Fed. **34** E2
Storozhynets' Ukr. **38** C2
Storsjön *l.* Sweden **40** C3
Storslett Norway **40** D1
Storuman Sweden **40** C2
Storuman *l.* Sweden **40** C2
Stour *r.* England U.K. **47** C3
Stour *r.* England U.K. **47** C4
Stout Lake Can. **114** A1
Stowbtsy Belarus **36** C3
Strabane U.K. **45** C1
Strakonice Czech Rep. **50** C3
Stralsund Ger. **50** C2
Stranda Norway **41** B3
Strangford Lough *inlet* U.K. **45** D1
Stranraer U.K. **44** B3
Strasbourg France **53** D2
Strasburg Ger. **49** F1
Stratford Can. **123** D2
Stratford N.Z. **106** B2
Stratford U.S.A. **127** C1
Stratford-upon-Avon U.K. **47** C3
Strathspey *val.* U.K. **44** C2
Straubing Ger. **50** C3
Strausberg Ger. **49** F1
Streaky Bay Austr. **104** A2
Streator U.S.A. **122** C2
Strehaia Romania **38** B3
Strœder Arg. **137** B5
Ströhen Ger. **49** D1
Stromboli, Isola *i.* Italy **56** C3
Stromness U.K. **44** C1
Strömsund Sweden **40** C3
Stronsay *i.* U.K. **44** C1
Stroud U.K. **47** B4
Stroud U.K. **47** B4
Struga Macedonia **59** B3
Strugi-Krasnyye Rus. Fed. **36** C2
Struis Bay S. Africa **98** B3
Strumica Macedonia **59** B2

Strydenburg S. Africa **98** B3
Stryy Ukr. **38** B2
Stuart Lake Can. **112** C2
Stull Lake Can. **113** F4
Stupino Rus. Fed. **37** E3
Sturgeon Lake Can. **114** A2
Sturgis *SD* U.S.A. **120** C2
Sturgis *SD* U.S.A. **120** C2
Sturt Creek *watercourse* Austr. **102** B1
Sturt Stony Desert Austr. **104** C1
Stutterheim S. Africa **99** C3
Stuttgart Ger. **50** B3
Stuttgart U.S.A. **124** B2
Stykkishólmur Iceland **40** [inset]
Styr *r.* Belarus/Ukr. **38** C1
Suaçuí Grande *r.* Brazil **139** D1
Suakin Sudan **92** B3
Suara, Mount Eritrea **82** A3
Subotica S.M. **58** A1
Suceava Romania **38** C2
Suck *r.* Ireland **45** B2
Sucre Bol. **136** B2
Sucuriú *r.* Brazil **138** B2
Suda Rus. Fed. **37** E2
Sudak Ukr. **39** D3
Sudan *country* Africa **93** A3
Sudbury Can. **114** B2
Sudd *swamp* Sudan **93** A4
Sudogda Rus. Fed. **37** F2
Suðuroy *i.* Faroe Is **42** B1
Sueca Spain **55** C2
Suez Egypt **92** B2
Suez, Gulf of Egypt **92** B2
Suez Canal Egypt **84** B2
Suffolk U.S.A. **123** E3
Şuhār Oman **83** C2
Sühbaatar Mongolia **72** D1
Suhl Ger. **49** E2
Suide China **74** B2
Suifenhe China **70** B2
Suihua China **73** E1
Suining China **74** A2
Suiping China **74** B2
Suiyang China **74** B2
Suizhou China **74** B2
Sujangarh India **78** B2
Sujanpur India **78** B1
Sujawal Pak. **78** A2
Sukabumi Indon. **64** B2
Sukadana Indon. **65** B2
Sukaraja Indon. **65** C2
Sukhinichi Rus. Fed. **37** E3
Sukhona *r.* Rus. Fed. **37** F2
Sukhothai Thai. **66** A2
Sukkur Pak. **78** A2
Sula *i.* Norway **42** D1
Sula, Kepulauan *is* Indon. **63** C3
Sulaiman Range *mts* Pak. **78** A1
Sulawesi *i.* Indon. *see* Celebes
Sullana Peru **134** A3
Sullivan U.S.A. **121** E3

Sulphur Springs U.S.A. **127** E2
Sulu Archipelago *is* Phil. **68** B3
Sulu Sea N. Pacific Ocean **68** A3
Sulzbach-Rosenberg Ger. **49** E3
Sumāil Oman **83** C2
Sumatera *i.* Indon. *see* Sumatra
Sumatra *i.* Indon. **64** A1
Šumava *mts* Czech Rep. **49** F3
Sumba *i.* Indon. **65** C2
Sumba, Selat *sea chan.* Indon. **65** C2
Sumbawa *i.* Indon. **65** C2
Sumbawanga Tanz. **95** D3
Sumbe Angola **96** A1
Sumburgh U.K. **44** [inset]
Sumburgh Head U.K. **44** [inset]
Sumenep Indon. **65** C2
Sumisu-jima *i.* Japan **71** D4
Summerside Can. **115** D2
Summit Lake Can. **112** C2
Šumperk Czech Rep. **51** D3
Sumqayıt Azer. **85** C1
Sumter U.S.A. **125** D2
Sumy Ukr. **39** D1
Sunan N. Korea **69** B2
Şunaynah Oman **83** C2
Sunbury Austr. **104** C3
Sunch'ŏn N. Korea **69** B2
Sunch'ŏn S. Korea **69** B3
Sun City S. Africa **99** C2
Sunda, Selat *str.* Indon. **64** B2
Sundance U.S.A. **120** C2
Sundarbans *coastal area* Bangl./India **79** C2
Sunderland U.K. **46** C2
Sundsvall Sweden **41** D3
Sundumbili S. Africa **99** D2
Sungaliat Indon. **64** B2
Sungaipenuh Indon. **64** B2
Sungai Petani Malaysia **64** B1
Sungurlu Turkey **84** B1
Sunndal Norway **42** E1
Sunndalsøra Norway **40** C3
Sunnyside U.S.A. **118** C1
Sunnyvale U.S.A. **119** B3
Sunyani Ghana **90** B4
Superior *NE* U.S.A. **121** D2
Superior *WI* U.S.A. **122** B1
Superior, Lake Can./U.S.A. **122** C1
Suponevo Rus. Fed. **37** D3
Süq ash Shuyūkh Iraq **85** C2
Suqian China **74** B2
Süq Suwayq Saudi Arabia **82** A2
Suqutrā *i.* Yemen *see* Socotra
Şür Oman **83** C2
Surab Pak. **78** A2
Surabaya Indon. **65** C2
Surakarta Indon. **65** C2
Surat India **78** B2
Suratgarh India **78** B2

at Thani Thai. 67 A3
azh Rus. Fed. 37 D3
dulica S.M. 58 B2
endranagar India 78 B2
gut Rus. Fed. 34 G2
ago Phil. 68 B3
n Thai. 67 B2
maue country S. America 35 D2
ulangun Indon. 64 B2
anino Rus. Fed. 37 F2
anville U.S.A. 118 B2
ethy Turkey 84 B1
ice Czech Rep. 49 F3
sex Can. 115 D2
tedt Ger. 49 D1
suman Rus. Fed. 87 L2
urluk Turkey 59 C3
ak Jammu and Kashmir B1
herland S. Africa 98 B3
ton Coldfield U.K. 47 C3
tsu Japan 70 D2
va Fiji 100
orov Rus. Fed. 37 E3
valki Pol. 51 E2
wannaphum Thai. 67 B2
wannee r. U.S.A. 125 D3
ways, Qanāt as canal Egypt
e Suez Canal
wŏn S. Korea 69 B2
edal' Rus. Fed. 37 F2
zhou Anhui China 74 B2
zhou Jiangsu China 74 C2
zu Japan 71 C3
eu-misaki pt Japan 71 C3
albard terr. Arctic Ocean
6 C1
atove Ukr. 39 E2
ay Riêng Cambodia 67 B2
eg Sweden 41 C3
elgen Norway 44 G2
nciğnys Lith. 36 C2
erdlovsk Rus. Fed. see
ekaterinburg
eti Nikole Macedonia 58 B2
ttaya Rus. Fed. 70 C1
atlogorsk Rus. Fed. 36 B3
atly Rus. Fed. 36 B3
atogorsk Rus. Fed. 41 F3
necea Mare, Vârful mt.
omania 38 B3
r' r. Rus. Fed. 37 E1
ishtov Bulg. 58 C2
tavy Czech Rep. 51 D3
tlovods'k Ukr. 39 D2
obodnyy Rus. Fed. 73 E1
olvaer Norway 40 C2
vyetlahorsk Belarus 36 C3
rakop watercourse Namibia
98 A1
rakopmund Namibia 96 A2
van Hill Austr. 104 C3
van Lake Can. 113 E2

Swan River Can. 113 E2
Swansea U.K. 47 B4
Swatow China see Shantou
Swaziland country Africa 99 D2
Sweden country Europe 41 D3
Sweetwater U.S.A. 127 D2
Swellendam S. Africa 98 B3
Świdnica Pol. 51 D2
Świdwin Pol. 51 D2
Świebodzin Pol. 51 D2
Świecie Pol. 51 D2
Swift Current Can. 110 E3
Swindon U.K. 47 C4
Świnoujście Pol. 50 C2
Switzerland country Europe
53 D2
Swords Ireland 45 C2
Syanno Belarus 36 C3
Sychevka Rus. Fed. 37 D2
Sydney Austr. 105 E2
Sydney Can. 115 D2
Syeverodonets'k Ukr. 39 E2
Syktyvkar Rus. Fed. 34 E2
Sylacauga U.S.A. 125 C2
Sylhet Bangl. 79 D2
Sylt i. Ger. 50 B2
Symi i. Greece 59 C3
Synel'nykove Ukr. 39 E2
Syracuse Italy 56 C3
Syracuse KS U.S.A. 120 C2
Syracuse NY U.S.A. 123 E2
Syrdar'ya r. Asia 80 B2
Syria country Asia 84 B2
Syrian Desert Asia 84 B2
Syros i. Greece 59 B3
Syzran' Rus. Fed. 35 D3
Szczecin Pol. 50 C2
Szczecinek Pol. 51 D2
Szczytno Pol. 51 E2
Szeged Hungary 51 E3
Székesfehérvár Hungary 51 D3
Szekszárd Hungary 51 D3
Szigetvár Hungary 51 D3
Szolnok Hungary 51 E3
Szombathely Hungary 51 D3

T

Tabas Iran 85 D2
Tābask, Kūh-e mt. Iran 85 D3
Tabelbala Alg. 90 B2
Taber Can. 113 D3
Tábor Czech Rep. 50 C3
Tabora Tanz. 95 D3
Tabou Côte d'Ivoire 90 B4
Tabriz Iran 85 C2
Tabūk Saudi Arabia 82 A2
Täby Sweden 36 A2
Tacheng China 81 F2
Tachov Czech Rep. 50 C3

Tacloban Phil. 68 B2
Tacna Peru 134 B4
Tacoma U.S.A. 118 B1
Tacuarembó Uru. 136 C4
Tacupeto Mex. 126 C3
Tadjoura Djibouti 93 C3
Tadmur Syria 84 B2
Tadoule Lake Can. 113 F2
Taegu S. Korea 69 B2
Taejŏn S. Korea 69 B2
Tafarqi China 73 E1
Tafalla Spain 55 C1
Tafi Viejo Arg. 136 B3
Taftān, Kūh-e mt. Iran 83 D2
Taganrog Rus. Fed. 39 E2
Taganrog, Gulf of Rus. Fed./Ukr.
39 E2
Tagbilaran Phil. 68 B3
Tagum Phil. 68 B3
Tagus r. Port. 54 B2
Tagus r. Spain 54 B2
Tahat, Mont mt. Alg. 91 C2
Tahe China 73 E1
Tahiti i. Fr. Polynesia 101
Tahlequah U.S.A. 127 F1
Tahoe, Lake U.S.A. 119 B3
Tahoe City U.S.A. 119 B3
Tahoua Niger 91 C3
Tahrūd Iran 83 C2
Tahsis Can. 112 C3
Tai'an China 74 B2
T'aichung Taiwan 75 C3
Taihape N.Z. 106 C2
Tailem Bend Austr. 104 B3
T'ainan Taiwan 75 C3
Taiobeiras Brazil 139 D1
T'aipei Taiwan 75 C3
Taiping Malaysia 64 B1
Taishan China 75 B3
T'aitung Taiwan 75 C3
Taivalkoski Fin. 40 F2
Taivaskero h. Fin. 40 E2
Taiwan country Asia 75 C3
Taiwan Strait China/Taiwan
75 B3
Taiyuan China 74 B2
Taizhou Jiangsu China 74 B2
Taizhou Zhejiang China 75 C3
Ta'izz Yemen 82 B3
Tajamulco, Volcán de vol. Guat.
129 C3
Tajikistan country Asia 81 E3
Taj Mahal tourist site India
79 B2
Tajo r. Spain see Tagus
Tak Thai. 66 A2
Takaka N.Z. 106 B3
Takamatsu Japan 71 B4
Takaoka Japan 71 C3
Takapuna N.Z. 106 B2
Takasaki Japan 71 C3
Takatokwane Botswana 98 B1

Takatshwaane *Ghanzi* Botswana 98 B1
Takayama Japan 71 C3
Takengon Indon. 64 A1
Takêv Cambodia 67 B2
Takhemaret Alg. 55 D2
Takikawa Japan 70 D2
Takla Lake Can. 112 C2
Takla Landing Can. 112 C2
Taklimakan Desert China 81 F3
Taklimakan Shamo *des.* China *see* Taklimakan Desert
Taku *r.* Can./U.S.A. 112 B2
Takua Pa Thai. 67 A3
Talachyn Belarus 36 C3
Talara Peru 134 A3
Talaud, Kepulauan *is* Indon. 63 C2
Talavera de la Reina Spain 54 C2
Talca Chile 137 A4
Talcahuano Chile 137 A4
Taldom Rus. Fed. 37 E2
Taldykorgan Kazakh. 81 E2
Talia Austr. 104 A2
Talisay Phil. 68 B2
Taliwang Indon. 65 C2
Tal'Afar Iraq 85 C2
Tallahassee U.S.A. 125 D2
Tallinn Estonia 36 B2
Tallulah U.S.A. 124 B2
Tal'ne Ukr. 38 D2
Talodi Sudan 93 B3
Taloqan Afgh. 78 A1
Talovaya Rus. Fed. 37 F3
Taloyoak Can. 110 F2
Talsi Latvia 36 B2
Taltal Chile 136 A3
Taltson *r.* Can. 113 D1
Talu Indon. 64 A1
Talwood Austr. 105 D1
Tamala Rus. Fed. 39 F1
Tamale Ghana 90 B4
Tamanrasset Alg. 91 C2
Tamar *r.* U.K. 47 A4
Tambacounda Senegal 90 A3
Tambelan, Kepulauan *is* Indon. 64 B1
Tambey Rus. Fed. 34 G1
Tambov Rus. Fed. 37 F3
Tamiahua, Laguna de *lag.* Mex. 129 C2
Tampa U.S.A. 125 D3
Tampa Bay U.S.A. 125 D3
Tampere Fin. 41 E3
Tampico Mex. 129 C2
Tamworth Austr. 105 E2
Tamworth U.K. 47 C3
Tana *r.* Kenya 95 E3
Tana, Lake Eth. 93 B3
Tanabe Japan 71 C4
Tana Bru Norway 40 F1
Tanahgrogot Indon. 65 C2
Tanahjampea *i.* Indon. 65 D2

Tanami Desert Austr. 102 C1
Tanan *r.* Italy 56 A1
Tanch'ŏn N. Korea 69 B1
Tandag Phil. 68 B3
Tāndārei Romania 38 C3
Tandil Arg. 137 C4
Tando Adam Pak. 78 A2
Tando Muhammad Khan Pak. 78 A2
Tanezrouft *reg.* Alg./Mali 90 B2
Tanga Tanz. 95 D3
Tanganyika, Lake Africa 95 C3
Tanger Morocco *see* Tangier
Tangermünde Ger. 49 E1
Tanggula Shan *mt.* China 79 D1
Tanggula Shan *mts* China 79 C1
Tangier Morocco 90 B1
Tangra Yumco *salt* l. China 79 C1
Tangshan China 74 B2
Taniantaweng Shan *mts* China 72 C2
Tanimbar, Kepulauan *is* Indon. 63 C3
Tanjay Phil. 68 B3
Tanjungbalai Indon. 64 A1
Tanjungpandan Indon. 64 B2
Tanjungpinang Indon. 64 B1
Tanjungredeb Indon. 65 C1
Tanjungselor Indon. 65 C1
Tanout Niger 91 C3
Tansen Nepal 79 C2
Tanțā Egypt 92 B1
Tanzania *country* Africa 95 D3
Taoudenni Mali 90 B2
Tapa Estonia 36 C2
Tapachula Mex. 129 C3
Tapajós *r.* Brazil 135 D3
Tapaktuan Indon. 64 A1
Tapauá Brazil 134 C3
Tapeta Liberia 90 B4
Tapi *r.* India 78 B2
Tapurucuara Brazil 134 C3
Taquari *r.* Brazil 138 A1
Taquari, Pantanal do *marsh* Brazil 138 A1
Taquari, Serra do *hills* Brazil 138 B1
Taquaritinga Brazil 138 C2
Tarābulus Libya *see* Tripoli
Tarakan Indon. 65 C1
Taran, Mys *pt* Rus. Fed. 36 A3
Taranaki, Mount *vol.* N.Z. 106 B2
Tarancón Spain 54 C1
Taranto Italy 57 C2
Taranto, Golfo di *g.* Italy 57 C2
Tarapoto Peru 134 B3
Tarasovskiy Rus. Fed. 39 F2
Taraszcá Brazil 134 B3
Taraszcá *r.* Brazil 134 C3
Tarawa *atoll* Kiribati 100
Taraz Kazakh. 81 E2
Tarazona Spain 55 C1
Tarbagatay, Khrebet *mts* Kazakh. 81 F2

Tarbert *Scotland* U.K. 44 B3
Tarbert *Scotland* U.K. 44 A2
Tarbes France 52 C3
Tarbet U.K. 44 B2
Tarcoola Austr. 104 A2
Taree Austr. 105 E2
Târgoviște Romania 38 C3
Targuist Morocco 54 C3
Târgu Jiu Romania 38 B2
Târgu Mureş Romania 38 B2
Târgu Neamţ Romania 38 C2
Tarif U.A.E. 83 C2
Tarija Bol. 136 B3
Tarim Yemen 83 B3
Tarim Basin China 81 F3
Tarim He *r.* China 81 F2
Tarim Pendi *basin* China *see* Tarim Basin
Taritatu *r.* Indon. 63 D3
Tarko-Sale Rus. Fed. 34 G2
Tarlac Phil. 68 B2
Tärnaby Sweden 40 D2
Tarnak *r.* Afgh. 78 A1
Târnăveni Romania 38 B2
Tarnobrzeg Pol. 51 E2
Tarnów Pol. 51 E2
Taroudannt Morocco 90 B1
Tarquinia Italy 56 B2
Tarragona Spain 55 D1
Tàrrega Spain 55 D1
Tarsus Turkey 84 B2
Tartagal Arg. 136 B3
Tartu Estonia 36 C2
Ţarţūs Syria 84 B2
Tarumirim Brazil 139 D1
Tashk, Daryācheh-ye *l.* Iran 85 D3
Tashkent Uzbek. 81 D2
Tasialujjuaq, Lac *l.* Can. 115 C1
Tasiat, Lac *l.* Can. 114 C1
Tasiujaq Can. 115 D1
Taskesken Kazakh. 81 F2
Tasman Bay N.Z. 106 B3
Tasmania *i.* Austr. 100
Tasmania *state* Austr. 103 D4
Tasman Mountains N.Z. 106 B3
Tasman Sea S. Pacific Ocean 103 E3
Tassili du Hoggar *plat.* Alg. 91 C2
Tassili n'Ajjer *plat.* Alg. 91 C2
Tatabe Indon. 65 D2
Tatabánya Hungary 51 D3
Tatarbunary Ukr. 38 C2
Tatarskiy Proliv *str.* Rus. Fed. 73 F1
Tathlina Lake Can. 112 D1
Tathlīth Saudi Arabia 82 B3
Tathlīth, Wādī *watercourse* Saudi Arabia 82 B2
Tathra Austr. 105 D3
Tatkon Myanmar 66 A1
Tatra Mountains Pol. 51 D3
Tatsinskiy Rus. Fed. 39 F2

'atta Pak. **78** A2
'atuí Brazil **138** C2
'atum U.S.A. **127** D2
'atvan Turkey **85** C2
'aua Brazil **138** E3
'aubaté Brazil **139** C2
'auberbischofsheim Ger. **49** D3
'aunggui Myanmar **66** A1
'aung-ngu Myanmar **66** A2
'aungup Myanmar **66** A2
'aunton U.K. **47** B4
'aunus hills Ger. **48** C2
'aupo N.Z. **106** C2
'aupo, Lake N.Z. **106** C2
'auranga N.Z. **106** C2
'auranga Turkey **84** B2
'aurus Mountains Turkey **84** B2
'avas Turkey **59** C3
'avda Rus. Fed. **34** F3
'avistock U.K. **47** A4
'avoy Myanmar **67** A2
'avşanli Turkey **59** C3
'aw r. U.K. **47** A4
'awas City U.S.A. **122** D2
'awau Malaysia **65** C1
'awitawi i. Phil. **68** A3
'axco Mex. **129** C3
'axiatosh Uzbek. **80** C2
'axkorgan China **81** E3
'ay r. U.K. **44** C2
'ay, Firth of est. U.K. **44** C2
'ayabas U.S.A. **127** E2
'aylorville U.S.A. **122** C3
'aymā' Saudi Arabia **82** A2
'aymyr, Ozero l. Rus. Fed. **87** I2
'aymyr, Poluostrov pen.
Rus. Fed. see Taymyr Peninsula
'aymyr Peninsula Rus. Fed.
87 H2
'ay Ninh Vietnam **67** B2
'aytay Phil. **68** A2
'az r. Rus. Fed. **34** G2
'za Morocco **90** B1
'zin Lake Can. **113** E2
'zoult Lambèse Alg. **55** E2
'bilisi Georgia **85** C1
'illisskaya Rus. Fed. **39** F2
'hibanga Gabon **94** B3
'ew Pol. **51** D2
'Anau N.Z. **106** A4
'Anau, Lake N.Z. **106** A4
'apa Mex. **129** C3
'Awamutu N.Z. **106** C2
'bessa Alg. **91** C1
'bingtinggi Sumatera Utara
Indon. **64** A1
'chiman Ghana **90** B4
'comán Mex. **128** B3
'coripa Mex. **128** B2
'cpan Mex. **129** B3
'cuala Mex. **128** B2
'cuci Romania **38** C2

Tedzhen Turkm. **80** D3
Teeli Rus. Fed. **81** G1
Tees r. U.K. **46** C2
Tefenni Turkey **59** C3
Tegal Indon. **64** B2
Tegucigalpa Hond. **130** B3
Teguidda-n-Tessoumt Niger
91 C3
Tehek Lake Can. **113** F1
Tehrān Iran **85** D2
Tehuacán Mex. **129** C3
Tehuantepec, Golfo de g. Mex.
129 C3
Tehuantepec, Istmo de isth. Mex.
129 C3
Teifi r. U.K. **47** A3
Tejo r. Port. see Tagus
Tekapo, Lake N.Z. **106** B3
Tekax Mex. **129** D2
Tekirdağ Turkey **59** C2
Te Kuiti N.Z. **106** C2
T'elavi Georgia **85** C1
Tel Aviv-Yafo Israel **84** B2
Telegraph Creek Can. **112** B2
Telémaco Borba Brazil **138** B2
Telford U.K. **47** B3
Telo Indon. **64** A2
Tel'pos-Iz, Gora mt. Rus. Fed.
34 E2
Telšiai Lith. **36** B2
Telukbatang Indon. **65** B2
Telukdalam Indon. **64** A1
Teluk Intan Malaysia **64** B1
Temagami Lake Can. **114** C2
Temba S. Africa **99** C2
Tembilahan Indon. **64** B2
Tembo Aluma Angola **94** B3
Temerluh Malaysia **64** B1
Temirtau Kazakh. **81** E1
Temora Austr. **105** D2
Temple U.S.A. **127** E2
Templemore Ireland **45** C2
Templin Ger. **49** F1
Tempoal Mex. **129** C2
Temryuk Rus. Fed. **39** E2
Temuco Chile **137** A4
Temuka N.Z. **106** B3
Tenabo Mex. **129** C2
Tenali India **77** C3
Tenasserim Myanmar **67** A2
Tendaho Eth. **93** C3
Tende France **53** D3
Ten Degree Channel India **67** A3
Tendō Japan **70** D3
Ténéré, Erg du des. Niger **91** D3
Ténéré du Tafassâsset des.
Niger **91** D2
Tenerife i. Canary Is **90** A2
Ténès Alg. **55** D2
Tengah, Kepulauan is Indon.
65 C2
Tengchong China **66** A1
Tenggarong Indon. **65** C2
Tengger Shamo des. China **74** A2

Tenke Dem. Rep. Congo **95** C4
Tenkodogo Burkina **90** B3
Tennant Creek Austr. **102** C1
Tennessee r. U.S.A. **124** C1
Tennessee state U.S.A. **124** C1
Tenosique Mex. **129** C3
Tenteno Indon. **65** D2
Tenterfield Austr. **105** E1
Teodoro Sampaio Brazil **138** B2
Teófilo Otôni Brazil **139** D1
Tepache Mex. **128** B2
Te Paki N.Z. **106** B1
Tepatitlán Mex. **128** B2
Tepelenë Albania **59** B2
Tepic Mex. **128** B2
Teplice Czech Rep. **50** C2
Tequila Mex. **128** B2
Teramo Italy **56** B2
Terebovlya Ukr. **38** C2
Terek r. Rus. Fed. **35** D4
Teresina Brazil **135** E3
Teresópolis Brazil **139** D2
Teressa Island India **67** A3
Tergnier France **48** A3
Terme Turkey **84** B1
Termini Imerese Italy **56** B3
Términos, Laguna de lag. Mex.
129 C3
Termiz Uzbek. **81** D3
Termoli Italy **56** B2
Ternate Indon. **63** C2
Terneuzen Neth. **48** A2
Terni Italy **56** B2
Ternopil' Ukr. **38** C2
Terpeniya, Mys c. Rus. Fed.
73 F1
Terpeniya, Zaliv g. Rus. Fed.
73 F1
Terrace Can. **112** C2
Terrace Bay Can. **114** B2
Terra Firma S. Africa **98** B2
Terre Haute U.S.A. **122** C3
Terschelling i. Neth. **48** B1
Tertenia Italy **56** A3
Teruel Spain **55** C1
Tervola Fin. **40** E2
Teseney Eritrea **82** A3
Teshio-gawa r. Japan **70** D2
Teslin Can. **112** B1
Teslin Lake Can. **112** B1
Tesouro Brazil **138** B1
Tessaoua Niger **91** C3
Tete Moz. **97** C1
Teteriv r. Ukr. **38** D1
Teterow Ger. **49** F1
Tetiyiv Ukr. **38** C2
Tétouan Morocco **90** B1
Tetovo Macedonia **58** B2
Teuco r. Arg. **136** B3
Tevere r. Italy see Tiber
Teviot N.Z. **106** A4
Tewantin Austr. **103** E2
Te Wharau N.Z. **106** C3
Texarkana U.S.A. **127** F2

Texas Austr. **105** E1
Texas *state* U.S.A. **127** E2
Texas City U.S.A. **127** F3
Texel *i.* Neth. **48** B1
Texoma, Lake U.S.A. **127** E2
Teykovo Rus. Fed. **37** F2
Teza *r.* Rus. Fed. **37** F2
Tezpur India **79** D2
Tezu India **66** A1
Tha-anne *r.* Can. **113** F1
Thabana-Ntlenyana *mt.* Lesotho
99 C2
Thabazimbi S. Africa **99** C1
Thabong S. Africa **99** C2
Thagyettaw Myanmar **67** A2
Thai Binh Vietnam **66** B1
Thailand *country* Asia **67** B2
Thailand, Gulf of Asia **67** B2
Thai Nguyên Vietnam **66** B1
Thakèk Laos **66** B2
Thalang Thai. **67** A3
Thal Desert Pak. **78** B1
Thale (Harz) Ger. **49** E2
Thamar, Jabal *mt.* Yemen **82** B3
Thamarit Oman **83** C3
Thames *r.* Can. **114** B2
Thames N.Z. **106** C2
Thames *r.* U.K. **47** D4
Thanbyuzayat Myanmar **67** A2
Thandwè Myanmar **66** A2
Thanh Hoa Vietnam **66** B2
Thanjavur India **77** B3
Thanlyin Myanmar **66** A2
Thar Desert India/Pak. **78** A2
Thargomindah Austr. **104** C1
Tharthār, Buhayrat *ath l.* Iraq
85 C2
Thasos *i.* Greece **59** B2
Thaton Myanmar **66** A2
Thaungdut Myanmar **67** A2
Thayawadi Myanmar **66** A2
Thayetmyo Myanmar **66** A2
Thazi Myanmar **66** A1
The Bahamas *country*
West Indies **131** C2
The Cheviot *h.* U.K. **46** B2
The Dalles U.S.A. **118** B1
The Fens *reg.* U.K. **47** C3
The Great Oasis Egypt *see*
Khārijah, Wāḥāt al
The Gulf Asia **83** C2
The Hague Neth. **48** B1
The Minch *sea chan.* U.K. **44** A1
Theodore Roosevelt *r.* Brazil
134 C3
The Pas Can. **113** E2
Thermaïkos Kolpos *g.* Greece
59 B2
Thermopolis U.S.A. **120** B2
The Rock Austr. **105** D3
Thessalon Can. **114** B2

Thessaloniki Greece **59** B2
Thetford U.K. **47** D3
The Triangle *mts* Myanmar
66 A1
Thévenet, Lac *l.* Can. **115** D1
Thibodaux U.S.A. **124** B3
Thicket Portage Can. **113** F2
Thief River Falls U.S.A. **121** D1
Thiers France **52** C2
Thika Kenya **95** D3
Thiladhunmathi Atoll Maldives
77 B4
Thimphu Bhutan **79** C2
Thionville France **53** D2
Thira *i.* Greece **59** C3
Thirsk U.K. **46** C2
Thisted Denmark **41** B4
Thlewiaza *r.* Can. **113** F1
Thoen Thai. **66** A2
Thohoyandou S. Africa **99** D1
Thomastown Ireland **45** C2
Thomasville U.S.A. **125** D2
Thompson Can. **113** F2
Thompson *r.* U.S.A. **112** D2
Thompson Falls U.S.A. **118** C1
Thompson Sound Can. **112** C2
Thorshavnheiane *reg.* Antarctica
107 C2
Thouars France **52** B2
Three Gorges Dam Project *resr*
China **75** B2
Three Pagodas Pass
Myanmar/Thai. **67** A2
Thuin Belgium **48** B2
Thule Greenland **111** H1
Thunder Bay Can. **114** B2
Thung Song Thai. **67** A3
Thüringer Wald *mts* Ger. **49** E2
Thurles Ireland **45** C2
Thurso U.K. **44** C1
Thurso *r.* U.K. **44** C1
Tianjin China **74** B2
Tianjin *mun.* China **74** B2
Tianlin China **75** A3
Tianmen China **74** B2
Tianshan China **74** C1
Tianshui China **74** A2
Tianzhu China **74** A2
Tiaret Alg. **55** D2
Tibagi *r.* Brazil **138** B2
Tibati Cameroon **94** B2
Tiber *r.* Italy **56** B2
Tiberias, Lake Israel *see*
Galilee, Sea of
Tibesti *mts* Chad **91** D2
Tibet *aut. reg.* China *see*
Xizang Zizhiqu
Tibet, Plateau of China **79** C1
Tibooburra Austr. **104** C1
Tibúrón, Isla *i.* Mex. **128** A2
Tichît Maur. **90** B3
Tichla Western Sahara **90** A2
Ticul Mex. **129** D2

Tidjikja Maur. **90** A3
Tiel Neth. **48** B2
Tieling China **74** C1
Tielt Belgium **48** A2
Tienen Belgium **48** B2
Tienen Belgium **48** B2
Tien Shan *mts* China/Kyrg.
72 B2
Tientsin China *see* Tianjin
Tierp Sweden **41** D3
Tierra Blanca Mex. **129** C3
Tierra del Fuego, Isla Grande
de *i.* Arg./Chile **137** B6
Tietê Brazil **138** C2
Tietê *r.* Brazil **138** B2
Tiflis Georgia *see* Tbilisi
Tifton U.S.A. **125** D2
Tigre *r.* Ecuador/Peru **134** B3
Tigris *r.* Turkey **85** C2
Tijuana Mex. **128** A1
Tikhoretsk Rus. Fed. **39** F2
Tikhvin Rus. Fed. **37** D2
Tikhvinskaya Gryada *ridge*
Rus. Fed. **37** D2
Tikokino N.Z. **106** C2
Tikrīt Iraq **85** C2
Tiksi Rus. Fed. **87** K2
Tilburg Neth. **48** B2
Tilcha Austr. **104** C1
Tilemsès Niger **90** C3
Tilos *i.* Greece **59** C3
Tilpa Austr. **104** C2
Timanskiy Kryazh *ridge* Rus. Fed.
34 D2
Timaru N.Z. **106** B3
Timashevsk Rus. Fed. **39** E2
Timbedgha Maur. **90** B3
Timber Creek Austr. **102** C1
Timbuktu Mali **90** B3
Timimoun Alg. **90** C2
Timiș *r.* Romania **58** B1
Timișoara Romania **58** B1
Timmins Can. **114** B2
Timokhino Rus. Fed. **37** E2
Timon Brazil **135** E3
Timor *i.* East Timor/Indonesia
63 C3
Timor Sea Austr./Indon. **62** C3
Timrå Sweden **41** D3
Tindouf Alg. **90** B2
Tingri China **79** C2
Tinian *i.* N. Mariana Is **63** D2
Tinos Greece **59** C3
Tinos *i.* Greece **59** C3
Tinqueux France **48** A3
Tinrhert, Plateau du Alg. **91** C1
Tinsukia India **66** A1
Tipasa Alg. **55** D2
Tipperary Ireland **45** B2
Tirana Albania **59** A2
Tiranë Albania *see* Tirana
Tiraspol Moldova **38** C2
Tire Turkey **59** C3

ree i. U.K. **44** A2
rich Mir mt. Pak. **78** B1
ruchchirappalli India **77** B3
runelveli India **77** B4
rupati India **77** B3
ruppatur India **77** B3
r8 a i. S.M. **58** B1
sdale Can. **113** E2
ssemsilt Alg. **55** D2
ticaca, Lake Bol./Peru **136** D2
tlagarh India **79** C2
tu Romania **38** C3
tusville U.S.A. **125** D3
verton U.K. **47** B4
voli Italy **56** B2
øl Ouzou Alg. **55** D2
εnit Morocco **90** B2
acotalpán Mex. **129** C3
apa Mex. **129** C3
axcala Mex. **129** C3
emcen Alg. **90** B1
skweng Botswana **99** C1
ad River Can. **112** C2
amasina Madag. **97** [inset] D1
ba, Danau i. Indon. **64** A1
ba and Kakar Ranges mts Pak. **78** A1

rbago i. Trin. and Tob. **131** D3
lbermory Can. **114** D2
lbermory U.K. **44** A2
rbat Lake Can. **113** E2
rboali Indon. **64** B2
rbol r. Kazakh./Rus. Fed. **80** D1
rbol'sk Rus. Fed. **34** F3
rcantins r. Brazil **135** E3
rccoa U.S.A. **125** D2
rce r. Italy **56** A1
rcopilla Chile **136** A3
rdos Santos Mex. **128** A2
rtf U.K. **44** [inset]
rgian i. Indon. **65** D2
rgian, Kepulauan is Indon.
65 D2
rgo country Africa **90** C4
r. U.S.A. **112** A1
rkara-rettö is Japan **71** A3
rkarevka Rus. Fed. **37** F3
rkelau terr. S. Pacific Ocean
101
rkmak Ukr. **39** E2
rkmok Kyrg. **81** E2
rkoroa N.Z. **106** C2
rksun China **81** F2
rkyö Japan **71** C3
rlaharo Madag. **97** [inset] D2
rledo Brazil **138** B2
redo Spain **54** D2
redo U.S.A. **122** D2
redo, Montes de mts Spain
54 C2

Toledo Bend Reservoir U.S.A.
124 B2
Toliara Madag. **97** [inset] D2
Tolitoli Indon. **65** D1
Tolmezzo Italy **56** B1
Tolosa Spain **52** B3
Toluca Mex. **129** C3
Tol'yatti Rus. Fed. **35** D3
Tomah U.S.A. **122** B2
Tomakomai Japan **70** D2
Tomar Port. **54** B2
Tomaszów Lubelski Pol. **51** E2
Tomaszów Mazowiecki Pol.
51 E2
Tomatlán Mex. **128** B3
Tombigbee r. U.S.A. **124** C2
Tombos Brazil **139** D2
Tombouctou Mali see Timbuktu
Tombua Angola **96** A1
Tom Burke S. Africa **99** C1
Tomingley Austr. **105** D2
Tomini, Teluk g. Indon. **65** D2
Tom Price Austr. **102** A2
Tomsk Rus. Fed. **86** H3
Tomtabacken h. Sweden **41** C4
Tonalá Mex. **129** C3
Tonantins Brazil **134** C3
Tender Denmark **50** B2
Tonga country S. Pacific Ocean
101
Tongatapu Group is Tonga **101**
Tongcheng China **75** B3
Tongchuan China **74** A2
Tongdao China **75** A3
Tongduch'ōn S. Korea **69** B2
Tongeren Belgium **48** B2
Tonghae S. Korea **69** B2
Tonghai China **75** A3
Tonghua China **69** B1
Tongjosŏn-man b. N. Korea
69 B2
Tongking, Gulf of China/Vietnam
75 A3
Tongliao China **74** C1
Tongling China **74** B2
Tongo Austr. **104** C2
Tongren China **75** A3
Tongshan China **74** B2
Tongshi China see Wuzhishan
Tongtian He r. China see Yangtze
Tongue U.K. **44** B1
T'ongyŏng S. Korea **69** B3
Tongzi China **73** E2
Tonk India **78** B2
Tonle Sap l. Cambodia **67** B2
Tonopah U.S.A. **119** C3
Tensberg Norway **41** C4
Tooleybuc Austr. **104** C2
Toowoomba Austr. **105** E1
Topeka U.S.A. **121** D3
Topolobampo Mex. **128** B2
Topozero, Ozero l. Rus. Fed.
40 C2
Toppenish U.S.A. **118** B1

Torbalı Turkey **59** C3
Torbat-e Heydariyeh Iran **80** C3
Torbat-e Jām Iran **80** D3
Tordesillas Spain **54** C1
Tordesilos Spain **55** C1
Torgau Ger. **49** F2
Torgelow Ger. **49** G1
Torhout Belgium **48** A2
Torino Italy see Turin
Tori-shima i. Japan **71** D4
Torixoréu Brazil **138** B1
Tor'kovskoye Vodokhranilishche
resr Rus. Fed. **37** F2
Tormes r. Spain **54** B1
Torneälven r. Sweden **40** E2
Torngat Mountains Can.
115 D1
Tornio Fin. **40** E2
Toro Spain **54** B1
Toronto Can. **114** C2
Tororo Uganda **95** D2
Toros Dağları mts Turkey see
Taurus Mountains
Torquay U.K. **47** B4
Torre mt. Port. **54** B1
Torrecerredo mt. Spain **54** C1
Torrelavega Spain **54** C1
Torrens, Lake salt flat Austr.
104 B2
Torrent Spain **55** C2
Torreón Mex. **128** B2
Torres Novas Port. **54** B2
Torres Strait Austr. **100**
Torres Vedras Port. **54** B2
Torrevieja Spain **55** C2
Torridon U.K. **44** B2
Torrington WY U.S.A. **120** C2
Tórshavn Faroe Is **42** B1
Tortolì Italy **56** A3
Tortosa Spain **55** D1
Toruń Pol. **51** D2
Tory Island Ireland **45** B1
Torzhok Rus. Fed. **37** D2
Tosca S. Africa **98** B2
Toscano, Arcipelago is Italy
56 A2
Tosno Rus. Fed. **37** D2
Tostado Arg. **136** B3
Tostedt Ger. **49** D1
Tot'ma Rus. Fed. **37** F2
Tottori Japan **71** B3
Touba Côte d'Ivoire **90** B4
Tougan Burkina **90** B3
Touggourt Alg. **91** C1
Toul France **53** D2
Toulouse France **52** C3
Tourcoing France **48** A2
Tournai Belgium **48** A2
Touros Brazil **135** F3
Tours France **52** C2
Tousside, Pic mt. Chad **91** D2
Towada Japan **70** D2

Townsend U.S.A. **118** D1
Townsville Austr. **103** D1
Town, Teluk *b.* Indon. **65** D2
Toxkan He *r.* China **81** F2
Tōya-ko *l.* Japan **70** D2
Toyama Japan **71** C3
Toyota Japan **71** C3
Tozeur Tunisia **91** C1
Tqvarch'eli Georgia **85** C1
Trablous Lebanon *see* Tripoli
Trabzon Turkey **84** B1
Trafalgar, Cabo *c.* Spain **54** B2
Trail Can. **112** D3
Trakai Lith. **36** B3
Tralee Ireland **45** B2
Tramore Ireland **45** C2
Trang Thai. **67** A3
Trangan *i.* Indon. **63** C3
Transantarctic Mountains
  Antarctica **107** H2
Transylvanian Alps *mts* Romania
  38 B2
Trapani Italy **56** B3
Traralgon Austr. **105** D3
Trat Thai. **67** B2
Traunstein Ger. **50** C3
Traverse City U.S.A. **122** C2
Třebíč Czech Rep. **51** D3
Trebinje Bos.-Herz. **57** C2
Trebišov Slovakia **51** E3
Trelew Arg. **137** B5
Trelleborg Sweden **41** C4
Tremblant, Mont *h.* Can.
  114 C2
Tremiti, Isole *i.* Italy **56** C2
Tremonton U.S.A. **118** D2
Tremp Spain **55** D1
Trenčín Slovakia **51** D3
Trenque Lauquén Arg. **137** B4
Trent *r.* U.K. **46** C3
Trento Italy **56** D1
Trenton Can. **123** F2
Trenton *MO* U.S.A. **121** D2
Trenton *NJ* U.S.A. **123** F2
Tres Arroyos Arg. **137** B4
Três Corações Brazil **139** D2
Três Lagoas Brazil **138** B2
Três Lagos Arg. **137** A5
Três Marias, Represa *resr* Brazil
  139 C1
Três Pontas Brazil **139** C2
Três Rios Brazil **139** D2
Treviglio Italy **56** A1
Treviso Italy **56** B1
Trevose Head U.K. **47** A4
Tricase Italy **57** C3
Trichur India **77** B3
Trida Austr. **105** D2
Trier Ger. **48** C3
Trieste Italy **56** B1
Triglav *mt.* Slovenia **56** B1
Trincomalee Sri Lanka **77** C4

Trindade Brazil **138** C1
Trindad Bol. **136** B2
Trinidad *i.* Trin. and Tob. **131** D3
Trinidad U.S.A. **120** C3
Trinidad and Tobago *country*
  West Indies **131** D3
Trinity Bay Can. **115** E2
Tripoli Greece **59** B3
Tripoli Lebanon **84** B2
Tripoli Libya **91** D1
Tristan da Cunha *i.*
  S. Atlantic Ocean **144** D8
Trivandrum India **77** B4
Trnava Slovakia **51** D3
Trogir Croatia **57** C2
Troisdorf Ger. **48** C2
Trois-Rivières, Cap des *c.*
  Morocco **54** C2
Trois-Rivières Can. **115** C2
Troitsko-Pechorsk Rus. Fed.
  34 E2
Trombetas *r.* Brazil **135** D3
Trompsburg S. Africa **99** D3
Tromsø Norway **40** D2
Trondheim Norway **40** C3
Trout Lake Can. **112** D2
Trout Lake *l.* N.W.T. Can.
  112 C1
Trout Lake *l.* Ont. Can. **114** A1
Trowbridge U.K. **47** B4
Troy *AL* U.S.A. **125** C2
Troy *NY* U.S.A. **123** F2
Troyes France **52** C2
Trubchevsk Rus. Fed. **37** D3
Trujillo Hond. **130** B3
Trujillo Peru **134** B3
Trujillo Spain **54** B2
Trumann U.S.A. **124** B1
Truro Can. **115** D2
Truro U.K. **47** A4
Truth or Consequences U.S.A.
  126 C2
Trutnov Czech Rep. **51** D2
Trysil Norway **41** C3
Tsagaannuur Mongolia **72** B1
Tsaratanana, Massif du *mts*
  Madag. **97** [inset] D1
Tsarevo Bulg. **58** C2
Tselina Rus. Fed. **39** F2
Tses Namibia **98** A2
Tsetseng Botswana **98** B2
Tsetserleg Mongolia **72** D1
Tshabong Botswana **98** B2
Tshane Botswana **98** B1
Tschikskoye Vodokhranilishche
  resr Rus. Fed. **39** E2
Tshela Dem. Rep. Congo **94** B3
Tshikapa Dem. Rep. Congo
  94 C3
Tshikapa *r.* Dem. Rep. Congo
  94 C3
Tshitanzu Dem. Rep. Congo
  94 C3

Tshuapa *r.* Dem. Rep. Congo
  94 C3
Tshwane S. Africa *see* Pretoria
Tsimlyanskoye
  Vodokhranilishche *resr*
  Rus. Fed. **35** D4
Tsingtao China *see* Qingdao
Tsna *r.* Rus. Fed. **37** F3
Tsu Japan **71** C4
Tsuchiura Japan **71** D3
Tsugarū-kaikyō *str.* Japan **70** D2
Tsumeb Namibia **96** A1
Tsumis Park Namibia **98** A1
Tsumkwe Namibia **96** B1
Tsuruga Japan **71** C3
Tsuruoka Japan **70** C3
Tsushima *is* Japan **71** A4
Tsuyama Japan **71** B3
Tswelelang S. Africa **99** C2
Tsyurupyns'k Ukr. **39** D2
Tual Indon. **63** C3
Tuam Ireland **45** B2
Tuamotu Archipelago *is*
  Fr. Polynesia **143** F6
Tuapse Rus. Fed. **35** D4
Tuatapere N.Z. **106** A4
Tuba City U.S.A. **126** B1
Tubarão Brazil **136** D3
Tübingen Ger. **50** B3
Tubruq Libya **91** E1
Tubuai Islands Fr. Polynesia **10**
Tubutama Mex. **128** A1
Tuchitua Can. **112** C1
Tucson U.S.A. **126** B2
Tucumcari U.S.A. **127** C1
Tucupita Venez. **134** C2
Tucuruí Brazil **135** E3
Tucuruí, Represa *resr* Brazil
  135 E3
Tudela Spain **55** C1
Tuela *r.* Port. **54** B1
Tugela *r.* S. Africa **99** D2
Tuguegarao Phil. **68** B2
Tui Spain **54** B1
Tukangbesi, Kepulauan *is* Indon
  63 C3
Tuktoyaktuk Can. **110** D2
Tukums Latvia **36** B2
Tula Rus. Fed. **37** E3
Tulancingo Mex. **129** C2
Tulare U.S.A. **119** C3
Tularosa U.S.A. **126** C2
Tulcea Romania **38** C2
Tul'chyn Ukr. **38** C2
Tulemalu Lake Can. **113** F1
Tulia U.S.A. **127** D2
Tulit'a Can. **112** C1
Tullahoma U.S.A. **125** C1
Tullamore Ireland **45** C2
Tulle France **52** C2
Tulsa U.S.A. **127** E1
Tuluksak U.S.A. **110** B2
Tumaco Col. **134** B2
Tumahole S. Africa **99** C2

nba Sweden 41 D4
nba, Lac l. Dem. Rep. Congo 4 B3
nbarumba Austr. 105 D3
nbes Peru 134 A3
nbler Ridge Can. 112 C2
nby Bay Austr. 104 B3
nen China 69 B1
nereng Guyana 134 C2
nindao i. Phil. 68 A3
nkur India 77 B3
nnin r. Rus. Fed. 73 F1
np Pak. 78 A2
nucumaque, Serra hills Brazil 135 D2
nut Austr. 105 D3
nbridge Wells, Royal U.K. 47 D4
aceli Turkey 84 B2
ncurry Austr. 105 E2
nduru Tanz. 95 D4
agsten Can. 112 C1
nia Tunisia 91 D1
nisia country Africa 91 C1
nja Col. 134 B2
ansjoen l. Norway 40 C3
nsjen l. Norway 40 C3
aaciguara Brazil 138 C1
nelo U.S.A. 124 C2
niza Bol. 136 B3
ni r. Rus. Fed. 87 I2
na r. Rus. Fed. 34 F3
abah Saudi Arabia 82 B2
ana, Khrebet mts Rus. Fed. ? K3
angi N.Z. 106 C2
an Lowland Asia 80 C3
rayf Saudi Arabia 82 A1
bat Pak. 78 A2
bo Col. 134 B2
da Romania 38 E2
fan China see Turpan
gay Kazakh. 80 D2
gutlu Turkey 59 C3
nhal Turkey 84 B1
la r. Spain 55 C2
in Italy 56 A1
iys'k Ukr. 38 B1
kana, Lake salt l. Eth./Kenya ? B4
kestan Kazakh. 81 D2
key country Asia/Europe 4 B2
kmenabat Turkm. 80 D3
kmenbashi Turkm. 80 C2
kmenistan country Asia 80 C2
ks and Caicos Islands terr. West Indies 131 C2
ku Fin. 41 E3
lock U.S.A. 119 B3
nagain, Cape N.Z. 106 C3
neffe Islands atoll Belize 129 D3

Turnhout Belgium 48 B2
Turnor Lake Can. 113 E2
Turnu Măgurele Romania 58 B2
Turpan China 81 F2
Turugart Pass China/Kyrg. 81 E2
Tuscaloosa U.S.A. 124 C2
Tuskegee U.S.A. 125 C2
Tuticorin India 77 B4
Tutume Botswana 96 B3
Tuvalu country S. Pacific Ocean 100
Tuwayra, Jabal hills Saudi Arabia 82 B2
Tuwayq, Jabal mts Saudi Arabia 82 B2
Tuwwal Saudi Arabia 82 A2
Tuxpan Nayarit Mex. 128 B2
Tuxpan Veracruz Mex. 129 C2
Tuxtla Gutiérrez Mex. 129 C3
Tuyên Quang Vietnam 66 B1
Tuy Hoa Vietnam 67 B2
Tuz, Lake salt l. Turkey 84 B2
Tuz Gölü salt l. Turkey see Tuz, Lake
Tuz Khurmātū Iraq 85 C2
Tuzla Bos.-Herz. 57 C2
Tuzlov r. Rus. Fed. 39 F2
Tweed r. U.K. 46 B2
Twee Rivier Namibia 98 A2
Twentynine Palms U.S.A. 119 C4
Twin Falls U.S.A. 118 D2
Twizel N.Z. 106 B3
Two Harbors U.S.A. 121 E1
Tyler U.S.A. 127 E2
Tynda Rus. Fed. 87 J1
Tynset Norway 41 C3
Tyre Lebanon 84 B2
Tyrnavos Greece 59 B3
Tyrrell, Lake dry lake Austr. 104 C3
Tyrrhenian Sea France/Italy 56 B2
Tyup-Karagan, Mys pt Kazakh. 80 C2
Tyumen' Rus. Fed. 34 F3
Tywi r. U.K. 47 A4
Tzaneen S. Africa 99 D1

U

Uamanda Angola 96 C3
Uapés Brazil 134 C3
Ubai Brazil 139 D2
Ubá Brazil 138 C2
Ubangi r. C.A.R./Dem. Rep. Congo 94 B3
Ube Japan 71 B4
Úbeda Spain 54 C2
Uberaba Brazil 138 C1
Uberlândia Brazil 138 C1

Ubombo S. Africa 99 D2
Ubon Ratchathani Thai. 67 B2
Ubstadt-Weiher Ger. 49 D3
Ucayali r. Peru 134 B3
Uchara Kazakh. 80 F2
Uchiura-wan b. Japan 70 D2
Uchur r. Rus. Fed. 87 K3
Ucluelet Can. 112 C3
Udaipur India 78 B2
Uday r. Ukr. 39 D1
Uddevalla Sweden 41 C4
Uddjaure l. Sweden 40 D2
Uden Neth. 48 B2
Udhampur India 78 B1
Udine Italy 56 B1
Udomlya Rus. Fed. 37 E2
Udon Thani Thai. 66 B2
Udupi India 77 B3
Ueda Japan 71 C3
Uekuli Indon. 65 D2
Uele r. Dem. Rep. Congo 94 C2
Uelen Rus. Fed. 110 A2
Uelzen Ger. 49 E1
Uere r. Dem. Rep. Congo 95 C2
Ufa Rus. Fed. 35 E3
Ugalla r. Tanz. 95 D3
Uganda country Africa 95 D2
Uglegorsk Rus. Fed. 73 F1
Uglich Rus. Fed. 37 E2
Uglovka Rus. Fed. 37 D2
Ugra Rus. Fed. 37 D3
Uherské Hradiště Czech Rep. 51 D3
Uhlava r. Czech Rep. 49 F3
Uig U.K. 44 A2
Uige Angola 94 B3
Üijŏngbu S. Korea 69 B2
Uinta Mountains U.S.A. 118 D2
Ŭisŏng S. Korea 69 B2
Uitenhage S. Africa 99 C3
Uithuizen Neth. 48 C1
Uivak, Cape Can. 115 D1
Ujjain India 78 B2
Ukholovo Rus. Fed. 37 F3
Ukhrul India 66 A1
Ukhta Rus. Fed. 34 E2
Ukiah U.S.A. 119 B3
Ukkusissat Greenland 111 I2
Ukmergė Lith. 36 B2
Ukraine country Europe 38 D2
Ulaanbaatar Mongolia see Ulan Bator
Ulaangom Mongolia 72 C1
Ulan Bator Mongolia 72 D1
Ulanhad China see Chifeng
Ulanhot China 73 E1
Ulan-Khol Rus. Fed. 35 D4
Ulan-Ude Rus. Fed. 73 D1
Ulan Ul Hu l. China 79 D1
Ulchin S. Korea 69 B2
Ulenurme Estonia 36 C2
Ulhasnagar India 77 B3
Uliastai China 73 D1
Uliastay Mongolia 72 C1

Ulithi *atoll* Micronesia **63** D2
Ulladulla Austr. **105** E3
Ullapool U.K. **44** B2
Ullswater *l.* U.K. **46** B2
Ullŭng-do *i.* S. Korea **69** C2
Ulm Ger. **50** B3
Ulsan S. Korea **69** B2
Ulsta U.K. **44** [inset]
Ulster *reg.* Ireland/U.K. **45** C1
Ultima Austr. **104** C3
Ulua *r.* Hond. **129** D3
Uludağ *mt.* Turkey **59** C2
Ulundi S. Africa **99** D2
Ulungur Hu *l.* China **81** F2
Uluru *h.* Austr. **102** C2
Ulverston U.K. **46** B2
Ul'yanovsk Rus. Fed. **35** D3
Ulysses U.S.A. **120** C3
Uman' Ukr. **38** D2
Umboi *i.* P.N.G. **63** D3
Umeå Sweden **40** E3
Umeälven *r.* Sweden **40** E3
Umet Rus. Fed. **39** F1
Umingmaktok Can. **110** E2
Umlazi S. Africa **99** D2
Umm Lajj Saudi Arabia **82** A2
Umm Ruwaba Sudan **93** B3
Umm Sa'ad Libya **91** E1
Umpqua *r.* U.S.A. **118** B2
Umtata S. Africa **99** C3
Umuarama Brazil **138** B2
Una *r.* Bos.-Herz./Croatia **57** C1
Unai Brazil **138** C1
Unalakleet U.S.A. **110** B2
'Unayzah Saudi Arabia **82** B2
Unecha Rus. Fed. **37** D3
Ungarie Austr. **105** D2
Ungarra Austr. **104** B2
Ungava, Péninsule d' *pen.* Can. **111** H2
Ungava Bay Can. **115** D1
Unggi N. Korea **69** C1
Unghenî Moldova **38** C2
Unguja *i.* Tanz. *see* Zanzibar Island
União di Vitória Brazil **138** B3
Unini *r.* Brazil **134** C3
Union City U.S.A. **124** C1
Uniondale S. Africa **98** B3
Uniontown U.S.A. **123** E3
United Arab Emirates *country* Asia **83** C2
United Kingdom *country* Europe **42** C2
United States of America *country* N. America **116** D3
Unst *i.* U.K. **44** [inset]
Unstrut *r.* Ger. **49** E2
Upa *r.* Rus. Fed. **37** E3
Upemba, Lac *l.* Dem. Rep. Congo **95** C3
Upington S. Africa **98** B2
Upper Alkali Lake U.S.A. **118** B2

Upper Arrow Lake Can. **112** D2
Upper Klamath Lake U.S.A. **118** B2
Upper Liard Can. **112** C1
Upper Lough Erne *l.* U.K. **45** C1
Upsala Sweden **41** D4
'Uqlat aş Şuqūr Saudi Arabia **82** B2
Ural *r.* Kazakh./Rus. Fed. **80** C2
Uralla Austr. **105** E2
Ural Mountains Rus. Fed. **35** F2
Uralsk Kazakh. **80** C1
Ural'skiy Khrebet *mts* Rus. Fed. *see* Ural Mountains
Urambo Tanz. **95** D3
Urana Austr. **105** D3
Uray Rus. Fed. **34** F2
Urengoy Rus. Fed. **34** G2
Urganch Uzbek. **80** D2
Urk Neth. **48** B1
Urla Turkey **59** C3
Urmia, Lake *salt l.* Iran **85** C2
Uroševac S.M. **58** B2
Uralchki Rus. Fed. **38** B2
Uraqu Brazil **135** E4
Uruapan Mex. **128** B3
Urucara Brazil **135** F3
Uruçui Brazil **135** C3
Uruguai *r.* Brazil **138** B3
Uruguaiana Brazil **136** C3
Uruguay *r.* Uru./Urg. **133**
Uruguay *country* S. America **137** C4
Ürümqi China **81** F2
Urup *r.* Rus. Fed. **39** F2
Uryupinsk Rus. Fed. **39** F1
Urziceni Romania **38** C3
Usa Japan **71** B4
Uşak Turkey **59** C3
Usakos Namibia **98** A1
Ushtobe Kazakh. **81** E2
Ushuaia Arg. **137** B6
Usinsk Rus. Fed. **34** E2
Uskhodni Belarus **36** C2
Usman' Rus. Fed. **37** E3
Usogorsk Rus. Fed. **34** D2
Ussel France **52** C2
Ussuriysk Rus. Fed. **70** B2
Ust'-Donetskiy Rus. Fed. **39** F2
Ustica, Isola di *i.* Italy **56** B3
Ust'-Ilimsk Rus. Fed. **87** I3
Ustka Pol. **51** D2
Ust'-Kamchatsk Rus. Fed. **87** M3
Ust'-Kamenogorsk Kazakh. **81** F2
Ust'-Kara Rus. Fed. **34** F2
Ust'-Kulom Rus. Fed. **34** E2
Ust'-Labinsk Rus. Fed. **39** E2
Ust'-Luga Rus. Fed. **36** C2
Ust'-Nera Rus. Fed. **87** L2
Ust'-Omchug Rus. Fed. **87** L2
Ust'-Ordynskiy Rus. Fed. **87** I3
Ust'-Port Rus. Fed. **34** H2

Ust'-Tsil'ma Rus. Fed. **34** E2
Ustyurt Plateau Kazakh./Uzbek. **80** C2
Ustyuzhna Rus. Fed. **37** E2
Usvyaty Rus. Fed. **37** D2
Utah *state* U.S.A. **119** D3
Utah Lake U.S.A. **118** D2
Utena Lith. **36** C2
Utica U.S.A. **123** E2
Utiel Spain **55** C2
Utikuma Lake Can. **112** D2
Utrecht Neth. **48** B1
Utrera Spain **54** B2
Utsjoki Fin. **40** F2
Utsunomiya Japan **71** C3
Uttaradit Thai. **66** B2
Uummannaq Greenland *see* Dundas
Uusikaupunki Fin. **41** E3
Uvalde U.S.A. **127** E3
Uvarovo Rus. Fed. **39** F1
Uvs Nuur *salt l.* Mongolia **72** C1
Uwajima Japan **71** B4
'Uwayrid, Harrat al *lava field* Saudi Arabia **82** A2
Uweinat, Jebel *mt.* Sudan **92** A2
Uyar Rus. Fed. **87** I3
Uyo Nigeria **91** C4
Uyuni Bol. **136** B3
Uyuni, Salar de *salt flat* Bol. **136** B3
Uzbekistan *country* Asia **80** D2
Uzerche France **52** C2
Uzès France **53** C3
Uzh *r.* Ukr. **38** D1
Uzhhorod Ukr. **38** B2
Užice S.M. **58** A2
Uzlovaya Rus. Fed. **37** E3
Uzunköprü Turkey **59** C2

Vaal *r.* S. Africa **99** B2
Vaal Dam S. Africa **99** C2
Vaasa Fin. **40** E3
Vác Hungary **51** D3
Vacaria Brazil **136** C3
Vacaria, Serra *hills* Brazil **138** B2
Vacaville U.S.A. **119** B3
Vacha Rus. Fed. **37** F2
Vadodara India **78** B2
Vadsø Norway **40** F1
Vaduz Liechtenstein **53** D2
Vágar *i.* Faroe Is **42** B1
Vágur Faroe Is **42** B1
Váh *r.* Slovakia **51** D3
Vaiaku Tuvalu **100**
Vaida Estonia **36** C2
Vail U.S.A. **120** B3
Valday Rus. Fed. **37** D2

ayskaya Vozvyshennost' hills
s. Fed. **37** D2
Mecañas, Embalse de resr
pain **54** B2
de-Meuse France **53** D2
lepeñas Spain **54** C2
de-Reuil France **47** D5
lés, Peninsula pen. Arg.
7 B5
Mez U.S.A. **112** A1
livia Chile **137** A4
l'Or Can. **114** C2
osta U.S.A. **125** D2
mount Can. **112** D2
ence France **53** C3
encia Spain **55** C2
encia Venez. **134** C1
ncia, Golfo de g. Spain
50 C1
anciennes France **48** A2
antine U.S.A. **120** C2
enzuela Phil. **68** B2
a Venez. **134** B2
avo S.M. **58** A2
a Latvia **36** C2
eakoski Fin. **41** E3
lenswaard Neth. **48** B2
y Ukr. **39** D2
yrie Dome ice feature
ntarctica **107** D2
adolid Mex. **129** D2
adolid Spain **54** C1
de Uxó Spain **55** C2
ovey France **41** B4
edupar Col. **134** B1
Hermoso Mex. **129** C2
ovo **41** B4
a Malta **91** D1
ey City U.S.A. **121** D1
ey Falls U.S.A. **118** B1
eyview Can. **112** D2
s Spain **55** D1
Marie Can. **120** B1
niera Latvia **36** C2
gnes France **47** C5
azhyn Belarus **36** E1
araíso Brazil **138** B2
araíso Chile **137** A4
, Tanjung c. Indon. **63** D3
sad India **78** B2
 apan S. Africa **98** B3
ryki Rus. Fed. **39** E1
del Camino Spain
i **58** D2
Turkey **85** C2
, Lake salt l. Turkey **85** C2
Buren U.S.A. **123** G1
couver Can. **112** D3
couver U.S.A. **118** B1
sand Island Can. **112** C3
dalia U.S.A. **122** C3
derhoof Can. **112** C2
dra Estonia **36** C2

Vänern l. Sweden **41** C4
Vänersborg Sweden **41** C4
Vangaindrano Madag. **97** [inset]
D2
Van Gölü salt l. Turkey see
Van, Lake
Van Horn U.S.A. **126** D2
Vanimo P.N.G. **63** D3
Vanino Rus. Fed. **73** F1
Vannes France **52** B2
Van Rees, Pegunungan mts
Indon. **63** D3
Vanrhynsdorp S. Africa **98** A3
Vantaa Fin. **41** E3
Vanua Levu i. Fiji **142** E6
Vanuatu country S. Pacific Ocean
100
Van Wert U.S.A. **122** D2
Vanwyksvlei S. Africa **98** B3
Van Zylsrus S. Africa **98** B2
Varanasi India **79** C2
Varangerfjorden sea chan.
Norway **40** F1
Varangerhalvøya pen. Norway
40 F1
Varaždin Croatia **57** C1
Varberg Sweden **41** C4
Varde r. Macedonia **59** B2
Varde Denmark **41** B4
Vardø Norway **40** G1
Varel Ger. **48** D1
Varèna Lith. **36** C2
Varese Italy **56** A1
Varginha Brazil **139** C2
Varkaus Fin. **41** F3
Varna Bulg. **58** C2
Värnamo Sweden **41** C4
Várzea da Palma Brazil **139** D1
Varzino Rus. Fed. **40** G2
Vasknarva Estonia **36** C2
Vaslui Romania **38** C1
Västerås Sweden **41** D4
Västerdalälven r. Sweden **41** D3
Västerhaninge Sweden **36** A2
Västervik Sweden **41** D4
Vasto Italy **56** B2
Vasyl'kiv Ukr. **38** D1
Vatan France **52** C2
Vatican City Europe **56** B2
Vatnajökull ice cap Iceland
40 [inset]
Vatra Dornei Romania **38** C2
Vättern l. Sweden **41** C4
Vaughn U.S.A. **126** C2
Vauvert France **53** C3
Vava'u Group is Tonga **101**
Vawkavysk Belarus **36** B3
Växjö Sweden **41** C4
Vaygach, Ostrov i. Rus. Fed.
34 E1
Vechta Ger. **49** D1
Vedea r. Romania **38** C3
Veendam Neth. **48** C1
Veenendaal Neth. **48** B1

Vegreville Can. **113** D2
Vejer de la Frontera Spain
54 B2
Vejle Denmark **41** B4
Velbüzhki Prokhod pass
Bulg./Macedonia **58** B2
Veldhoven Neth. **48** B2
Velebit mts Croatia **56** B2
Velenje Slovenia **56** C1
Veles Macedonia **57** D2
Vélez-Málaga Spain **54** C2
Velhas r. Brazil **139** D1
Velika Plana S.M. **58** B2
Velikaya r. Rus. Fed. **36** C2
Velikiye Luki Rus. Fed. **37** D2
Velikiy Novgorod Rus. Fed.
37 D2
Velikiy Ustyug Rus. Fed.
34 D2
Veliko Tŭrnovo Bulg. **58** C2
Veli Lošinj Croatia **56** B2
Velizh Rus. Fed. **37** D2
Vellberg Ger. **49** D3
Vel'sk Rus. Fed. **34** D2
Velykyy Burluk Ukr. **39** E1
Venceslau Bráz Brazil **138** C2
Vendôme France **52** C2
Venev Rus. Fed. **37** E3
Venezia Italy see Venice
Venezuela country S. America
134 C2
Venezuela, Golfo de g. Venez.
134 B1
Venice Italy **56** B1
Venice U.S.A. **125** D3
Venice, Gulf of Europe **56** B1
Venray Neth. **48** B2
Venta r. Latvia/Lith. **36** B2
Ventnor U.K. **47** C4
Ventspils Latvia **36** B2
Ventura U.S.A. **119** C4
Venustiano Carranza, Presa resr
Mex. **127** D3
Vera Spain **55** C2
Veracruz Mex. **129** C3
Veraval India **78** B2
Verbania Italy **56** A1
Vercelli Italy **56** A1
Vercors reg. France **53** D3
Verdalsøra Norway **40** C3
Verde r. Goiás Brazil **138** B1
Verde r. Mato Grosso do Sul Brazil
138 B2
Verde r. U.S.A. **126** B2
Verde Grande r. Brazil **139** D1
Verden (Aller) Ger. **49** D1
Verdinho, Serra do mts Brazil
138 B1
Verdun France **53** D2
Vereeniging S. Africa **99** C2
Verín Spain **54** B1
Verkhnebakanskiy Rus. Fed.
39 E3

247

Verkhnetulomskiy Rus. Fed. 40 F2
Verkhniy Mamon Rus. Fed. 39 F1
Verkhnov'ye Rus. Fed. 37 E3
Verkhovyna Ukr. 38 B2
Vermilion U.S.A. 121 D2
Vermont state U.S.A. 123 F2
Vernon Can. 112 D2
Vernon U.S.A. 127 E2
Vero Beach U.S.A. 125 D3
Veroia Greece 59 B2
Verona Italy 56 B1
Versailles France 52 C2
Vertou France 52 B2
Verviers Belgium 48 B2
Verzy France 48 B3
Vescovato France 53 D3
Veselaya, Gora mt. Rus. Fed. 35 F3
Vesele Ukr. 39 D2
Veselovskoye Vodokhranilishche resr Rus. Fed. 39 F2
Veselyy Rus. Fed. 39 F2
Veshenskaya Rus. Fed. 39 F1
Vesoul France 53 D2
Vesterålen is Norway 40 C2
Vestfjorden sea chan. Norway 40 C2
Vesuvius vol. Italy 56 B2
Ves'yegonsk Rus. Fed. 37 E2
Vetlanda Sweden 41 D4
Veurne Belgium 48 A2
Vevey Switz. 53 D2
Veydelevka Rus. Fed. 39 E1
Vezirköprü Turkey 84 B1
Viana Brazil 138 E3
Viana do Castelo Port. 54 B1
Viangchan Laos see Vientiane
Vianópolis Brazil 138 C1
Viareggio Italy 56 B2
Viborg Denmark 41 B4
Vibo Valentia Italy 57 C3
Vic Spain 55 D1
Vicente Guerrero Mex. 128 A1
Vicenza Italy 56 B1
Vichuga Rus. Fed. 37 F2
Vichy France 52 C2
Vicksburg U.S.A. 124 B2
Viçosa Brazil 139 D2
Victor Harbor Austr. 104 B3
Victoria r. Austr. 102 C1
Victoria state U.S.A. 104 C3
Victoria Can. 112 C3
Victoria Chile 137 A4
Victoria Seychelles 99
Victoria U.S.A. 127 E3
Victoria, Lake Africa 95 D3
Victoria, Lake salt l. Austr. 104 C2
Victoria, Mount Myanmar 66 A1

Victoria, Mount P.N.G. 63 D3
Victoria Falls Zambia/Zimbabwe 96 B1
Victoria Island Can. 110 E2
Victoria West S. Africa 98 B3
Victorville U.S.A. 119 C4
Videle Romania 38 C3
Viðidalsá Iceland 40 [inset]
Viedma Arg. 137 B5
Viedma, Lago l. Arg. 137 A5
Vienenburg Ger. 49 E2
Vienna Austria 51 D3
Vienne France 52 C2
Vienne r. France 52 C2
Vientiane Laos 66 B2
Viersen Ger. 48 C2
Vierzon France 52 C2
Vieste Italy 57 C2
Vietnam country Asia 66 B2
Việt Tri Vietnam 66 B1
Vigan Phil. 68 B2
Vigevano Italy 56 A1
Vigo Spain 54 B1
Vijayawada India 77 C3
Vík Iceland 40 [inset]
Vikeyri Norway 42 E1
Vila Franca de Xira Port. 54 B2
Vilagarcía de Arousa Spain 54 B1
Vilalba Spain 54 B1
Vila Nova de Gaia Port. 54 B1
Vilanova i la Geltrú Spain 55 D1
Vila Real Port. 54 B1
Vilar Formoso Port. 54 B1
Vila Velha Brazil 139 D2
Vilcabamba, Cordillera mts Peru 134 B4
Vil'cheka, Zemlya i. Rus. Fed. 86 G1
Vilhelmina Sweden 40 D3
Vilhena Brazil 134 C4
Viljandi Estonia 36 C2
Vilkaviškis Lith. 36 B3
Villa Ahumada Mex. 128 B1
Villablino Spain 54 B1
Villach Austria 50 C3
Villa Flores Mex. 129 C3
Villagrán Mex. 129 C2
Villa Insurgentes Mex. 128 A2
Villa María Arg. 136 B4
Villa Montes Bol. 136 B3
Villanueva de la Serena Spain 54 B2
Villa Ocampo Arg. 136 C3
Villarrica Para. 136 C3
Villarrobledo Spain 54 C2
Villa Unión Arg. 136 B3
Villa Unión Durango Mex. 128 B2
Villa Unión Sinaloa Mex. 128 B2
Villavicencio Col. 134 B2
Villazon Bol. 136 B3

Villefranche-sur-Saône France 50 A3
Villena Spain 55 C2
Villeneuve-sur-Lot France 52 C3
Ville Platte U.S.A. 124 B2
Villeurbanne France 53 C2
Vilnius Lith. 36 C3
Vil'nohirs'k Ukr. 39 C2
Vil'nyans'k Ukr. 39 E2
Vilvoorde Belgium 48 B2
Vilyeyka Belarus 36 C3
Vimmerby Sweden 41 D4
Viña del Mar Chile 137 A4
Vinaros Spain 55 D1
Vincennes U.S.A. 122 C3
Vineland U.S.A. 123 E3
Vinh Vietnam 66 B2
Vinh Long Vietnam 67 B2
Vinita U.S.A. 127 E1
Vinnytsya Ukr. 38 C2
Vinson Massif mt. Antarctica 107 K2
Vinstra Norway 41 B3
Virac Phil. 68 B2
Virden Can. 113 E3
Vire France 52 B2
Virei Angola 96 A1
Virgem da Lapa Brazil 139 D1
Virgin r. U.S.A. 126 B1
Virginia S. Africa 99 C2
Virginia U.S.A. 121 E1
Virginia state U.S.A. 123 E3
Virginia Beach U.S.A. 123 E3
Virginia City U.S.A. 119 C3
Virgin Islands (U.K.) terr. West Indies 131 D3
Virgin Islands (U.S.A.) terr. West Indies 131 D3
Virovitica Croatia 57 C1
Virton Belgium 48 B3
Virtsu Estonia 36 B2
Vis i. Croatia 57 C2
Visaginas Lith. 36 C2
Visalia U.S.A. 119 C3
Visayan Sea Phil. 68 B2
Visby Sweden 41 D4
Viscount Melville Sound sea chan. Can. 110 E2
Visé Belgium 48 B2
Višegrad Bos.-Herz. 57 C2
Viseu Port. 54 B1
Vishakhapatnam India 77 C3
Viški Latvia 36 C2
Visoko Bos.-Herz. 57 C2
Vistula r. Pol. 51 D2
Viterbo Italy 56 B2
Viti Levu i. Fiji 142 E6
Vitim r. Rus. Fed. 87 J3
Vitória Brazil 139 D2
Vitória da Conquista Brazil 135 E4
Vitoria-Gasteiz Spain 54 C1
Vitré France 52 B2

-le-François France **53** C2
ebsk Belarus **37** D2
ria Italy **56** B3
ro Spain **54** B1
aino, Sierra *mts* Mex.
3 A2
Turkey **58** C2
nagaram India **77** C3
rdingen Neth. **48** B2
kavkaz Rus. Fed. **35** D4
imir Rus. Fed. **37** F2
vostok Rus. Fed. **70** D2
and *i.* Neth. **48** B1
iingen Neth. **48** A2
6 Albania **59** A2
Kenya **95** D3
en France **53** D2
ny Bay Can. **115** D1
ns Denmark **50** B1
odina *prov.* S.M. **58** A1
navolok Rus. Fed. **40** G3
ano Bay Japan *see*
miura-wan
a Norway **42** E1
a Rus. Fed. **37** E2
a *r.* Rus. Fed. **37** E2
odonsk Rus. Fed. **35** D4
oprad Rus. Fed. **35** D4
nov Rus. Fed. **37** E2
hov *r.* Rus. Fed. **37** D1
ovakha Ukr. **39** E2
chys'k Ukr. **38** C2
darsk Rus. Fed. **37** F2
dars'ke Ukr. **39** E2
dymyrets' Ukr. **38** C1
dymyr-Volyns'kyy Ukr.
C1
dymyr-Volyns'kyy Ukr.
B1
gda Rus. Fed. **37** E2
kolamsk Rus. Fed. **37** E2
konovka Rus. Fed. **39** E1
is Greece **59** B3
sovo Rus. Fed. **36** C2
r Rus. Fed. **37** D2
ak Rus. Fed. **35** D3
a, Lake *resr* Ghana **90** C4
Redonda Brazil **139** D2
hskiy Rus. Fed. **35** D4
aafjörður Iceland **40** [inset]
nava Belarus **36** C3
aioi Sporades *is* Greece
s A2
kuta Rus. Fed. **37** F2
nsi *i.* Estonia **36** B2
na *r.* Rus. Fed. **39** F1
nezh Rus. Fed. **37** E3
nezh *r.* Rus. Fed. **37** E3
ontsovka Rus. Fed. **39** F1
skla *r.* Rus. Fed. **39** D2
sjärv *i.* Estonia **36** C2
i Estonia **36** C2

Vosburg S. Africa **98** B3
Vosges *mts* France **53** D2
Voskresensk Rus. Fed. **37** E2
Voss Norway **41** B3
Vostochno-Sibirskoye More *sea*
Rus. Fed. *see* East Siberian Sea
Vostochnyy Sayan *mts* Rus. Fed.
87 I3
Vostok Rus. Fed. **70** C1
Votkinsk Rus. Fed. **34** E3
Votuporanga Brazil **138** C2
Vouziers France **48** B3
Voynitsa Rus. Fed. **40** G2
Voznesens'k Ukr. **39** D2
Voznesenskoye Rus. Fed. **37** F3
Vrangel' Rus. Fed. **70** B2
Vrangelya, Ostrov *i.* Rus. Fed. *see*
Wrangel Island
Vranje S.M. **58** B2
Vratnik *pass* Bulg. **58** C2
Vratsa Bulg. **58** B2
Vrbas *r.* Bos.-Herz. **57** C1
Vrbas S.M. **58** A1
Vredenburg S. Africa **98** A3
Vredendal S. Africa **98** A3
Vršac S.M. **58** B1
Vryburg S. Africa **98** B2
Vryheid S. Africa **99** D2
Vučitrn S.M. **58** B2
Vukovar Croatia **57** C1
Vuktyl' Rus. Fed. **34** E2
Vukuzakhe S. Africa **99** C2
Vulcano, Isola *i.* Italy **56** B3
Vung Tau Vietnam **67** B2
Vyatka Rus. Fed. *see* Kirov
Vyaz'ma Rus. Fed. **37** D2
Vyazniki Rus. Fed. **37** F2
Vyerkhnyadzvinsk Belarus
36 C2
Vyksa Rus. Fed. **37** F2
Vylkove Ukr. **38** C2
Vynohradiv Ukr. **38** B2
Vypolzovo Rus. Fed. **37** D2
Vyritsa Rus. Fed. **37** D2
Vyselki Rus. Fed. **39** E2
Vyshhorod Ukr. **38** D1
Vyshniy-Volochek Rus. Fed.
37 D2
Vyškov Czech Rep. **51** D3
Vytegra Rus. Fed. **34** C2

Wa Ghana **90** B3
Waal *r.* Neth. **48** B2
Waalwijk Neth. **48** B2
Wabasca *r.* Can. **112** D2
Wabasca-Desmarais Can.
112 D2
Wabash *r.* U.S.A. **122** C3
Wabē Gestro *r.* Eth. **93** C4

Wabē Shebelē Wenz *r.* Eth.
93 C4
Wabowden Can. **113** F2
Waccasassa Bay U.S.A. **125** D3
Wächtersbach Ger. **49** D2
Waco U.S.A. **127** E2
Wad Pak. **78** A2
Waddān Libya **91** D2
Waddenzee *sea chan.* Neth.
48 B1
Waddington, Mount Can.
112 C2
Waddinxveen Neth. **48** B1
Wadena Can. **113** E2
Wadena U.S.A. **121** D1
Wadgassen Ger. **48** C3
Wad Halfa Sudan **92** B2
Wad Medani Sudan **92** B3
Wafangdian China **74** C2
Wageningen Neth. **48** B2
Wagga Wagga Austr. **105** D3
Wahoo U.S.A. **121** D2
Wahpeton U.S.A. **121** D1
Waiau *r.* N.Z. **106** B3
Waigeo *i.* Indon. **63** C3
Waikabubak Indon. **65** C2
Waikerie Austr. **104** B2
Waimate N.Z. **106** B3
Wainganga *r.* India **79** B3
Waingapu Indon. **65** D2
Wainwright Can. **113** D2
Wainwright U.S.A. **110** B2
Waiouru N.Z. **106** C2
Waipara N.Z. **106** B3
Waipawa N.Z. **106** C2
Wairau *r.* N.Z. **106** B3
Wairoa N.Z. **106** C2
Waitaki *r.* N.Z. **106** B3
Waitara N.Z. **106** B2
Waiuku N.Z. **106** B2
Wajir Kenya **95** E2
Wakasa-wan *b.* Japan **71** C3
Wakatipu, Lake N.Z. **106** A4
Wakayama Japan **71** C4
WaKeeney U.S.A. **120** D3
Wakefield N.Z. **106** B3
Wakefield U.K. **46** C3
Wake Island *terr.* N. Pacific Ocean
100
Wakkanai Japan **70** D1
Walbrzych Pol. **51** D2
Walcha Austr. **105** E2
Walchum Ger. **48** C1
Walcz Pol. **51** D2
Wales *admin. div.* U.K. **47** B3
Walgett Austr. **105** D2
Walker Lake U.S.A. **119** C3
Walla Walla U.S.A. **118** C1
Walldürn Ger. **49** D3
Wallendbeen Austr. **105** D2
Wallis and Futuna Islands *terr.*
S. Pacific Ocean **101**
Walney, Isle of *i.* U.K. **46** B2
Walsall U.K. **47** C3

Walsenburg U.S.A. **120** C3
Walsrode Ger. **49** D1
Walterboro U.S.A. **125** D2
Walvis Bay Namibia **96** C2
Wamba Dem. Rep. Congo **95** C2
Wanaaring Austr. **104** C1
Wanaka N.Z. **106** A3
Wanaka, Lake N.Z. **106** A3
Wanda Arg. **138** B3
Wanda Shan *mts* China **70** B1
Wanding China **66** A1
Wanganui N.Z. **106** C2
Wangaratta Austr. **105** D3
Wangqing China **69** B1
Wan Hsa-la Myanmar **66** A1
Wanning China **75** B4
Wanxian China **74** C2
Wanyuan China **74** A2
Warangal India **77** B3
Warburg Ger. **49** D2
Warburton Austr. **102** B2
Warburton *watercourse* Austr.
104 B1
Wardha India **79** B2
Ward Hill U.K. **44** C1
Ware Can. **112** C2
Waren Ger. **49** F1
Warendorf Ger. **48** C2
Warialda Austr. **105** E1
Warmbad Namibia **98** A2
Warm Springs U.S.A. **119** C3
Warner Lakes U.S.A. **118** C2
Warner Robins U.S.A. **125** D2
Warracknabeal Austr. **104** C3
Warrego *r.* Austr. **105** D2
Warren Austr. **105** D2
Warren *AR* U.S.A. **124** B2
Warren *OH* U.S.A. **123** D2
Warren *PA* U.S.A. **123** E2
Warrenpoint U.K. **45** C1
Warrensburg U.S.A. **121** E3
Warrenton S. Africa **98** B2
Warri Nigeria **91** C4
Warrington U.K. **46** B3
Warrnambool Austr. **104** C3
Warsaw Pol. **51** E2
Warszawa Pol. *see* Warsaw
Warta *r.* Pol. **51** C2
Warwick Austr. **105** E1
Warwick U.K. **47** C3
Wasco U.S.A. **119** C3
Washburn U.S.A. **120** C1
Washington *DC* U.S.A. **123** E3
Washington *IA* U.S.A. **121** E2
Washington *IN* U.S.A. **122** C3
Washington *MO* U.S.A. **121** E3
Washington *NC* U.S.A. **125** E1
Washington *PA* U.S.A. **123** D2
Washington *state* U.S.A. **118** B1
Washington, Mount U.S.A.
123 F2
Washuk Pak. **78** A2
Waskaganish Can. **114** C1

Waskaiowaka Lake Can.
113 F2
Waswanipi, Lac *l.* Can. **114** C2
Watampone Indon. **65** D2
Waterbury U.S.A. **123** F2
Waterbury Lake Can. **113** E2
Waterford Ireland **45** C2
Waterford Harbour Ireland
45 C2
Waterloo Can. **121** E2
Waterpoort S. Africa **99** C1
Watertown *NY* U.S.A. **123** E2
Watertown *SD* U.S.A. **121** D2
Watertown *WI* U.S.A. **122** C2
Waterville U.S.A. **123** G2
Watford U.K. **47** C4
Watford City U.S.A. **120** C1
Wathaman *r.* Can. **113** E2
Watonga U.S.A. **127** E1
Watsa Dem. Rep. Congo **95** C2
Watsi Kengo Dem. Rep. Congo
94 C3
Watson Lake Can. **112** C1
Watsonville U.S.A. **119** B3
Wau Sudan **93** A4
Wauchope Austr. **105** E2
Waukegan U.S.A. **122** C2
Wausau U.S.A. **122** C2
Waveney *r.* U.K. **47** D3
Waverly U.S.A. **121** E2
Waycross U.S.A. **125** D2
Wayne U.S.A. **121** D2
Waynesboro *GA* U.S.A. **125** D2
Waynesboro *VA* U.S.A. **123** E3
Wazirabad Pak. **78** B1
Wear *r.* U.K. **46** C2
Weatherford U.S.A. **127** E2
Webequie Can. **114** B1
Webi Shabeelle *r.* Somalia **93** C4
Webster U.S.A. **121** D1
Wee Waa Austr. **105** D2
Wegorzewo Pol. **51** E2
Weiden in der Oberpfalz Ger.
49 F3
Weifang China **74** B2
Weihai China **74** C2
Weilmoringle Austr. **105** D1
Weimar Ger. **49** E2
Weinan China **74** A2
Weinsberg Ger. **49** D3
Weipa Austr. **103** D1
Weishan China **66** B1
Weißenburg in Bayern Ger.
49 E3
Weißenfels Ger. **49** E2
Weißkugel *mt.* Austria/Italy
50 C3
Wejherowo Pol. **51** D2
Wekweti Can. **112** D1
Weldiya Eth. **93** B3
Welkom S. Africa **99** C2
Welland *r.* U.K. **47** C3
Wellesley Islands Austr. **103** C1

Wellington Austr. **105** D2
Wellington N.Z. **106** B3
Wellington U.S.A. **121** D3
Wellington, Isla *i.* Chile **137** A8
Wellington, Lake Austr. **105** D3
Wells U.K. **47** B4
Wells U.S.A. **118** D2
Wells, Lake *salt flat* Austr.
102 B2
Wellsford N.Z. **106** B2
Wells-next-the-Sea U.K. **46** D3
Wels Austria **50** C3
Welshpool U.K. **47** B3
Wemindji Can. **114** C1
Wenatchee U.S.A. **118** B1
Wenchang China **75** B4
Wendelstein Ger. **49** E3
Wendeng China **74** C2
Wengyuan China **75** B3
Wenling China **75** C3
Wenshan China **75** A3
Wentworth Austr. **104** C2
Wenzhou China **75** C3
Wepener S. Africa **99** C2
Werda Botswana **98** B2
Werdau Ger. **49** F2
Werder Ger. **49** F1
Wernberg-Köblitz Ger. **49** F3
Wernigerode Ger. **49** E2
Werra *r.* Ger. **49** D2
Werris Creek Austr. **105** E2
Wertheim Ger. **49** D3
Wesel Ger. **48** C2
Wesendorf Ger. **49** E1
Weser *sea chan.* Ger. **49** D1
Wessel Islands Austr. **103** C1
Wesselton S. Africa **99** C2
West Antarctica *reg.* Antarctica
107 I2
West Bank *terr.* Asia **84** B2
West Bromwich U.K. **47** C3
Westerburg Ger. **48** C2
Western Australia *state* Austr.
102 B2
Western Cape *prov.* S. Africa
98 B3
Western Desert Egypt **92** A2
Western Ghats *mts* India **77** B3
Western Sahara *terr.* Africa
90 A2
Westerschelde *est.* Neth. **48** A2
Westerstede Ger. **48** C1
Westerwald *hills* Ger. **48** C2
West Falkland *i.* Falkland Is
137 B6
West Frankfort U.S.A. **122** C3
West Frisian Islands Neth. **48** B1
West Indies *is* Caribbean Sea
131 D2
Westlock Can. **112** D2
Westmalle Belgium **48** B2
West Memphis U.S.A. **124** B1
Weston-super-Mare U.K. **47** B4
West Palm Beach U.S.A. **125** D3

t Plains U.S.A. **121** E3
Point U.S.A. **121** D2
port N.Z. **106** B3
port Ireland **45** B2
tray Can. **113** E2
ray i. U.K. **44** C1
: Siberian Plain Rus. Fed.
Zapadno Sibirskaya Ravnina
t-Terschelling Neth. **48** B1
t Town Ireland **45** B1
: Virginia state U.S.A.
3 D3
t Wyalong Austr. **105** D2
: Yellowstone U.S.A. **118** D2
askiwin Can. **112** D2
clar Ger. **49** D2
vak P.N.G. **63** D3
ford Ireland **45** C2
burn Can. **110** F3
ne Ger. **49** D1
mouth U.K. **47** B4
katane N.Z. **106** C2
le Cove Can. **113** F1
lsay i. U.K. **44** [inset]
ngarei N.Z. **106** B2
rf U.K. **46** C3
a Ti Can. **112** D1
atland U.S.A. **120** B2
eler Peak NM U.S.A.
6 C1
eeler Peak NV U.S.A.
6 D3
eeling U.S.A. **123** D2
rnside h. U.K. **46** B2
stler Can. **112** C2
by U.K. **46** C2
er Can./U.S.A. **112** B1
te r. U.S.A. **124** B2
te, Lake salt flat Austr.
2 B2
te Bay Can. **115** E2
te Butte mt. U.S.A. **120** C1
te Cliffs Austr. **104** C2
tecourt Can. **112** D2
tefish U.S.A. **118** D1
tehaven U.K. **46** B2
tehorse Can. **112** B1
te Lake U.S.A. **124** B3
te Mountain Peak U.S.A.
9 C3
te Nile r. Sudan/Uganda
8 B3
te Sea Rus. Fed. **34** C2
te Sulphur Springs U.S.A.
8 D1
teville U.S.A. **125** E2
tewater Baldy mt. U.S.A.
26 C2
tewater Lake Can. **114** B1
thorn U.K. **44** B3
tianga N.Z. **106** C2
tney, Mount U.S.A. **119** C3
tsunday Island Austr.
03 D2

Whyalla Austr. **104** B2
Wichita U.S.A. **121** D3
Wichita Falls U.S.A. **127** E2
Wick U.K. **44** C1
Wickenburg U.S.A. **126** B2
Wicklow Ireland **45** C2
Wicklow Head Ireland **45** D2
Wicklow Mountains Ireland
45 C2
Widnes U.K. **46** B3
Wiehengebirge hills Ger. **49** D1
Wien Austria see Vienna
Wiener Neustadt Austria **51** D3
Wieringerwerf Neth. **48** B1
Wiesbaden Ger. **48** D2
Wiesloch Ger. **49** D3
Wiesmoor Ger. **48** C1
Wieżyca h. Pol. **51** D2
Wight, Isle of i. U.K. **47** C4
Wijchen Neth. **48** B2
Wilcannia Austr. **104** C2
Wild Coast S. Africa **99** C3
Wilge r. S. Africa **99** C2
Wilhelm, Mount P.N.G. **100**
Wilhelmshaven Ger. **48** D1
Wilkes-Barre U.S.A. **123** E2
Wilkes Land reg. Antarctica
107 G2
Willcox U.S.A. **126** C2
Willebroek Belgium **48** B2
Willemstad Neth. Antilles
131 D3
William, Mount Austr. **104** C3
William Creek Austr. **104** B1
Williams U.S.A. **126** B1
Williamsburg U.S.A. **123** E3
Williams Lake Can. **112** C2
Williamson U.S.A. **122** D3
Williamsport U.S.A. **123** E2
Williamston U.S.A. **125** E1
Williston S. Africa **98** B3
Williston U.S.A. **120** C1
Williston Lake Can. **112** C2
Willits U.S.A. **119** B3
Willmar U.S.A. **121** D1
Willowmore S. Africa **98** B3
Willowvale S. Africa **99** C3
Wills, Lake salt flat Austr.
102 B2
Willunga Austr. **104** B3
Wilmington Austr. **104** B2
Wilmington DE U.S.A. **123** E3
Wilmington NC U.S.A. **125** E2
Wilnsdorf Ger. **48** D2
Wilson U.S.A. **125** E1
Wilson's Promontory pen. Austr.
105 D3
Wiluna Austr. **102** B2
Winchester U.K. **47** C4
Winchester KY U.S.A. **122** D3
Winchester VA U.S.A. **123** E3
Wind r. Can. **112** B1

Windermere l. U.K. **46** B2
Windhoek Namibia **98** A1
Windom U.S.A. **121** D2
Windorah Austr. **103** D2
Wind River Range mts U.S.A.
120 B2
Windsor Can. **105** E2
Windsor Can. **114** B2
Windward Islands Caribbean Sea
131 D3
Windward Passage Cuba/Haiti
131 C3
Winfield U.S.A. **121** D3
Winisk Can. **114** B1
Winisk r. Can. **114** B1
Winisk Lake Can. **114** B1
Winnebago, Lake U.S.A. **122** C2
Winnemucca U.S.A. **118** C2
Winner U.S.A. **120** C2
Winnfield U.S.A. **124** B2
Winnibigoshish, Lake U.S.A.
121 E1
Winnipeg Can. **113** F3
Winnipeg r. Can. **113** F2
Winnipeg, Lake Can. **113** F2
Winnipegosis, Lake Can.
113 E2
Winnipesaukee, Lake U.S.A.
123 F2
Winnsboro U.S.A. **124** B2
Winona MN U.S.A. **121** E2
Winona MS U.S.A. **124** C2
Winschoten Neth. **48** C1
Winsen (Aller) Ger. **49** D1
Winsen (Luhe) Ger. **49** E1
Winslow U.S.A. **126** B1
Winston-Salem U.S.A. **125** D1
Winterberg Ger. **49** D2
Winter Haven U.S.A. **125** D3
Winterswijk Neth. **48** C2
Winterthur Switz. **53** D2
Winton Austr. **103** D2
Winton N.Z. **106** A4
Wirrabara Austr. **104** B2
Wisbech U.K. **47** D3
Wisconsin r. U.S.A. **122** B2
Wisconsin state U.S.A. **122** C2
Wisconsin Rapids U.S.A.
122 C2
Wisła r. Pol. see Vistula
Wismar Ger. **50** C2
Witbank S. Africa **99** C2
Witney U.K. **47** C4
Wittenberge Ger. **49** E1
Wittingen Ger. **49** E1
Wittlich Ger. **48** C3
Wittmund Ger. **48** C1
Wittstock Ger. **49** F1
Witvlei Namibia **98** A1
Witzenhausen Ger. **49** D2
Władysławowo Pol. **51** D2
Włocławek Pol. **51** D2
Wodonga Austr. **105** D3
Woippy France **48** C3

Wokam *i.* Indon. **63** C3
Woking U.K. **47** C4
Woldegk Ger. **49** F1
Wolfen Ger. **49** F2
Wolfenbüttel Ger. **49** E1
Wolfhagen Ger. **49** D2
Wolf Point U.S.A. **120** B1
Wolfsburg Ger. **49** E1
Wolfville Can. **115** D2
Wolgast Ger. **50** C1
Wolin Pol. **50** C2
Wollaston Lake Can. **113** E2
Wollaston Lake *l.* Can. **110** F3
Wollaston Peninsula Can. **110** E2
Wollongong Austr. **105** E2
Wolmirstedt Ger. **49** E1
Wolvega Neth. **48** C1
Wolverhampton U.K. **47** B3
Wŏnju S. Korea **69** B2
Wonowon Can. **112** C2
Wŏnsan N. Korea **69** B2
Wonthaggi Austr. **105** D3
Woocalla Austr. **104** B2
Woodah, Isle *i.* Austr. **103** C1
Woodbridge U.K. **47** D3
Woodroffe, Mount Austr. **102** C2
Woods, Lake *salt flat* Austr. **102** C1
Woods, Lake of the Can./U.S.A. **121** E1
Woods Point Austr. **105** D3
Woodstock Can. **123** G1
Woodville N.Z. **106** C3
Woodward U.S.A. **127** E1
Woolgoolga Austr. **105** E2
Woomera Austr. **104** B2
Worcester S. Africa **98** A3
Worcester U.K. **47** B3
Worcester U.S.A. **123** F2
Wörgl Austria **50** C3
Workington U.K. **46** B2
Worksop U.K. **46** C3
Worland U.S.A. **120** B2
Worms Ger. **49** D3
Wörth am Rhein Ger. **49** D3
Worthing U.K. **47** C4
Worthington U.S.A. **121** D2
Wotu Indon. **65** D2
Wowoni *i.* Indon. **65** D2
Wrangel Island Rus. Fed. **87** D2
Wrangell U.S.A. **112** C2
Wrangell Mountains U.S.A. **110** B3
Wrath, Cape U.K. **44** B1
Wray U.S.A. **120** C2
Wreck Point S. Africa **98** A2
Wrexham U.K. **46** B3
Wrightmyo India **67** A2
Wrigley Can. **112** C1
Wrocław Pol. **51** D2
Września Pol. **51** D2
Wudu China **74** A2

Wuhai China **74** A2
Wuhan China **75** B2
Wuhu China **74** B2
Wukari Nigeria **91** C4
Wuli China **79** D1
Wuliang Shan *mts* China **66** B1
Wuliaru *i.* Indon. **63** C3
Wumeng Shan *mts* China **75** A3
Wunnummin Lake Can. **114** B1
Wunsiedel Ger. **49** F2
Wunstorf Ger. **49** D1
Wuntho Myanmar **66** A1
Wuppertal Ger. **48** C2
Würzburg Ger. **49** D3
Wurzen Ger. **49** F2
Wuwei China **74** A2
Wuxi *Chongqing* China **74** A2
Wuxi *Jiangsu* China **74** C2
Wuxing China see Huzhou
Wuyishan China **75** B3
Wuyi Shan *mts* China **75** B3
Wuyuan China **74** A1
Wuzhishan China **75** A4
Wuzhong China **74** A2
Wuzhou China **75** B3
Wyangala Reservoir Austr. **105** D2
Wycheproof Austr. **104** C3
Wye *r.* U.K. **47** B4
Wyndham Austr. **102** B1
Wynne U.S.A. **124** B1
Wynyard Can. **113** E2
Wyoming *state* U.S.A. **120** B2
Wyszków Pol. **51** E2

X

Xaafuun Somalia **93** D3
Xaignabouli Laos **66** B2
Xai-Xai Moz. **97** C2
Xamba China **74** A1
Xam Nua Laos **66** B1
Xanagas Botswana **98** B1
Xangongo Angola **96** A1
Xankändi Azer. **85** C2
Xanthi Greece **59** B2
Xanxerê Brazil **138** B3
Xapuri Brazil **134** C4
Xátiva Spain **55** C2
Xiamen China **75** B3
Xi'an China **74** A2
Xianfeng China **75** A3
Xiangfan China **74** B2
Xianggelila China **66** A1
Xianghuang Qi China see Xin Bulag
Xiangkhoang Laos **66** B2
Xiangtan China **75** B3
Xiantao China **75** B2
Xianyang China **74** A2
Xiaogan China **75** B2

Xiao Hinggan Ling *mts* China **73** E1
Xiaoshan China **75** C2
Xichang China **66** B1
Xifeng *Gansu* China **74** A2
Xigazê China **79** C2
Xilinhot China **74** B1
Xin Bulag China **74** B1
Xinghai China **72** C2
Xinghua China **74** B2
Xingning China **75** B3
Xingping China **74** A2
Xingtai China **74** B2
Xingu *r.* Brazil **135** D3
Xingyi China **75** A3
Xining China **72** C2
Xinjiang Uygur Zizhiqu *aut. reg.* China **79** C1
Xinmin China **69** A1
Xinning China **75** B3
Xintai China **75** B2
Xinxiang China **74** B2
Xinyang China **74** B2
Xinyu China **75** B3
Xinzhou *Hubei* China **74** B2
Xinzhou *Shanxi* China **73** D2
Xinzo de Limia Spain **54** B1
Xiqing Shan *mts* China **72** C2
Xi Ujimqin Qi China see Bayan Ul Hot
Xiushan China **75** A3
Xiuying China **75** B3
Xizang Zizhiqu *aut. reg.* China **66** A1
Xo'jayli Uzbek. **80** C2
Xuanhai China **74** B2
Xuanwei China **75** A3
Xuchang China **74** B2
Xuddur Somalia **93** C4
Xun Jiang *r.* China **75** B3
Xuwen China **75** B3
Xuyong China **75** A3

Y

Ya'an China **75** A2
Yabēlo Eth. **93** B4
Yablonovyy Khrebet *mts* Rus. Fed. **73** D1
Yadkin *r.* U.S.A. **125** D1
Yagnitsa Rus. Fed. **37** E2
Yahk Can. **112** D3
Yahualica Mex. **128** B2
Yahyalı Turkey **84** B2
Yaizu Japan **71** C4
Yakima U.S.A. **118** B1
Yakumo Japan **70** D2
Yakutat U.S.A. **112** B2
Yakutat Bay U.S.A. **112** A2
Yakutsk Rus. Fed. **87** K2
Yakymivka Ukr. **39** E2
Yala Thai. **67** B3

urn Austr. **105** D3
ra Turkey **59** C2
. Ukr. **39** D3
Jiang r. China/N. Korea
A1
agata Japan **70** D3
guchi Japan **71** B4
ati, Poluostrov pen. Rus. Fed.
Yamal Peninsula
al Peninsula Rus. Fed. **34** F1
ba Austr. **105** E1
oio Sudan **93** A4
bol Bulg. **58** C2
burg Rus. Fed. **34** G2
ethin Myanmar **66** A1
oussoukro Côte d'Ivoire
B4
pil' Ukr. **38** C2
una r. India **79** C2
zho Yumco r. China **79** D2
a r. Rus. Fed. **87** L2
an China **74** A2
ou' al Baḥr Saudi Arabia
A2
cheng China **74** C2
chep Austr. **102** A3
gchun China **75** B3
gdok N. Korea **69** B2
jiang China **75** B3
gön Myanmar see Rangoon
guan China **74** B2
gtze r. Qinghai China **72** C2
gtze r. China **75** B3
gtze r. China **66** B1
gtze, Mouth of the China
C2
zhou China **74** B2
i China **69** B1
xton U.S.A. **121** D2
skiy Zaliv g. Rus. Fed. **87** L2
al China **74** C2
undé Cameroon **94** B3
i. Micronesia **63** D2
en i. Indon. **63** D3
en, Selat sea chan. Indon.
C3
ui r. Mex. **128** A2
nsk Rus. Fed. **34** D3
m Nauru **100**
n Yemen **82** B3
ung Zangbo r. China **72** C3
oslavl' Rus. Fed. **37** E2
oslavskiy Rus. Fed. **70** B2
am Austr. **105** D3
sevo Rus. Fed. **37** D2
nogorsk Rus. Fed. **37** E3
othon Thai. **67** B2
n Austr. **105** D2
gan Turkey **59** C3
kyed Lake Can. **113** F1
sushiro Japan **71** B4
ari r. Brazil/Peru **134** C3
atmal India **79** B2

Yavoriv Ukr. **38** B2
Yawatahama Japan **71** B4
Yazd Iran **85** D2
Yazoo City U.S.A. **124** B2
Ydra i. Greece **59** B3
Ye Myanmar **67** A2
Yecheng China **81** E3
Yécora Mex. **128** B2
Yefremov Rus. Fed. **37** E3
Yegorlyk r. Rus. Fed. **39** F2
Yegorlykskaya Rus. Fed. **39** F2
Yegor'yevsk Rus. Fed. **37** E3
Yei Sudan **93** B4
Yekaterinburg Rus. Fed. **34** F3
Yelets Rus. Fed. **37** E3
Yell i. U.K. **44** [inset]
Yellowknife Can. **112** D1
Yellow Sea N. Pacific Ocean **73** E2
Yellowstone r. U.S.A. **118** E1
Yellowstone Lake U.S.A.
120 A2
Yel'sk Belarus **36** C3
Yemen country Asia **82** B3
Yemva Rus. Fed. **34** E2
Yenakiyeve Ukr. **39** E2
Yenangyaung Myanmar **66** A1
Yên Bai Vietnam **66** B1
Yendi Ghana **90** B4
Yeovil U.K. **47** B4
Yerevan Armenia **85** G2
Yeymentau Kazakh. **81** E1
Yermish' Rus. Fed. **37** F3
Yershov Rus. Fed. **35** D3
Yesil' Kazakh. **81** D1
Yeşilova Turkey **59** C3
Yetman Austr. **105** E1
Ye-U Myanmar **66** A1
Yeu, Île d' i. France **52** B2
Yevlax Azer. **35** D4
Yevpatoriya Ukr. **39** D2
Yeysk Rus. Fed. **39** E2
Yezyaryshcha Belarus **36** C2
Yibin China **74** B2
Yichang China **74** B2
Yichun Heilong. China **73** E1
Yichun Jiangxi China **75** B3
Yilan China **70** A1
Yıldız Dağları mts Turkey **58** C2
Yıldızeli Turkey **84** A2
Yinchuan China **74** A2
Yingde China **75** B3
Yingkou China **74** C1
Yingshan Sichuan China **74** A2
Yingtan China **75** B3
Yining China **81** F2
Yirga Alem Eth. **93** B4
Yitong China **69** B1
Yiwu China **72** C2
Yixing China **74** B2
Yiyang China **75** B3
Yizhou China **75** A3
Yli-Kitka i. Fin. **40** F2
Ylitornio Fin. **40** E2
Ylivieska Fin. **40** E3

Yogyakarta Indon. **65** C2
Yokohama Japan **71** C3
Yola Nigeria **91** D4
Yonezawa Japan **71** D4
Yong'an China **75** B3
Yongchun China **75** B3
Yongdeng China **74** A2
Yongsheng China **66** B1
Yongzhou China **75** B3
Yopal Col. **134** B2
York Austr. **102** A3
York U.K. **46** C3
York NE U.S.A. **124** D3
York PA U.S.A. **123** E3
York, Cape Austr. **63** D3
Yorke Peninsula Austr. **104** B3
Yorketown Austr. **104** B3
Yorkshire Wolds hills U.K. **46** C3
Yorkton Can. **110** F3
Yoshkar-Ola Rus. Fed. **35** D3
Youghal Ireland **45** C3
Young Austr. **105** D2
Younghusband Peninsula Austr.
104 B3
Youngstown U.S.A. **123** D2
Youvarou Mali **90** B3
Yozgat Turkey **84** B2
Ypé-Jhú Para. **138** A2
Yreka U.S.A. **118** B2
Yr Wyddfa mt. U.K. see Snowdon
Ystad Sweden **41** C4
Ysyk-Köl salt l. Kyrg. **81** E2
Ytri-Rangá r. Iceland **40** [inset]
Yuan Jiang r. China **66** B1
Yuba City U.S.A. **119** B3
Yucatán pen. Mex. **129** C5
Yucatan Channel Cuba/Mex.
130 B2
Yuendumu Austr. **102** C2
Yueyang China **75** B3
Yugorsk Rus. Fed. **34** F2
Yukagirskoye Ploskogor'ye plat.
Rus. Fed. **87** M2
Yukon r. Can./U.S.A. **112** B1
Yukon Territory admin. div. Can.
110 C2
Yulin Guangxi China **75** B3
Yulin Shaanxi China **74** A2
Yulong Xueshan mt. China
66 B1
Yuma AZ U.S.A. **126** B2
Yuma CO U.S.A. **120** C2
Yumen China **72** C2
Yunak Turkey **84** B2
Yuncheng China **74** B2
Yunnan prov. China **75** A3
Yunta Austr. **104** B2
Yunyang China **74** B2
Yurungkax He r. China **79** C1
Yur'yevets Rus. Fed. **37** F2
Yü Shan mt. Taiwan **75** C3
Yushkozero Rus. Fed. **40** G3
Yutian China **79** C1
Yuxi China **66** B1

Yuzha Rus. Fed. **37** F2
Yuzhno-Kuril'sk Rus. Fed. **70** E2
Yuzhno-Sakhalinsk Rus. Fed. **70** D1
Yuzhnoukrayinsk Ukr. **39** D2
Yuzhou China **74** B2
Yvetot France **52** C2

Z

Zaandam Neth. **48** B1
Zabid Yemen **82** B3
Zābol Iran **83** D1
Zāboli Iran **83** D2
Zacapa Guat. **129** D3
Zacapu Mex. **128** B3
Zacatecas Mex. **128** B2
Zacatlán Mex. **129** C3
Zacharo Greece **59** B3
Zacoalco Mex. **128** B2
Zadar Croatia **56** C2
Zadetkyi Kyun i. Myanmar **67** A3
Zadonsk Rus. Fed. **37** E3
Za'farānah Egypt **84** B2
Zafra Spain **55** B2
Zagreb Croatia **57** C1
Zagros, Kūhhā-ye mts Iran see Zagros Mountains
Zagros Mountains Iran **85** C2
Zāhedān Iran **83** D2
Zahlé Lebanon **84** B2
Zahrā Saudi Arabia **82** B3
Zahrez Chergui salt pan Alg. **55** D2
Zaječar S.M. **58** B2
Zākhō Iraq **85** C2
Zakynthos Greece **59** B3
Zakynthos i. Greece **59** B3
Zalaegerszeg Hungary **51** D3
Zalău Romania **38** B2
Zalim Saudi Arabia **82** B2
Zalmā, Jabal az mt. Saudi Arabia **82** A2
Zama City Can. **122** D3
Zambeze r. Angola see Zambezi
Zambezi r. Angola **97** B1
Zambezi Zambia **96** B1
Zambia country Africa **96** B1
Zamboanga Phil. **68** B3
Zamboanga Peninsula Phil. **68** B3
Zamora Spain **54** B1
Zamora de Hidalgo Mex. **128** B3
Zamość Pol. **51** E2
Zanda China **79** C2
Zandvliet Belgium **48** B2
Zanesville U.S.A. **122** D3
Zanjān Iran **85** C2
Zanskar Mountains India **79** B1
Zante i. Greece see Zakynthos

Zanzibar Tanz. **95** D3
Zanzibar Island Tanz. **95** D3
Zaokskiy Rus. Fed. **37** E3
Zaouatallaz Alg. **91** C2
Zaozhuang China **74** B2
Zapadnaya Dvina r. Europe **37** D2
Zapadnaya Dvina Rus. Fed. **37** D2
Zapadno Sibirskaya Ravnina plain Rus. Fed. **34** H2
Zapadnyy Sayan reg. Rus. Fed. **72** B1
Zapata U.S.A. **127** D3
Zapolyarnyy Rus. Fed. **40** G2
Zaporizhzhya Ukr. **39** E2
Zara Turkey **84** B2
Zaragoza Spain **55** C1
Zarand Iran **83** C1
Zaranj Afgh. **78** A1
Zarasai Lith. **36** C2
Zaraysk Rus. Fed. **37** E3
Zaraza Venez. **134** C2
Zaria Nigeria **91** C3
Zarichne Ukr. **38** C1
Zarqān Iran **85** C2
Zarubino Rus. Fed. **70** B2
Żary Pol. **50** D2
Zastron S. Africa **99** C3
Žatec Czech Rep. **49** F2
Zavitinsk Rus. Fed. **73** E1
Zawiercie Pol. **51** D2
Zdolbuniv Ukr. **38** C1
Zealand i. Denmark **41** C4
Zeebrugge Belgium **48** A2
Zeerust S. Africa **99** C2
Zeil, Mount Austr. **102** C2
Zeitz Ger. **49** F2
Zelenogorsk Rus. Fed. **41** F3
Zelenograd Rus. Fed. **37** E2
Zemmora Alg. **55** D2
Zempoltépetl, Nudo de mt. Mex. **129** C3
Zengfeng Shan mt. China **69** B1
Zenzach Alg. **55** D2
Zereh, Gowd-e depr. Afgh. **78** A2
Zermatt Switz. **53** D2
Zernograd Rus. Fed. **39** F2
Zeulenroda Ger. **49** E2
Zeven Ger. **49** D1
Zevenaar Neth. **48** C2
Zeya Rus. Fed. **87** K3
Zeydābād Iran **83** D2
Zeyskoye Vodokhranilishche resr Rus. Fed. **87** K3
Zgierz Pol. **51** D2
Zhabinka Belarus **36** B3
Zhaltyr Kazakh. **81** D1
Zhanaozen Kazakh. **80** C2
Zhangjiajie China **75** B3
Zhangjiakou China **74** B1
Zhangping China **75** B3

Zhangshu China **75** B3
Zhangwu China **69** A1
Zhangye China **72** C2
Zhangzhou China **75** B3
Zhanibek Kazakh. **80** B2
Zhanjiang China **75** B3
Zhao'an China **75** B3
Zhaoqing China **75** B3
Zhaotong China **75** A3
Zhari Namco salt l. China **79**
Zharkent Kazakh. **81** F2
Zharkovskiy Rus. Fed. **37** D2
Zhashkiv Ukr. **38** D2
Zhejiang prov. China **75** C3
Zhelaniya, Mys c. Rus. Fed. **86** G1
Zheleznogorsk Rus. Fed. **37**
Zhenba China **74** A2
Zheng'an China **75** A3
Zhengzhou China **74** B2
Zhenyuan China **75** A3
Zherdevka Rus. Fed. **37** F3
Zheshart Rus. Fed. **34** D2
Zhezkazgan Karagandinskaya Oblast' Kazakh. **80** D2
Zhezkazgan Karagandinskaya Oblast' Kazakh. **81** D2
Zhicheng China see Qingzhou
Zhigansk Rus. Fed. **87** K2
Zhitikara Kazakh. **80** D1
Zhlobin Belarus **36** C3
Zhmerynka Ukr. **38** C2
Zhob Pak. **78** A1
Zhongba China **79** C2
Zhongning China **74** A2
Zhongshan China **75** B3
Zhongwei China **74** A2
Zhoukou China **74** B2
Zhoushan China **75** C2
Zhovti Vody Ukr. **39** D2
Zhovtneve Ukr. **39** D2
Zhukovka Rus. Fed. **37** D3
Zhukovskiy Rus. Fed. **37** E2
Zhumadian China **74** B2
Zhuzhou Hunan China **75** B3
Zhuzhou Hunan China **75** B3
Zhydachiv Ukr. **38** B2
Zhytkavichy Belarus **36** C3
Zhytomyr Ukr. **38** C1
Žiar nad Hronom Slovakia **51** D3
Zibo China **74** B2
Zielona Góra Pol. **51** D2
Zigaing Myanmar **66** A1
Zigong China **74** A2
Ziguinchor Senegal **90** A3
Žilina Slovakia **51** D3
Zillah Libya **91** D2
Zima Rus. Fed. **83** H1
Zimapán Mex. **129** C2
Zimbabwe country Africa **97** C1
Zimmi Sierra Leone **90** A4
Zimnicea Romania **38** C3
Zinder Niger **91** C3

...uaro Mex. **129** B3
...i Ger. **50** C2
...ust Rus. Fed. **35** E3
...zech Rep. **51** D3
...evka Rus. Fed. **37** E3
...v Ukr. **39** E2
...henka *Orlovskaya Oblast'*
..., Fed. **37** E3
..."yanka Ukr. **39** D2
...no Czech Rep. **51** D3
...hiv *Kharkivs'ka Oblast'* Ukr.
...E1
...hiv *L'vivs'ka Oblast'* Ukr.
...B2
...onosha Ukr. **39** D2

Zolotukhino Rus. Fed. **37** E3
Zomba Malawi **97** C1
Zonguldak Turkey **84** B1
Zossen Ger. **49** F1
Zouar Chad **91** D2
Zouérat Maur. **90** A2
Zrenjanin S.M. **58** B1
Zubtsov Rus. Fed. **37** D2
Zug Switz. **53** D2
Zugdidi Georgia **85** C1
Zumbo Moz. **97** C1
Zumpango Mex. **129** C3
Zuni Mountains U.S.A.
   126 C1
Zunyi China **75** A3

Županja Croatia **57** C1
Zürich Switz. **53** D2
Zutphen Neth. **48** C1
Zuwārah Libya **91** D1
Zvenyhorodka Ukr. **38** D2
Zvishavane Zimbabwe **97** C2
Zvolen Slovakia **51** D3
Zwedru Liberia **90** B4
Zweibrücken Ger. **48** C3
Zwettl Austria **50** D3
Zwickau Ger. **49** F2
Zwolle Neth. **48** C1
Zyryanka Rus. Fed. **87** M2